THE SUPERNATURAL WORLDVIEW

EXAMINING PARANORMAL, PSI, AND THE APOCALYPTIC

CRIS PUTNAM

DEFENDER

CRANE, MISSOURI

Supernatural Worldview

Crane, Missouri 65633

©2014 by Cris Putnam

All rights reserved. Published 2014.

Printed in the United States of America.

ISBN: 978-0-9856045-6-1

A CIP catalog record of this book is available from the Library of Congress.

Cover illustration and design by Daniel Wright: www.createdwright.com.

Acknowledgments

I wish to acknowledge the following people without whose friendship, inspiration, and moral support this book could not have been written: my lovely wife, Michelle (Shelley) Putnam; my mom, Majel Hyers; publisher Tom Horn; John Warwick Montgomery, Gary Habermas, Michael Heiser, and Chuck Missler; and Tom Innes and all of my church family PBC in Raleigh, NC.

CONTENTS

FOREWORD

By Chuck Missler

Clearly, the entire world is plunging into an era of turmoil in every sphere of perception and involvement.

The global economy is in unprecedented turmoil as politicians ignore the realities of excessive debt: Every single hour of every single day, the U.S. government spends about $200 million that it doesn't have—every hour, every day, seven days a week, day and night, 365 days a year.[1] There is a desperate (and widespread) attempt to forestall the recognition that the United States has become the world's largest debtor and is currently bankrupt. There appears to be a high likelihood of a major collapse facing the unprepared.

And there are other paradigm shifts threatening our fundamental foundations as well. Numerous other uncertainties continue to pervade every aspect of our lives and our awareness. Scientists, the primary priesthood in our society, now recognize that even the "constants" of physics are changing, which implies—in their words, not ours—"that our reality is but a shadow of a larger reality."[2] (No kidding! That's what the Bible has declared all along.[3])

As stochastic electrodynamics are beginning to displace the traditional "quantum electrodynamics," when confronted with the realities of the overlooked (and rediscovered) zero-point energy,[4] our very foundational physical constructs now appear myopic and insufficient.

As gravity is eclipsed by electromagnetic forces at intergalactic distances,[5] our perceptions of the universe are being replaced by an "electric" sky, and are accompanied by speculations that the entire universe is some kind of superhologram, which further challenges any concept of boundaries to our perceived reality.

As "evolution" (or, more specifically, biogenesis) is increasingly acknowledged by experts as insufficient and erroneous as an explanation of our origins, the resulting tensions in our society are challenging the very existence of "truth" and the role of design throughout the universe.[6]

So it should not surprise us to see refugees from a bankrupt materialism being subsequently driven into mysticism and the paranormal, lunging even farther away from the empirically verifiable. The panorama of alternatives provides a spectrum of confusion in which a biblical perspective will be increasingly difficult to maintain within the avalanche of the paradigm changes emerging in so many (mutually orthogonal) directions.

Fortunately, it is a great and refreshing encouragement to encounter a skill and an aptitude that appear unique to the occasion. Cris Putnam's previous work on *Exo-Vaticana*[7] demonstrated a depth of scholarship and perspicacity in addressing what has to be one of the most difficult areas to research competently. As one well informed in that specialized area, I can attest to his work as unmatched as a milestone in its field. I believe that this current work will prove equivalent and essential to the serious thinker as we all face the emerging turmoil on our collective horizons.

How will *you* deal with empirical validations of extrasensory perceptions? Of near-death experiences? Nonbiblical spirits? Evidence that the mind goes far beyond the organ we know as the brain?

If our eschatological perceptions have any validity, the current trends toward a "Supernatural Worldview" will prove to be a critical challenge to those who take their personal destiny seriously, and we can certainly anticipate that our adversaries will exploit these challenges to advance their own agendas. There is, indeed, a cosmic climax emerging on our near horizon.

We need to understand where our own personal perspectives fit in. This authoritative study will provide a sound foundation to meet the very critical challenges facing all of us in the turbulence ahead. Put on your armor and prepare for a provocative ride.

In the service of our Coming King,
Chuck Missler

Notes

1. The first law of holes is to stop digging!
2. "The Constancy of Constants," *Scientific American,* June 2005.
3. Hebrews 11:3. (Four dimensions listed in Ephesians 3:18; cf.
    1 Corinthians 15:39–57.)
4. Zero-point energy: The remaining energy of evacuated space
    cooled to -273°C, initially dismissed as a convenient mathematical
    construct, now empirically confirmed and precipitating a
    reexamination of Quantum Electrodynamics (QED), the basis of the
    "standard model," now being replaced by Stochastic Electrodynamics
    (SED); cf. *Cosmology and the Zero Point Energy, Natural Philosophy
    Alliance Monograph Series,* No. 1, 2013, Barry Setterfield, Natural
    Philosophy Alliance, 2013, ISBN 978-1-304-19508-1.
5. Electromagnetic forces are 10^{36} times as powerful as gravity. Gravity
    further suffers by being divided by the square of the distance between
    the masses, minimizing its relevance at intergalactic distances; cf.
    Donald E. Scott, *The Electric Sky* (Portland, OR: Mikamar, 2006).
6. The very definition of "entropy" (randomness) is frequently
    inverted through mathematical carelessness, and is the inverse of
    "information" (design). To confuse the two terms simply manifests
    ignorance of their antithetical definitions.
7. Thomas Horn and Cris Putnam, *Exo-Vaticana* (Crane, MO:
    Defender, 2013).

PARANORMAL WITNESS TO GOSPEL WITNESS

The Supernatural Worldview will ultimately eclipse all others. A key theme of the book in your hands is that the paranormal is the new normal. It follows that the supernatural is experiencing a cultural renaissance. Supernatural beings, stories, and themes have invaded America's entertainment choices, from movies such as *The Conjuring, The Rite, Insidious, The Sixth Sense,* and *The Exorcism of Emily Rose,* to television programs like *Supernatural, The Vampire Diaries, Charmed,* and *Ghost Whisperer,* to children's books like the Harry Potter and Goosebumps series, and even to video games like Diablo, Resident Evil, and The Darkness. But it is not the fictional entertainment media that sparks my interest as an investigative writer and a Christian, but rather the unprecedented new genre of paranormal reality programming.

Ghost Hunters, Paranormal Witness, and *Ghost Adventures* all feature paranormal investigators collecting evidence for the existence of alleged disembodied humans. Even the Animal Planet network is in the mix with *The Haunted,* a show featuring ghost stories and paranormal investigations involving animals. Syfy premiered some new shows in 2013, including *Ghost Mine* and *Stranded.* These programs all feature similar bumps in the night intensified by dramatic editing and high production values. While some episodes are more compelling than others, a healthy skepticism is warranted. Other paranormal "reality" shows are more harmful.

Long Island Medium on TLC seems to have picked up where John Edward's *Crossing Over* left off, taking Theresa Caputo's spiritualist-medium act on the road and into our living rooms via reality television. Attorney Bill Weld has a website dedicated to exposing Caputo "as a soothsaying charlatan rather than a legitimate psychic."[1] *The Dead Files* on the Travel Channel features a physical medium, Amy Allan, and retired NYPD homicide detective, Steve Di Schiavi, who team up to investigate unexplained paranormal phenomena in haunted locations across America. While Schiavi relies on his detective experience to search for physical evidence, Amy communicates with the dead, even reliving their deaths. At the show's end, the two investigators share their findings. If genuine, the parallels between their discoveries are often compelling. However, communicating with the dead is prohibited in Scripture in the strongest possible language (Deuteronomy 18:11–12). By delivering messages from specific deceased individuals, mediums are making a much stronger claim than the typical paranormal investigator.

Of course, debunkers abound, and it isn't difficult to find refutations of popular mediums on the Internet. I suggest that the skeptics aren't always asking the right questions. Rather than asking whether or not these mediums are really making contact, perhaps one should consider, even if they are, whether anyone should seek their counsel in the first place. Mediums will be discussed in chapter 9, but, for now, the salient point is the widespread acceptance and promotion of spiritualism and ghost belief in the early twenty-first century.

I don't think you should take any of these programs at face value. Obviously, the networks are in the business of selling advertising, and the shows need to be entertaining or they won't sell many Cheetos and Toyotas. This creates an enormous incentive to exaggerate and even stage scenes for the camera. While exaggeration and staging in these programs are nearly impossible to prove, I do have a personal example. The fall 2012 season premiere of *Ghost Hunters* featured The Atlantic Paranormal Society (TAPS) crew investigating the Old Charleston Jail in South Carolina. During the investigation of the run-down, dangerous-looking, old building, one of the female team members was allegedly scratched repeatedly by an invisible entity. Her colleagues pulled up the back of her shirt to reveal a long, red mark down her back. This level of physical activity, if real, should leave little doubt in even the most hardened skeptic's mind—that is, if it could be proven beyond a reasonable doubt.

When the show aired, my wife and I were vacationing at Myrtle Beach only a short drive away. As one of the oldest cities in the United States, Charleston, South Carolina, is also held to be one of the most haunted. I couldn't resist, so to help with my research for this book, I scheduled two tours: one of haunted Charleston and another of the Old Jail. My wife and I were scheduled to go on the latest possible tour of that facility, which was at 10:00 p.m.

Our first tour, the one of haunted Charleston, took us through the streets, cemeteries, back alleyways, and churches of the historic city. We enjoyed hearing the lore concerning local ghosts, haunted houses, voodoo, and various superstitions.

The highlight of that tour was access to the Provost Dungeon under the Old Exchange Building at 122 East Bay St., which dates back to 1771, when the Old Exchange was built in the center of the waterfront. As a hub of international trade for our burgeoning nation, Charleston was the most active port in the South during this time. The Old Exchange was built to accommodate the booming trade and collateral industry. Directly beneath the hustle-bustle of genteel southern society, prisoners were shackled to walls in brutal conditions, often never again to see the light of day. Under British rule, patriots and pirates received the same treatment. Conditions in the dungeon were repugnant. Wharf rats, insects, disease, filth, and rancid food were characteristic amenities. The bodies of prisoners who died were frequently left to decompose alongside live prisoners. Many people have reported paranormal activity in the dungeon. While there was some excitement on our tour when a security rope began to swing, I can't say that I witnessed anything out of the ordinary.

However, as the ten o'clock hour loomed, the Old Charleston Jail promised the paranormal. Operational from 1802 until 1939, the facility housed Charleston's most infamous criminals, nineteenth-century pirates, and Civil War prisoners. Our tour guide was a sleek, young, goth female dressed in all-black attire. The art of storytelling is the craft of ghost tourism, and she was good at it. As she led us around the jail, she would unexpectedly pound on a door and the entire group would jump.

The jail had been a real horror in its heyday. A breeding ground for disease, conditions were inhuman and the temperature in the cells would reach 120 degrees during the humid summers. Many men were hung to their deaths on the grounds, and those who survived likely left a piece of themselves behind. The facility held some of America's most notorious criminals, including Lavinia Fisher, the first female mass murderer in America. She and her husband owned the Six Mile Wayfarer House, a hotel in which the couple poisoned guests in order to steal their property.

Another person of note involved with the jail was a particularly sadistic warden who, by popular accounting, is the source of the scratching and poltergeist-type activity at the jail. Some visitors even claim to smell the smoke of his cigars.

What made the jail tour anticlimactic occurred as we were climbing the stairs of a dark corridor and bright light beamed through cracks around some of the locked doors. My wife, the curious woman that she is, peeked through one of the wider cracks as the rest of the group was fumbling around in the dark. To her surprise, she saw a group of college students studying in a large, modern lounge. As it turns out, the building is being remodeled by the American College of the Building Arts, which purchased it in 2000. In other words, the impression of a spooky, run-down, abandoned building was mostly made for television and ghost tourism. It turns out that people were living and studying inside the whole time. I think they were giggling at us, too.

To be fair, I am not implying that the jail isn't haunted. It's as good a candidate as any, housing some of the most evil malcontents in history as well as hosting their agonizing executions. In 2011, the *Ghost Adventures* show also investigated the jail (season 5, episode 3), and allegedly recorded an electronic-voice phenomenon (EVP) of mass murderer Fisher saying "the devil"—the last two words she uttered before the hangman's noose broke her neck. The television program's cast members also reported seeing misty orbs appearing in front of them throughout the whole investigation.

Many people probably have had strange experiences in the jail, but my point is that the TV shows tend to dramatize by leaving out contrary information like the building's use as a school. If people were being preternaturally scratched on a regular basis, then I doubt the students would have been so comfortable. For these reasons, investigative programs centered on cases with testimony from reliable witnesses seem more compelling than shows that are trying to capture new, live, paranormal footage every week. It is just too tall an order to deliver.

Paranormal Witness, a Syfy network documentary television series made by a British production company, is described as featuring eyewitness testimony from everyday people who claim to have experienced paranormal activity. The series premiered on September 7, 2011, was picked up for a second season with twelve new episodes in 2012, and is currently in its third season—scheduled for twenty episodes that began airing on June 5, 2013, and are ongoing as this book hits the press. The show is unique in the genre in that the cases are usually reported by reliable witnesses and supported with evidence that can be verified or dismissed through research.

One case in particular captured my attention because it encapsulates in one story multiple instances of paranormal and, indeed, supernatural phenomena. That episode was called "Haunted Highway" (season 1, episode 102),[2] and originally aired on September 14, 2011, to an audience of 1.36 million viewers.[3]

Haunted Highway: The Amazing Rescue of Nick Skubish

Actually, the same case originally ran on the February 21, 1997, episode of *Unsolved Mysteries,* and its reuse by *Paranormal Witness* testifies to its utterly unique combination of events and phenomena. It is an amazing case. The story centers on twenty-four-year-old Christine Skubish and her three-year-old son, Nick, who went missing off Highway 50 in the Sierra Nevada Mountains of California about fifteen miles outside of Placerville. A single mother, Christine had recently earned her paralegal certification and was moving to start a new career. She was also hopeful about marrying her son's father, who lived in that area. When she left her family's home near Sacramento on Sunday, June 5, 1994, her hopes were high.

Christine and Nick Skubish[4]

According to the show's version of events, Dave Stautzenbach, Christine's stepfather, received a telephone call on Wednesday, June 8, from one of her friends, who said she had expected Christine to arrive in town on Monday—but it was now Wednesday morning. Worried, Stautzenbach called the police to make a missing-persons report and started checking with hospitals along the route Christine would have traveled.

Regrettably, his effort was to no avail. Deputy Rich Strasser told viewers, "There's people reported missing all the time, everyday, throughout this country. There was nothing out of the ordinary. I thought it was just another, I hate to say it, routine missing-persons report."[5]

Of course, the vast majority of cases do turn out to be nonevents when the missing person shows up after an unplanned excursion. However, this case was anything but routine, and it qualifies as one of the most diverse paranormal cases in history.

I contacted Christine Skubish's aunt, Karen Nichols, whose story is also featured on "Haunted Highway." According to her, the report isn't very accurate. On the program, Karen calls Dave Stautzenbach and recounts a strange dream that included Christine and Nick, as well as the number sixteen repeated over and over. Karen told me that the TV version is mostly fiction, because the number sixteen was *not* part of her dream. Somehow, the details of her dream got mixed up with other details, and the show presented a falsehood. It is not clear whether the inaccuracy was intentional.

Perhaps this was because Karen refused to participate in either *Unsolved Mysteries* or *Paranormal Witness,* even though both programs offered her money. Why did Karen decline the monetary offer? She said she is a born-again Christian who felt it was wrong to sensationalize the tragedy. She wrote to me, "I declined their offer because I didn't see how this could in any way glorify the church. I didn't feel it in my spirit."[6]

You might ask why Karen spoke to me; by the end of this chapter, the answer to that will be clear. She had several extrasensory dreams, and this is the first time they have ever been accurately described to the public. We will now set the record straight.

Karen Nichols' Extrasensory Dreams

Despite the errors, however, "Haunted Highway" did report at least a few details about Karen's dreams that were correct. For example, on the show, Stautzenbach commented concerning Karen's dream: "She had premonitions before, but this was so real, she knew that she was going to find him."[7] This is absolutely true; Karen has written in detail about her lifelong experience with premonitions, visions, and precognitive dreams. In fact, she once warned a relative concerning cancer weeks before it was diagnosed and accurately predicted a close family member's demise.

It is important to note that having these dreams and premonitions is not something Karen tries to do. They just happen to her unexpectedly. She states that she repented from occult involvement by dedicating her life to Christ many years ago.

This is Karen's account of the first dream she had on the night of the accident:

Monday morning about 3 a.m., June 6, 1994, I had a dream of riding in the backseat of a car at night. I could see the silhouette of a child in the passenger seat and a girl driving. I could see the reflection of the headlights and the hood of the car. I could tell we were on a dark road because there were no streetlights, and outside it seemed to be mountainous.

That morning, I spoke to my mother and my sister and asked if they had heard from Chrissy. They said, "No," but I knew she was going to stop by a friend's house in Carson City, Nevada. So, even though I felt a bit uneasy, I continued to push it out of my mind and told myself everything was OK.[8]

The above dream probably occurred at the time of the accident or shortly after. Interestingly, it seems to transport Karen into the car with her niece and young Nick. The setting is correct: It was a dark mountain road.

That morning, Karen called her sister, Brenda, and asked if she had heard from Christine—the answer was no. The following night and into Tuesday morning, Karen had a similar dream:

That night when I went to sleep, I had the same dream, exactly as the night before, and I repeated the same activities as the day before, calling to check on Christine, with the same disappointing result. It was now Tuesday, June 7, and my concern grew stronger, and I felt very anxious. My heart felt heavy, and I had a sick feeling in my stomach. I knew that something was very wrong.

With no word from Christine on Tuesday, Karen was distraught. The character of the third dream might reflect this mental state, but the content suggests the supernatural: The spirit of Christine Skubish was contacting Karen in her dreams in order to save Nick, who was still in the woods.

Karen's third dream is much more disturbing (keep in mind that Karen calls Christine her "sister" because they were so close, but technically, she is Christine's aunt):

That night I had another dream that was different than the other two. This dream was more of a catastrophic nature. I was in my sister's house and there was a horrible wind. This wind had so much force that the trees were completely bent in half. I was standing in front of the window and looking out into the yard. It was a big yard, as my sister lived on sixteen acres with many tall pine trees. It was nighttime, and all of a sudden, the winds increased to hurricane-like winds. I could hear the sound of glass breaking and popping and metal scraping. I could see sparks.

I looked over in the yard and I could see Nicky standing in the middle of the yard. I also saw my sister trying to get to him.

There was so much debris blowing around and glass shattering and metal that looked like it was curled up. I was trying to help my sister, but I couldn't find my shoes. I was barefooted, and I knew I wouldn't be able to make it to her because of all the glass that was on the ground. I finally found them, and when I opened the door, the wind stopped. I ran to her and she was just standing there with Nicky.

Nervously, I was laughing, and I turned her towards me and asked if she was all right. When I looked in her eyes, they were blank and there was no life in them. Her face was inexpressive. She looked like she was in a trance, because she didn't look at me but through me.

I asked if she was okay, and she said, "No."

I said, "Are you going to be okay?"

She looked at me with very haunting eyes and with a melancholy expression and again said, "No."

This dream seems to meet the definition of what experts call an after-death communication (ADC), because Christine is telling Karen that she (Christine) is deceased, but that Nick needs help. This was early on Wednesday morning, June 8, 1994, and nobody had any evidence about a car accident. However, Karen was now absolutely sure that something was amiss.

At this point, I woke up to hear a loud screaming sound and a pounding like a loud bang. I sat up. My heart was racing; I could hear the sound of my heart beating. It was hard to breathe. It felt like someone hit me hard in the pit of my stomach. It felt like all the blood had rushed to my head. It was brutal. It was the kind of dream that shakes you to the very core, and it wasn't going to go away. There was no shaking this dream. This was probably about the same time of night as the other two dreams I had previously.

Now this is Wednesday, June 8. I couldn't go back to sleep. I got ready for work and still my gut hurt. My heart felt heavy. My chest felt tight. My head felt swollen. I felt completely out of sorts. When I got to work, it was really hard to concentrate on my work. I told my coworker about the dream and how I couldn't shake it. I kept having a chill that ran down my back. I made it through the day, but I felt really tired.

When I got home, my daughter asked, "Mom, did you hear that Chrissy is missing?"

I said, "No," I hadn't heard, but I flippantly said, "Chris isn't missing. How can you miss Chris? She was too loud to miss."

As I said that, I took a couple of steps and stopped dead in my tracks. I knew that this was it. Chrissy was supposed to have arrived today, and I still hadn't heard from her.

The dream occurred the morning of Wednesday, June 8, and it was that evening when Deputy Strasser got the missing-persons report. Thursday came and went with no new developments. Karen was convinced that her entire immediate family should be scouring the roadside, but she had no car. She asked her husband to rent one. Karen continued:

I was trying to convince my family that if she had been in a wreck, there was a good possibility that Nicky could have survived. I could feel him. I could feel that he was alive. I didn't feel Chrissy, but I did feel Nick. But still, no one would help.

*My sister did make fliers and hand them out and post them
with a picture of Chris.*

Increasingly concerned, the family printed up fliers and began
distributing the fliers along Highway 50. Karen, who lived five hundred miles away, was finally able to rent a car in order to start searching the roadside with her husband.

Karen described the search:

> *On Friday, June 10, I knew the window of opportunity
> was closing for Nicky. I was desperate. The car rental [com-
> pany] called to tell me that the car we were to pick up had
> been returned vandalized and we would have to wait on
> another car to come in. Well, it finally came in, and by the
> time we picked up the car, it [was] around 8 to 9 p.m. We
> had about a seven-hour drive ahead of us, so on our way, we
> stopped and bought a spotlight so that we would be able to see
> if we arrived before sunup.*
>
> *As we left on our journey, I was praying, and continued to
> pray all the way. We were probably about two hours into our
> drive, and I just couldn't find the words to pray. Then there
> was a groaning in my spirit, and I began to hear an utterance
> that I couldn't understand. I believe it was the Holy Spirit. I
> began to hear a man's voice; it was dynamic and forceful, and
> he was praying. He was demanding and he was rebuking.
> Even though it was strange, I understood every word.*
>
> *He was covering Chrissy and Nicky with the blood of
> Jesus. He was sending God's angels to surround them. It
> sounded like heaven was being called down with all the glory
> and love and protection. I do not believe I ever experienced*

such power before. I felt like I was enveloped in peace and warmth. I heard this for what seemed the entire trip, but then, at one point, I couldn't feel Nicky any longer. I told my husband he could slow down…it was over. Nicky was gone. I could no longer feel him.

This sounds like a mystical experience of the spiritual warfare variety. Enveloped in power, Karen heard a male voice commanding angels to protect Christine and Nick. However, then something happened and Nick dropped off the radar. Did Nick lose his grip on this world for a brief time? The extrasensory mechanism assuring her that Nick was alive no longer detected his life force. Karen believes that Nick actually died at this time—and there is some startling confirmation of that from Nick himself after his rescue.

Meet Nick Skubish

The great miracle of this case is three-year-old Nick's unlikely survival. The serpentine highway winds its way through the Sierra Nevada Mountains from Sacramento to Lake Tahoe. Because there were no skid marks, the police hypothesize that Christine fell asleep just prior to reaching the corner known as Bullion Bend. Running off the road with no guard rails, the car plunged forty feet down an embankment, making it invisible to passing motorists. Of course, no one really knows what happened. However, if a third party ran her off the road, or even if an animal ran onto the highway, one would expect to find skid marks.

I was able to locate, contact, and interview Nick, who will be twenty-three by the time this book hits the street. He actually remembers quite a bit, considering that he was only three at the time of the tragedy.

By the end of this chapter, I hope it is clear that finding Nick was more from divine providence than my investigative journalism. Of course, this accident was an extremely traumatic and life-altering event that affects his life to this day. With that in mind, I endeavored to maintain a degree of sensitivity with the questions I asked.

CRIS: Nick, do you actually remember the accident?

NICK: Oh, the accident? Absolutely…but I don't remember anything before the accident, and I don't even remember the hospital at all, like recovering. But I remember the accident quite a bit actually.

CRIS: Tell me what you remember.

NICK: I remember almost every night; I don't remember the days too much, but I remember the night we wrecked. I remember the car flipping. I remember hitting tree after tree after tree… And I remember when the roof of the car got ripped off. I remember seeing my mom. I remember getting out of the car. I remember climbing up that forty-foot embankment and sliding down on pine needles. I remember seeing the lights. I remember every night, pretty much. I just don't remember the days at all. If anything, I feel like I was sleeping, but I don't remember the days at all.

CRIS: Did you have any water or anything?

NICK: Not that I remember. I know we wrecked at two o'clock in the morning, June sixth, and they found us sometime in the afternoon on June eleventh.

CRIS: So, a little over five days and six nights counting the night of the accident.

NICK: That sounds right.

CRIS: That's a long time to go without food and water.

NICK: Yeah, I had a severe concussion; matter of fact, I still have a scar. I'd say a good three inches long on the side of my head, more of an indentation really, and I went through severe malnutrition and severe dehydration.[9]

The Apparition by the Road

Paranormal Witness called this story "Haunted Highway" for a good reason. The second episode of the first season featured an interview with Deborah Hoyt, an unrelated traveler, who adds another paranormal element to the Skubish story. She describes awakening in the middle of night—the early morning hours of Saturday, June 11—with an overwhelming urgency to go home. Based on the vague but powerful premonition, she persuaded her husband to wake and drive up Highway 50. On the way home to Lake Tahoe, Deborah was astonished to see a naked, apparently deceased, young woman on the side of the road. She described the woman as young, dark-haired, attractive, and endowed with large breasts—features matching Christine Skubish. Because this was the age before cell phones, Deborah and her husband drove to the closest gas station to call 911. When an officer arrived, Deborah led him to Bullion Bend...but there was no sign of the ghostly white, nude woman.

Deborah related her disappointment: "[The police officer] had a big spotlight and he was looking, and then he came back down and told me they hadn't found anything and that we should go home. I told my husband that I didn't think they believed me and that they thought I was crazy and they would probably just stop the search."[10]

Apparently, the police were led back to Bullion Bend later that night, but that information has never been disclosed to the public— that is, until now. That will be explained shortly. For now, we return to Nick.

Nick's Angels

In the meantime, deep down the precipitous embankment, three-year-old Nick was in the car next to his deceased mother's broken body. After talking to the officer who responded to Deborah Hoyt, Deputy Strasser was increasingly convinced that the apparition and the Skubish disappearance were connected. But there's more. While thirsty and starving, Nick was strangely *not* alone.

CRIS: Do you believe you saw angels at the scene of the accident?

NICK: Yes, only at night.

CRIS: Can you describe them for me?

NICK: Sure. Take the silhouette of a person, just the form, if you will. And make that form an essence of light, just light radiating from the form, but no physical features, no hands, no clothes…just light.

CRIS: So just a shape of a body glowing light?

NICK: Yes, exactly.

A Supernatural Worldview allows one to postulate that the spirit of Christine Skubish was desperately trying to save her child. In contrast, skeptics have suggested that perhaps the body on the side of the road was actually Nick. While it's hard to imagine a three-year-old boy being misidentified as a busty adult female, it offers a nonparanormal possibility. As a matter of fact, Nick remembers climbing up to the road, but after no cars came, not knowing what to do, he returned to the car and his mom.

CRIS: You remember making it to the road?

NICK: Yes. I definitely got up to the road a couple times.

CRIS: Is it possible the naked body people saw was you?

NICK: I don't know. Honestly, I don't ever remember laying up there, but anything is possible. I just remember what I remember, and other people saw what they say they saw.

CRIS: Do you think the naked apparition seen at the road might have been your mother?

NICK: I would say…yeah. I think, if my Mom were playing a part in what happened, she might have to go about things in different ways with different people to get them to perceive what was actually going on. Maybe their mind would've told them it wasn't real. But a woman lying on the side of the road was a real possibility; therefore, Deborah Hoyt saw it when she did.

CRIS: It seems like that was a big part of what saved you: People reported a naked woman's body on the side of the road. Deborah Hoyt definitely saw a female, and she seemed pretty sure about it. So it's hard to believe it was you, but I suppose a skeptic might say that, so I wanted to ask. Some people just do not want to believe in anything supernatural.

NICK: That is one thing I have found throughout the years. A lot of people I have met have a hard time believing in anything big at all. People think they do, but not everyone generally believes what they think they do, I have found.

CRIS: That is what this book is about: how the presuppositions you hold, the things that you believe about reality, will mold your opinion about everything else. If you don't believe in the possibility of miracles or supernatural things, then you will always try to come up with an explanation that excludes them, no matter how fanciful. In this way, opinions are really a product of worldview as much as facts. People always interpret facts through their worldview. It's like the lens that you view the world through.

NICK: It is. You know what? I really like what you're talking about. I've read a lot of books on spiritual things; I read a lot. I am definitely interested in this book that you are writing.

Ghost or no ghost, a naked woman lying on the side of the high-way is hard to ignore. Nick believes his mom was doing what was necessary to get a reaction. His great aunt Karen also believes that the apparition was her niece's post-mortem effort to save her son. She offered:

> *Some say that to be absent from the body is to be present with the Lord. But if there was any possible way to make this happen, I know Chrissy could. She had such a great love for the Father and Jesus and she was so strong-willed and determined that nothing would stop her from making sure her baby was safe. She loved him so much. He was all she had in this world. He was her everything, and there were no boundaries where he was concerned. Her love remained even in death— even if it meant taking her clothes off to attract someone to the site of the wreck.*

I asked Nick for more details about the angels that were with him at night. Perhaps they had something to do with apparition sightings? Interestingly, this led Nick back to Karen's dreams.

Cris: These beings of light that you saw, were they close to you? Were they only at a distance? Did you interact with them?

NICK: One of them was next to the car the whole time, and one of them was next to the road. I've been told by a lot of people that when I was in the hospital—and, like I said earlier, I don't remember the hospital, I don't remember the recovery at all—I was told by a lot of people that I told them I saw the angels. I told them a lot of other things, too. I told my aunt [Karen] a few things. I don't know what show you saw, but one that goes way back *[Unsolved Mysteries]* talks about my aunt having visions; that's the same aunt. She had multiple dreams, I guess, at the time it was going on. She has actually had quite a few paranormal experiences. A lot of people in my family have had paranormal experiences—on that side of the family at least.

Cris: Your aunt had a dream, and she reported it, and others saw a naked body by the road—and it was those things put together that helped them find you, correct?

Nick: My aunt's dreams never get focused on because she did not want to be involved in any of the television programs. So the next show that covered it *[Paranormal Witness]* was because my grandfather submitted it, and it was the first one I took part in since the accident.

An important idea developed in *The Supernatural Worldview* is that some folks, like Karen Nichols, are more inclined to perceive the spirit realm than others. This doesn't make them guilty of witchcraft or of practicing the occult arts. It isn't something Karen asked for or intentionally developed, but rather is an inherent ability. In her third dream, an after-death communication from Christine led Karen to conclude that her niece was deceased, but that Nick was in desperate need of rescue. The dream featured broken glass and tearing metal—details that are consistent with the actual mangled automobile. Karen's actions support her story as well. Desperate, she and her husband rented a car to drive five hundred miles as they scoured the roadside for any small sign. Karen described the journey and a remarkable event that was spiritually perceived and later confirmed:

> *I was praying as we left on our journey and continued to pray all the way. We were probably about two hours into our drive, and I just couldn't find the words to pray, and there*

came a groaning in my spirit, and I began to hear an utterance that I couldn't understand. I believe it was the Holy Spirit, and I began to hear a man's voice. It was dynamic and forceful, and he was praying, he was demanding, he was rebuking. I understood his every word; he was covering Chrissy and Nicky with the blood of Jesus. He was sending God's angels to surround them. It sounded like heaven was being sent down with all the glory and love and protection. I do not believe I have ever experienced such power before. I felt like I was enveloped in warmth and peace. I heard this for what seemed the entire trip, but then at one point I couldn't feel Nicky any longer, and I told my husband he could slow down. It was over; Nicky was gone…I couldn't feel him.

Karen believes that Nick briefly departed this life. This odd detail is especially interesting in light of what she later learned at the hospital. For now, we return to the search as described by Karen:

I knew that there would be something of Chrissy's or Nicky's on the road or at a turn out that would let me know where they were. So I began looking on the side of the road. If I didn't have a clear view, I would have my husband stop so I could get out and physically look over the side. There was so much vegetation on Highway 50, a very mountainous highway that leads to Lake Tahoe.

The timing of the discovery is amazing, because it seems that Karen and Deputy Strasser arrived at the scene within minutes of each other. The Associated Press reported: "Strasser had spotted the boy's tennis shoe on the side of the highway Saturday, and then found the car. He believes the boy at some point climbed from the car to the highway, and then returned to the car. That is the only explanation for the shoe being on the road, Strasser said."[11] Just minutes after Deputy Strasser had followed the shoe to locate the car, Karen and her husband spotted Nick's shoe on the road and pulled up next to the patrol car.

Karen continues:

> As we were looking, I saw a little tennis shoe lying on the side of the road and also noticed that the patrol car had stopped there. I told my husband, "She's here; stop the car!" I got out of the car and started to run, but the deputy stopped me and told me that I couldn't go down there. By "down there," I mean there was a drop-off about twenty feet down and I could see Chrissy' car. I was yelling Chrissy's name. The deputy said that Chrissy was gone. I remember it felt like my legs turned to rubber, and I and my husband hit the ground.
>
> Nicky was alive, but barely. He looked like a little bird that had [fallen] out of a nest: His skin was dark and baggy, his little eyes [were] filled with muck. His lips were parched; he was marked and curled up in a fetal position next to Chris. When his name was called, he responded quietly. I left to go to Marshall Medical Center in Placerville to wait for the ambulance to bring Nicky there.
>
> When I was finally able to see Nicky, he was alert but weak. I knew something miraculous had taken place, but at that time I wasn't sure what it was. Later that morning when they were able to stabilize him, they transferred him to UC Davis. His organs were shutting down. They said he only had thirty minutes, maybe less, of life left because his kidneys were

shutting down and they still weren't sure if they would be able to reverse the damage. So we left Marshall Hospital and went to UC Davis in Sacramento.

When I walked in the hospital room, Nicky sat straight up and looked at me, his little eyes as big as saucers, and said, "Aunt Kiki, Aunt Kiki, my mommy died!"

I said, "Yes, Nicky she did."

Then he said, "I died too, but I wasn't afraid because I was with Jesus and His angels, but I couldn't stay. I had to come back here."

He also said that Jesus' angels were there with him in the car. I asked where they were, and he said, "There were three— there was two by the car and one on the road."

I didn't say anything. I couldn't speak. I just held him and thought back to the time when I couldn't feel him anymore, and said, "Well there it is."

I thought to myself, "He is only three and a half years old; how would he know these things?" He wasn't old enough to be influenced by anyone.

This corroboration from Nick suggests that when Karen could no longer feel Nick's life force, he actually had a near-death experience (NDE). This possibility brings the number of paranormal phenomena associated with this case to five: 1) Karen's extrasensory perception (ESP) dreams; 2) Christine's after-death communication to Karen; 3) Apparition on side of the road seen by multiple witnesses; 4) Nick's angels; and 5) Nick's NDE. Of course, the atheist fundamentalists and debunkers cannot allow a case this strong to stand uncontested.

E.D.S.O. CORONERS REPORT:

VICTIM: SKUBISH, CHRISTINE DAWN   D.O.B. OCT. 24, 1969

DETAILS OF INVESTIGATION:

On June. 11, 1994 Approx. 0612 hours the EL Dorado Sheriff's
Dispatch contacted me by phone at home regarding a pending coroners
case. I was advised that there was a fatal vehicle accident on
state Highway 50 in the area of Bullion Bend and the Emergency
personnel at the scene requested that the Deputy Sheriff Coroner
respond to that location. I arrived at the scene at approx. 0708
hours and contacted Deputy R. Strasser; No. 3D281 at that location.
Dep. Strasser stated that on June. 09, 1994 there was a missing
persons report filed with the EL Dorado County Sheriff's Department
on the Decedent, Ms. Skubish, Catherine Dawn; Dob. Oct. 24, 1969
and her Son, Nick Anthony Skubish; Dob. Jan. 05, 1991 by their
family members and a friend. Please refer to the two attached M\P
reports Case No.s 94-11621 and 94-11585 for further information
regarding that matter.

Dep. Strasser further stated that Det. Hogland; No.3K208 who
was working the M\P Case on Ms. Skubish and her (3) year old Son,
Nick Skubish had provided him and the other patrol units with the
M\P Information. Dep. Strasser advised that on 06-11-94 approx.
0310 hours E.D.S.O. Units received a citizens report of a naked
lady laying along HWY 50 in the Bullion Bend area. The E.D.S.O.
Deputies and C.H.P. Officers reportedly checked the indicated area
in response to the citizens report but were unable to locate the
described subject or any other suspicious circumstances at that
time. While Dep. Strasser was rechecking the area in the day light
at approx. 0605 hours, he observed a child's boot laying next to
HWY 50 at the scene. Dep. Strasser located Ms. Skubish and her
Son, Nick Skubish with the list vehicle Calif. Lic. No. 2XBY018 at
the scene. Dep. Strasser on 06-11-94 confirmed Ms. Skubish's death
at approx. 0610 Hours and requested Emergency aid for Nick Skubish
at approx. 0612 hours. Nick Skubish was first transported to
Marshall Hospital and then on to the U.C. Davis Hospital for
further medical treatment.

Official Coroner's Report for Christine Skubish

10 — Lodi News-Sentinel — Tuesday, June 14, 1994

Tot's rescue still an enigma

McClatchy News Service

SACRAMENTO — The toddler who survived a horrendous auto crash and five days without food and water was told Monday that his mother was dead.

Nicky Skubish "buried his little head in my chest, grabbed onto me and cried," grandmother Brenda Stautzenbach said of the 3-year-old boy's reaction to the news. "We talked and we talked about his mother going to heaven."

Christene Dawn Skubish, 24, died June 6 when the car she was driving plunged off Highway 50 near Pollock Pines in the Sierra Nevada foothills and barrel-rolled into a stand of trees some 40 feet down an embankment.

It wasn't until Saturday morning that the wreckage was found, Nicky huddling naked in the passenger seat beside his mother. Stautzenbach said she and her husband,

David, were advised Monday by child social services personnel that Nicky should be told of his mother's death in order to begin the healing process.

"They met with us today and told us they felt Nicky needed to know what happened. He was there with her for five days," Stautzenbach said.

While the family is concentrating on comforting Nicky, the reality of Christene's death has begun to sink in, Stautzenbach said.

Brenda's mother, Betty, has donated to Christene her burial plot at Forest Lawn in Anaheim. "My dad and Chrissy were very, very close," Stautzenbach explained.

While the miracle of Nicky's recovery continues, its mystery remains.

Sheriff's deputy Rich Strasser was led to the scene of the crash by an early-morning report from a passing motorist that there was a nude

NICKY SKUBISH   CHRISTENE SKUBISH

woman on the roadside.

"I just started screaming and screaming," said Deborah Hoyt, 34, of Lake Tahoe, who said she was returning home with her husband when she saw on the roadway "a naked lady, lying on her side, bent legs together with an arm over her head."

Hoyt said she now believes what she saw was an apparition, "some kind of spirit" sent by God.

Local paper corroborates the story[12]

Skepticism vs. the Supernatural Worldview

According to the police, the female apparition matching Christine's description was undoubtedly what first led them to Bullion Bend, where it was eventually discovered that the car ran off the road. This is obviously not a mere coincidence, but skeptics can't accept the idea of supernatural intervention. One callous online cynic suggested that the apparition was invented by Deborah Hoyt in order to conceal the fact that she and her husband had run Christine off the road. To escape responsibility, the cynic asserted, she concocted the ghost as a way to alert the police to the location without incriminating herself or the driver. Such a libelous accusation offers the anti-supernaturalist a plausible escape—a disparaging tactic common to paranormal debunkers. However, the absence of skid marks reveals that Christine never hit the brakes. Even more, the skeptical slander is controverted by evidence not included on the television shows. These are new details never reported before.

After Nick's rescue, a California highway patrolman, Jack Greenwood, gave Karen astonishing information not reported on any of the television programs. He even told her that "something supernatural took place." She recalled the conversation between her and her husband and Greenwood shortly after Nick's rescue:

> *We met with Jack, and when we first met, his eyes were big and he spoke very precisely. He began with a deep breath and started by saying, "I'm not a religious man. I'm not a Christian man."*
>
> *Then he said, "I am Catholic, but I'm not religious. I have to tell you something happened here that I can't explain."*
>
> *He was on duty the night before Christine was found,*

and there had been not one but actually three calls. The first call was about a woman lying on the side of the road. They reported she was naked, had dark brown hair, was petite with big breasts, and her skin looked real white, like she had been in the cold for a long time.

[Greenwood] said he went out to the area to investigate and found nothing. Later that night, he received another report of a woman lying on the side of the road with the same description in the same area. Again, he went to investigate and found nothing. Later that morning, he received another call with the same report of a naked woman of the same description. He said he told the caller that he had been out twice and there was nothing there.

The man replied, "The hell there isn't!" He told Jack that he was sitting on the side of the road with his cell phone watching her from his rear view mirror and that she was running frantically back and forth like she looking for something. He said, "I'm watching her as we speak."

Again, [Greenwood] found nothing. He went on to say that later that morning, he was still on duty and received the call on the accident and he was the one that responded.

Greenwood reported that *three different people* had reported seeing a naked woman by the side of the road. In fact, one witness had seen her pacing back and forth! This unprecedented information substantially changes the case in favor of a Supernatural Worldview. Karen continued with her recollection of the conversation:

He went on to say that he had been a highway patrolman for over twenty-eight years and had seen a lot of accidents where people had been in the elements for days. He said that when the body deteriorates, the abdomen will usually swell and burst, and that is what he expected to find. The days all that week had been very hot, about 106 degrees in the daytime. He was the CHiP officer who went to the site of the accident. It was a wilderness area. He said the insects were awful. They were being bitten by mosquitoes and other bugs. There were lots of varmints and wild animals in that area, but the strange thing was that when they got to the car, it was as though a tent or a veil had been placed over the car. He said there wasn't one insect bite, no blowfly larva, no animal bites, no sign of anything.

Nicky's clothes had been folded and placed on the hood of the car. There were signs that Nicky had been out of the car, and when he was picked up and put on the gurney, he had been sitting on a book of Bible stories, and you could see the imprint of his little bottom on it. [Greenwood] then said that he was the one that took Christine out of the car, and her tummy was just as flat as if she had just died. There was no sign of deterioration or decay; she only had a little trickle of blood from her nose. [Greenwood said] that she had probably died at impact; it was obvious that she had broken her neck from the protrusion of the cervical spine. He said that there was only one tiny spot on her elbow that showed any sign of deterioration. He said that when he took her out and looked at her, she fit the total description of the girl that had been reported.

He said, "I don't know what happened, but something supernatural took place here, folks." He said we should report to Unsolved Mysteries.

These details have also never previously been revealed. Of course, Greenwood's final piece of advice came to pass, and the case premiered on *Unsolved Mysteries* (season 9, episode 16) as: "Highway 50 Phantom" on February 21, 1997. But what about the other unreported details? It seems unlikely that a toddler bothered to fold his clothes after he stripped them off in the sweltering summer heat. Did the angels fold his clothes, or did his mother's ghost do it? I suppose we'll never know. What about Christine's body? If we count its (and Nick's) unexpected preservation, we have seven paranormal phenomena.

1. Karen had ESP dreams (view from inside the car).
2. Christine and Karen experienced after-death communication with one another.
3. At least three witnesses reported an apparition pointing to the scene of the accident. Deborah Hoyt's account is on record; the accounts of two others were verified by officer Jack Greenwood.
4. Angels (figures of light) were seen near the car and by the road at night.
5. Nick had a possible near-death experience.
6. Christine Skubish's body was inexplicably preserved.
7. Nick was able to survive without food and water for five days in temperatures over 100 degrees.

From Paranormal to Gospel

As we come full circle in this first chapter, one might wonder why it is titled "Paranormal Witness to Gospel Witness." According to

Karen Nichols, Christine had her challenges, but was a Christian who loved the Lord. While recovering in the hospital, Nick said he was briefly with Jesus and His angels in heaven. Officer Greenwood related that Nick was discovered sitting on a book of Bible stories in the torturously wrecked car. Without food or water, Nick was miraculously preserved through scorching heat that reached more than 100 degrees Fahrenheit. Despite the loss, God's hand of provision can be seen through the tragedy.

How can evangelical Christians respond to a story like this? All too often, it ends up being "demonize first, ask questions later" (that is, if ever). It seems disingenuous and inconsistent coming from folks whose central message involves the resurrection of the dead. In this case, it appears that God allowed a departed mother's spirit to intercede with passing motorists and to communicate in the dreams of her aunt. Why should this stretch plausibility for those with a biblical worldview? I don't believe it should, but it often appears that way. If Karen hadn't been informed by dreams, and if the apparition hadn't been reported, Nick would not have been found in time. At least one ghost story has yielded good fruit.

During the process of interviewing Nick Skubish in 2013, I suggested to him that God must have an important plan for his life. We all know that many young children are killed in car accidents. The odds for the toddler's survival in the wilderness for five days were exceedingly low. Nick quickly agreed, and told me he is still experiencing unusual events to this day. I shared my personal testimony and asked Nick to read the gospel of John.

After he read it, I asked for his reaction. Nick responded, "I thought it was a good example of how consuming sin really is. Seems like the people's pride in their own opinion or religious views prevented them from seeing who He was and why He was even here."

Needless to say, I was very impressed with his answer, since this was his first reading of the book of John.

I did my best to explain why his response about the consuming nature of sin was so accurate: "We need saving because God's judgment against sin is real. But the really cool thing He did was to provide a way for imperfect sinners like you and me to make it. He took the punishment we deserve. The really important passage is: 'For God so loved the world, that he gave his only Son, that whoever believes in him should not perish but have eternal life. For God did not send his Son into the world to condemn the world, but in order that the world might be saved through him. Whoever believes in him is not condemned, but whoever does not believe is condemned already, because he has not believed in the name of the only Son of God'"(John 3:16–18).

I asked, "So do you know that you have experienced that rebirth that Jesus was telling Nicodemus about?" Nick responded that he has never really experienced it. We prayed together, and Nick accepted the gospel over the phone. Nick has moved from "paranormal witness" to "gospel witness." He has a challenging path before him. Please pray for Nick.

Despite the desperate last gasps by the drowning neoatheists, the paranormal is the new normal in Western culture. I endeavor to empower you with astonishing new findings that suggest a paradigm shift of biblical proportions…possibly even heralding the end of the age.

Notes

1. "Is the Long Island Medium a Fake?" Long Island Medium Fake. com, http://www.longislandmediumfake.com/main.html (accessed 09/26/13).
2. Paranormal Witness, "Haunted Highway," Syfy, http://www.syfy. com/paranormalwitness/episodes/season/1/episode/102/haunted_ highway_kentucky_ufo_chase (accessed 09/26/13).
3. Bill Gorman, "Syfy's New Hit Series 'Paranormal Witness' Spooks 1.63 Million Total Viewers, Up 29% Versus Last Week's Premiere," TV by the Numbers, September 15, 2011 (accessed 09/26/13).
4. Nick and christine scoobish.jpg, Unsolved Mysteries Wiki, http:// unsolvedmysteries.wikia.com/wiki/Christine_Scoobish?file=Nick_ and_christine_scoobish.jpg.
5. Paranormal Witness, season 1, episode 2, "Haunted Highway/ Kentucky UFO Chase," Daily Motion, http://www.dailymotion. com/video/xl3oef_paranormal-witness-haunted-highway-kentucky-ufo-chase-s01-e02_shortfilms (5:57–6:09).
6. Personal communication from Karen Nichols to Cris Putnam via Facebook private message, September 26, 2013.
7. Paranormal Witness (8:13–8:20).
8. Personal communication from Karen Nichols to Cris Putnam via Facebook private message, August 23, 2013.
9. Interview transcribed from recorded phone call between author and Nick Skubish, July 19, 2013.
10. Paranormal Witness (15:17–15:54).
11. Associated Press, "Boy, 3, Recovering After 5 Days in Car With Dead Mother," *Los Angeles Times,* June 14,1994, http://articles.

latimes.com/1994-06-14/news/mn-3969_1_dead-mother (accessed
02/07/14).

12. McClatchy News Service, "Tot's Rescue Still an Enigma," *Lodi News
Sentinel,* June 14, 1994, http://news.google.com/newspapers?id=EGo
zAAAAIBAJ&sjid=pjIHAAAAIBAJ&pg=7130%2C5551853.

THE SUPERNATURAL WORLDVIEW OF REALITY

Reality is merely an illusion, albeit a very persistent one.

—ALBERT EINSTEIN

The Supernatural Worldview entails understanding and perceiving what exists through a supernatural lens. Although the term "supernatural" implies that nature is not all there is, most of Western culture now assumes nature's completeness. Like in Eastern religions in which "all is one," our universities teach that nature, consisting of matter and energy, is all encompassing. Antithetical to the cultural consensus, the Supernatural Worldview entails presuppositions derived from ancient prophetic texts as well as cutting-edge science. It holds that nature is not ultimate and that a Creator God brought it into being. If this is indeed true, then there is much more than meets the eye, and reality is not only much stranger than commonly recognized; it is much more wonderful.

Truth is that which corresponds to reality. Reality is what exists regardless of human opinion. For example, I believe atheists are still immortal, immaterial spirits created by God—whether they believe that or not. Their unbelief does not change that reality. I still want to lead them to Christ. I want them to understand that the brief lifetime they experience within this material realm is a flash in the pan of cosmic time. Nevertheless, today's decisions have eternal ramifications. God is our greatest ally when we choose to follow Him. In contrast, there are dark, nonhuman adversaries plotting behind the scenes, manipulating and steering history toward malevolent ends. Often they are forgotten in lieu of human conflicts involving politics, religion, and ideology. Even so, secrets long buried will surface to the light of day, and, in the end, there will be ultimate justice. God is always watching. This is the wisdom behind the "fear of the Lord" extolled in the Proverbs. All is not one; there is a transcendent *Other*. This is the Supernatural Worldview. One's worldview is often assumed and unexamined. This necessitates defining terms carefully.

Supernatural

The term "supernatural" originates in sixteenth-century, medieval Latin: *supra*, which means "above," plus *naturalis*, meaning "nature." Thus, it describes transcendence of the natural realm. It is defined in a standard dictionary as:

1) Of or relating to an order of existence beyond the visible observable universe; especially: of or relating to God or a god, demigod, spirit, or devil. 2) a: departing from what is

usual or normal especially so as to appear to transcend the laws of nature; b: attributed to an invisible agent (as a ghost or spirit).[1]

Of course, modern sophisticates recoil at the suggestion of supernatural intervention in the world. Accordingly, the supernatural has been demoted to superstition in the academy, but, even so, most people claim some sort of transcendent spirituality. The definitive question comes down to oneness—as in monism—or, as New Testament scholar Peter Jones explains it, twoness entailing "the Creator of nature, namely God, is a completely different being, whose will determines the nature and function of all created things."[2]

This book is unabashedly written from the perspective of Christian theism in that the triune God of the Bible transcends all because He created all things. Exception is taken with former NASA astronaut-turned-Institute of Noetic Sciences (IONS) founder, Edgar Mitchell, who contends, "There are no unnatural or supernatural phenomena, only very large gaps in our knowledge of what is natural."[3] He believes that "all is one" within nature. This form of oneness (monism) is based on "promissory naturalism" in that a natural explanation is promised in the future but remains, for now, unknown. It goes something like, "Well, science cannot yet explain it, but due to its remarkable past success, we have faith that one day it will." The problem is that some realities lie outside the purview of science. Science is not only incapable of finding ultimate answers concerning the origin of nature; it is utterly impotent to even begin to address the existence of the supernatural.

A common mistake made by skeptics is to assume science has disproven supernatural phenomena. It is formally called a "category error." Science, by definition, deals with the natural; thus, the supernatural is outside of its purview. Christian philosopher Gregory Koukl makes a colorful illustration by asking, "Can you weigh a chicken with a yardstick?"[4] Of course, this is manifestly absurd, because a yardstick doesn't measure weight, but rather length. The salient point is that science by definition only examines natural phenomena in the same way a yardstick only measures distance. Thus, science is incapable of making any determination whatsoever when it comes to phenomena outside of nature. It is impotent. Jones compares it to the new perspective earth science was given from the space program:

> Geophysics got a lot easier once we could study the globe from the outside. But scientists cannot fly outside the universe to send back pictures of the cosmos, as the astronauts did when they took those stunning pictures of the blue planet earth. We cannot roam the outer reaches of our mental world, either—standing outside ourselves, our world, our brains—to make meaningful statements about the whole of life.[5]

When a scientist says the supernatural does not exist, he is making a category error along the lines of trying to weigh a chicken with a yardstick. Also, because nature has not always existed, the supernatural must exist to get it started.

The twentieth century marked a paradigm shift from the belief in an eternal universe to the mathematical certitude of a temporal one. This strongly implies the existence of God. The cosmological argument states: 1) Everything that begins to exist has a cause; 2) The universe began to exist; 3) Therefore, the universe has a cause. What modern cosmology labels as the "Big Bang" is what Christians call "Creation." Because nature is within the universe, a cause outside of nature is necessary; so, it is supernatural by definition. It follows logically that bangs need "bangers,"—in this case, one of unimaginable power. Also, because the constants of nature are extremely fine tuned to chance-defying precision, this cause must be exceedingly intelligent.[6] Furthermore, the cause chose to bring everything into existence, including man as a personal conscious being. The answer to the philosopher's conundrum of "Why is there something rather than nothing?" is that a choice was made. Impersonal forces do not make choices, and persons always come from other persons. Thus, one derives a supernatural, personal, conscious being of unimaginable power and intelligence responsible for creating the universe. It seems that Moses was three thousand years ahead of modern cosmology when he wrote, "In the beginning, God created the heavens and the earth" (Genesis 1:1).

Paranormal

When an entity outside of nature (God, angels, demons, spirits) interacts with the natural world, that interaction is by definition a supernatural intervention. While the term "paranormal" is often used synonymously, an important distinction is drawn. More in line with Edgar Mitchell's hope, paranormal is better defined as "not scientifically explainable."[7] While supernatural phenomena are always paranormal, the paranormal are not always supernatural. For example, if extrasensory perception (ESP) is a human ability, then it is paranormal but not supernatural. In contrast, God sending a spirit to speak through a prophet would be supernatural (1 Kings 22:22). Sometimes, God uses natural mechanisms to accomplish a supernatural miracle. For example, a strong wind parted the Red Sea (Exodus 14:21). The wind was natural, but its behavior was not. The important distinction is that while the supernatural is also outside the purview of science, the paranormal may eventually be scientifically explained. According to sociologist Marcello Truzzi, the term "para-normal" was originally coined in order to preserve the distinction:

> If something is rare or extraordinary in science but it is explainable, we call it abnormal. The term paranormal refers to something that science can explain some day but at the present moment cannot. These are the scientific frontiers. However, there are things that are fundamentally inexpli-cable by science, the supernatural.[8]

Scientific and spiritual ideas converge in the paranormal, and some of those ideas are explored within. As a Christian theist, I have directed my focus in this volume primarily on the supernatural, but many paranormal phenomena are examined as well, because they may turn out to be supernatural. Let's examine the opposition to the Supernatural Worldview.

Naturalism and Material Reductionism

The worldview taught in our universities today is philosophical natu-ralism, the position that says nature is the ultimate reality. Naturalists are typically atheists who collaterally deny the existence of angels and demons.[9] Also, they typically deny the existence of a soul or afterlife and necessarily contend that consciousness is a phenomenon of the brain. The remarkable progress of science based on methodological naturalism in medicine has undone a great deal of superstition about disease and has afforded great progress. For this reason, it is entirely understandable that modern people, including Christians, have a tendency to think in naturalistic ways. Yet, naturalism is unsatisfying, because it cannot even begin to address the big questions, the sorts of questions a child might ask, like "Why am I here?" or a philosophical ultimate, like "Why is there something rather than nothing?" The Bible answers these with authority; nevertheless, it is also replete with demon possession, mystical experiences, and the resurrection of the dead. The skeptic will default to naturalism when interpreting these passages, but this is not a viable track for those who accept the inspiration and inerrancy of the Bible. One cannot be a Christian and a naturalist.

A corollary of naturalism is reductive materialism. This is the idea that all of reality is explained by matter and energy interacting according to the laws of chemistry and physics. This implies that everything reduces down to matter and the natural laws, hence reductionism. Physicalism is often used synonymously for materialism, but the two terms are distinguished in the following way: Materialists believe that only matter exists, while physicalists accept the existence of matter *and* energy. Because of the ever-shifting goal posts in science, some contemporary physicalists define their position defensively as "the theory that the ultimate constituents of reality are whatever ultimate particles or entities are accepted by physics."[10] This is as unfalsifiable as any religious faith statement. Neither view allows for the existence of God, the soul, or the supernatural. Now we examine the concept of worldview.

Worldview

The term "worldview" is derived from a German word, *weltanschauung*, which means a "look onto the world." An academic definition is "the comprehensive set of basic beliefs in which one views the world and interprets experiences."[11] It is the lens through which we interpret reality. Consciously or not, everyone has a worldview. It consists of our presuppositions that define reality. Most often, our worldview is formed by upbringing, education, nationality, and culture. It is fueled by books, music, art, and movies. Arguably, for the majority of people, their worldview is simply something they have acquired unintentionally by "osmosis." It is absorbed from popular culture.

Seven Worldview Questions

Dr. James Sire is an author and college professor of English literature, philosophy, and theology. His classic introductory text on worldviews, *The Universe Next Door*, published in 1976, is now in its fifth edition, having sold more than 350,000 copies. He defines a worldview as a committed spiritual orientation that is expressed as a set of presuppositions (that may or may not be true and consistent) concerning the basic makeup of the world. These entail answers to the basic questions a child might ask, like "Why am I here?" The way we answer these questions forms our worldview. An atheist might say, "There is no reason why," whereas a Christian might answer, "To glorify God and enjoy Him forever."

Sire wrote that worldviews all answer seven basic questions: (1) What is really real? (2) What is the nature of external reality, the world around us? (3) What is a human being? (4) What happens to a person after death? (5) Why is it possible to know anything at all? (6) How do we know what is right and wrong? (7) What is the meaning of human history?[12] The answers to these questions reflect one's philosophical and/or spiritual commitments. Each question is examined to reveal the issues involved:

1. What is really real? This first worldview question addresses the nature of reality and whether there is such a thing as the supernatural. It deals with such questions as:

- Does God exist? If there is, what is He like?
- If there is no God, why is there something rather than nothing?
- Does free will exist, or is everything determined?

2. What is the nature of external reality? This question deals with the observable world and what it consists of. Some Eastern worldviews argue that it is an illusion, but most people agree that the external world exists in some form. For instance, even idealists acknowledge that matter exists, but qualify that it is ultimately derived from consciousness rather than independently existing stuff.

- Does it exist? Is it all an illusion?
- Is the external world made of matter (materialism)?
- Is the external world ultimately derived from consciousness (idealism)?
- It is created or uncreated?
- It is orderly or chaotic?
- It is personal or impersonal?
- It is eternal or temporal?

3. What is a human being? Different worldviews have radically divergent views on the nature of humankind. The answer to this question has vast implications for how one treats other people. Some commonly held answers include:

- A highly evolved biological robot (the dominant view of Western science)
- A god or potential god (Mormons, transhumanists, New Age)
- Energy that changes forms; part of god (reincarnation, Buddhism, Hinduism)
- An embodied spirit (a material-spiritual being) bearing the image of God in a body created by God (the biblical answer)

4. What happens to a person after death? Even though denied by atheistic worldviews, the answer to this question has profound implications. For example, since the atheist denies the afterlife, what incentive is there for denying a pleasurable indulgence no matter how selfish or harmful to others—especially if it is unlikely one will ever get caught? Why not? Similarly, if a jihadist is motivated by a postmortem harem of seventy-two virgins, then why not strap a bomb to his body to glorify Allah? Some common answers include:

- People cease to exist.
- People reincarnate into other people or animals based on karma.
- All people become spirits and enter directly into heaven.
- People can become spirits stuck in a ghostly existence on earth.
- People become spirits; some enter heaven and are later given glorified bodies. Others, after periods, are given bodies, face judgment, and enter hell for eternity.

Note that some worldviews might allow for more than one of these answers depending on circumstances.

5. Why is it possible to know anything at all? Knowledge is best defined as justified true belief. Epistemology is the branch of philosophy that studies the nature of knowledge—in particular, its foundation, scope, and rationality. Different people have different ways of defining truth and knowledge, ranging from holding all knowledge to be relative and subjective to absolute and objective. These are some of the ways that various worldviews deal with the issue of knowledge:

- Consciousness and reason are developed through a long process of evolution.
- Consciousness and reason are an illusion.
- Humans are made in the image of God, who is the basis of all reason and knowledge.

6. How do we know what is right and wrong? This question addresses the source of moral values. Even when people and cultures disagree on specific issues, most acknowledge that they exist. Here are some of the ways that various worldviews address morality:

- Morality evolved as a survival mechanism.
- Morals are dictated by society.
- Morals are determined by personal preference.
- God defined morality and has revealed what is right.

7. What is the meaning of human history? The search for meaning and significance is probably the most profound issue that human beings wrestle with. It addresses hope. A survey of suicide notes reveals that a bad answer to this question has dire implications. Worldview dictates one's answer by asserting:

- Humans are accidents of matter and energy. There is no meaning to human history.
- Meaning is what we decide it to be.
- Meaning involves realizing that all is one.
- God has a plan and purpose for our lives. Meaning results from discovering and fulfilling that mission.

It is important to understand the nature of these questions so that you might carefully consider your own answers. Are you consistent? Perhaps after thinking these questions through, you realize the culture has influenced you more than you first thought. A 2009 Barna Group survey sought to determine how many Americans hold a biblical worldview. For the survey, a biblical worldview was defined as follows:

Believing that absolute moral truth exists; the Bible is totally accurate in all of the principles it teaches; Satan is considered to be a real being or force, not merely symbolic; a person cannot earn their way into Heaven by trying to be good or do good works; Jesus Christ lived a sinless life on earth; and God is the all-knowing, all-powerful creator of the world who still rules the universe today.[13]

The data revealed that less than 9 percent of Americans have a biblical worldview. Even amongst folks who claim the title "born again," the percentage was a dismal 19 percent. If most self-proclaimed Christians do not have a Supernatural Worldview, our evangelism faces a serious challenge.

Also, the questions are most useful for effectively interacting with people who believe differently than you. If you want to persuade someone with a different worldview, you must start by addressing the presuppositions that undergird his or her beliefs. Most often a good deal of preliminary work is needed. For example, unless someone is open to the existence of God, the gospel message will not gain much traction. Some folks might not be able to fully address these seven questions comprehensively, so four simple ones serve a similar diagnostic function.

Four Basic Questions

The seven questions provide metaphysical details, but most average people have never considered how to answer them. For that reason, simpler evaluations have been offered based on four questions everyone faces:

1) **Who are we?**
2) **Where are we?**
3) **What is wrong?**
4) **What is the answer?**

These offer a quick way to start thinking about the issues, and they make for an efficient analysis. For example, let's compare answers from secular worldview to those from a Christian perspective:

Secular Worldview

1. **Who are we?** Human beings are the primate species *homo sapiens* that evolved from lesser hominids (or great apes).
2. **Where are we?** We are on earth, a mediocre planet amongst many that support intelligent life.
3. **What is wrong?** There is a lack of education and resources. Therefore, people are frustrated and suffer from low self-esteem.
4. **What is the answer?** The solution is more education and equitable distribution of resources by a benevolent world government.

Biblical Worldview

1. **Who are we?** Human beings are embodied spirits bearing the image of God in a body created by God.
2. **Where are we?** We are on earth, an utterly unique planet in a finely tuned universe created to fantastically precise specifications to sustain intelligent life and maintained moment to moment by an omnipotent, sovereign God.
3. **What is wrong?** A powerful serpentine being called the *nachash* (a Hebrew word implying a shining serpentine entity) lured the first humans into sin. Sin is defined as humankind's disobedience to God and rebellion against His moral standards. Sin broke our relationship with our Creator, and humankind is perplexed, incomplete, and dissatisfied. We need our relationship with God restored in order to feel whole. Although most people are oblivious, mankind is in a state of war with the *nachash* and his ilk (see Genesis 3:15; Ephesians 6:12; and 2 Corinthians 4:4, 10:4).
4. **What is the answer?** The answer is the gospel, the good news. Jesus Christ, God's unique, eternal Son, came into the world in human form and gave His life as a sacrifice for our sins. God endows us with the grace to believe, and we believe God raised Jesus from the dead, we accept His sacrifice, and we make Him Lord of our life. By paying our debt, His perfect character is credited to those who believe and follow Him through faith alone.

Reality: Uppercase vs. Lowercase

REALITY is everything, but reality is only the part you are aware of. Consider that sentence carefully, because "REALITY" and "reality" are not the same. The uppercase-versus-lowercase distinction is not my own. I would like to acknowledge Christian anthropologist Dr. Charles Kraft for his excellent worldview book, *Christianity with Power.* He teaches a "two-realities position," or, alternately, *critical realism,* defined in this way:

> It holds that there are two realities. There is a REALITY "out there." The world outside ourselves existing both materially and nonmaterially. It is REAL. But there is also a perceptual reality inside our minds. That, too, is real, but it is different in nature from REALITY as God knows it to be.[14]

In other words, we perceive only a portion of the external world and, even then, some of that may be incorrect. This idea is supported by scriptural texts that promise the believer a fuller picture in the afterlife: "For now we see in a mirror dimly, but then face to face. Now I know in part; then I shall know fully, even as I have been fully known" (1 Corinthians 13:12). While we observe REALITY, we perceive only a portion of it as lowercase reality, and our subjective perception is largely based on our worldview. If we do not believe it exists, we will not likely perceive it, *even when it's there.*

Kraft defines worldview as "culturally structured assumptions, values, and commitments underlying a people's perception of REALITY."[15] This is why two people can look at the same evidence and come to radically different conclusions. Many Western Christians are rendered powerless by their worldview. Their lowercase reality has no place for miracles, healings, and spiritual entities. When one becomes a Christian, many things change quickly, but there are usually stubborn areas of unbelief and skepticism. It is hard to believe what you haven't yet experienced. Some of the theological underpinnings like cessationism and amillennialism in various denominations reinforce these strongholds of unbelief. Kraft writes of paradigms as a "sizable segment of reality" that composes a worldview.[16] The next chapter will present evidence that Western culture as a whole in undergoing a paradigm shift, but even Christians as individuals experience stages of transformation as perceived reality expands.

Often, growth in Christianity is a series of paradigm shifts as one's lowercase reality becomes a clearer more accurate picture of REALITY. For example, I recently maintained a healthy skepticism about speaking in tongues until I met privately with Sid Roth after appearing on his television show, *It's Supernatural,* in April of 2013.[17] In a private session, Roth and his associate laid hands and prayed over me, and, somewhat unexpectedly, I spoke in an unknown language. I believed it was possible and was open to the experience; it is a new component of my perceived reality. I hope my commitments are transparent. I believe God has spoken and that we should derive our overarching view of REALITY from His Word. The Christian worldview is committed to the authority of divine revelation in Scripture. It is a "revealed" worldview, hence it is *apocalyptic.*

Apocalyptic

Even though it is usually associated with the end times, the word "apocalypse" means "revelation." The term occurs eighteen times in the New Testament in the Greek noun form *apokalupsis* and twenty-six times in the verb form *apokalupto.* These Greek terms derive from the combination of the preposition *apo* and the verb *kalupto,* resulting in the definition "to reveal, to disclose, to make fully known, revelation."[18] The Supernatural Worldview is based on revealed truth from God. Because God has revealed Himself verbally in the Bible, scripturally informed followers of Jesus have answers to those fundamental questions about REALITY that evade competing worldviews. Ask yourself if you can answer Sire's seven questions—but, even more, ask if you can defend your answers. How might those answers mold the four simpler worldview questions? Do you really believe miracles are possible? Why should anyone else believe it? Chances are the world has influenced you more than you realize. The Bible presents a radically different picture than our post-Enlightenment culture whose sole authority is science.

Theologian Neil Andersen writes:

The Christian worldview perceives life through the grid of Scripture, not through culture or experience. And Scripture clearly teaches that supernatural, spiritual forces are at work in this world. For example, approximately one-fourth of all the healings recorded in the Gospel of Mark were actually deliverances.[19]

Would it even occur to you that an ill person might need deliverance rather than medicine? Does your church engage in deliverance? If Jesus thought it was important, shouldn't we?

As His followers, Christians should adopt and defend the worldview of Jesus. Unfortunately, many in the church have adopted a form of naturalism that relegates all supernatural activity to the biblical era. It is commonly called cessationism, based on the idea that spiritual sign gifts and miraculous forms of intervention ceased after the biblical canon closed. As a result, many times, the secular paranormal enthusiast's beliefs are more consistent with revealed REALITY replete with angels and demons interacting with humans than some of those who claim to believe the Bible. This is unacceptable.

The dilemma facing the Christian is finding the appropriate level of suspicion when faced with supernatural claims. The culture is abounding with everything from ghosts to space aliens and all sorts of fantastic nonsense. No one wants to be gullible. Unfortunately, all too often the baby is thrown out with the bathwater. Dr. Michael Brown has argued, "And as much as discernment is a good thing, the general attitudes of skepticism and cynicism are not."[20]

We will look at some surprising evidences that support a supernatural worldview. This doesn't mean that we accept every supernatural claim. We're commanded to seek supernatural gifts (1 Corinthians 12:31) and test the spirits (1 John 4:1). These commands make no sense unless there really are gifts to acquire and spirits to question.

Skeptics classify the Bible in the same category as paranormal nonsense (or, as they like to call it, "woo"), yet the existence of counterfeit does not preclude the genuine article; in fact, it assumes it. Let's face it: Christians are making some fantastically supernatural claims. The cornerstone of the Christian faith is the resurrection of Jesus Christ from the dead after three days in the tomb. The historical evidence supporting that event will be examined in chapter 12. For most evangelicals, the experience of the Holy Spirit provides individual confirmation and assurance, but this is subjective, and many other religions make similar claims (like Mormonism's "burning the bosom").

So, why should a reasonable person accept the authority of the Bible? Fulfilled Bible prophecy provides convincing evidence for the supernatural inspiration of the Bible. Future events described in advance suggest authorship that transcends time. While fulfilled prophecy could make a complete book of its own, a basic argument from prophecy is offered here.

The Seventy Weeks: A Minimal Facts Approach

Daniel chapter 9 contains a famous "seventy-weeks" prophecy delivered to Daniel by an angel:

> Seventy weeks are decreed about your people and your holy city, to finish the transgression, to put an end to sin, and to atone for iniquity, to bring in everlasting righteousness, to seal both vision and prophet, and to anoint a most holy place. Know therefore and understand that from the going out of the word to restore and build Jerusalem to the coming of an anointed one, a prince, there shall be seven weeks. Then for sixty-two weeks it shall be built again with squares and moat, but in a troubled time. And after the sixty-two weeks, an anointed one shall be cut off and shall have nothing. And the people of the prince who is to come shall destroy the city and the sanctuary. Its end shall come with a flood, and to the end there shall be war. Desolations are decreed. (Daniel 9:24–26)

While there are several interpretations of this prophecy held by sincere, Bible-believing scholars, nearly all evangelicals and even some Jewish scholars agree it is messianic. In fact, this prophecy alone has led many Jews to accept Yeshua (Jesus) as their Messiah. Because my purpose here is to merely demonstrate that the future was written in advance, I present a minimal-facts case from four key points:

- First, the prophecy was unquestionably written down before Jesus was born. Conservative scholars like Dr. Bruce Waltke at Knox Theological Seminary argue vigorously for dating the book to sixth century BC as it internally claims.[21] However, even the most liberal scholars late date it to the second century BC during the Maccabean period (over three hundred years later than the book claims). A total of eight fragmentary copies of the book of Daniel were found at Qumran amongst the Dead Sea Scrolls (DSS), but none is complete due to the effects of extreme age. However, between them, they preserve text from eleven of Daniel's twelve chapters (chapter 12 is missing but quoted in another DSS work). The discovery labeled 4QDane (4Q116) contains part of chapter 9. All eight manuscripts were copied within 175 years, ranging from 125 BCE (4QDan) to about AD 50 (4QDan). The mere fact that it was accepted as canonical at Qumran means it was necessarily composed long before the oldest date in the second century.

- Second, any coherent reading must account for the elements in verse 24: 1) Finish the transgression; 2) Make an end of sins; 3) Make reconciliation for iniquity; 4) To bring in everlasting righteousness; 5) To seal up the vision and prophecy; and 6) To anoint the Most Holy.

- Third, there is scholarly debate on whether the "commandment to rebuild" is the decree to Ezra in 458 BC (Ezra 7:11–26), Sir Robert Anderson's date of 445 BC widely popularized in his book, *The Coming Prince*,[22] or 444 BC, as purposed by Waltke and others.[23] Because I am making a minimal-facts case, the exact date isn't important. No one disputes that there was a command to rebuild between 458 and 444 BC.

- Fourth, the prophecy predicts the Messiah will be cut off after sixty-nine weeks of years (483 years). Some object to the translation of *mashiach* as "the Messiah," because the Hebrew can also mean "anointed one" and also because the definite article "the" is not in the original text. However, the oldest Jewish translation, the Septuagint, translates *mashiach* as *tou christou* ("the anointed one"), which is where the word "Christ" derives. Furthermore, *mashiach nagid* is a priest and a king (or prince), but the Old Testament law separated those duties for Israelites and predicts that they are to be uniquely combined in the Messiah (Isaiah 9:6–7). For this reason, many rabbis hesitantly acknowledge the seventy-weeks prophecy as Messianic.[24]

• Fifth, after the Messiah is "cut off," the city and sanctuary will be destroyed. That Jesus was crucified between AD 30–AD 33 is virtually uncontested. Even secular Roman historians like Tacitus wrote about His crucifixion.[25] It is also an undisputed historical fact that the Roman army led by Titus Vespasian destroyed Jerusalem and the temple in AD 70.[26]

Based on these well-established facts, one must ask if there is another viable candidate for the Jewish Messiah who was "cut off" just prior to the destruction of Jerusalem in AD 70. The six goals listed in the second bullet point only make sense in light of Jesus of Nazareth's atoning sacrifice at Calvary. There is simply no other historical event that can claim to satisfy those six requirements like the cross did. As a representative example of how some scholars calculate the numbers, Bruce Waltke is cited:

Daniel, in addition to predicting that Rome will succeed Greece, also predicts the very date that Israel's Messiah will be crucified. In Daniel 9:24 the writer predicts that 69

"weeks" (= 483 years) after the decree to restore and rebuild
Jerusalem Messiah will be 'cut off'. Artaxerxes issued this
decree in the month Nisan of his twentieth year of 444 B.C.
(Neh. 2:2). Hoehner demonstrates that Jesus Christ was crucified on the Passover in the year A.D. 33. The time interval
between the first of Nisan (444 B.C.) and the Passover (A.D.
33) is 173,880 days (476 x 365 = 173,740 days; March 4
[1 Nisan] to March 29 [the date of the Passover in A.D. 33]
= 24 days; add 116 for leap years). Now a prophetic year
(also a lunar year) is 360 days (cf. Rev. 11) and 483 years
multiplied by that figure also equal 173,880 days.[27] Here
then is confirmatory proof that the book contains genuine
predictions.[28]

Because even skeptical scholars concede the prophecy was written
before Jesus of Nazareth lived, we are rational to conclude that the
future was revealed to Daniel. It is a supernatural claim rather than a
paranormal one, because this prophecy was reportedly delivered by a
messenger of God identified as the angel Gabriel (Daniel 9:21). Next,
one might examine Isaiah 53 (dated to the seventh century BC) in
light of the Gospel narratives. Many of the details are confirmed by
extrabiblical sources like the Jewish historian Flavius Josephus and
secular Roman historians, so the Gospel authors cannot be accused
of crafting their narratives to conform to Isaiah.[29] My great hope is
that the uninitiated agnostic will start to see that the Bible is a unique
collection of ancient texts (sixty-six books by more than forty authors
written over a period of more than fifteen hundred years) packed with
precisely fulfilled prophecies demonstrably written down before they
came to pass. It stands head and shoulders above all other religious
literature and demands one to rise to its challenge.[30]

Christianity Is a Challenging Worldview

Many skeptics view Christianity as a metaphorical *crutch*. The thinking on the street is that faith is something weak people adopt because death is too scary and they need a useful fiction to lean against. Accordingly, the infamous communist Karl Marx called religion "the opium of the people."[31] Adopting this view, Joseph Stalin and Chairman Mao set about bulldozing churches in Russia and China respectively. As a result, militant atheism claimed nearly two hundred million lives, and it isn't over yet. While the opium remark correctly applies to some folks, is it a comprehensive criticism? Is religious faith merely an emotional response to the uncertainty of death?

It seems the opium rationale better applies to the oneist, the postmodern pluralist. It is popular to say, "I'm spiritual but not religious." This usually reflects the smorgasbord approach based on preference. Perhaps sprinkle the ethical teachings of Jesus with a pinch of Hindu relativism. Just add a smidgeon of Buddhist meditation, a dash of yoga, and, if you're feeling a little perturbed with your neighbor, a smidge of Zoroastrian dualism. What is most revealing about this common approach is that the final product always ends up reflecting the person who is doing the choosing—it is utterly subjective. It becomes one's lowercase reality, but does not truly reflect REALITY. No one adopting this subjective approach ends up with a deity resembling the God of the Bible. "Spiritual but not religious" is about convenience. It never requires a major lifestyle change or personal sacrifice, especially in areas of pleasure and affluence. It amounts to creating God in one's own image and, truthfully, this nebulous spirituality *is* the opiate of the people. Christianity is not like this. Jesus makes demands.

The God of the Bible is called "holy," which means "set apart."

Christianity is quite inconvenient because believers are also called to be holy. It is not designed to make life easier; far from that, it is actually a colossal challenge that *changes everything*. Don't get me wrong: Jesus will meet any sinner right where he or she is and accept him or her unconditionally, but that is merely the beginning. What ensues is a radical program of reprogramming one's entire value system to that of the kingdom. While there is great joy along the way, it is usually an extremely difficult and painful process. Accordingly, Jesus asks us to count the cost: "If anyone would come after me, let him deny himself and take up his cross daily and follow me" (Luke 9:23). This is not a easy way out, but rather a serious challenge.

Even more, Christians are called to enter into Christ's suffering (Philippians 1:29; 2 Timothy 1:8; 1 Peter 4:13). This doesn't entail monastic flagellation, but rather endurance of the world's chastisement for the sake of the gospel. It also necessitates a struggle against one's sin nature. To that end, Paul exhorted believers to offer themselves as a living sacrifice (Romans 12:1). It is an inside job, a spiritual process called sanctification accomplished by the indwelling Holy Spirit. Still, it takes effort and endurance. True followers of Jesus know Christianity is true because they experience radical, life-altering changes that cannot be explained apart from God. Christian faith isn't a crutch or wishful thinking. It is trusting in God's process.

Often maligned, the term "faith" has been culturally redefined in a manner inconsistent with the biblical worldview. Mark Twain popularized a Pudd'nhead cartoon's definition: "Faith is believing what you know ain't so."[32] In a similar vein, outspoken atheist Richard Dawkins argues that faith is merely "belief without evidence," or a process of intentional nonthinking.[33] These definitions are disingenuous. Even science must assume many basic beliefs that cannot be proved empirically. Much is taken for granted. For example, the regularity of nature and the laws of logic are simply assumed by science. According to a theological dictionary, faith refers both to intellectual belief and to relational trust or commitment.[34] Biblical faith is more akin to an earned trust like that between a husband and wife. In the case of my marriage, I have faith based on an earned trust in my spouse's character. My faith is based on evidence from past performance.

There are several kinds of evidence that undergird the Christian faith. In the social sphere, Christianity demonstrably changes lives. Criminals become honest, alcoholics get sober, and skeptics become evangelists. I am one of them. I have experienced God's undeniable power in my life. (My testimony is recorded online, and you can follow the link in the endnote to read it and listen to it.[35]) Christian missionaries feed the starving, nurse the infirm, and minister in areas of the world that few people want to enter. In charity and altruism, Christianity is second to none.

In the intellectual sphere, there are rigorous philosophical arguments for the existence of God: cosmological, ontological, teleological, and moral.[36] These provide an intellectually robust foundation for believers and, although skeptics might pick at each one in isolation, their cumulative punch is overwhelming. Philosophers like Alvin Plantinga, J. P. Moreland, and Richard Swineburne are recognized as some of the top minds in the discipline. Anyone who has witnessed William Lane Craig debate an atheist is aware that the Christian faith can hold its own.[37] In fact, the next chapter will reveal that atheistic naturalism is waning due to mounting contrary evidence from science.

Historically, the biblical texts span a period of more than fifteen hundred years yet present a coherent, complementary account of God's actions and plan. Furthermore, the writings of the early church fathers corroborate and codify the New Testament. These historical accounts are increasingly corroborated by archeology, and many accounts thought mythological have been vindicated. Chapter 12 will demonstrate that the arguments for Jesus' resurrection are compelling, but the alternative theories lack force. While there are shelves of apologetics texts concerning the social, philosophical, and historical proofs, this book explores *controversial new evidences.* Accordingly, authentic faith is supported by many different lines of evidence and is more akin to an established trust than a blind leap.

Consequently, Christians should be careful in characterizing their faith. Do not concede to the world's definition of a blind leap. The Gospel of John is an evidential argument based on the signs done by Jesus that is designed to produce a faith response (John 20:38). Contrary to the opinions of skeptics, the Bible is a proven entity. It is not one book, but, as mentioned earlier, it is a collection of sixty-six different books by over forty different authors written over a period exceeding fifteen hundred years in three different languages, on three different continents. Its vast scope makes the internal coherence of the metanarrative (overarching story) all the more astounding. In other words, for those with ears to hear, a unified voice is speaking across the entire book. Once we make this discovery, the text comes alive. It has stood the test of time for thousands of years and continues to radically change lives. We can prove it to ourselves by putting trust in it. This requires an investment of studious effort. It merits trust from its coherence to metaphysical reality, accurate assessment of the human condition, proven historical veracity, fulfilled prophecy, and the transcendent self-authenticating quality of Jesus' teachings. Accordingly, biblical faith is more akin to earned trust than the blind leap that skeptics argue. In fact, faith as derived from the Hebrew prophet Habakkuk is a cornerstone of New Testament theology.

The famous quote from Habakkuk reads, "the righteous shall live by his faith" (Habakkuk 2:4b). It is quoted by Paul in Galatians 3:11 and Romans 1:17, and arguably also by Paul in Hebrews

10:38. When read together devotionally, the phrase seems to connect the three books. In fact, Martin Luther used this passage to start the reformation theology of "justification by faith." It seems that the Catholic Church had become like the errant Galatians in thinking that they must earn God's favor. Martin Luther was a man who wanted to please God, but he knew that he never measured up. He pursued mysticism and relentless confession, but never felt any assurance that he was justified before God. After studying the first chapter of Romans, Luther concluded that the "justice of God" doesn't exclusively refer to the punishment of sinners. Rather, the "justice" or "righteousness" of the righteous is not their own, but God's. The "righteousness of God" is that which is freely given to those who live by faith.

Luther's idea coheres nicely with the theme from Galatians that we are not saved by works of the law; rather, the law becomes our taskmaster. Men like to take credit for their accomplishments, which is why the gospel is so counterintuitive. According to Scripture, we cannot justify ourselves; God does it for us by His grace. The central message of Galatians is "a person is not justified by works of the law but through faith in Jesus Christ" (2:16). That distinguishes Christianity from man-made religions. Men would never make this up since they cannot take credit. Furthermore, living by Christian ethics requires considerable faith. Consider the paradoxical nature of biblical ethics:

- Living is dying and dying is living (Mark 8:35; John 12:24; 1 Corinthians 15:36).
- Save your life and you will lose it; lose your life and you will save it (Matthew 10:39).
- The best self-love is to not be self-centered (Matthew 6:33; Mark 12:29–31).

- Loving yourself requires denying yourself (Luke 9:23; 1 Corinthians 10:24).
- There is honor in shame and joy in persecution (Matthew 5:12; Hebrews 12:2; James 1:2).
- Please God and you will have pleasures forevermore (Psalms 16:11; Matthew 6:33).
- Please yourself and you will never be satisfied (Proverbs 27:20 and 30:15; Ecclesiastes 5:10).
- The way up is down; exaltation requires humility (Ezekiel 21:26; Luke 14:8–9; 1 Peter 5:6).
- The way down is up; self-promotion leads to humiliation (Ezekiel 21:26; Matthew 23:12).
- Having is giving and giving is having (Ecclesiastes 11:1; Mark 4:24; Luke 6:38).
- Reward comes from expecting nothing (Luke 6:35).[38]

These don't seem to be the sort of principles that humans would come up with on their own. The counterintuitive nature of Christian righteousness implies a supernatural source. While biblical faith is clearly not a crutch, it is the shield of the believer's spiritual armor (Ephesians 6:10–20). Armor is necessary because the secular world is currently in the hands of an evil overlord whose designs are nearing their fruition. The biblical philosophy of history posits a definite trajectory and goal to world affairs.

Christianity Is a Providential Worldview

How one answers the third and fourth simple worldview questions, "What is wrong?" and "What is the answer?" is determined by one's philosophy of history. The difference between a biblical philosophy of history and a secular one is that Christians believe history has an ultimate goal in the return of Jesus Christ. Until that time, we are in a spiritual war. People without a biblical framework often perceive their lives as a series of accidents and self-determination. There are two basic ways to interpret the world. One is the coincidental or accidental view and the other is the providential or, if I dare say, a conspiratorial view. In the coincidental view, one interprets the existence of the universe, the origin of life, the rise and fall of empires, and wars as the result of natural events and serendipity. We are all either victims or champions of circumstance. Life just happens to us, and there's no real rhyme or reason. While it seems to accurately describe events like natural disasters and weather, it doesn't provide a convincing explanation for historical events or a satisfying framework for interpreting life.

Christians believe history is pointed toward a particular plan that is laid out in Scripture. Those who take prophecy seriously believe there is a conspiracy to bring forth the Antichrist. You might be thinking, "Wait a minute! You don't expect me to sport a fedora from the aluminum-wear haberdashery do you?" Not really... But what if the version of world history the universities are peddling is misleading? History is not only written by the victors, but also by those *in charge*. In most cases, it is not intentionally sinister, but rather a product of academic conditioning by the same world system. This book argues that the world system is part of a vast cosmic conspiracy influencing sinful men. This was not my idea; it is the worldview of the biblical authors and Jesus Himself. The New Testament uses the language of war, and Christians are positioned as fighting against the greatest and most fantastic conspiracy imaginable. When one truly holds a biblical worldview and takes it to heart, life is no longer mundane. It is an epic cosmic struggle in which everything counts. Actually, it is the oldest story in the world.

The Bible teaches that God created man to be in intimate fellowship with Him but humankind made a bad choice when a rebel usurper, the *nachash*, lured them into disobedience (Genesis 3). Whereas most translations render the Hebrew as "serpent" or "snake," they do not have vocal chords and cannot speak. Semitic language expert Michael Heiser explains that the Hebrew root means "bright" as an adjective. Thus, he argues, "Eve was not talking to a snake. She was speaking to a bright, shining upright being who was serpentine in appearance, and who was trying to bewitch her with lies."[39] This threw the whole of creation into a tailspin—even leading the very first fraternal relationship into homicide. Sides were drawn between the spiritual offspring of the woman and the spiritual progeny of the serpentine usurper. By his clever ruse, dominion of this world was taken from man. The battle is still raging, and Christians live in enemy territory. According to the apostle John, "that ancient serpent" the *nachash,* is Satan (Revelation 12:9), and chapter 10 is devoted to him and his minions. However, the very first prophecy in the Bible, the protoevangelium, promised a Redeemer who would crush the head of the evil tempter and restore God's original utopian design (Genesis 3:15).

Not of the World, but in the World

In the New Testament, the term *kosmos* ("world") is used for an evil system opposed to God. It is led by Satan, and we are born into and are unwittingly under its influence unless we overcome through Jesus Christ. The apostle John warned that the whole world is in the power of the evil one (1 John 5:19). He recorded Jesus acknowledging the devil's present authority by describing him as "the prince

(Greek: *archon*) of this world" (John 14:30; 16:11). Like the serpent in the garden, the devices of the devil are deception and obfuscation. The apostle Paul wrote that this lowercase-"g" god blinds the minds of unbelievers to keep them from seeing the truth of Jesus' message.

The educators who are indoctrinating our youth with naturalism are unwittingly participating in the conspiracy. Paul also warned believers to "see to it that no one takes you captive by philosophy and empty deceit, according to human tradition, according to the elemental spirits of the world, and not according to Christ" (Colossians 2:8). The Greek term *stoicheia*, translated "elemental spirits," refers to our cosmic enemies. In the ancient world, this term was widely used for spirits in Persian religious texts, magical papyri, astrological documents, and many Jewish texts. Paul is likely using it here to refer to demonic spirits. At the end of his apostolic career, Paul still regarded those opposing the gospel as having fallen into a snare of the devil, "who has taken them captive to do his will" (2 Timothy 2:26). It is interesting that the deception occurs largely in the mind through philosophy and tradition, supporting the notion that spiritual warfare is a battle for the mind. The primary arena of battle is in the realm of ideas and beliefs—i.e., worldview.

The foundational spiritual warfare text is found in the last chapter of Paul's letter to the Ephesians. He argues that "we do not wrestle against flesh and blood, but against the rulers, against the authorities, against the cosmic powers over this present darkness, against the spiritual forces of evil in the heavenly places" (Ephesians 6:12). More will be said about this text later, particularly in chapter 11, but for this present discussion, we note that in this definitive text on spiritual warfare, we don't find special rituals or prayers to recite for casting out demons. Rather, the tools of spiritual warfare are the belt of truth, which derives from a stalwart commitment to big-"R"

REALITY; the shield of faith, which is akin to well-placed trust; the helmet of salvation, a free gift; and the sword of the spirit, which is the Word of God in Scripture that is highly accessible for study. Our primary offensive weapon is a command of sound doctrinal truth from the study of Scripture and prayer. In other words, the more you are familiar with the truth, the more impenetrable your spiritual armor. The majority of our warfare is in the realm of ideas, Scripture, and philosophy. If we know the word of God and have a firm grip on the truth, we are to engage in the battle for hearts and minds.

Accordingly, a biblically consistent Christian is necessarily watching for spiritual deceptions and distrusts humanistic philosophies. The Bible is replete with warnings concerning false prophets, false christs (Matthew 24:5), false gospels (Galatians 1:6–10), and false teachings (Acts 20:28–31). For these reasons, believers are told to "test the spirits" (1 John 4:1). The mandate to test is predicated on the fact that many false prophets have gone out into the world. It is no wonder that Christians are wary of outside spiritual and paranormal claims. It's not that Christians enjoy judging others; it is simply that they take the biblical teachings seriously. In this way, savvy believers are *de facto* conspiracy theorists. The Bible is unequivocal from cover to cover in stating that there is spiritual conspiracy afloat that will culminate at the return of Jesus Christ entailing fearsome judgment of the world system's natural (unbelievers) and supernatural (spirits) elements. The enemy is pulling out all the stops in order to obfuscate the Bible's prophetic warnings. This is why the dominant worldview promoted in institutes of higher learning today excludes the supernatural. Naturalists answer the seven worldview questions basically like this:

1. **What is really real?** God does not exist. Only material things exist. The universe is purposelessly driven by deterministic physical processes.

2. **What is the nature of external reality?** The material world is all that is real. Immaterial things are an illusion.

3. **What is a human being?** Humans are highly evolved biological machines determined by genetics.

4. **What happens to a person after death?** After death, people cease to exist.

5. **Why is it possible to know anything at all?** Knowledge is possible because of consciousness and reason developed through a long process of evolution.

6. **How do we know what is right and wrong?** Morality has evolved as a survival mechanism.

7. **What is the meaning of human history?** Humans are accidents of matter and energy. There is no meaning to human history.

I believe the naturalistic worldview is based on a pernicious myth—meaning an idealized conception or "just-so story" that affirms the assumed worldview. It is pernicious because it leads men to perdition. It is a fictional myth because it fails to address obvious facts. Because materialism (physicalism) fails to explain fundamental realities like consciousness and the origin of life, its adherents regularly invoke promissory naturalism to suggest that one day science will provide the answer. However, this is an empty promise. Immaterial realities like consciousness cannot be reduced to physical laws acting on matter. Life has never been observed to come from nonlife. Consequently, the mythology of promissory naturalism pushes the problem out into the future so the naturalist faithful can comfortably ignore it. This amounts to a blind faith in naturalism. The next chapter discusses why some former true believers have become agitated enough to abandon naturalism. REALITY has a way of ruining comfortable mythology, *especially when it's demonstrably false.*

Since materialists believe there are no true spiritual realities, only natural phenomena, they assume that there must be a natural explanation behind every religious belief, paranormal phenomenon, and supernatural claim. Thus, they assert that scientifically ignorant people create myths and religious symbols for natural phenomena they do not understand. For instance, if a culture doesn't understand thunder, it reinterprets thunder to represent a deity roaring in the heavens in order to make sense of it. While this is true for some primitive beliefs, it doesn't explain away all the evidence for theism. The naturalist simply presupposes that the supernatural does not exist. Screenwriter and Christian apologist Brian Godawa has argued that naturalism has its own mythology:

> The art of demythologizing is itself a mythology that believes there are no preternatural or transcendent mysteries to life, so it interprets what it cannot understand or does not know in terms of its own naturalistic cause-and-effect bias.[40]

Chapter 3 will examine how the success of reductionist science in the natural realm has led many to accept elements of this atheistic worldview. Even the church has allowed the demythologizing project to slip in the back door undetected. Even so, the evidence is mounting against naturalism. I believe we are in the midst of a massive paradigm shift. The naturalist consensus is facing serious challenges from, ironically, science and secular philosophy. Unfortunately, it will most likely soon give way to a flood of deceptive spiritualism.

Notes

1. "Supernatural," Merriam-Webster.com, http://www.merriam-webster.com/dictionary/supernatural.
2. Peter Jones, *One or Two: Seeing a World of Difference* (Escondido, CA: Main Entry Editions, 2010) Kindle edition, 155–157.
3. Edgar Mitchell cited in Peter A. Sturrock, *A Tale of Two Sciences: Memoirs of a Dissident Scientist*, book excerpt at IONS, http://noetic.org/noetic/issue-three-october/a-tale-of-two-sciences-memoirs-of-a-dissident-scie/ (accessed 09/25/12).
4. Greg Koukl, "Bad Arguments Against Religion," http://store.str.org/ProductDetails.asp?ProductCode=CD302.
5. Jones, 1180–1183.
6. Hugh Ross, "Fine-Tuning For Life in the Universe," Reasons to Believe, February 13, 2009, http://www.reasons.org/articles/fine-tuning-for-life-in-the-universe (accessed 10/19/13).
7. "Paranormal," Merriam Webster.com, http://www.merriam-webster.com/dictionary/paranormal.
8. Marcello Truzzi, "Reflections on the Reception of Unconventional Claims in Science," Colloquium presented by Marcello Truzzi, PhD, professor of sociology at Eastern Michigan University at Ypsilanti, Michigan, and director, Center for Scientific Anomalies Research, Ann Arbor, Michigan, November 29, 1989, http://www.ufoevidence.org/documents/doc1226.htm (accessed 09/03/13).
9. C. Stephen Evans, *Pocket Dictionary of Apologetics & Philosophy of Religion* (Downers Grove, IL: InterVarsity Press, 2002) 79.
10. Ibid., 92.
11. Ibid., 124.
12. James Sire, "What Is a Worldview? "Christianity.com, http://www.christianity.com/christian-life/worldview/what-is-a-worldview-11627153.html?p=0 (accessed 05/23/13).

13. "Barna Survey Examines Changes in Worldview among Christians
    over the Past 13 Years," March 6, 2009, Barna Group, https://www.
    barna.org/barna-update/21-transformation/252-barna-survey-
    examines-changes-in-worldview-among-christians-over-the-past-13-
    years#.UvghxLRUYw8 (accessed 02/09/14).

14. Charles H. Kraft, *Christianity with Power: Your Worldview and Your
    Experience of the Supernatural,* reprint ed. (Eugene, OR: Wipf &
    Stock, 2005) 15.

15. Ibid., 20.

16. Ibid., 87.

17. "Tom Horn and Cris Putnam Part I," Sid Roth's It's Supernatural!
    & Messianic Vision, sidroth.org, April 1, 2013, http://sidroth.org/
    television/tv-archives/tom-horn-and-cris-putnam-part-1.

18. Johannes P. Louw and Eugene Albert Nida, *Greek-English Lexicon of
    the New Testament: Based on Semantic Domains*, vol. 1, electronic ed.
    of the 2nd ed. (New York: United Bible Societies, 1996) 338.

19. Neil T. Anderson, *The Bondage Breaker* (Eugene, OR: Harvest
    House, 2006) 33.

20. Michael L. Brown, *Authentic Fire: A Response to John MacArthur's
    Strange Fire* (Lake Mary, FL: Excel, 2013) Kindle edition,
    3222–3223.

21. Bruce K. Waltke, "The Date of the Book of Daniel," *Bibliotheca
    Sacra,* 133:532 (October 1976): 329. Journal article available here:
    https://www.galaxie.com/article/bsac133-532-04.

22 Sir Robert Anderson, *The Coming Prince,* 59. Note: This book is
    widely available for download online; print versions available at www.
    amazon.com and other online booksellers.

23. Waltke, 329.

24 Michael L. Brown, *Answering Jewish Objections to Jesus: Messianic
    Prophecy Objections,* vol. 3 (Grand Rapids, MI: Baker, 2003) 89.

25. The Roman historian and Senator Tacitus referred to Jesus Christ,

His execution by Pontius Pilate, and the existence of early Christians in Rome in his final work, *Annals* (written ca. AD 116), book 15, chapter 44.

26. Flavius Josephus, book 7, chapter 1.1, *The Wars of the Jews or History of the Destruction of Jerusalem.*

27. Cited in Waltke, Harold Hoehner, "Chronological Aspects of the Life of Christ; Part 6: Daniel's Seventy Weeks and New Testament Chronology," *Bibliotheca Sacra* 132 (January–March 1975) 47–65.

28. Waltke, 329.

29. See "The Historicity of Jesus Christ: Did He Really Exist?" The Divine Evidence, http://thedevineevidence.com/jesus_history.html.

30. For further prophecy study, I recommend: J. Barton Payne, *Encyclopedia of Biblical Prophecy* (Nashville: Baker, 1980).

31. Karl Marx, *A Contribution to the Critique of Hegel's Philosophy of Right* (1843) http://www.marxists.org/archive/marx/works/1843/critique-hpr/intro.htm (accessed 05/23/13).

32. Mark Twain, *Following the Equator: A Journey around the World* (New York: American, 1898) 132.

33. Richard Dawkins, "Is Science a Religion?" American Humanist Association, http://www.thehumanist.org/humanist/articles/dawkins. html (accessed 06/19/11).

34. Stanley Grenz, David Guretzki, and Cherith Fee Nordling, *Pocket Dictionary of Theological Terms* (Downers Grove, IL: InterVarsity Press, 1999) 50.

35 Cris Putnam, "My Testimony & Interview on NTR with Chris White," http://www.logosapologia.org/?p=3099 (accessed 09/25/13).

36. See Appendix 4.

37. William Lane Craig vs. Frank Zindler, "Atheism vs. Christianity: Which Way Does the Evidence Point?," YouTube, http://youtu.be/ HuCA4rIX4cE (accessed 05/23/13).

38. Daniel R. Heimbach, "Notes Lecture 3 Introduction to Christian

Ethics" (Wake Forest, NC: Southeastern Baptist Theological Seminary, 2013).

39. Michael S. Heiser, "The Nachash and His Seed: Some Explanatory Notes on Why the 'Serpent' in Genesis 3 Wasn't a Serpent" (Dept. of Hebrew and Semitic Studies, University of Wisconsin-Madison), 2. Available here: http://www.scribd.com/doc/68024391/Serpent-Seed-Dr-Michael-S-Heiser.

40. Brian Godawa, *Hollywood Worldviews: Watching Films with Wisdom & Discernment* (Intervarsity Press, 2009) Kindle edition, 750–751.

THE PARANORMAL PARADIGM SHIFT

Satan is exciting all his energies and using all kinds of
means to stir up the latent power of the soul in religionists,
mental scientists, and even Christians.
—WATCHMAN NEE

The paranormal has become the new normal among
certain sectors of the religious demographic in America.
—DR. RON RHODES,
PRESIDENT, REASONING FROM THE SCRIPTURES MINISTRIES[1]

While the term "paranormal" has been adequately explained, the
notion of a paradigm shift needs unpacking. Thomas Kuhn is an
acclaimed philosopher of science whose influential 1962 book,
The Structure of Scientific Revolutions, introduced the concept of
"paradigm shift" into the common vernacular.[2] Rather than thinking of science as a steady process of increasing knowledge, Kuhn
argued that events like the sixteenth-century Copernican revolution demonstrate more abrupt alterations, changes that not only

defy the previous theories, but that even redefine the questions being asked, consequently rendering terminology and theories from the old paradigm obsolete. Once the shift has occurred, the two paradigms are called "incommensurable," meaning the new paradigm cannot be proven or disproven by the rules of the old paradigm, and vice versa. The transformation is so radical that the adherents of the old and new paradigms speak a different language. A paradigm shift involves a worldview transformation.

Kevin Barrett writes, "Paradigm-shifters are issues where mainstream discourse says one thing, and reality says another; and where accepting reality would radically change the way we see the world... and presumably shock us enough to change our behavior."[3] At the dawn of the twenty-first century, we're living in the middle of a radical paradigm shift. What was once called paranormal is becoming normal. To understand what is occurring, the Copernican revolution is an instructive model.

In Ptolemy's second-century model of the solar system, cycles and epicycles were used for modeling the movements of the stars and planets around a stationary earth at its center. As more and more astronomical data came in, the complexity of the system increased. While the system worked, it became horrendously difficult. This suggested a problem. The honored principle known as Occam's razor dictates, all things being equal, that a simpler explanation is better than a more complex one. When Copernicus proposed a new cosmology with the sun at the center, solar mechanics were greatly simplified and, slowly, a paradigm shift occurred. When the paradigm shift was complete, all of the Ptolemaic science was relegated to the garbage heap—albeit with great protest from the old guard. Many believe we are in a similar shift today and the strident cries of the "new atheists"—Richard Dawkins, Christopher Hitchens, Sam

Harris, and Daniel Dennett—represent naturalism's death throes rather than resurgence. Once ardent materialists like the dominant atheist philosopher of the twentieth century, Oxford philosophy professor Anthony Flew, are now changing their minds.[4]

Hard science is increasingly revealing that material reductionism is bankrupt. In the previous chapter, it was shown how Big-Bang cosmology makes a supernatural, powerful, intelligent, and personal Creator of the universe the most reasonable conclusion from the data. The problem for materialism is showcased in descriptions of the Big Bang. In a book about the burgeoning area known as string theory, *The Elegant Universe*, Brian Greene, a physicist and Rhodes Scholar, extrapolated back to the moment of creation:

> As we imagine running the clock backward from the age of the presently observed universe, about 15 billion years, the universe as we know it is crushed to an ever smaller size. The matter making up everything—every car, house, building, mountain on earth; the earth itself; the moon; Saturn, Jupiter, and every other planet; the sun and every other star in the Milky Way; the Andromeda galaxy with its 100 billion stars and each and every other of the more than 100 billion galaxies—is squeezed by a cosmic vise to astounding density. And as the clock is turned back to ever earlier times, the whole of the cosmos is compressed to the size of an orange, a lemon, a pea, a grain of sand, and to yet tinier size still. Extrapolating all the way back to "the beginning," the universe would appear to have begun as a point—an image we will critically re-examine in later chapters—in which all matter and energy is squeezed together to unimaginable density and temperature. It is believed that a cosmic fireball, the big

bang, erupted from this volatile mixture spewing forth the seeds from which the universe as we know it evolved.[5]

Greene is tap dancing around the coherence problem for matter by saying it began "as a point." What exactly is a point? In a later chapter, he refers to "zero dimensional point-particles."[6] While scientists accuse theologians of abstraction, one marvels at the absurdity of a particle with no dimensionality. Technically, such an entity does not exist. It is truly an abstraction that makes the physicists' mathematical formulas resolve, but that has no physical substance. Greene acknowledges the issue by posing a question:

But just as string theory shows that the conventional notion of zero-dimensional point particles appears to be a mathematical idealization that is not realized in the real world, might it also be the case that an infinitely thin one dimensional strand is similarly a mathematical idealization?[7]

Again, I am not aware of anything real that can be said to have one dimension. It seems to me that these are only abstract ideas. They are theoretical entities that yield satisfying mathematical solutions—but at bottom, they are truly only ideas. There is no material stuff with zero or one dimension. It seems safe to say that science points to a universe that was created from nothing and is fundamentally made up of immaterial ideas.

If materialism is a coherent worldview, then matter is its fundamental reality. But Greene admits that matter is an uncertain entity:

Quantum mechanics, on the contrary, injects the concept of probability into the universe at a far deeper level. According to [Max] Born and more than half a century of subsequent experiments, the wave nature of matter implies that matter itself must be described fundamentally in a probabilistic manner.[8]

There is no escaping the fact that by its own methods science has undermined materialism. In fact, the damage is fatal. Its fundamental entity, "matter," is only a vague shadow of reality. Sure, the big things—like cars and elephants—seem stable enough, but the truth is that they are mostly empty space—and even the tiny particles that give the illusion of solidity aren't made of anything particularly tangible. The deeper we look, the more we discover that reality is fundamentally *immaterial*. This idea is picked up again and examined more thoroughly in chapter 12.

As if that were not enough, scientists have come to the disquieting realization that they can only account for a small percentage of the measured gravity in space. Over the last decade, astronomers have discovered that every galaxy is surrounded by super-massive, yet invisible, gravity sources. They detect these massive sources from observing that galaxies rotate too quickly for the amount of matter they contain. Something huge and invisible is exerting a powerful gravitational force on these star clusters. Because it is invisible, they call it dark matter. Theoretical astrophysicist David Spergel, a leader of the Wilkinson Microwave Anisotropy Probe space mission, concedes:

"From our experiments, the periodic table which comprises the atoms or normal matter that are said to make up the entire universe actually covers only 4.5 percent of the whole," lead theorist Spergel said. "Students are learning just a tiny part of the universe from their textbooks. It would be dark matter and dark energy that comprise the next 22 percent and 73.5 percent of the universe."[9]

In other words, science only accounts for less than 5 percent of REALITY, and given quantum mechanics, they hardly understand it. Considering this astonishing lack of knowledge, one marvels at the enduring pathological denial regarding the supernatural. Consequently, many former naturalists are losing their faith in promissory materialism. This extends to evolutionary biology as well.

Thomas Nagel, an influential philosopher at New York University, just published *Mind & Cosmos: Why the Materialist Neo-Darwinian Conception of Nature Is Almost Certainly False.* The title is self explanatory and marks an important milestone. When an accomplished academic atheist points to naturalism, screaming "the emperor has no clothes," it implies a paradigm shift. For decades, we've heard about the overwhelming evidence for the naturalistic Darwinian account of life. Yet, here is Nagel breaking ranks:

The argument from the failure of psychophysical reductionism is a philosophical one, but I believe there are independent empirical reasons to be skeptical about the truth of reductionism in biology. Physico-chemical reductionism in biology is the orthodox view, and any resistance to it is regarded as not only scientifically but politically incorrect. But for a long time I have found the materialist account of how we and our fellow organisms came to exist hard to believe, including the standard version of how the evolutionary process works. The more details we learn about the chemical basis of life and the intricacy of the genetic code, the more unbelievable the standard historical account becomes.[10] This is just the opinion of a layman who reads widely in the literature that explains contemporary science to the nonspecialist. Perhaps that literature presents the situation with a simplicity and confidence that does not reflect the most sophisticated scientific thought in these areas. But it seems to me that, as it is usually presented, the current orthodoxy about the cosmic order is the product of governing assumptions that are unsupported, and that it flies in the face of common sense.[11]

This is strong language coming from a respected secular academic. Nagel is arguing that there is "no free lunch" and that matter cannot account for all of reality. A cause must be sufficient for its alleged effect, and the mechanistic processes of physics, chemistry, and evolutionary biology are simply not adequate for explaining life, consciousness, reasoning, and morality. Even so, Nagel has a hard time accepting God. He wrote in the *New York Times*, "Even though the theistic outlook, in some versions, is consistent with the available scientific evidence, I don't believe it, and am drawn instead to a naturalistic, though non-materialist, alternative."[12] This clearly reveals how worldview dictates one's interpretation of the evidence. In other words, even though the scientific evidence points to God as the most reasonable explanation, he is hoping for a naturalistic alternative that is yet to be conceived—another milestone along the way of the paranormal paradigm shift.

Another prime example is Dr. Eben Alexander, a celebrated neurosurgeon and academic who earned his MD at Duke University School of Medicine in 1980. With 150 published articles and chapters and two textbooks to his credit, he worked at the top of his field. Like the majority of his colleges, he once held to the materialist reductionist worldview, that is, until a near-death experience (NDE) radically changed his paradigm. In response, he wrote the best-selling *Proof of Heaven: A Neurosurgeon's Journey into the Afterlife*, in which he describes his 2008 NDE and asserts that science can and will determine that heaven really does exist. Dr. Alexander explains:

> In my view, what I think is going to happen is that science in the much broader sense of the word and spirituality which will be mainly an acknowledgement of the profound nature of our consciousness will grow closer and closer together. We will all move forward into a far more enlightened world. One thing that we will have to let go of is this kind of addiction to simplistic, primitive reductive materialism because there's really no way that I can see a reductive materialist model coming remotely in the right ballpark to explain what we really know about consciousness now.
>
> Coming from a neurosurgeon who, before my coma, thought I was quite certain how the brain and the mind interacted and it was clear to me that there were many things I could do or see done on my patients and it would eliminate consciousness. It was very clear in that realm that the brain gives you consciousness and everything else and when the brain dies there goes consciousness, soul, mind—it's all gone. And it was clear.
>
> Now, having been through my coma, I can tell you that's exactly wrong and that in fact the mind and consciousness are independent of the brain. It's very hard to explain that, certainly if you're limiting yourself to that reductive materialist view.[13]

While Alexander's theological conclusions face critical analysis in chapter 5, his change of heart is indicative of the ongoing paradigm shift. Will this make science obsolete?

An interesting thing about paradigm shifts is that although the new paradigm may seem unintelligible from within the old paradigm, once the new paradigm is adopted, the old one is still accessible. The great missiologist and theologian Lesslie Newbigin made this observation:

> Whatever valid criticisms may be made of [Thomas] Kuhn, however, he does demonstrate that shifts such as that from the physics of Newton to that of Einstein do not arise from any step-by-step reasoning from within the presuppositions of the earlier view but from a new vision that calls for a kind of conversion. My point here is simply this: while there is radical discontinuity in the sense that the new theory is not reached by any process of logical reasoning from the old, there is also a continuity in the sense that the old can be rationally understood from the point of view of the new. In Einstein's physics, Newtonian laws are still valid for large bodies in slow motion. Newtonian physics is still valid for mechanics. Thus, to recognize a radical discontinuity between the old and the new is not to surrender to irrationality. Seen from one side there is only a chasm; seen from the other there is a bridge.[14]

This means that, while one can never arrive at the new paradigm from the presuppositions of the old one, there is backward compatibility from the new paradigm to the old. This means that empirical methods of science will continue to have value even after naturalism has been discredited as a worldview. In fact, I predict, most ironically, that empirical evidence will ultimately destroy naturalism.

The notion that destroyed Alexander's naturalism is that the mind is not contained in the brain. He experienced an otherworldly reality while his brain was clinically dead. Naturalistic science proposes that the mind is a product or epiphenomenon of the brain. In this view, consciousness is merely the result of chemical reactions and electrical impulses from neurons. According to naturalism, human beings are biological robots determined by physical law. This book explores several lines of evidence that contradict mind/brain uniformity. These include: 1) the evidence for extrasensory perception, also called *psi*—a controversial area for Christian apologetics (more on psi in chapter 6); 2) the near-death experience, which implies that consciousness survives bodily death; and 3) the evidence for spirits and apparitions, whether of human or nonhuman origin. Included are interviews with respected academics engaged in deliverance ministry as well as Christians who have investigated paranormal phenomena like ghosts. While any one of these serves as a defeater for naturalism, the biblical worldview can account for all of the above.

Indeed, this is an argument for biblical theism, albeit an unconventional one. There are many excellent books available arguing for miracles,[15] the veracity of the Bible,[16] the historical evidence of the resurrection of Jesus,[17] and intelligent design and creation.[18] I also recommend *I Don't Have Enough Faith to Be an Atheist* by Norman Geisler and Frank Turek as a comprehensive case for biblical Christianity. However, the book in your hands right now trades on more radical ideas from the fringes of science and theology that could become mainstream very quickly. I have a deep concern that many Western Christians are not prepared for the burgeoning paradigm shift.

To really understand and accurately represent another world-view, it is best to go to the source. In order to gain a working knowledge of parapsychology, I enrolled as a student at the Rhine Education Center, the teaching arm of the Rhine Research Center in Durham, North Carolina (what remains of the famous Duke Parapsychology Lab founded by J. B. and Louisa Rhine). I earned a certificate in parapsychology under Nancy Zingrone, PhD, another in paranormal investigation with Loyd Auerbach, MA, and completed specialized coursework on premonitions and precognition with Carlos Alvarado, PhD, and Zingrone. All are academically credentialed parapsychologists doing legitimate scientific research. They impressed me as honest intellectuals searching for truth. While this may raise the hackles of a few legalistic fundamentalists, the biblical worldview has more in common with parapsychology than naturalism, and we have much to learn from the research.

My conviction is that the Christian has nothing to fear from the pursuit of truth, even from unconventional (or antagonistic) sources. However, many members of my faith tradition have buried their heads in the sand. Dean Radin describes a remarkable shared skepticism between Christians and naturalist skeptics:

> On the religious side, within the Judeo-Christian-Islamic traditions, only God (or those he appoints) is allowed to perform miracles. Ordinary folks who perform such feats are considered suspect (by theists) if they're lucky and heretical if they're not. And on the scientific side, there is a widely held (but incorrect, as we'll see) assumption that these phenomena cannot exist because they violate one or more scientific principles.[19]

While there are good reasons to hold some with suspicion, my goal was to learn about evidence for paranormal and supernatural phenomena and the worldview promoted by parapsychology. My concern is that many Christians are too insulated in their faith communities to adequately understand and address what is coming. While I urge caution when exploring these topics, my hope is that this book serves as a wake-up call to the Christian apologetics community. We have excluded areas of knowledge that work in our favor, but we're also threatened by a blind spot. The new paradigm promotes a radical pluralism positioning Christian exclusivism as the odd man out.

The New Babylon

Nearly everyone recognizes that the world is in the midst of a transition. Powerful forces are at work to bring about world government. Technology facilitates communication and commerce to such a degree that global governance is soon to be a necessity. Recent economic collapses seem to be driving toward a global financial system. For globalism to be successful, the sovereign nation state must go the way of the dinosaur. Conservative analysts have documented a moral decline in Western culture and America specifically. I have noticed it in my lifetime. Former United States Court of Appeals judge, Robert H. Bork, wrote *Slouching towards Gomorrah: Modern Liberalism and American Decline* in 1996. The title is a play on the final couplet of Yeats' poem, "The Second Coming," which reads:

And what rough beast, its hour come round at last,
Slouches towards Bethlehem to be born?[20]

Bork contends that the rough beast of decadence is sending us slouching to our new home, which is not Bethlehem, but rather *Gomorrah*. He argues that Western culture and specifically the United States is declining as a result of modern liberalism and the rise of the so-called New Left. Bork traces the swift rise of modern liberalism since the 1960s, arguing that this legacy of radicalism shows that the precepts of modern liberalism are antithetical to traditional American thought. He exposes the incoherent nature of simultaneously exalting a thorough-going individualism alongside a radical egalitarianism. His arguments persuade, but something is missing.

While he rightly bemoans increased violence, perversion-saturated media, abortion, divorce, euthanasia, feminism, and the decline of religion as evidence of cultural degeneracy, he does not account for the demonic spiritual assault behind it. British New Testament scholar, Dr. Peter Jones, came to America in the early sixties and then took a teaching assignment in France for nearly twenty years. Upon his return, he marveled at how America had changed during his absence:

Does the average Christian know what is going on in our ostensibly civilized society? Pagan ideology, sometimes of the most radical and anti-Christian nature, is taught in university departments of religion, theological seminaries, mainline church agencies, feminist networks and wicca covens across the land. It adopts the name of Christianity, but will render our world unrecognizable…. If you doubt the success of this revolution (1960s), note the following statistic: in 1994, seventy-one percent of Americans and forty percent of those calling themselves "evangelicals" no longer believed in absolute truth.[21]

We aren't turning pagan because we are politically and socially liberal; rather, we are more leftist because we are increasingly spiritually pagan. Jones is correct that the 1960s were the turning point. However, few scholars of his stature will acknowledge the dark spiritual element involved. On the front lines, Pastor Russ Dizdar, author of *The Black Awakening*, a book based on a discovered occultist meme forecasting a violent Judgment Day, writes:

> Occult historian, James Charles Napier Webb, declared in his work, *The Occult Establishment: The Dawn of the New Age and the Occult Establishment*, that the second largest proliferation of occult literature was released in the 1960s in the U.S. The first was unleashed in pre-Nazi Germany. What a spinning decade the '60s were! We saw The Beatles, anti-war movement, the sexual revolution, eastern mysticism, and the 1966 establishment of the modern "Church of Satan" with the release of self-proclaimed dark pope Anton LaVey's *The Satanic Bible* (1969). That book spelled out for many, sex, destruction, and even death rituals. The '60s was only the first dark steps of even darker left-hand path rituals. (Perhaps it was Alistair Crowley or the "Babylon Working" ritual by U.S. rocket scientist, Jack Parsons, that helped open the doors to the modern rise of these dark rituals and manifesting dark powers?)[22]

The conservative's overemphasis of political ideology is illustrative of rationalism and secularism that has blinded conservatives to the spiritual decay, a topic examined in chapter 4 on demythologization. It seems that the radicalism of the sixties was the impetus for inclusivism ("all spirituality leads to salvation") from Vatican II,

Billy Graham, and across the board to the resurgence of overt pagan universalism. For example, Graham said this when interviewed by Robert Schuller on the *Hour of Power* television show:

> I don't think that we're going to see a great sweeping revival that will turn the whole world to Christ at any time. I think James answered that, the Apostle James in the first council in Jerusalem, when he said that God's purpose for this age is to call out a people for His name. And that's what God is doing today, He's calling people out of the world for His name, whether they come from the Muslim world, or the Buddhist world, or the Christian world or the non-believing world, they are members of the Body of Christ because they've been called by God. They may not even know the name of Jesus but they know in their hearts that they need something that they don't have, and they turn to the only light that they have, and I think that they are saved, and that they're going to be with us in heaven.[23]

If Graham is correct, then a good Muslim earns salvation through his works and missionaries have been throwing their lives away for nothing. If this is really the case, it seems there was no reason for Christ to die. Nonetheless, Jesus believed there was no other way (Matthew 7:13–29; John 14:6; Acts 20:28; Romans 3:21–26, 5:9; Ephesians 1:7, 2:13; Colossians 1:20; Hebrews 9:12, 22). Jesus was an exclusivist, whereas the above inclusivism is nothing short of blatant anti-Christian theology coming from the lips of one of its most famous evangelists.[24]

A new book by Kurt Johnson and David Robert Ord, *The Coming Interspiritual Age,* illustrates the new Christianized paganism.

They argue that we are in the midst of a massive paradigm shift entailing a new interspiritual age. Dr. Johnson is a former monk of the Anglican Order of the Holy Cross, now widely known as an evolutionary biologist, comparative religionist, and social activist. Coauthor David Ord is a former Presbyterian (USA) minister and graduate of San Francisco Theological Seminary. Their vision of the future entails the eradication of world religions toward a global spirituality. They explain how the concept emerged from Roman Catholic mysticism:

> The word "interspirituality" was nonexistent until it was coined in 1999 by a Roman Catholic lay monk and pioneer interfaith leader, Brother Wayne Teasdale, in a book aptly entitled *The Mystic Heart: Discovering a Universal Spirituality in the World's Religions*. By 2004, when Brother Teasdale and colleagues introduced the perspective at the Parliament of the World's Religions in Barcelona, Spain, the term was still hardly known. Yet today an internet search for "interspirituality" or "interspiritual" calls up over 100,000 hits.
>
> It's obvious to many that interspirituality—a more universal experience of the world's religions, emphasizing shared experiences of heart and unity consciousness—represents part of the world's ongoing movement toward globalization and multiculturalism. It can be seen as an inevitable response to globalization…. Brother Teasdale predicted that interspirituality would become the global spiritual view of our era.[25]

In remarkable similarity to the New Age of the 1980s and '90s, the two ostensibly Christian authors extrapolate a metaphysic—in which everything is ultimately the same—from quantum physics and monastic mysticism. The result is the same as the pantheistic monism asserting "Nirvana" or "Brahman" found in Eastern religions, the "Omega Point" of Jesuit mystic Pierre Teilhard de Chardin, extraterrestrial disclosure for the UFO community, and the technological singularity of transhumanism. "All is one," labeled "oneism" by Peter Jones, is the prevailing spiritual idea of our age. It seems most unlikely that these diverse philosophies would converge on this *oneism* by chance.

I contend it is by design and leading toward the *sine qua non* of cosmic history—the return of Jesus Christ to judge the world—described in the book of Revelation. Accordingly, we will be examining how monism (oneism) is promoted by near-death-experience researchers, the paranormal community, and parapsychology. The global spiritual convergence is nothing less than the metaphorical rebuilding of the tower of Babel—brick by brick—in which man's creative ideas and endeavors, whether spiritual or scientific, reach for greatness, or even for godhood.

This world religion is symbolized in Scripture by "the great prostitute who is seated on many waters" (Revelation 17:1) and by the "woman sitting on a scarlet beast that was full of blasphemous names" (Revelation 17:3). It appeals to everyone because it provides a broad, redemptive road. It reinforces the popular belief that diverse world religions are God's way of communicating to different cultures at different moments in history. Thus, there are many equally valid paths to God. While this is politically correct theology, it is logically incoherent because the various religions make contradictory truth claims. Despite endorsements by theologians once identified with Christianity, interspirituality amounts to the New Age dressed up in red robes and a fish hat. The ongoing religious convergence coincides with more and more people adopting paranormal beliefs. If the real, Bible-believing church cannot provide adequate answers, people will increasingly turn to parapsychology and spiritualism. We would do well to have a command of the terminology and ideas associated with those areas of inquiry.

Historically, parapsychology grew out of the spiritualist movement in the nineteenth century. During Charles Darwin's day, dissatisfaction with Christian theism and naturalistic science converged and captured the hearts and minds of many intellectuals. In truth, Alfred Russel Wallace was as well known, if not more so, than Darwin. Wallace looked at the impact of philosophical materialism on ethics and rightly rejected it in order to retain traditional Victorian morality. Since he saw no substitute for Darwinism, he sought a spiritual science—even if it entailed a leap of faith into the occult and spiritualism. A leading parapsychology textbook explains:

> Within a few years the message of spiritualism had spread throughout America and to Europe. Its growth was soon to accelerate dramatically as people found wanting alternative worldviews based solely on an agnostic science or on a Christianity under siege from Darwin's theory of evolution. Spiritualism offered an appealing compromise, for here was a religious movement that claimed to put religion on an empirical footing, most particularly by seeking direct "scientific proof" of its central tenets through communication with the spirit world.[26]

Thus, many formerly naturalist scientists founded the *Society for Psychical Research* (SPR), which included notables like William James and Sir Arthur Conan Doyle. Faced with the hopelessness of the Darwinian paradigm, these men had noble intentions. Like Thomas Nagel cited earlier, they were desperately looking for a new science to give naturalistic justification for consciousness and the afterlife in order to preserve the hope and values previously provided by the Christianity that they believed Darwin had undone.

They weren't too far astray, because if naturalism is true, there really is no hope. Given the Darwinian paradigm, life is nothing but brutal, tooth-and-claw survival. When you die, you just cease to exist, and, accordingly, everything is ultimately meaningless. It is hardly surprising that naturalists cannot live consistently with the philosophical conclusions of their worldview. As a result, they inevitably leap into an irrational hope that will preserve elements of the Christian worldview without its God. This is why a literary genius and man of science like Doyle lived out his last days being duped out of his royalties by every two-bit medium and spiritualist sham artist in Britain. While some of the work done by the SPR remains compelling, modern parapsychology has distanced itself from its forerunner.

In the early twentieth century, Duke University psychologist Joseph B. Rhine and his wife, Dr. Louisa Rhine, were the most important academic advocates of the controversial new science called parapsychology. While Louisa compiled thousands of spontaneous, real-world cases for statistical analysis, J. B. earnestly sought to make parapsychology a legitimate science by severing its connection to spiritualism and its questionable associations. He moved it into the laboratory and sought to establish the existence of what he called ESP (extrasensory perception) through repeatable scientific experiments. However, like his predecessors, the tension between his religious longings and the scientific worldview was what drove him. Rhine explained:

> Dissatisfied with the orthodox religious belief which had at one time impelled me toward the ministry and dissatisfied, except as a last resort with a materialistic philosophy, I

was obviously ready to investigate any challenging fact that might hold possibilities of new insight into human personality and its relations to the universe.[27]

Rhine's early ministry ambitions reveal that a frustrated Christian theism compelled his search. Like most rational people, he intuited that materialism was inadequate and sought a way to prove it. His underlying aspiration to answer the basic worldview questions is laid bare:

My interest in psychic research had grown out of my desire, common, I think, to thousands of people, to find a satisfactory philosophy of life, one that could be regarded as scientifically sound and yet could answer some of the urgent questions regarding the nature of man and his place in the natural world.[28]

Although most mainstream scientists today reject his data, few have really examined it. Even more, an increasing number of respectable academics believe that Rhine proved the existence of ESP and that recent work has replicated and confirmed his conclusions. (Those details are unpacked in chapters 6 and 7 on psi.) As materialism goes extinct, one should expect the controversial science (or its successor) to experience a renaissance.

Interestingly, parapsychologist George P. Hansen has observed that throughout history, "the paranormal and supernatural become prominent during times of transition. Charismatic leaders may arise who demonstrate paranormal powers, attracting followers, and challenging the legitimacy of the establishment."[29] He came to this conclusion from an exhaustive historical survey of paranormal and supernatural beliefs in his work, *The Trickster and the Paranormal.* Hansen believes that paranormal events, such as sightings of strange creatures, UFOs, and ghosts occur when the society is in disorder and during times of transition. He also ascribes this to agency rather than coincidence by writing, "The paranormal encompasses everything from levitating monks to ESP, from spirits to cattle mutilations—an incredible and unsavory hodgepodge. The mix seems incoherent. But the trickster makes sense of it."[30] While we will address the trickster within (see chapter 10), it is demonstrable that paranormal beliefs are not only becoming more common, but are rising to unprecedented levels.

Paranormal Is the New Normal

The Pew Forum on Religion and Public Life released a report on December 9, 2009, titled "Many Americans Mix Multiple Faiths."[31] The report shows that many Americans now "blend Christianity with Eastern or New Age beliefs such as reincarnation,"[32] and that significant numbers of all major religious groups (including evangelicals) report having supernatural experiences like seeing ghosts and contacting the dead through spirit mediums. A Lutheran scholar recently sounded an alarm in a 2013 book on demon possession, stating: "The western world is in transition with paganism on the rise. Spiritualism is progressively becoming a dominant religious preference within a postmodern age."[33] Americans are having mystical visions and experiences like at no other time in our history. According to the data, the number of Americans who report having a mystical experience surpassed the numbers who have not.[34] Interestingly, that number has been on the rise continually since prayer

was removed from the public schools in 1962. Back then, 78 percent
said they had not had a mystical experience. Many Christian authors
have described the 1960s as an occult explosion.

Christian apologist Ron Rhodes concluded:

In some sectors of our society, the paranormal has become
the new normal. Indeed, tens of millions of people have
rejected Christianity and replaced it with belief in ghosts,
spirit guides, psychic phenomena, out-of-body experiences,
and the like. Psychics are currently communicating messages
from these spirit entities that blatantly contradict the teachings of the Bible.[35]

One of my favorite defenders of faith saw it coming many years
ago.

In my opinion, Francis Schaeffer was the greatest theologian
of the twentieth century. Through regular contacts with European
students at his L'Abri Fellowship, Schaeffer understood the culture
better than most academics. In 1979, Schaeffer and Surgeon General C. Everett Koop wrote *Whatever Happened to the Human Race?*
Within, they commented on the emergent paranormal worldview as
a desperate search for hope:

People are hungry for something which will give them hope
in life. They are tired of the empty platitudes that politicians
and many theologians have made: endless exhortations to be
good, to be good, to be good! They are also afraid. Things
really do seem hopeless, even on the level of everyday life
with its threats of a lower standard of living, of a growing
authoritarianism, of famine and ecological disaster, of dev-

astating war. And they are looking for any answer. So the UFOs are messengers of a friendly race from another planet. "Do not fear—the Force is with you!"—to borrow from a current science fiction film. And so people believe it irrationally. If they used their minds, they would see no evidence for friendly people from outside. But the feeling of experience as they read about this or see it on a screen is enough. It does not matter if there is any reality to it.

What about the growth of occultism, witchcraft, astrology? Is it simply economics that has put the signs of the zodiac in shops from one end of our society to the other? In part it is economics, but, once again, the real reason is deeper. People are looking for answers—answers they can experience....

Wherever we look, this is what confronts us: irrational experience. We must be careful not to be bewildered by the surface differences between these movements. We are not saying they are all the same. Of course there are differences. The secular existentialists, for example, disagree with one another. Then, too, secular existentialists differ with religious existentialists; the former tend to be pessimistic, the latter optimistic. Some of the movements are serious and command our respect. Some are just bizarre. There are differences. Yet, all of them represent the new mysticism![36]

Not only did Schaeffer perceive the common thread connecting ostensibly diverse movements, he is beseeching us to ask the deeper questions while offering a strong caution to trust our experiences. Far too often, well-meaning Christians trade their supernatural experiences for a more respectable scientific explanation, but not necessarily in line with REALITY. The next chapter will explain Schaeffer's two-story truth concept by which people place their hopes in demons and the occult. Secular psychologists have tracked this worldview shift as well.

Dr. Kenneth Ring is a professor emeritus of psychology at the University of Connecticut and past president of the International Association for Near-Death Studies (IANDS). He is the author of *Heading Toward Omega: In Search of the Meaning of the Near-Death Experience* and *The Omega Project: Near-Death Experiences, UFO Encounters, and Mind at Large,* two books with terrific application to the subject at hand. His fascination with the Omega Point is borrowed directly from the writings of the Jesuit mystic Pierre Teilhard de Chardin, who conceived of the idea that evolution was progressing to a goal—the maximum level of complexity and consciousness—called the Omega Point. Along with the Ukrainian geochemist Vladimir Ivanovich Vernadsky, he also developed the concept of *noosphere,* an innovative term denoting the numinous sphere of collective human thought. During his prime, Chardin was condemned as a heretic because his mystical Darwinian syncretism severely conflicted with the teaching magisterium of the Catholic Church, particularly regarding human origins and the doctrine of original sin. His primary book, *The Phenomenon of Man,* presented an evolutionary account of the unfolding of the cosmos that abandoned biblical theology for an occult pantheistic monism. However, today his thought is mainstreamed in the Jesuit order and was endorsed repeatedly in the theological writings of Pope Benedict XVI.[37]

Borrowing deeply from Chardinian concepts like noogenesis, Ring employed the tools of psychological research to document the worldview shift resulting from transformative encounters like NDEs and alien abduction. He concluded these phenomena are instigating a paradigm shift entailing the "shamanizing of modern human-ity."[38] Of course, a shaman is typically a tribal leader who contacts the spirit world and practices magic. Like Chardin, Ring frames it as an extension of evolution. However, Ring has tabulated a lot of data that suggests we are within "a major shift in the levels of conscious-ness that will eventually lead to humanity being able to live in two worlds at once—the physical and the imaginal."[39] He concludes that humankind is merging with "Mind at Large."[40] This corresponds quite neatly with the converging monistic aspirations of the inter-spiritual age discussed above. Recent poll data supports the trend toward shamanization.

The paranormal has deeply penetrated American culture. It now is the mainstream. A 2005 Gallup poll revealed that three in four Americans believe in the paranormal. Put another way, that is 75 percent of Americans[41]—or around 235,425,000 people. Also, 37 percent believe houses can be haunted and 21 percent believe they can personally communicate with the dead. Thus, out of the current population estimate of roughly three hundred million Americans, one hundred eleven million people believe in hauntings, and sixty-three million Americans believe they can communicate with the dead! To put that figure in visual terms, imagine a large superdome football stadium that holds fifty thousand people. Think about this: It would take *1,260* of those stadiums to hold the number of Ameri-cans who believe it is possible to communicate with the dead! That entails a lot of necromantic tailgating. What is more disturbing to a Christian apologist is that many of these folks claim to be Bible believers.

Astonishingly, 20 percent of Protestants and 28 percent of Catholics believe in reincarnation, an idea foreign to biblical theol-ogy, but, as we will examine, very popular in NDE research, parapsychology, and the new pantheism. Close to the same percentages of Protestants and Catholics practice yoga as spiritual discipline, believe in astrology, and hold a belief in spiritual energy arising from objects such as mountains, trees, or crystals. This extends into areas traditionally associated with witchcraft. Seventeen percent of Catholics and 16 percent of Protestants and believe people can use the "evil eye" to "cast curses or spells that cause bad things to happen."[42] Reports of ghosts have *doubled!* The percentage of Americans who report seeing a ghost has doubled from 9 percent to 18 percent over thirteen years prior to the 2009 survey. The percentage who said that they were in touch with a dead person has increased from 18 percent to 29 percent. Given this data, should Christian apologists be spending most of their time addressing atheistic naturalism? I think not. There is a much more pressing need in addressing the occult/paranormal worldview. This is a wakeup call. However, the warning gong was rung by a Christian martyr and watchman on the wall who saw it coming from his study of biblical prophecy.

Watchman Nee's Warning

On November 4, 1903 in Swatow, China, a baby boy, Nee Shu-Tsu, was born. His name means "he who proclaims his ancestors' merits."[44] After the boy's life mission became apparent to his mother, an early Chinese Christian, she gave him a new name, To-Sheng, meaning "the sound of a gong."[45] The new name implies that he would be a watchman who would bang the gong to warn the people of God. Hence, his name was anglicized to "Watchman

Watchman Nee[43]

Nee," and he lived up to his name by issuing early warnings concerning the ongoing paranormal paradigm shift.

Watchman Nee (1903–1972) was a Christian teacher and church leader in China during the first half of the twentieth century. He established churches throughout China and taught countless disciples. During his thirty years of service, Nee published over a hundred books expounding the Bible,[46] including *The Normal Christian Life*, his best-known book that sold over one million copies worldwide and became a Christian classic. Following the Communist Revolution, he was persecuted and imprisoned for his faith. He spent the last twenty years of his life in prison and died a Christian martyr at the hands of militant atheism. Nee was named one of the "100 Most Influential Christians of the Twentieth Century" by *Christianity Today* magazine, and was officially honored for his contributions to Protestant Christianity by the United States House of Representatives.[47]

Nee not only predicted the current paranormal paradigm shift, but he offered a shocking explanation for it: mankind's latent soul power apprehended in the last days for Satan's diabolic ends. Nee held to the belief that man is tripartite. In Christian theology, the tripartite view holds that man is a composite of three distinct components: body, soul, and spirit. New Testament passages—like "may your whole spirit and soul and body be kept blameless at the coming of our Lord Jesus Christ" (1 Thessalonians 5:23b) and "For the word of God is living and active, sharper than any two-edged sword, piercing to the division of soul and of spirit" (Hebrews 4:12a)—support this view. Michael A. Harbin is a modern trichotomist who explains spiritual death at the Fall by appealing to the distinction between soul and spirit diagrammed like this:

Humankind after the Fall is spiritually dead.[48]

In contrast, the bipartite view holds that "soul" and "spirit" are different terms for the same component. This is because some contemporary scholars argue that spirit and soul seem to be used interchangeably in other passages. Even so, Hebrews 4:12 strongly supports the tripartite distinction. Nee explained the division in this way:

> What is the spirit? That which makes us conscious of God and relates us to God is the spirit. What is the soul? It is that which relates us to ourselves and gives us self-consciousness. What is the body? It causes us to be related to the world.[49]

Furthermore, he believed the soul was the interface between spirit and body and that before the Fall it was the seat of Adam's ability to converse and walk with God. Nee stated:

> The living soul, which is the result of the coming together of the spirit and the body, possesses unthinkable supernatural

power. At the fall, though, the power which distinguishes Adam from us is lost. Yet this does not mean there is no longer such power; it only denotes that though this ability is still in man, it is nonetheless "frozen" or immobilized.[50]

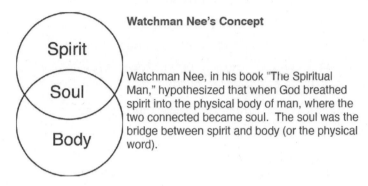

Watchman Nee's Concept

Watchman Nee, in his book "The Spiritual Man," hypothesized that when God breathed spirit into the physical body of man, where the two connected became soul. The soul was the bridge between spirit and body (or the physical word).

Thologian Michael Lake has illustrated and explained Nee's view like this.[51]

While some of his exegesis is questionable according to modern scholarship, still his overarching thesis deserves careful consideration. It cannot be disputed that he predicted much of what we see happening today. Within this volume, we will examine some of Nee's ideas in greater depth to "test everything; hold fast what is good" (1 Thessalonians 5:21). But for now, let us hear him as a prophetic watchman:

In Revelation 18 things are mentioned which shall come to pass in the last days. I indicated at the very beginning how man's soul will become a commodity in Babylon— that which can be sold and bought. But why is man's soul treated as a commodity? Because Satan and his puppet the Antichrist wish to use the human soul as an instrument for their activities at the end of this age. When Adam fell in the garden of Eden his power was immobilized. He had not lost this power altogether, only it was now buried within him. He had become flesh, and his flesh now enclosed tightly this marvelous power within it. Generation has succeeded generation with the result that this primordial ability of Adam has become a "latent" force in his descendants. It has turned to become a kind of "hidden" power. It is not lost to man, it is simply bound up by the flesh.

Today in each and every person who lives on earth lies this Adamic power, though it is confined in him and is not able to freely express itself. Yet such power is in every man's soul just as it was in Adam's soul at the beginning. Since today's soul is under siege by the flesh, this power is likewise confined by the flesh. The work of the devil nowadays is to stir up man's soul and to release this latent power within it as a deception for spiritual power. The reason for my mentioning these things is to warn ourselves of the special relationship between man's soul and Satan in the last days.[52]

Watchman Nee believed that humans have extrasensory abilities as a remnant of their pre-Fall status entailing freer access to God and the supernatural realm. Whether his exegetical inferences are perfectly sound is beside the larger point, being that this soul power is an inherent talent, some having more than others. There is a great deal of scientific evidence demonstrating this power examined in chapters 6 and 7. More troublesome, Nee believed that mankind's greatest supernatural enemy would seek to encourage and harness this psychic power for his own evil ends: "But it is Satan's desire to develop this latent ability so as to make man feel he is as rich as God in accordance with what Satan had promised. Thus will man worship himself, though indirectly it is a worship of Satan."[53] From the facts examined in this chapter that are further developed within, it is reasonable to conclude this strategy is already in play.

Notes

1. Ron Rhodes. *The Truth Behind Ghosts, Mediums, and Psychic Phenomena* (Eugene, OR: Harvest House, 2006) Kindle edition, 19.

2. T. S. Kuhn, *The Structure of Scientific Revolutions*, 1st. ed. (Chicago: University of Chicago Press, 1962).

3. Kevin Barrett, "Book Review: Dean Radin's 'Supernormal' Could (and Should) Destroy the Dominant Western Paradigm," *Veterans Today*, August 27, 2013, http://www.veteranstoday.com/2013/08/27/radin/ (accessed 11/28/13).

4. Antony Flew and Roy Abraham Varghese, *There Is a God: How the World's Most Notorious Atheist Changed His Mind* (New York: HarperOne, 2008) 114.

5. Brian Greene, *The Elegant Universe: Superstrings, Hidden Dimensions, and the Quest for the Ultimate Theory* (New York: W. W. Norton, 2003) 42.

6. Ibid., 77.

7. Ibid.

8. Ibid., 51.

9. "WMAP Space-Mission Survey of the Universe After the Big Bang Completed—Its Results Hint at a Far Stranger Cosmos," *The Daily Galaxy*, October 8, 2010, http://www.dailygalaxy.com/my_weblog/2010/10/-wmap-space-mission-survey-of-the-universe-after-the-big-bang-completed-but-its-results-may-hint-at-.html.

10. Nagel cites Dawkins as an example of the standard account that he doubts. See Richard Dawkins, *The Blind Watchmaker: Why the Evidence of Evolution Reveals a Universe without Design* (New York: Norton, 1986).

11. Thomas Nagel, *Mind and Cosmos: Why the Materialist Neo-Darwinian Conception of Nature Is Almost Certainly False* (Oxford: Oxford University, 2012) Kindle edition, 5.

12. Thomas Nagel, "The Core of 'Mind and Cosmos,'" *New York Times,* August 18, 2013, http://opinionator.blogs.nytimes. com/2013/08/18/the-core-of-mind-and-cosmos/?_r=0 (accessed 10/29/13).

13. Eben Alexander, quoted from interview at Skeptiko podcast, November 22, 2011, http://www.skeptiko.com/154-neurosurgeon-dr-eben-alexander-near-death-experience/ (accessed 04/25/12).

14. Lesslie Newbigin, *Foolishness to the Greeks: The Gospel and Western Culture* (Grand Rapids, MI: Eerdmans, 1986) Kindle edition, 676–681.

15. Craig S. Keener. *Miracles: The Credibility of the New Testament Accounts* (Grand Rapids, MI: Baker, 2011) Kindle edition, 2827–2828.

16. Greg Koukl, "Ancient Words, Ever True," *Solid Ground,* September/ October 2011, Stand to Reason, http://www.str.org/Media/Default/ Publications/DigitalSG_0911_New-1.pdf.

17. Gary Habermas and Michael Licona, *The Case for the Resurrection of Jesus* (Grand Rapids, MI: Kregel, 2004).

18. Lee Strobel, *The Case for a Creator: A Journalist Investigates Scientific Evidence that Points Toward God* (Grand Rapids, MI: Zondervan, 2005).

19. Dean Radin, *Supernormal: Science, Yoga, and the Evidence for Extraordinary Psychic Abilities* (Deepak Chopra, 2013) Kindle edition, 26.3/669.

20. William Butler Yeats. "The Second Coming," http://www.potw.org/ archive/potw351.html (accessed 09/21/13).

21. Peter Jones, *Spirit Wars: Pagan Revival in Christian America* (Mukilteo, WA: Winepress, 1997) 35.

22. Russ Dizdar, "Dark Rituals/Dark Powers," in Thomas Horn, et. al, *God's Ghostbusters* (Crane MO: Defender, 2011) Kindle edition, 3658–3664.

23. Hour of Power, program 1426, "Billy Graham and Robert Schuller 'Say "Yes" to Possibility Thinking,'" May 31, 1997. Clip available here: http://www.youtube.com/watch?v=axxlXy6bLH0.

24. John MacArthur rebuked Graham here: "A Wideness to God's Mercy?" Grace to You, February 28, 2010, http://www.gty.org/blog/B100228.

25. "The Journey: Where Interspirituality Came From," The Coming Interspiritual Age, http://www.thecominginterspiritualage.com/quotations/2.

26. Harvey J. Irwin and Caroline A. Watt, *An Introduction to Parapsychology*, 5th ed. (Jefferson, NC: McFarland, 2007) Kindle edition, 412–415.

27. J. B. Rhine, *New Frontiers of the Mind: The Story of the Duke Experiments* (New York: Farrar & Rinehart, 1937) 51. Available here: http://www.scribd.com/doc/6490627/JB-Rhine-New-Frontiers-of-the-Mind.

28. Ibid., 50–51.

29. George P. Hansen, *The Trickster and the Paranormal* (Bloomington, IN: Xlibris, 2001) Kindle edition, 2026–2034.

30. George P. Hansen, "The Trickster and the Paranormal Overview," http://www.tricksterbook.com/ (accessed 09/04/13).

31. "Many Americans Mix Multiple Faiths," Pew Research, December 9, 2009, http://www.pewforum.org/2009/12/09/many-americans-mix-multiple-faiths/#1 (accessed 09/04/2013).

32. Ibid.

33. Robert H. Bennett, *I Am Not Afraid: Demon Possession and Spiritual Warfare* (St. Louis, MO: Concordia, 2013). Kindle edition, 290–291.

34. "Many Americans Mix Multiple Faiths."

35. Rhodes, 18.

36. C. Everett Koop and Francis A. Schaeffer, *Whatever Happened to the Human Race?*, rev. ed. (Westchester, IL: Crossway, 1983) 103.

37. Pope Benedict XVI, *Credo for Today: What Christians Believe* (San Francisco: Ignatius, 2009) 34, 113.

38. Kenneth Ring, *The Omega Project: Near-Death Experiences, UFO Encounters, and Mind at Large* (New York: William Morrow, 1992) 239.

39. Ibid., 240.

40. Ibid., 246.

41. David W. Moore, "Three in Four Americans Believe in Paranormal," Gallup, June 16, 2005, http://www.gallup.com/poll/16915/Three-Four-Americans-Believe-Paranormal.aspx (accessed 08/11/2011).

42. "Eastern or New Age Beliefs, 'Evil Eye,'" Pew Research, December 9, 2009, http://www.pewforum.org/2009/12/09/many-americans-mix-multiple-faiths/#1 (accessed 09/4/13).

43. "File: W_Nee.jpg," http://en.wikipedia.org/wiki/File:W_Nee.jpg.

44. Dana Roberts, *Secrets of Watchman Nee* (Orlando, FL: Bridge-Logos, 2005) 6.

45. Ibid.

46. His works are listed here: http://www.watchmannee.org/publications.html.

47. Christopher H. Smith, "Acknowledgement of Watchman Nee in the House of Representatives," United States Government Publishing Office, July 30, 2009, p. E2110, http://thomas.loc.gov/cgi-bin/query/z?r111:E31JY9-0052 (accessed 09/04/13).

48. Diagrams based on those in Michael A. Harbin, *The Promise and the Blessing: A Historical Survey of the Old and New Testaments* (Grand Rapids, MI: Zondervan, 2005) 72–73.

49. Watchman Nee, *The Latent Power of the Soul* (Christian Literature Crusade, 1980) 10.

50. Ibid., 13.
51. Michael Lake, "A Kingdom Paradigm about Reality," *Biblical Life Assembly*, August 10, 2013, http://www.biblicallifeassembly.org/library/weekly.htm. (Notes and diagram shared with author via email.)
52. Nee, 14–15.
53. Ibid., 21.

THE ETHOS OF DEMYTHOLOGIZATION
AND THE EXCLUDED MIDDLE

There are three classes of people: Those who see.
Those who see when they are shown.
Those who do not see.
—LEONARDO DA VINCI, RENAISSANCE POLYMATH

In the nineteenth-century short story, "The Generous Gambler," by Charles Baudelaire, the narrator plays cards with the devil, but doesn't believe until it is too late, and he loses his soul. Upon his woeful epiphany, he recalls a neglected pastoral: "Never, my brethren, forget, when you hear enlightenment vaunted, that the neatest trick of the devil is to persuade you that he does not exist."[1] This was recycled in the 1995 film, *The Usual Suspects* starring Kevin Spacey, as: "The greatest trick the devil ever pulled was convincing the world he didn't exist."[2] Through the work of philosophers like David Hume, the Enlightenment era was the period that disabused Western culture of some unhelpful superstitions, but it also led to a sweeping suspicion of anything supernatural. Evangelical philosophers have answered the skepticism of David

Hume, but the siren song of progressive pragmatism is subtly irresistible. Pragmatism is a way of thinking concerned with practical results rather than ethics or theoretical principles. Pragmatism is the Enlightenment ethos—its fundamental character. The thesis argued in this chapter is that the Enlightenment ethos has surreptitiously exchanged Western evangelical belief in a dynamic spirit realm replete with angels and demons for a largely theoretical one, a mere afterglow of the biblical worldview.

It is widely conceded that Western culture has entered a post-Christian era. In the 1960s, A. W. Tozer wrote, "Secularism, materialism, and the intrusive presence of things have put out the light in our souls and turned us into a generation of zombies."[3] Since his lament, the situation has deteriorated significantly, with a split into postmodern and naturalistic camps. Beginning with Francis Schaeffer, the Western church has engaged in rigorous worldview apologetics, but it is steadily losing ground. As stated in the previous chapter, a recent Barna Group survey revealed only 19 percent of professing born-again believers hold a biblical worldview.[4] This suggests something has been overlooked or a problem in methodology—or both. We are facing a serious problem. At the same time that the culture is embracing the paranormal, the church is largely uninformed and incredulous. The answers we provide concerning phenomena like ghosts and ESP are often circular and unsatisfactory. As argued in later chapters, they often are not entirely biblical, either. This is largely due to demythologization and well-intended pragmatism. It didn't happen overnight.

While the Enlightenment bolstered science as the exclusive avenue to objective truth, higher criticism increasingly questioned biblical revelation until it was marginalized and relegated to the private sphere of belief. The large-scale defections from historic orthodoxy bore fruit in nineteenth-century, theological liberalism's social gospel. The focus became "this worldly" in order to foster social justice rather than heavenly treasure by making disciples. Into the twentieth century, this progressively polarized conservative Christians, and they withdrew from the academy and culture at large. As the Bible believers left the discussion, unbelievers had free rein in academia and the majority influence on the next generation. This was a fatal error and a failure to heed the Lord's command to "occupy till I come" (Luke 19:13, KJV).

Demythologizing: The Spirit of the Old Guard

In the 1940s, Rudolf Bultmann, a German Lutheran theologian and biblical scholar, sought to interpret the New Testament through the existentialist philosophy of Martin Heidegger, and began to call this interpretive technique "demythologizing."[5] He explained, "To de-mythologize is to reject not Scripture or the Christian message as a whole, but the world-view of Scripture."[6] Bultmann's antisupernatural agenda was laid bare in his writings: "Now that the forces and the laws of nature have been discovered, we can no longer believe in spirits, whether good or evil."[7] Of course, because God is a spirit (John 4:24), the *reductio ad absurdum* of this line of thinking entails the "death of God" theology, which flourished in the 1960s.[8] Accordingly, Bultmann rejected the Supernatural Worldview this book endorses. Many academics have adopted his approach. Writing as acting chair of the theology department at the University of Notre Dame, Roman Catholic theologian Richard McBrien wrote that the idea of a personal Satan is "premodern and precritical."[9] On the Protestant side, a Methodist theologian at Auburn Theological

Seminary, Walter Wink, wrote: "It is as impossible for most of us to believe in the real existence of demonic or angelic powers as it is to believe in dragons, or elves, or a flat world."[10] Unfortunately, the mainline denominational churches[11] have been taken captive by the spirit of the age.

This is also true of postmodern "evangelicals," aka the emergent church movement led by the likes of Brian McLaren, Gregory Boyd, and Rob Bell. McLaren is postmodern to the depths of denying the gospel in adopting a radical inclusivism. Boyd is an open theist—holding a position that states God does not infallibly know the future. Bell—aptly described as classic theological liberalism in skinny jeans[12]—created a firestorm of controversy by denying the reality of hell and promoting universalism in his best seller, *Love Wins,* but given his previous questioning of the virgin birth, it was not a big surprise. Of course, no inerrancy-affirming evangelical would assent to the above ideas derivative of Bultmann's classic proclamation: "It is impossible to use electric light and the wireless and to avail ourselves of modern medical and surgical discoveries, and at the same time to believe in the New Testament world of spirits and miracles."[13] Bultmann defined an almost complete split between history and faith, writing that only the bare fact of Christ crucified was necessary for Christian faith, and the above postmoderns are his heirs apparent.

In contrast, people who hold to the Supernatural Worldview of the Bible stand and defend the fundamentals. Often maligned, the term "fundamentalist" started out simple enough. Because it has been distorted beyond its original meaning, I would like to offer a corrective. In 1846, the Evangelical Alliance was formed to unite all believers who saw nineteenth-century rise of "social gospel" theological liberalism as a denial of the faith. At a meeting in Niagara

Falls, New York, the alliance listed the five "fundamentals" that could not be denied without falling into the error of liberalism. Those five were: (1) inerrancy of Scripture, (2) the divinity of Jesus, (3) the virgin birth, (4) Jesus' death on the cross as a substitute for our sins, and (5) His physical Resurrection and impending return. In light of recent attacks, I propose to add (6) the doctrine of the Trinity[14] and (7) the existence of Satan, angels, and spirits to the list for a total of seven.

Those doctrines are what separate the sheep from the goats. The church I attend affirms all of them. If yours does not, consider finding a new place to worship. While it is argued here that they are all essentials, numbers two, four, five, and six cannot be denied while in any meaningful way remaining a Christian. After all, we worship a triune God with Christ at the center of Christianity, the gospel is His death and resurrection, and the great hope of the believer is His promise to return and eternal life (Hebrews 9:28; Titus 2:13; Matthew 25:46). Even the outspoken antitheist Christopher Hitchens had a better understanding of Christianity than what most liberal, mainline Christians express. For example, this excerpt from an interview of Hitchens by Unitarian minister Marilyn Sewell concerning Hitchens' book, *God Is Not Great*, reveals the bankruptcy of demythologized nominal Christianity:

> **Sewell:** The religion you cite in your book is generally the fundamentalist faith of various kinds. I'm a liberal Christian, and I don't take the stories from the scripture literally. I don't believe in the doctrine of atonement (that Jesus died for our sins, for example). Do you make and distinction between fundamentalist faith and liberal religion?

Hitchens: I would say that if you don't believe that Jesus of Nazareth was the Christ and Messiah, and that he rose again from the dead and by his sacrifice our sins are forgiven, you're really not in any meaningful sense a Christian.[15]

It is terribly unfortunate that an ardent antitheist like Hitchens understands Christianity better than a so-called minister. While conservative Christians differ in principle, it seems that Bultmann may have been more correct than first assumed.

Cessationism: Demythologizing the Work of the Holy Spirit

Surely, one might think, the conservative resurgence in the Southern Baptist Convention and the *Chicago Statement of Biblical Inerrancy* safeguarded the man in the pew from the conclusions of higher criticism. Although conservative Christians have taken a valiant stand against liberalism, they have endorsed a form of supernatural skepticism out of seeming necessity. Charles Kraft explains how the corrosive ethos diminishes one's ability to mount a reasonable defense of the Bible when facing its critics:

> Instead of attempting to return to at least the more reasonable aspects of the supernaturalism that the Enlightenment overturned, evangelicals have often argued against the liberal positions from the same rationalistic basis. We, like they, have often seen little of God's hand in the present and conducted our defense purely on the basis of what God used to do.[16]

Kraft is pointing out how a large part of Western evangelicalism doesn't believe the Holy Spirit is actively revealing Himself, as reported in the New Testament, through speaking in tongues, healing by the laying on of hands, and prophetic utterances. Although these gifts are described as ongoing, unbelief has been baptized as cessation theology—the threefold idea that 1) the Holy Spirit's purpose for the "sign gifts" was finished in the first century; 2) the sign gifts were given exclusively to the original twelve apostles, so that the sign gifts and apostleship are inextricably linked; and 3) the gift of apostleship no longer exists. The most-often cited proof text is: "Love never ends. As for prophecies, they will pass away; as for tongues, they will cease; as for knowledge, it will pass away. For we know in part and we prophesy in part" (1 Corinthians 13:8–9). According to cessationists, "the perfect" refers to the New Testament implying that, upon the closing of the canon, the sign gifts cease. However, this is a far-fetched twisting of Scripture, as "the perfect" more likely denotes the return of Christ. John Piper explains:

Let's take the two halves of the verse one at a time. First it says, "Now we see in a mirror dimly, but then face to face." Is it more likely that Paul is saying, "Now before the New Testament is written, we see in a mirror dimly; but then when the New Testament is written, we shall see face to face"? Or is it more likely that he is saying, "Now in this age we see in a mirror dimly; but then when the Lord returns, we shall see face to face"? In the Old Testament there are half a dozen references to seeing God "face to face." Revelation 22:4 says that in heaven we shall see God's face. 1 John 3:2 says that when Jesus appears, we shall be like him for we shall see him as he is.[17]

The cessationist interpretation makes little sense in context. Even so, from this dubious foundation, cessationists argue that: 1) the sign gifts have ceased, and 2) they should not be expected to return. Although sincere believers hold this view, it is easily refuted by Scripture and a survey of church history.

The first point ignores the purpose of the power described in Luke 24:49: "Stay in the city until you are clothed with power from on high," and Acts 1:8, "But you will receive power when the Holy Spirit has come upon you, and you will be my witnesses in Jerusalem and in all Judea and Samaria, <u>and to the end of the earth</u>" (underline added). The power is to aid the completion of *global evangelization*. The task of world evangelization is not yet complete. The power is for authenticating the gospel—the resurrection of Jesus—not the apostles. The disputed long ending of Mark, while likely not original, still preserves the opinion of the early church, and it states: "And these <u>signs</u> will accompany those who believe" (Mark 16:17a, underline added).

In Peter's sermon on the day of Pentecost, he added the words "in the last days" to Joel 2:28–32. The last days he spoke of are not just the end times, but were inaugurated at Pentecost (1 Corinthians 10:11; 2 Timothy 3:1; Hebrews 1:2; James 5:3; 2 Peter 3:3) and will continue until Christ's return. Peter included gifts like prophecy, dreams, and visions, which most cessationists deny: "And in the last days it shall be, God declares, that I will pour out my Spirit on all flesh, and your sons and your daughters shall prophesy, and your young men shall see visions, and your old men shall dream dreams" (Acts 2:17). Also, Paul wrote to the Corinthian church: "so that you are not lacking in <u>any gift</u>, as you wait for the revealing of our Lord Jesus Christ" (1 Corinthians 1:7, underline added), implying that all of the gifts are for the entire period up until Jesus' return. Thus,

point one must be false, because there is no scriptural reason to sus-
pect the sign gifts have ceased and many to the contrary.

As to the second point that the sign gifts were only for the original twelve apostles, there is not even a hint of that in the Bible. The
same sign gifts were displayed by Stephen (Acts 6:8) and Philip (Acts
8:13), who were not of the original twelve. In 1 Corinthians 14,
Paul gives detailed instructions about the use of tongues. Though
he warns sharply against many abuses of tongues, he doesn't outlaw
their use. Instead, he explicitly says, "Do not forbid to speak with
tongues" (v. 39b). He teaches that they are a sign for unbelievers
and that prophecy is a sign for believers: "Thus tongues are a sign
not for believers but for unbelievers, while prophecy is a sign not
for unbelievers but for believers" (1 Corinthians 14:22, underline
added). Obviously, Paul did not teach cessationism but rather the
continuation of the sign gifts.

From there, we see a steady stream into the second century. Justin Martyr wrote in an apologetic to a Jew named Trypho, stating:
"For the prophetical gifts remain with us, even to the present time.
And hence you ought to understand that [the gifts] formerly among
your nation have been transferred to us."[18] In addition, the charis-
mata bestowed upon the apostolic church were not extinct in the
days of Irenaeus (second century, AD 202). He was a student of
Polycarp, who was a disciple of the apostle John. He wrote in his
Against Heresies:

Wherefore, also, those who are in truth His disciples, receiving grace from Him, do in His name perform [miracles],
so as to promote the welfare of other men, according to the
gift which each one has received from Him. For some do
certainly and truly drive out devils, so that those who have

thus been cleansed from evil spirits frequently both believe [in Christ], and join themselves to the Church. Others have foreknowledge of things to come: they see visions, and utter prophetic expressions. Others still, heal the sick by laying their hands upon them, and they are made whole. Yea, moreover, as I have said, the dead even have been raised up, and remained among us for many years. (underline added)[19]

Irenaeus even offered his own personal recollection of some who had been raised from the dead living on as witnesses to the Christian faith. Furthermore, he mentioned that tongues were an ongoing sign gift in the second century:

In like manner we do also hear many brethren in the Church, who possess prophetic gifts, and who through the Spirit speak all kinds of languages, and bring to light for the general benefit the hidden things of men, and declare the mysteries of God, whom also the apostle terms "spiritual," they being spiritual because they partake of the Spirit, and not because their flesh has been stripped off and taken away, and because they have become purely spiritual.[20]

Even Augustine (AD 354–430), initially a cessationist, later changed his mind because of all of the supernatural miracles he witnessed. He mentioned a blind man restored to sight: "The miracle which was wrought at Milan when I was there, and by which a blind man was restored to sight, could come to the knowledge of many."[21] A woman with terminal breast cancer got baptized and was subsequently ruled to be miraculously healed by a physician: "When he had examined her after this, and found that she who, on his former examination, was afflicted with that disease was perfectly cured."[22]

He lists miraculous healing after healing and astonishing accounts of demonic possession, like this one:

There is a country-seat called Victoriana, less than thirty miles from Hipporegius. At it there is a monument to the Milanese martyrs, Protasius and Gervasius. Thither a young man was carried, who, when he was watering his horse one summer day at noon in a pool of a river, had been taken possession of by a devil. As he lay at the monument, near death, or even quite like a dead person, the lady of the manor, with her maids and religious attendants, entered the place for evening prayer and praise, as her custom was, and they began to sing hymns. At this sound the young man, as if electrified, was thoroughly aroused, and with frightful screaming seized the altar, and held it as if he did not dare or were not able to let it go, and as if he were fixed or tied to it; and the devil in him, with loud lamentation, besought that he might be spared, and confessed where and when and how he took possession of the youth. At last, declaring that he would go out of him, he named one by one the parts of his body which he threatened to mutilate as he went out and with these words he departed from the man. But his eye, falling out on his cheek, hung by a slender vein as by a root, and the whole of the pupil which had been black became white. When this was witnessed by those present (others too had now gathered to his cries, and had all joined in prayer for him), although they were delighted that he had recovered his sanity of mind, yet, on the other hand, they were grieved about his eye, and said he should seek medical advice. But his sister's husband, who had brought him there, said, "God, who has banished the devil, is able to restore his eye at the

prayers of His saints." Therewith he replaced the eye that
was fallen out and hanging, and bound it in its place with
his handkerchief as well as he could, and advised him not to
loose the bandage for seven days. When he did so, he found
it quite healthy. Others also were cured there, but of them it
were tedious to speak.[23]

Even more amazing, Augustine reported that the dead were still
being raised:

There, too, the son of a man, Irenaeus, one of our tax-gath-
erers, took ill and died. And while his body was lying lifeless,
and the last rites were being prepared, amidst the weeping
and mourning of all, one of the friends who were consoling
the father suggested that the body should be anointed with
the oil of the same martyr. It was done, and he revived.[24]

Augustine lamented there were so many divine miracles performed he could not record them all:

What am I to do? I am so pressed by the promise of finish-
ing this work, that I cannot record all the miracles I know.…
For when I saw, in our own times, frequent signs of the presence of divine powers similar to those which had been given
of old, I desired that narratives might be written, judging
that the multitude should not remain ignorant of these
things. (underline added)[25]

Augustine called these "signs," similar to those of old, which
were occurring frequently in fourth and fifth centuries—long after
the apostles had lived. While allowing the third point in the cessa-

tionists' syllogism that true apostleship entailed being an eyewitness to the resurrected Lord, this testimony from the early church fathers soundly discredits the second pillar of the cessationists' argument. With the first two premises proven false beyond a reasonable doubt, the argument for cessationism fails.

Cessationism is a product of the Enlightenment ethos. Frankly, it amounts to a sanctified form of unbelief. Certainly, cessationists argue that their unbelief is justified by abusive charlatans, and there are many. Nevertheless, phonies more properly warrant increased discernment rather than sweeping dismissal. Of course, we should not accept every supernatural claim, but it seems fair to point out that we run the danger of creating a self-fulfilling theology because even Jesus would not work miracles when faced with stubborn unbelief: "And he did not do many mighty works there, because of their unbelief" (Matthew 13:58). There are voluminous reports by missionaries from South America, Asia, India, and Africa that support the tongues phenomenon still serves as a sign to unbelievers. As a trained physicist-turned-Anglican clergyman, John Polkinghorne, points out, "It might be that other cultures provide, through their different practice and different kinds of openness, regimes more conducive than ours to certain types of experience."[26] It seems that where belief flourishes, miracles still occur—even in the West.

New Testament scholar Craig Keener has documented thousands of cases in his massive, two-volume set: *Miracles: The Credibility of the New Testament Accounts.* Against David Hume-inspired skepticism, Keener lists two theses for the book. The primary thesis is that eyewitnesses still do make miracle claims like those in the New Testament, and the secondary thesis is that supernatural explanations should be welcome on the scholarly table along with other explanations, rather than being perfunctorily excluded. The case for point one is so overwhelming that no intellectually honest reader can

leave Keener's work unconvinced. The second point is more controversial: "That we are not obligated to begin with the a priori assumption that none of these events could involve intelligent suprahuman
causation."[27] Even so, it does not entail naïve acceptance, but rather
fair-mindedly following the evidence where it leads.

As one example among thousands of modern-day reports of
miraculous healings, the case of Kayla Knight stands out for its cor-
roborating scientific evidence. In 2008, Kayla, an eleven-year-old
girl, had a massive brain tumor that covered nearly a fourth of her
brain. A local news station reported Kayla's mother, Amy, saying:

> We both hit our knees and we were praying. That was actu-
> ally on a Wednesday so when we got to church we had a
> good 30 people or more lay hands on her and it just...you
> could feel God. I can't say we prayed as much before. I mean
> we did...but not like this. Not like we do now.[28]

Two days after the prayer and laying on of hands by the church,
Kayla was sent to Baylor Hospital in Dallas for emergency surgery to
save her life. In preparation to remove the tumor, the doctors took
another MRI and were astounded.

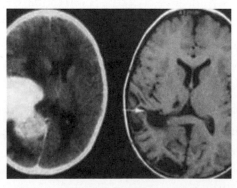

Tumor seen on left is completely missing on right two days later.[29]

The tumor was completely gone. Amy described the doctor's confusion:

> He said, "It's got to be a mistake, it has to be. We are going to schedule another test, there is no way it's just gone," and just the whole time he is stuttering and there is just this look on his face like: I don't understand. I don't know. We did another one and it was gone and his words were, "It was truly a miracle, this has to be the act of God."[30]

This case validates the Supernatural Worldview of the Bible. While cessationists pray for healing, how many would have the courage to allow thirty folks to lay on hands when faced with such an illness? Of all the supernatural sign gifts, prophecy is the most important.

The most ironic thing about the gift of prophecy is that many ostensibly cessationist pastors are exercising it without knowing it. Charles H. Spurgeon, a seminal figure in the Reformed Baptist tradition, was known as the "prince of preachers." It is estimated that in his lifetime, he preached to around ten million people. Given his reformed pedigree, it is safe to say he was a cessationist. However, his autobiography contains surprising instances of supernatural prophecy. On one occasion, Spurgeon interrupted his sermon and pointed at a young man, announcing: "Young man, those gloves you are wearing have not been paid for: you have stolen them from your employer."[31] Later, a dumbfounded and convicted youth asked to speak to Spurgeon privately. Placing the pilfered gloves on the table, he said, "It's the first time I have robbed my master, and I will never do it again. You won't expose me, sir, will you? It would kill my mother if she heard that I had become a thief."[32] Spurgeon wrote, "I could tell as many as a dozen similar cases in which I pointed at somebody in the hall without having the slightest knowledge of the person, or any idea that what I said was right, except that I believed I was moved by the Spirit to say it."[33] Something similar led to my own conversion.

When I first attended Providence Baptist Church in my hometown of Raleigh, North Carolina, I went only to appease my mother. I was at the end of my rope, having pursued a "rock-star" lifestyle to the point of demoralizing addiction to drugs and alcohol. I had tried treatment centers and twelve-step programs, only to fail repeatedly. Church was the last stop on the block, and I had no expectation that it would help. As I sat in the pew, Pastor David Horner seemed to read my mind. At one point, he exclaimed, "Maybe someone out there has been telling God that you are going to commit suicide because your life is no longer worth living. God says He can make you a new creation. Do you think you know better than God?" It wasn't just a general statement that coincidently matched my disheartened state; I was thinking that exact thought precisely when he said it. I believe God spoke directly to me through him. Paul wrote about this phenomenon: "But if all prophesy, and an unbeliever or outsider enters, he is convicted by all, he is called to account by all, the secrets of his heart are disclosed, and so, falling on his face, he will worship God and declare that God is really among you" (1 Corinthians 14:24–25). Even though Pastor Horner didn't know it at the time, it was a true sign miracle that led me to the gospel. Things began to change rapidly after that, and today I am a seminary-trained Christian author. (My testimony is available online by following the link in the endnote.[34]) Sign miracles do still happen today, but Western Christianity suffers from a lack of belief that is perpetuated by Satan's clever use of counterfeit.

It is logical that Satan would direct his attacks to the sector of

Christendom that threatens him most. If so, charismatic Christianity is his greatest fear. Thus, he seeks to discredit it by promoting phonies. Most cessationism is a reaction to widespread abuses seen on the fringes of the Charismatic movement. Ironically, it is based on contemporary experience rather than biblical exegesis. While false teaching deserves rebuke, all too often the baby is thrown out with the filthy bathwater. Satan seeks to disempower the church so that he may control the middle realm. By inciting disgust with the false prophets, he promotes cessationism. However, counterfeit always assumes the genuine. No criminal in his right mind would print three-dollar bills. Satan is not stupid. Accordingly, false signs and wonders closely parallel the genuine article in order to discredit it.

Many mature, believing scholars support the responsible use of tongues and other sign gifts, John Piper, J. P. Moreland, Sam Storms, Adrian Warnock, Gordon Fee, Wayne Grudem, and Michael Brown being high-profile examples. Moreland notes that, "Fewer and fewer Christian scholars hold to cessationism, and it may fairly be called an increasingly marginalized viewpoint."[35] He admits that growing consensus does not prove cessationism false, but adds, "At the very least, the direction of Evangelical thought on these matters should cause cessationists to lower the degree of strength they take themselves to have regarding the truth of their position."[36] Unfortunately, rather than the humility Moreland suggested, an overconfident enmity is being promoted by John MacArthur as this book goes to press.[37] For someone who claims a Supernatural Worldview, he promotes a very strange fire of hostility toward charismatics. Might he unwittingly be playing into Satan's hands? As the return of Christ grows closer, there very well may be an increase in bona fide prophetic words in the fashion of prophets of old. Hard-line cessationists will unwittingly close themselves off. Even so, alleged prophets, however, should still be tested (1 Thessalonians 5:20–21), and the test is the same now as it's always been (Deuteronomy 18:22). This begs the question, "Will the cessationist church have ears to hear?" It has excluded the middle through a corrosive ethos to be explained below.

The Corrosive Ethos of Pragmatism

The discounting of the biblical worldview need not be so intentional. The Western ethos of progress, defined as increased convenience and efficiency, entails a demythologizing program of its own. Professor of religion, culture, and social theory at the University of Virginia, James Davidson Hunter, emphasizes that worldview entails "our understanding of time, space, and identity—the very essence of reality as we experience it."[38] He criticizes the popular evangelical worldview approach to cultural revitalization as naïve idealism that ignores the institutional cultural power structures that only change from the top down. He asserts that all of the Christian worldview revitalization strategies based political activism will fail.[39] Hunter is a social scientist, and his criticism is convincing but clinical. Alternately, he suggests a "faithful presence" strategy entailing the love of Christ realized incarnationally through us, in our relationships, within vocations, and within our circle of influence. Rather than pursuing political power, Jesus' emphasis is on social or relational power, the power one finds in ordinary life.[40] Yet for the West today, ordinary life is mediated through the lens of technology, which exacts a price.

Social critic Neil Postman argues that Western society is now a "technopoly," a culture that worships technology. One look at the excitement surrounding the release of the latest iPhone substantiates his assertion. He attributes this to scientism—the idea that science alone determines truth—and a constant progression of newer, improved technology fueling an ostensibly better quality of life. It seems we just cannot get enough new technology. My philosophy professor at Southeastern Baptist Theological Seminary, Bruce Little, explains that the assumption "newer is better" has been uncritically adopted by evangelicals, allowing a corrosive ethos into the church.[41] For example, when ministry success is quantified in secular terms, the world's methods reinforce the naturalistic worldview that produced them. While ministries have done this with the best of intentions, they have naïvely conceded ground to philosophical naturalism.

Postman argues that in a technopoly, "people are conceived of not as children of God or even as citizens but as consumers—that is to say, as markets."[42] Whereas ministries surely do not intend to adopt such a view, their methods may smuggle it in the back door. James Hunter writes that powerful commercial interest embedded in our institutions makes "resistance to their effects nearly impossible."[43] Accordingly, he argues that a "worldview never transcends the environment that surrounds it," and as a result, "it is difficult to imagine that there is a spiritual reality more real than the material world we live in."[44] This demythologization by default is readily seen in world missions when missionaries faced with demon possession realize they have unwittingly neglected the spirit realm in their preparation for ministry.

The Flaw of the Excluded Middle

Westerners typically view belief in the spirit realm of demons and angels as prescientific. However, in respect to the demonic, non-Westerners are often much closer to the biblical worldview than the missionaries who bring them the gospel. Christian anthropologist Charles Kraft observes:

In comparison to other societies, Americans and other North
Atlantic peoples are naturalistic. Non-Western peoples are
frequently concerned about the activities of supernatural
beings. Though many Westerners retain a vague belief in
God, most deny that other supernatural beings even exist.
The wide-ranging supernaturalism of most of the societies
of the world is absent for most of our people…. Our focus is
on the natural world, with little or no attention paid to the
supernatural world.[45]

This default naturalism led a missionary to India, Lesslie Newbigin, to argue, "Western Christian missions have been one of the
greatest secularizing forces in history."[46] Did you get that? Missionaries are a *secularizing* influence. Devout Christians with a strong
faith in God have a blind spot due to Western education and living
in technopoly. Anthropologist and missiologist Paul Hiebert wrote
concerning the error of the excluded middle:

I had excluded the middle level of supernatural but this-
worldly beings and forces from my own world view. As a
scientist, I had been trained to deal with the empirical world
in naturalistic terms. As a theologian, I was taught to answer
ultimate questions in theistic terms. For me the middle zone
did not really exist.[47]

By "excluded middle," he does not mean the one used in logic
that argues a statement must be true or false, allowing no middle
position, but rather the middle realm between God and man. In
other words, many in the West have a two-tiered view of reality with
religion (God, miracles) over science (natural laws, matter), but the
realm between has been excluded (demons, angels, spirits).

Religion - Belief in God
- miracles
- faith
- sacred

Excluded Middle - Angels, Demons, Spirits
- paranormal
- mysticism
- charismatic

Science - Matter, Energy, Physical Laws
- natural order
- observations
- secular

Whereas fewer than 18 percent of Christians in 1900 lived outside Europe and North America, today more than 60 percent do, and an estimated 70 percent will by 2025.[48] These Christians, largely charismatic, have no problem seeing and dealing with the activity of the middle realm. This means the Western, "excluded middle," cessationist worldview is, in fact, on the fringe minority of the majority church. In his treatment of African religion, Dr. John S. Mbiti notes that Western scholars "expose their own ignorance, false ideas, exaggerated prejudices and a derogatory attitude"[49] when they fail to take seriously genuine supernatural experiences pervasive in Africa. Whereas evangelical leaders are fairly open to hearing this sort of criticism in a missionary context, I am strongly suggesting it applies even more to our North American outreach to people coming from an occult background facing spiritual warfare. Some Christian counselors will likely suggest that these people see a psychiatrist for medication rather than offer deliverance. It is no wonder many have a hard time taking Western churches seriously when the excluded middle is on display.

In 2013, Rev. Dr. Robert Bennett's book, *I Am Not Afraid:*

Demon Possession and Spiritual Warfare, set a new standard in conservative Lutheran scholarship dealing with spiritual warfare. It provides his firsthand account of the dynamic spiritual warfare within the Lutheran Church of Madagascar. Part one provides an introduction into the Malagasy Lutheran Church and the traditional Malagasy worldview and discusses how the Western worldview varies radically from how Christianity is understood in most other parts of the world. Part two handles the biblical material as well as various aspects of Lutheran thought. Bennett suggests that the Enlightenment ethos has promoted an overconfident dismissal of spiritual warfare. Recognizing the paranormal paradigm shift underway in our own culture, he suggests we learn from these third-world contexts:

> As the western worldview continues to shift toward animism and the philosophy surrounding post-modernity, western views of rationalism appear to be on the decline and a new acceptance of the spiritualism seems to be the way of the future. If this is true, the Malagasy Lutheran Church's methods of contextualized catechesis and exorcism may lead the way to reach the lost within the western world.[50]

For those ministering within confessional Lutheranism, this work is sure to be helpful for what is around the corner. Most denominations have missionaries sounding a similar alarm.

Of course, things were not always this way. The middle realm has captured the hearts and minds of many great thinkers throughout history. Even modern science grew out of alchemy and occultism. For example, Isaac Newton, widely heralded as the father of modern science, was deeply involved in the quest for the philosopher's stone. After purchasing and studying Newton's alchemical works in

1942, economist John Maynard Keynes, for example, opined that "Newton was not the first of the age of reason, he was the last of the magicians."[51]

Paul Hiebert explained, "Belief in the middle level began to die in the 17th and 18th centuries with the growing acceptance...of a science based on materialistic naturalism. The result was the secularization of science and the mystification of religion."[52] What an interesting paradox we now face in that today we find an exact reversal with the secularization of religion through demythologization and the mystification of science via quantum theory.

The excluded middle seems applicable to Western Christianity as a whole. A new nationwide survey conducted by the Barna Group suggests that Americans who consider themselves to be Christian have been strongly influenced by technopoly:

> Four out of ten Christians (40%) strongly agreed that Satan "is not a living being but is a symbol of evil." An additional two out of ten Christians (19%) said they "agree somewhat" with that perspective. A minority of Christians indicated that they believe Satan is real by disagreeing with the statement: one-quarter (26%) disagreed strongly and about one-tenth (9%) disagreed somewhat. The remaining 8% were not sure what they believe about the existence of Satan.[53]

Adding the two skeptical categories "strongly agree" and "agree somewhat" together yields a shocking 59 percent of professing American *Christians* who do not believe Satan is real. The "greatest trick the devil ever pulled" turns out to be much more than a clever line. Views on the Holy Spirit are just as dismal, with the survey indicating that "38% strongly agreed and 20% agreed somewhat that the

Holy Spirit is 'a symbol of God's power or presence but is not a living entity.'"[54] Taken together, these statistics suggest that spiritual warfare has largely been abdicated in favor of worldly activism and politics.

While some Western evangelicals give verbal assent to the existence of the powers and principalities in Paul's letters, few reflect such belief in their methodology. It seems fair to argue that the major evangelical ministries are more prone to political activism than spiritual warfare. Rather than working in such a way that assents to Paul's teaching, "For we do not wrestle against flesh and blood" (Ephesians 6:12a), American evangelicals have frequently overemphasized politics that do just that.

Reflective of the excluded middle, the public witness of the church has been political and largely negative. Jeff Sharlet's book, *The Family: The Secret Fundamentalism at the Heart of American Power*, details how an elite group of neoconservative insiders organized the well-attended weekly prayer meetings for members of Congress and annual National Prayer Breakfasts attended by most presidents as a means to promote ostensibly Christian values.[55] However, the book exposes that their methods are more manipulative and worldly than Christ-like. Hunter argues that this political strategy has not only failed, it has diminished Christian influence. Accordingly, he advises "for the church and for Christian believers to decouple the 'public' from the 'political.'"[56] The single-minded quest for political power overlooks the spiritual warfare aspect of biblical theology. Refreshingly, Hunter acknowledges that the narrative of the Gospels reflects spiritual warfare between Jesus and the powers. By "the powers," he really means supernatural agents who influence the power structures of this world and cites passages acknowledging the devil as holding sway for now (John 12:31, 16:11; 2 Corinthians 4:4; 1 John 5:19). Breaking stride with naturalistic social science, Hunter interprets the culture war through a Supernatural Worldview:

Much of the gospel story, of course, can be read as a commentary on Christ's relationship to power and "the powers" generally. Consider the period of Christ's temptations in the wilderness at the start of his ministry. Here Satan offered to Jesus "all the kingdoms of the world and their splendor" (Matt. 4:8). Satan's implicit claim was that he possessed a ruling authority in and over the world. The biblical narrative makes clear that the scope and time of Satan's power were limited by God's sovereignty, and yet within those parameters he declared that power in the world was his to wield. Importantly, Jesus did not take issue with this claim. Indeed, Christ himself called the evil one "the prince of this world" (John 12:31; 16:11). This is a description that Paul, in his letter to the Corinthians, asserts as well, describing Satan as "the god of this world" (2 Cor. 4:4). It is also an account affirmed by John's first letter where he declares, "that the whole world is under the control of the evil one" (1 John 5:19). If this reading is right then the spirit that animates worldly power—whether held by individuals, social groups, communities, institutions, or social structures—naturally tends toward manipulation, domination, and control. Rooted in the deceptions of misdirected desire, it is a power that in its most coarse expressions would exploit, subjugate, and even enslave. Within a fallen humanity, then, all power is tainted, infected by the same tendencies toward self-aggrandizing domination. The natural disposition of all human power is to its abuse.[57]

This supernatural-saturated critique coming from an elite social scientist like James Hunter is to be commended. His argument suggests that the evangelical church, in its quest for political power, has played right into a cosmic bait and switch. Adding to the problem of demythologization is that many otherwise conservative pastors are taught that Satan was so completely defeated at the cross (Colossians 2:15) that they do not have to concern themselves with him. While his defeat was secured for the future, it is not yet fully realized, and, for now, we are still at war. Consider than when God gave Israel the Promised Land they still had to fight the occupying Nephilim and Canaanite hordes. Our situation is similar. Years after the cross, Peter wrote that our adversary, the devil, "prowls around like a roaring lion, seeking someone to devour" (1 Peter 5:8), and Paul called him "the prince of the power of the air, the spirit that is <u>now at work</u> in the sons of disobedience" (Ephesians 2:2, underline added). Also, as Hunter mentioned above, John was perhaps strongest of all in offering "the whole world lies in the power of the evil one" (1 John 5:19b). Making a modern analogy, Kraft has aptly pointed out that during World War II, D-Day had assured the Nazis' defeat, but the war didn't end for eleven more months—during which time more Allied troops were killed than in all the previous months combined.[58] In like fashion, please do not doubt that Christians today still face a very serious challenge. Satan is alive and well and more active than ever because he knows his time is short (Revelation 12:12).

Furthermore, readers should be shocked to learn that Paul N. Temple, an alleged Christian leader of "the family," the supposedly Christian political lobby group, is also the chairman emeritus and cofounder of the Institute of Noetic Sciences (IONS), a group promoting occultism, to be discussed in chapter 7.[59] The overemphasis of politics also explains the shocking ease with which a Christian school like Liberty University allowed a bishop from within the demonic cult of Mormonism to deliver its 2012 commencement address.[60] The corrosive ethos promoted pragmatism over spiritual faithfulness, and Liberty students will not easily transcend their leadership's failure. Worse yet, the Billy Graham organization purged all references to Mormonism as a cult from its websites.[61] The powers and principalities have subverted the church's mission by diverting it into partisan politics while convincing the rest of the West they do not exist.

The Ethos of Demythologization

The ethos of demythologization has infiltrated evangelical biblical exegesis, which, of course, affects theology and filters down to ministry. For many, the acid test is Genesis 6:1–4, a passage trained biblical scholars nearly unanimously agree refers to middle-realm "sons of God," or angels procreating with human women who consequently gave birth to giants. Hebrew Bible scholar Michael Heiser explains:

> Genesis 6:1–4 is one of those texts that, for many, is best left alone. Many contemporary evangelical Bible scholars have gone to great lengths to strip the "mythology" out of it (i.e., the supernatural elements) so as to make it more palatable. But one has to wonder how bending supernatural language to human reason is consistent with the testimony of affirming a supernatural worldview.[62]

The idea of angels procreating with human women appears to be too disturbing. However, it is beyond question that the ancient view entailed divine beings doing just that to produce the giants seen throughout the Hebrew Bible (Numbers 13:33; Deuteronomy 1:28, 2:10–11, 9:2; 1 Samuel 17:4; 1 Chronicles 20:4–8). The "sons of

God" are divine beings elsewhere in the Pentateuch (Deuteronomy 32:8; Job 1:6, 2:1), and the Septuagint rendering of "nephilim" is *gigantes,* Greek for "giants." The majority of Semitic language scholars, even unbelievers, do not question the supernatural intent of the passage. According to Gordon J. Wenham, writing for the scholarly *Word Biblical Commentary:*

> The "angel" interpretation is at once the oldest view and that of most modern commentators. It is assumed in the earliest Jewish exegesis (e.g., the books of 1 Enoch 6:2ff; Jubilees 5:1, LXX, Philo De Gigant 2:358), Josephus (Ant. 1.31) and the Dead Sea Scrolls (1QapGen 2:1; CD 2:17–19). The NT (2 Pet 2:4, Jude 6, 7) and the earliest Christian writers (e.g., Justin, Irenaeus, Clement of Alexandria, Tertullian, Origen) also take this line.[63]

It seems that only incredulous evangelicals—who are supposed to affirm a Supernatural Worldview—try to explain it away using fanciful eisegesis to replace the middle-realm spirits with humans. This sort of thing occurs in New Testament scholarship as well.

An example is the term *stoicheia,* properly rendered "elemental spirits" in the ESV translation, which was widely used for demonic spirits in ancient Jewish thought.[64] A growing consensus in Pauline scholarship recognizes:

> When Paul speaks of *ta stoicheia tou kosmou* in both Galatians and Colossians, they appear in a linguistic context in which they are associated with references to personal spiritual forces (angels, principalities and powers, gods who are not gods) and, in Colossians 2:8, set in contrast with Christ.[65]

Even so, many modern translations prefer a more naturalistic rendering—e.g., "elementary principles of the world" (NASB) and "basic principles of the world" (NKJV). Thus, when Paul warned, "See to it that no one takes you captive by philosophy and empty deceit, according to human tradition, according to the elemental spirits of the world, and not according to Christ" (Colossians 2:8), the emphasis is solely on the human element, when spiritual warfare is more likely Paul's overarching trajectory.

It Is Time to Remythologize

In the one area where the church is supposed to have specialized mastery, it is failing to be salt and light. Through either ignorance, incredulity, or both, we're not providing convincing answers when it comes to paranormal phenomena. Naturalism has not convinced a large portion of the population who are now turning to the occult. Research indicates that a large portion of the population believes in paranormal phenomenon like: extrasensory perception (60.1 percent); extraterrestrials visiting earth (35.2 percent); precognition (42.4 percent); and ghosts (45.5 percent).[66] Some phenomena are more consistent with a biblical worldview (Acts 16:16) than others and likely have a factual basis. Even the more fanciful variety could still be demonic deceptions that deserve a thoughtful analysis. Lost in a sea of naturalistic nihilism, it shouldn't be so surprising that non-Christians make the existential leap to a sort of upper-story hope.

In his groundbreaking work, *Escape from Reason*, Francis Schaeffer explained the divided-truth concept by making an analogy to a two-story building. The upper story, nonreason, hosts spiritual beliefs and morality while the lower story, reason, still claims to have universal, objective truth.[67] The divide can be diagrammed like this:

Non-reason

Subjective, Relative, Nonrational

Reason

Objective, Universal, Rational

Rather than holding a holistic concept of truth, modern man has divided it. The two-story grid functions as a gatekeeper defining what can be taken seriously as genuine knowledge and what should be dismissed as irrational. All spiritual claims are relegated to the upper story as subjective opinions that can be true for you but not for me. Nevertheless, because secular folks cannot live without some sort of hope, they inevitably make a leap into the upper story of nonreason. Schaeffer observed how the occult attracts the secular world:

> Though demons do not fit into modern man's concepts on the basis of his reason, many moderns would rather have demons than be left with the idea that everything in the universe is only one big machine. People put the occult in the upper story of nonreason in the hope of having some kind of meaning, even if it is a horrendous one.[68]

Why should we allow the devil a supernatural demesne? The church actually has the one thing the secular world does not and desperately needs: *the truth about the supernatural realm*. However, Western evangelicalism's assimilation into technopoly has diminished its ability to speak such truth into the culture. Most pastors are not equipped to handle questions about the occult. Hiebert's missional concern applies at home: "Because the Western world no longer provides explanations for questions on the middle level, it is not surprising that many Western missionaries have no answers within their Christian world view."[69] It seems likely that Western churches don't have those answers for their own people concerning the paranormal. Even so, the Bible implies that the middle realm is more active than we expect, "for thereby some have entertained angels unawares" (Hebrews 13:2b). The obliviousness to angels implies that we are inclined toward a blind spot.

As a result, spiritual warfare considerations are often low on the list of ministry priorities. Keith Ferdinando, a theology professor in Zaire, observed: "The skepticism of society has often been reflected in the life of the church and its theology too, in practice if not in theory."[70] The spiritual weapons and armor listed by Paul seem ethereal and impractical by worldly standards (Ephesians 6:12–18). All too often, Christian counselors concede to the world's methods steeped in naturalism. As implied in my discussions with Tom Sappington, a BIOLA New Testament scholar and Indonesian missionary, we are unnecessarily medicating thousands of folks who need deliverance.[71] Even among conservative Bible believers, we're hesitant to ascribe events to supernatural agency.

This also plays out as an overemphasis on political and social activism. Conflating faith and political conservatism lead to an inevitable confusion between the two. Schaeffer recognized this tendency, presciently arguing that fighting the world with worldly means will ultimately fail. He allowed, "They may bring some results—activism does have its results—but they will not be the ones the Lord wants."[72] He further explained:

In this war if Christians win a battle by using worldly means, they have really lost. On the other hand, when we seem to lose a battle while waiting on God, in reality we have won. The world may mistakenly say, "They have lost." But if God's people seem to be beaten in a specific battle, not because of sin or lack of commitment or lack of prayer or lack of paying a price, but because they have waited on God and refused to resort to the flesh, then they have won.[73]

Recent victories by the radical left in the United States bear this out. Schaeffer's teaching has a premillennial flavor, suggesting the meek really shall inherit the earth (Matthew 5:5). While Hunter's faithful presence construct carries his strategy forward, recent Evangelical Theology Society president, Clinton Arnold, stressed, "The powers of darkness are real, we need to be conscious of their influence, and we need to respond to them appropriately."[74] His own books on the topic are a great place to begin reeducation.[75]

Conclusion

This chapter argued that Western evangelicals have effectively demythologized the spirit realm. It sought to illustrate that this has occurred more by default than intent as a product of living in a technopoly. Disgust with modern excesses and fraud has led to a demythologization of the Holy Spirit known as cessationism. However, counterfeit always presumes the genuine. As a result, an inordinate focus is placed on political solutions to the detriment of the spiritual. The relationship between these points was shown. In the end, these points support the idea that Western evangelicals should adopt the faithful-presence strategy promoted by Hunter while working to revitalize their understanding of the middle realm, carefully reexamining the biblical position concerning charismatic gifts, and developing a rigorous spiritual warfare strategy involving deliverance.

Some of the strongest scientific evidence against naturalism is coming from near-death experience research. However, often that research is used to promote a worldview antagonistic to biblical Christianity. Because it is a major influence in the paranormal paradigm shift, the near-death experience is the subject of the next chapter.

Notes

1. Charles Baudelaire, "The Generous Gambler," *Paris Spleen: Little Poems in Prose*, trans. Keith Waldrop (Middletown, CT: Wesleyan University, 2009) 59.
2. "The Usual Suspects (1995) Quotes," IMDB, http://www.imdb.com/title/tt0114814/quote (accessed 10/29/13).
3. A. W. Tozer, *The Knowledge of the Holy: The Attributes of God, Their Meaning in the Christian Life* (San Francisco: HarperOne, 1978) 18.
4. Barna Group, "Barna Survey Examines Changes in Worldview among Christians over the Past 13 Years," March 6, 2009, Barna Group, https://www.barna.org/barna-update/21-transformation/252-barna-survey-examines-changes-in-worldview-among-christians-over-the-past-13-years#.UvghxLRUYw8 (accessed 02/09/14).
5. Walter A. Elwell, *Evangelical Dictionary of Theology:* 2nd ed. (Grand Rapids, MI: Baker, 2001) 194.
6. Rudolf Bultmannm, *Jesus Christ and Mythology* (New York: Scribner's, 1958) 35.
7. Rudolf Bultmann, "New Testament and Mythology," *Kerygma and Myth: A Theological Debate,* vol. 1 (London: SPCK, 1964) 10.
8. S. N. Gundry, "Death of God Theology," *Evangelical Dictionary of Theology,* 2nd ed. (Grand Rapids, MI: Baker, 2001) 326.
9. Philip Elmer-DeWitt, "No Sympathy for the Devil," *Time,* March 19, 1990, 55–56.
10. Walter Wink, *Naming the Powers* (Philadelphia: Fortress, 1984) 4.
11. United Methodist Church, Evangelical Lutheran Church in America, Presbyterian Church (USA), Episcopal Church, United Church of Christ, Christian Church (Disciples of Christ).
12. James White, "Rob Bell's Love Wins Chapter 4 Examined,"

YouTube, March 31, 2011, http://www.youtube.com/ watch?v=29J4JGJz6Dg (accessed 10/30/13).

13. Bultmann, "New Testament and Mythology," 10.

14. See "Reply to Rob Skiba on the Denial of the Personhood of the Holy Spirit," http://www.logosapologia.org/?p=5144.

15. "The Hitchens Transcript," *Portland Monthly*, December 17, 2009, http://www.portlandmonthlymag.com/arts-and-entertainment/ category/books-and-talks/articles/christopher-hitchens/ (accessed 09/29/11).

16. Charles Kraft, *Christianity with Power: Your Worldview and Your Experience of the Supernatural* (Ann Arbor, MI: Servant, 1989) 41.

17. John Piper, "When Will Prophecy Cease?," *Desiring God*, March 18, 1990, http://www.desiringgod.org/sermons/when-will-prophecy-cease (accessed 01/28/14).

18. Justin Martyr, "Dialogue of Justin with Trypho, a Jew," in *The Ante-Nicene Fathers: The Apostolic Fathers with Justin Martyr and Irenaeus*, eds. Alexander Roberts, James Donaldson, and A. Cleveland Coxe, vol. 1 (Buffalo, NY: Christian Literature, 1885) 240.

19. Irenaeus, *Against Heresies* 2.32.4 in *The Ante-Nicene Fathers Vol. I: Translations of the Writings of the Fathers Down to A.D. 325*, eds. Alexander Roberts, James Donaldson and A. Cleveland Coxe, (Oak Harbor, WA: Logos Research Systems, 1997) 409.

20. Ibid., 531.

21. Augustine, *City of God*, 8.22, *The Nicene and Post-Nicene Fathers Vol. II*, ed. Philip Schaff (Oak Harbor, WA: Logos Research Systems, 1997) 485.

22. Ibid., 486.

23. Philip Schaff, *The Nicene and Post-Nicene Fathers Vol. II*, St. Augustin's City of God and Christian Doctrine (Oak Harbor: Logos Research Systems, 1997) 487.

24 Ibid., 489.

25 Ibid.

26. John Polkinghorne, *Science and Providence: God's Interaction with the World*, 1st Shambhala ed. (Boston: Shambhala, 1989) 56.

27. Craig S. Keener. *Miracles: The Credibility of the New Testament Accounts*, (Grand Rapids, MI: Baker Book Group, 2011) Kindle edition, 2827–2828.

28. Clint Yeats, "Power of Prayer: Kayla Knight," KLTV, July 20, 2008, http://www.kltv.com/Global/story.asp?S=8699200 (accessed 10/30/13).

29. KLTV images, KLTV.com, http://kltv.images.worldnow.com/images/8699200_BG3.jpg.

30. Yeats.

31. Charles H. Spurgeon, *Autobiography: The Full Harvest, 1860–1892*, vol. 2 (Edinburgh: Banner of Truth Trust, 1973) 60.

32. Ibid.

33. Ibid., 227.

34. "My Testimony and Interview on NTR with Chris White," Logos Apologia, December 6, 2011, http://www.logosapologia.org/?p=3099.

35. J. P. Moreland, *Kingdom Triangle: Recover the Christian Mind, Renovate the Soul, Restore the Spirit's Power* (Grand Rapids, MI: Zondervan, 2012) Kindle Edition, 175.

36. Ibid., 176.

37. Strange Fire, http://www.tmstrangefire.org/ (accessed 10/30/13).

38. James Davison Hunter, *To Change the World: The Irony, Tragedy, and Possibility of Christianity in the Late Modern World* (New York: Oxford University Press, 2010) 33.

39. Ibid., 27.

40. Ibid., 186.

41. Bruce Little, "Pilgrim and Progress" in forthcoming "For the Love of God" class handout, PHI6520 (2013) 7.

42. Neil Postman, *Technopoly: The Surrender of Culture to Technology.* (New York: Random House, 2011) Kindle edition, 610–612.

43. Hunter, 209.

44. Ibid., 210.

45. Kraft, 27.

46. Lesslie Newbigin, *Honest Religion for Secular Man* (Philadelphia: Westminster, 1966), cited in Paul G. Hiebert, "The Flaw of the Excluded Middle," *Missiology* 10, 1 (1982) 44.

47. Ibid., 43.

48. Jehu J. Hanciles, *Beyond Christendom: Globalization, African Migration, and the Transformation of the West* (Maryknoll, NY: Orbis, 2009) 121.

49. John S. Mbiti, *African Religions and Philosophy,* 2nd rev. and enl. ed. (Oxford: Heinemann, 1992) 253.

50. Robert H. Bennett, *I Am Not Afraid: Demon Possession and Spiritual Warfare* (St. Louis: Concordia, 2013) Kindle edition, 3406–3408.

51. John Maynard Keynes, "Newton, the Man," http://www-history. mcs.st-and.ac.uk/Extras/Keynes_Newton.html (accessed 11/04/13).

52. Hiebert, 43.

53. "Most American Christians Do Not Believe that Satan or the Holy Spirit Exist," April 10, 2009, Barna Group, http://www.barna. org/barna-update/article/12-faithspirituality/260-most-american-christians-do-not-believe-that-satan-or-the-holy-spirit-exis (accessed 04/30/13).

54. Ibid.

55. Jeff Sharlet, *The Family: The Secret Fundamentalism at the Heart of American Power* (New York: Harper Perennial, 2009).

56. Hunter, 185.

57. Hunter, 187.

58. Charles Kraft, *Defeating Dark Angels: Breaking Demonic Oppression in the Believer's Life*, (Ventura, CA: Regal, 2011) 21.

59. IONS Directory Profile: Paul N. Temple, http://noetic.org/directory/person/paul-temple/(accessed 02/12/14).

60. "Gov. Mitt Romney to Deliver 2012 Commencement Address," Liberty University News Service, April 19, 2012, http://www.liberty.edu/news/index.cfm?PID=18495&MID=53438 (accessed 10/29/13).

61. Daniel Burke, "After Romney Meeting, Billy Graham Site Scrubs Mormon 'Cult' Reference," *Christianity Today*, October 16, 2012, http://www.christianitytoday.com/ct/2012/october-web-only/after-romney-meeting-billy-graham-site-scrubs-mormon-cult-r.html (accessed 02/13/14).

62. Michael Heiser, *The Myth That Is True*, (unpublished manuscript, 2012) 75. Available here: http://www.michaelsheiser.com/ResearchPDFs.html.

63. Gordon J. Wenham, *Word Biblical Commentary: Genesis 1–15*, vol. 1 (Dallas: Word, 2002) 139.

64. Richard R. Melick, *Philippians, Colossians, Philemon: The New American Commentary*, vol. 32, (Nashville: Broadman & Holman, 1991) 253.

65. Daniel G. Reid, "Elements/Elemental Spirits of the World," *Dictionary of Paul and His Letters,* eds. Gerald F. Hawthorne, Ralph P. Martin, and Daniel G. Reid (Downers Grove, IL: InterVarsity Press, 1993) 230.

66. Douglas S. Krull and Eric S. McKibben, "Skeptical Saints and Critical Cognition: On the Relationship between Religion and Paranormal Beliefs," archive for the Psychology of Religion 28 (2006) 269.

67. Francis A. Schaeffer, *Escape from Reason: A Penetrating Analysis of Trends in Modern Thought* (Downers Grove, IL: IVP, 2006).

68. Francis A. Schaeffer, *How Should We Then Live? The Rise and Decline of Western Thought and Culture* (Wheaton, IL: Crossway, 1983) 171.

69. Hiebert, 45.

70. Keith Ferdinando, "Screwtape Revisted: Demonology Western, African, and Biblical," in A. N. S. Lane, ed., *The Unseen World: Christian Reflections on Angels, Demons and the Heavenly Realm* (Grand Rapids, MI: Baker, 1997) 104.

71. In a personal phone conversation with author, Dr. Sappington implied that he has performed deliverance on many Western Christians who were able to discontinue psychiatric medications afterward. He also added that many of the demonized have connections to Freemasonry in the USA.

72. Francis A. Schaeffer, *No Little People* (Wheaton, IL: Crossway, 2003) 72.

73. Ibid.

74. Clinton E. Arnold, *Powers of Darkness: Principalities & Powers in Paul's Letters* (Downers Grove, IL: IVP Academic, 1992) 182.

75. Books by Clinton E. Arnold: *Powers of Darkness: Principalities & Powers in Paul's Letters; Three Crucial Questions about Spiritual Warfare; Ephesians: Power and Magic; The Concept of Power in Ephesians in Light of its Historical Setting.*

NEAR-DEATH-EXPERIENCE SCIENCE
DRIVES THE PARADIGM SHIFT

What we call life is a journey to death.
What we call death is the gateway to life.
—Anonymous

One of the near-death experience truths is that each
person integrates their near-death experience into
their own pre-existing belief system.
—Jody Long

Maria had never been to Seattle. America was everything she had
imagined and more. Although the rain never stopped, that crazy,
flying-saucer-looking building epitomized American excess. *En la
parte superior!* However, this visit was only a brief respite from
the arduous picking season. Like most other migrant workers, she
sent her hard-earned wages home. She came to this country for
the work. *Flash!* ...shooting pain, shortness of breath, darkness,
sirens, traffic, and blinding overhead lights. A too-skinny nurse
said she had a heart attack. She had been admitted to the Harborview Hospital coronary care unit.

While lying in the metal-railed bed, everything seemed white, clean; a bleachy aroma prevailed. Surely she would be up again soon. It came again—like a cannon shot. The pain in her chest exploded her up and out of her body. Really out—she was out of her body. Looking down, she saw the panicked staff rush to her bedside amidst the clamor of squawking alarms. Everything was realer than real... hyper-real, high-definition, holographic, multidimensional immersion. She was floating. As the staff was screaming and equipment was buzzing and beeping, she felt a blissful peace. She rose through the ceiling, through the roof, and looked down on the hospital. Floating, she thought, "Now that is odd." On a window ledge, she saw a single, tattered, blue tennis shoe sitting on its frayed lace. She wondered, "How did it get way up here on the third floor?" It had a hole in the pinky toe. All of sudden, she shot back into her body and felt an icy hot pain as she looked up and saw the doctor holding the defibrillator paddles.

Kimberly Clark was working as a social worker in Harborview Hospital when an unconscious cardiac arrest patient, Maria, was admitted. She had arrested again in the hospital, flatlining for a minute or two, but was resuscitated within the three-minute window. As part of her customary follow-up, Clark visited her the same day, whereupon Maria related her out-of-body experience (OBE) floating above the hospital. In addition to describing Maria's perspective looking down on her body and then rising through the building, Clark recorded, "Maria proceeded to describe being further distracted by an object on the third floor ledge on the North end of the building. She 'thought her way' up there and found herself 'eyeball to shoelace' with a tennis shoe, which she asked me to find for her."[1] Anxious to prove that she wasn't crazy, Maria desperately wanted her social worker to find the shoe.

Incredulous but sympathetic, Clark investigated and with some effort found a shoe that perfectly matched Maria's description. They were precise details that exclude coincidence, like the fact that the shoe had a hole in the pinky toe facing out from the ledge, and that it was sitting on top of its lace. This marked a paradigm shift for Kim Clark. She would never again doubt the existence of the immaterial soul. She explained, "The only way she could have had such a perspective was if she had been floating right outside and at very close range to the tennis shoe. I retrieved the shoe and brought it back to Maria; it was very concrete evidence for me."[2] This is called a *veridical* near-death experience (NDE), meaning that the experience has objective external evidence confirming it. It really happened, and has stood up well under the scrutiny of peer review.

Philosopher Dr. Gary Habermas not only verified those details, he discovered that Maria had just arrived in Seattle, was unfamiliar with area, and had never before been in that hospital. Also, the shoe could not be seen from the ground, and there were no buildings nearby that provided a vantage point from which it could be seen. Even more astonishing, neither the hole in the toe nor the position of the lace could be seen from the window where Sharp had retrieved it.[3] In other words, the perspective that Maria described from her bed could only be realized by floating in the air looking toward the building! As astonishing as this seems, this is one of many such cases with confirming external evidence.

The Near-Death Experience

This chapter will address the NDE and the increasingly popular worldview associated with it. This presentation will first give a broad overview and summary of the NDE and its associated literature. Then two well-evidenced cases will be presented as examples. While the veridical NDE serves as a defeater for naturalism, there are a variety of interpretations of the otherworldly aspects, some more coherent with Christian theology than others. The prevailing theological expression found in the more recent literature like Dr. Jeffrey Long's *Evidence of the Afterlife* (2011), Dr. Pim van Lommel's *Consciousness Beyond Life: The Science of the Near-Death Experience* (2007), and Dr. Eben Alexander's *Proof of Heaven* (2012) is the Omega Point worldview: the idea that "all is becoming one"—oneism—or monistic pantheism. This chapter examines how the NDE worldview answers the four basic worldview questions and critiques the answers. Then a final section on the life review will offer a Christian response with several key points of analysis. Although NDEs defeat the scientific notion that we are biological robots, they are far too mystical and subjective to derive reliable theological conclusions about the afterlife.

The expression "near-death experience" denotes an assortment of personal experiences associated with brief intervals of clinical death or impending death, hence the term *"near*-death experience." There are a multitude of documented cases, occurring in clinical environments, involving full cardiac arrest and flat EEG brainwave activity. Astonishingly, people describe vivid, conscious experiences when, under the normal standards of neuroscience, they should not be conscious. Of course, this presents a huge problem for naturalism and mind/brain identity. Accordingly, the NDE has enormous worldview implications. For example, it not only raises questions about who we are, but also suggests that our fundamental assumptions about "where we are" could be drastically oversimplified. Is it possible to be on a hospital table and traveling through the sky at the same time? Given the evidence, it seems so. Yet, the NDE evidence is profoundly religious in nature. After all, it offers an encouraging answer to a fundamental question all human beings share: What happens when we die? Accordingly, there is an abundance of literature available.

NDE Research

For more than thirty years, beginning in 1976 with the publication of philosopher and psychiatrist Raymond Moody's book, *Life After Life,* millions of people have become fascinated with the subject of life after death and enthralled by the accounts of NDEs. The early literature was largely anecdotal, and, while interesting, it was easily dismissed by skeptical naturalists and doubted by Bible-believing theologians. Cardiologist Michael Sabom, an evangelical Christian, was one of the first to attempt to document the phenomenon using rigorous scientific protocols. As the subject gained widespread attention, more serious researchers from the medical community got involved. The International Association for Near Death Studies (IANDS) was formed in 1981 and became a multidisciplinary nexus for scholarly work through its peer reviewed *Journal of Near-Death Studies.*[4] Through the work of these researchers, there now is a large body of peer-reviewed, academically rigorous, scientific research pointing to the existence of the immaterial soul. This is the most important aspect for Christian apologetics. Other aspects of NDE science are deeply troubling and discourage theologians from exploring the data.

The NDE research community shares much with the spiritist or spiritualist movement of the nineteenth century. Like their predecessors, they want a new science to replace traditional religion.

However, in so doing, they seem all too willing to accept occult theological content from unknown entities. Christian authors John Ankerberg and Robert Weldon argue, "The occult messages frequently conveyed by the 'being of light' and the alleged spirits of the dead prove that they are lying spirits."[5] Robert Morey also implies that all NDEs are in this category.[6] These writers base their accusation of deceptive spirituality on the following themes conveyed by many NDEs: 1) Death is good and there is no judgment; 2) There is no hell and everyone will go to heaven; 3) The Bible is wrong and the Eastern/occult view of death is correct; and 4) Occult practice is beneficial. The prevalence of these antibiblical messages leads Christians to overgeneralize, but understandably so. While these are common themes, they do not account for all NDEs.

While the NDE researchers' proclivity toward occult practices does not necessarily discredit their scholarly work, it seems many Christian apologists make broad, sweeping generalizations. Christians can celebrate the data confirming the immaterial soul, but it does not follow that they tacitly endorse the occult worldview. Satan is an imitator of God. Simply because some, even a majority, of NDEs promote occult ideas, it doesn't follow that all NDEs do. American artist and university professor Howard Storm's case is a fascinating counterexample.

Storm was on a teaching trip to Paris when he was overwhelmed by excruciating pain, put in an ambulance, and rushed to a nearby hospital. For a short while, he was clinically dead. As an atheist, Storm expected oblivion at death. To his astonishment, he was suddenly out of his own body, looking down on the hospital room. Then, rather than going toward the light, he was forcibly dragged down to horrific demesnes of darkness, where monstrous evil entities tortured him in revolting ways. Later rescued and transported to heaven, he encountered angels and the Creator God of the Bible. He described a "life review" and an interesting conversation with God. Storm was sent back with a new mission to proclaim the gospel. Today he is a pastor.[7] Interestingly, aspects of Storm's NDE life review match the more theologically problematic ones, a detail explored at the close of this chapter.

Although accounts vary, there seems to be a general consensus concerning the typical NDE. Dr. Jeffrey Long, a radiation oncologist who founded the Near Death Experience Research Foundation (NDERF), lists twelve elements common to most NDEs: 1) out-of-body experience; 2) separation of consciousness from the body; 2) heightened senses; 3) intense positive emotions or feelings; 4) passing into or through a tunnel; 5) encountering a mystical or brilliant light; 6) encountering other beings, either mystical beings or deceased relatives or friends; 7) a sense of alteration of time or space; 8) life review; 9) encountering unworldly ("heavenly") realms; 10) encountering or learning special knowledge; 11) encountering a boundary or barrier; and 12) a return to the body, either voluntarily or involuntarily.[8] While this may represent the majority of reported cases, it excludes widely reported negative NDEs. Even so, Long's landmark NDERF study surveyed more than 1,300 experiencers via Internet questionnaire and represents some of the most current data available.

Long derives nine lines of evidence from the data collected on the NDERF website. First, the unlikelihood of a lucid experience while unconscious or clinically dead is convincing. NDErs describe something more powerful than vivid dreams. Second, NDErs see and hear real events while out of body. This point implies that the soul has a conscious existence separate from the body. Third, NDEs occur when the anesthesia alone should preclude consciousness. Fourth, blind people can see (often for the first time) during NDEs. Fifth, the life review accurately reflects the person's life, even events that were forgotten. Sixth, virtually all encountered beings are deceased, and they are usually relatives. Astonishingly, some meet unknown relatives for the first time and are able to identify them later from a series of random photos. Seventh, the similarity between accounts from very young children and adults seems to exclude the influence of preexisting beliefs. One would not expect young children to reflect such a sophisticated cultural meme. Eighth, although there is literature challenging the notion, Long argues that NDEs have a consistency across cultures. Ninth, experiencers are seemingly transformed for the better.[9]

Long's case is very persuasive. Accordingly, he makes some pretty bold claims, like, "We have found some answers to humankind's oldest and deepest questions about the afterlife."[10] Because of their medical qualifications and exhaustive research, this chapter will rely heavily on data from Long's work and that of Pim van Lommel.

Van Lommel, a Dutch cardiologist, conducted a twenty-year hospital study published in 2001 in the renowned medical journal *The Lancet,* which is considered a landmark. His 2007 book, *Consciousness beyond Life,* offers that research to the English-speaking world at a popular level.[11] As a practicing cardiologist in a teaching hospital, his access afforded him the opportunity to collect scientifically rigorous data. For instance, his staff was often in a position to interview patients shortly after resuscitation, as opposed to Long's web-based data collection. Consequently, this study provides clinical evidence that the NDE represents a genuine experience that cannot be attributed to natural causes like oxygen deprivation, imagination, or psychosis. While his book ostensibly promotes monism, its title shows more restraint than Long. Van Lommel simply claims consciousness beyond life rather than life after death. It demonstrates beyond a reasonable doubt that consciousness does not always coincide with brain function, and can even be experienced apart from the body. There are various ways of classifying this consciousness.

Dr. Sabom divided the experience into two parts: autoscopic and transcendental.[12] The former entails viewing the material world and is also referred to as the veridical NDE. The latter involves passing through a void into an otherworldly realm. This distinction is paramount when considering truth claims. The autoscopic or veridical NDE is one of the most compelling evidences, because it involves verifiable data. The accounts suggest an answer to the mind/body problem that has daunted philosophers since the days of René Descartes. The evidence is strong enough to convince a neuroscientist like Eben Alexander to abandon philosophical naturalism even though his colleagues demur. As discussed in chapter 3, fundamental paradigm shifts meet decades of resistance, and there is a reluctance to accept the data, no matter how rigorous the protocol. This may appear like an exaggerated claim, but the evidence is overwhelmingly supportive of immaterial survival. If this evidence is accepted, the physicalism that dominates the Western academy is dead. In order to demonstrate this contentious claim, one of the better known veridical cases is surveyed.

Veridical NDEs

As exemplified by Maria's experience with the shoe, veridical NDEs are cases in which people have observed events or gathered information while outside of their bodies during a period of time when they should not have been conscious. These observations are verified by independent witnesses upon the experiencer's return to consciousness. The gold standard of veridical accounts is that of singer-songwriter Pam Reynolds.

Reynolds endured an exotic surgical procedure called "Operation Standstill" to remove a life-threatening aneurysm on her brain stem. The procedure entails stopping the heart, and the blood is drained from the brain to allow the aneurysm to be removed. Even more, the body temperature is lowered to 60 degrees while fully anesthetized with sound-emitting earplugs to verify flat brainwave activity on an EEG. Reynolds describes waking to the sound of Dr. Robert F. Spetzler, the surgeon, sawing her skullcap open, causing her to realize that she was observing herself from over his shoulder.

Upon returning to consciousness, she was able to accurately describe the surgical saw as looking like an "electric toothbrush" and coming from a "socket wrench case."[13] Sabom, the cardiologist who interviewed her, first thought she was mistaken, thinking, "An 'electric toothbrush' with 'interchangeable blades'? No way!"[14] However, while transcribing the tape of Reynolds' interview, he phoned the medical supplier to get the manual for the bone saw used in her procedure. The incredulous doctor was forced to admit, "I was shocked with the accuracy of Pam's description of the saw as an 'electric toothbrush' with 'interchangeable blades' and with a 'socket wrench case' in which this equipment is kept."[15] Not only that, but she accurately reported detailed conversations that took place in the operating room while she was under anesthesia, with a level of specificity that precludes guesswork.

After she was deemed unconscious, Reynolds overheard an operating room conversation concerning the placement of a catheter in her leg. She accurately recounted that one doctor, near her feet, had complained that her veins were small and that another, near her head, suggested changing from one leg to the other. These statements were subsequently verified by the astonished personnel. How is this explainable apart from her actually observing her operation at a time when her heart was stopped and her brain drained of blood? Neuroscientist Mario Beauregard argues that her case suggests that "mind, consciousness and self can continue when the brain is no longer functional and the clinical criteria of death have been reached."[16] In other words, this seriously challenges the materialist paradigm, which entails that the mind is simply a product of electrochemical brain processes. While this case is unique because of its stringent clinical conditions, it is by no means the only case with solid veridical verification.

Evangelical Response

The evangelical response to the growing body of evidence has been lukewarm. Many Christians are understandably incredulous because of the dubious theological claims associated with the phenomenon. Even so, reformed theologian R. C. Sproul has written:

> It shouldn't shock the Christian when people undergoing clinical death and being revived come back with certain recollections. I've tried to keep an open mind, and I hope that this interesting phenomenon will get the benefit of further research, analysis, and evaluation. Too many of these experiences have been reported for us to simply dismiss them as imaginary or hoaxes.[17]

As far as Christian appraisals, Sabom is very well respected in the NDE research community, and his books offer a Christian interpretation. J. P. Moreland and Gary Habermas' *Beyond Death* (1998) ranks at the top of the list, and more recently, Dinesh D'Souza's *Life After Death* (2009) serves as a seeker-sensitive case based solely on evidence. Others, like Maurice Rawlings, Douglas Groothuis, John Ankerberg, Robert Weldon, and Robert Morey see something more sinister at play.[18] There is a strong possibility that the NDE is a key component in a supernatural subterfuge leading to the paranormal paradigm shift.

To the world at large, the wide road of universalism is preferable to the narrow way of Christ: "Enter by the narrow gate. For the gate is wide and the way is easy that leads to destruction, and those who enter by it are many. For the gate is narrow and the way is hard that leads to life, and those who find it are few" (Matthew 7:13–14). Even Christians struggle with this teaching because we love and care about folks who take the wide road. Because the majority of NDEs promote the wide road, we should be careful. The devil appeals to what people want to hear, and his beguiling usually suggests a compromise of ethics, morals, and truth. The subjective components in NDEs offer extremely useful foil.

The otherworldly, transcendental NDE elements are necessarily subjective and open to interpretation. While there are a variety of religious features reported, the overarching message coming from bestsellers by Alexander, Long, and van Lommel is problematic for Christian truth claims. For example, Alexander extrapolates universalism from a painting of Jesus' Last Supper:

> And most important, a painting of Jesus breaking bread with his disciples evoked the message that lay at the very heart of my journey: that we are loved and accepted unconditionally by a God even more grand and unfathomably glorious that the one I'd learned of as a child in Sunday school.[19]

However, he neglects that Judas was in attendance at that meal as well. Far from unconditional acceptance, Jesus said, "The Son of Man goes as it is written of him, but woe to that man by whom the Son of Man is betrayed! It would have been better for that man if he had not been born" (Matthew 26:24). It has also been well documented by Groothuis in handling the case of Betty Eadie, whose NDE and subsequent best-selling book, *Embraced by the Light,* affirmed her Mormon theology mixed with Eastern pantheistic monism.[20] Likewise, there is a demonstrable tendency for most folks to interpret the NDE through presuppositions.

While in "heaven," Muslims see Allah, but Hindus see Krishna, Christians see Jesus, and so forth. This suggests that at least some of the experience is generated by the person's mind and is not reflective of a genuine spiritual reality. While claims of encountering the divine are common, often only a generic "being of light" is described. Whereas there is a superficial similarity, it is not at all clear that everyone is actually in the same place communicating with the same entity. In light of biblical revelation, this entity often presents very dubious theology, which demands discernment. Paul's admonition to the Corinthians stands in sharp relief: "Satan disguises himself as an angel of light" (2 Corinthians 11:14). This suggests the possibility of a satanic deception to promote universalism.

Biblical Assessment

The general consensus of conservative theologians supports an intermediate state between death and the resurrection body. Baptist theologian Millard Erickson argues, "There is no inherent untenability about the concept of disembodied existence. The human being is capable of existing in either a materialized (bodily) or immaterialized condition."[21] In the Old Testament, Isaiah 14:9–10 describes disembodied souls as *rephaim,* meaning "ghosts of the dead" or "the dead inhabitants of the netherworld" called *sheol.*[22] It is used in this way three times in Isaiah (14:9; 26:14; 26:19) and three times in Proverbs (2:18; 9:18; 21:16), as well as in Psalm 88:10 and Job 26:5. The writer of Ecclesiastes infers that all souls return to God (Ecclesiastes 12:7). These Old Testament passages establish a basis for a disembodied state, and the subject of ghosts is explored in chapters 8 and 9.

In the New Testament, Jesus clearly taught the idea, "And fear not them which kill the body, but are not able to kill the soul: but rather fear him which is able to destroy both soul and body in hell" (Matthew 10:28; cf. Luke 16:9). Also, the incorporeal state is seen in the white robe-adorned Tribulation martyrs: "I saw under the altar the souls of them that were slain for the word of God, and for the testimony which they held" (Revelation 6:9). Likewise, Paul addresses the issue of what happens to Christians when they die in 2 Corinthians 5:8 when he says, "We would rather be away from the body and at home with the Lord." This second letter to the church in Corinth has much more to offer.

Paul's second epistle to the Corinthians has far-reaching implications for the NDE. The overall context is Paul's response to a good report by Titus concerning the Corinthians' repentance. However, in chapters 10–13, Paul's tone changes dramatically in response to false teachers who were challenging his authority. He calls them "false apostles" who are "masquerading as apostles of Christ" (2 Corinthians 11:12). He argues, "And no wonder, for Satan himself masquerades as an angel of light. It is not surprising, then, if his servants also masquerade as servants of righteousness" (2 Corinthians 11:14–15a).

Though this has very troublesome implications for NDErs who see a "being of light," chapter 12 is where Paul addresses heavenly visions and revelations of the Lord.

It is in this section that Paul relates an astonishing account of his journey to heaven. Paul says he was "caught up," using the same Greek word, *harpazo*, as in Acts 8:39, Revelation 12:5, and the famous Rapture passage found in 1 Thessalonians 4:17.[23] He says he went to the "third heaven" (v. 2) and "paradise" (v. 3), seemingly equating the two. This is likely a Semitic synthetic parallelism in which the second term, "paradise," defines "third heaven."[24] The word "paradise" is used in the Septuagint for the "garden of God" (Ezekiel 28:13, 31:8) and refers to God's abode in the New Testament (Luke 23:43; Revelation 2:7). Paul's brooding as to whether it was "in the body or out of the body" indicates uncertainty, but implies that OBEs are consistent with biblical theology (a fact seldom recalled when apologists argue from incredulity). Scholars are divided; some material supports bodily (2 Kings 2:11; Hebrews 11:5) and other material supports outside the body (Revelation 4:2). Paul also says he heard things so great that mere knowledge of them put him in danger of conceit. If Paul would not speak of such things, what about the NDErs' eagerly expressed theological wisdom and metaphysical pontification? To assess that question, this presentation will now examine and evaluate the typical worldview associated with the NDE.

The NDE Worldview

Although the veridical portion is neutral, there is an emergent paranormal worldview associated with the NDE. As a form of universalism, it holds that all spiritual systems flow together into one. An appropriate academic classification is pantheistic monism. It reflects the Hindu belief that "Atman is Brahman," where Atman is basically the soul and Brahman is the single ultimate reality from which the multiplicitous world springs forth. Thus, the pantheist reasons that the soul of every person is a piece of the same universal soul, and individuality is a pernicious illusion. In reading through hundreds of NDE accounts, although counterexamples exist, this perspective is ubiquitous. Oneism is now arguably the dominant religious point of view in the West.

Even so, Gary Habermas has argued that NDEs are worldview neutral, precisely because they seem to occur across cultural barriers and differences. He argues this way because he only considers the autoscopic or veridical aspect as useful data. Indeed, there is a marked difference between that which is veridical and that which is subjective. Habermas and J. P. Moreland argue:

Where we have no evidence (as with the identity of religious figures whose presence is claimed), we have grounds to question the claims. In this sense, we think that NDEs are incapable of judging the truth or falsity of religious worldviews. While they may something rather generic concerning the very existence of an afterlife, they present no real grounds for judging between the options.[25]

This is advantageous for evidencing substance dualism with NDEs, but lacks adequate scope for dealing with the troublesome worldview issues. For instance, Long cites the cross-cultural aspect as the eighth line of evidence and concludes that all religions are equal paths to God. Because NDErs draw great significance from the transcendent aspect, there is a worldview associated with the NDE.

When Habermas was interviewed by Alex Tsakiris on the *Skeptiko* podcast, he was challenged by the host on this issue.[26] Tsakiris, well known in the parapsychology and NDE research communities, serves as a textbook example of the worldview in question.[27] He has also interviewed biblical scholar Michael Heiser, and also challenged him on Christian exclusivism.[28] For this reason, Tsakiris' comments will be interspersed with material from paradigmic NDE accounts. For instance, Dr. Long promotes the NDE theology derived from a Colombian woman named Hafur as wisdom that "sums up the message of NDEs worldwide."[29] Hafur's conclusions will be generously cited, but this composite does not represent any particular person's view in total. Because all worldviews answer basic questions— 1) Who are we? 2) Where are we? 3) What is wrong? and 4) What is the answer?—this presentation will first present the NDE worldview and then offer critique.

Who Am I?

A typical NDEr might answer, "I am a spiritual being endowed with special knowledge from the afterlife." Now armed with certain knowledge that death is not the end, she has returned by divine appointment to help humanity evolve spiritually. In this way, it is related to gnosticism. Family members confirm that relationships initially improve, as NDErs seem more compassionate and loving. NDErs are also keenly interested in NDE research, especially research disproving the folly of naturalistic reductionism. Very often, they not only believe in psychic phenomena, they claim they have acquired paranormal abilities. While there is usually a newfound altruism and selflessness, it still seems fair to think they might believe, "We are the enlightened ones." The accounts bear witness that NDErs feel they are specially chosen people with special knowledge—i.e., *gnosis.*

P. M. H. Atwater, herself an NDEr, is a primary player in the research community, definitely promoting a sort of enlightened elitism. Working as counselor for NDErs, she also became a practicing spirit medium.[30] She compiled data from thousands of interviews inferring that 80 to 90 percent of NDErs report the following aftereffects: losing the fear of death; becoming more spiritual/less religious; becoming more generous and charitable; handling stress easier; becoming more philosophical; becoming more open and accepting of the new and different; developing a disregard for time and schedules; regarding things as new even when they're not (boredom levels decrease); forming expansive concepts of love while at the same time being challenged to initiate and maintain satisfying relationships; becoming psychic/intuitive; knowing things (closer connection to deity/God, prayerful); dealing with bouts of depression; and becoming less competitive.[31]

Widespread belief in the post-NDE acquisition of paranormal abilities reflects the shamanization process mentioned by Kenneth Ring in chapter 3. Ankerberg and Weldon found:

> Many researchers have noted that the NDE frequently leads to the development of psychic powers…[and] conclude that the NDE can precipitate psychic powers and experiences as if the event itself had somehow opened the door to the psychic world—reminiscent of what occurs in occult initiations of all types. [32]

While this is alarming, the improvement in character and personality appears to authenticate the experience. This makes the task of disputing dubious theology and philosophy more challenging. Long and van Lommel's recent books certainly affirm these aftereffects, including psychic abilities. Hafur concludes, "I was everything and everything was me, without essential differences other than in earthly appearances," and "That 'I' includes 'we.'"[33]

Evaluation

The worldview is classic pantheistic monism. The concept of self is ultimately an illusion. In the end, one is absorbed into the whole and ceases to exist. Rather than affirming the value of people as unique individuals, this worldview devalues human life to a meaningless triviality to be absorbed into the ultimate and forgotten. In this way, the promised knowledge and significance is deceptive. Often, it leads to occult practice and results in an identity crisis.

Atwater has done the most scholarly work on cataloging the aftereffects of NDEs. While initially positive, she reveals the experience is so life altering that close to 75 percent of experiencers end up divorced. Also, experiencers rebel against classical Christianity in favor of pantheism. In an interview with Jim Harold on the Paranormal Podcast, Atwater recounted the following example as typical:

> Let me give you an example because examples go a long way, this was a woman from Arkansas or Missouri. She was a minister's wife. She had a several children. She had a near death experience. When I was talking to her she confided, she could no longer go to church. She could not be in the audience or congregation when her husband gave the sermon. And I said, "Why?" And she said, "Because he is lying. I know better and he is lying. And I cannot sit there and listen to what he tells these people." So she said, "I just invent reasons to stay home on Sunday mornings."[34]

This experiencer, who once identified as Christian, has been shamanized by NDE gnosis. It affirms the antibiblical theological content that seems to characterize the experience. Even more telling is the woeful personal example Atwater related with pride in the same interview:

I have three kids, one son, two daughters and the oldest daughter, her name is Natalie. And it was after my experience, sometime after my experience. And she sat me down one day, and you know, I come from Idaho and we're very independent outspoken people out there, I mean we are… and Natalie is well moo coo…ha ha. She sat me down one day and put her hands on her hips and said, "Well…well, you are easier to talk to now than you used to be but…you know, you're not Mom. I want Mom back!" We both looked for the woman, never did find her. Yeah, I don't know what happened to her. She's gone and Natalie was hurting. She missed her mother. I'm sitting there, same face, same body but I'm literally not the same person and she wanted her Mom back. [35]

While this is disturbing on a number of levels, this sort of transformation is all too common. It seems to activate the soul power Watchman Nee warned us about: "Since the fall, God has forbidden man to again use his original power of the soul. It is for this reason that the Lord Jesus often declares how we need to lose our soul life, that is, our soul power. God wishes us today not to use this soul power at all." [36]

Unchecked, the NDE has strong tendency to alienate family and initiate one into the occult. Atwater went on to become a psychic

medium and occult practitioner. Her emphasis on the transformative paranormal aftereffects suggests an entity attachment, a hypothesis discussed in Appendix 3 about Paul's thorn. Strangely, the "who"
and "where" questions blend together in pantheistic thought.

Where Am I?

The dominant answer to this question is monistic as well. Everything in creation is heading toward a convergence. The "where" will
be absorbed into the "one" until there is no "where." In the modern West, this idea was popularized by the Catholic mystic, Teilhard
de Chardin. In *The Phenomenon of Man*, he wrote concerning the
evolution of the material cosmos, from primordial particles to the
origin of life and human beings. Consciousness evolves into the
noosphere—the sum total of sentient thought—and finally to the
Omega Point, which is "pulling" everything towards it. In Chardinian thought, the second coming of Christ is really this consummation of pantheistic monism as advocated by Pope Benedict XVI:

> From this perspective the belief in the second coming of
> Jesus Christ and in the consummation of the world in that
> event could be explained as the conviction that our history
> is advancing to an "omega" point, at which it will become
> finally and unmistakably clear that the element of stability
> that seems to us to be the supporting ground of reality, so to
> speak, is not mere unconscious matter; that, on the contrary,
> the real, firm ground is mind. Mind holds being together,
> gives it reality, indeed is reality: it is not from below but from
> above that being receives its capacity to subsist. That there is
> such a thing as this process of "complexification" of material

being through spirit, and from the latter its concentration into a new kind of unity can already be seen in the remodeling of the world through technology.[37]

Many people will be surprised that Pope Benedict XVI was fond of ideas so caustic to biblical Christianity, but not many Catholics are aware of their leadership's affinities. Chardin was a leading proponent of orthogenesis, the idea that evolution occurs in a directional, goal-driven way. The former pope used the term "complexification" coined by Chardin, and his technological allusions suggest affinity to transhumanism and Ray Kurzweil's parallel to the Omega Point called "Singularity." Pun aside, many divergent schools of thought converge on monism.

The NDE literature is remarkably similar to Chardin's mystic Darwinism. NDErs return to life with a developing new worldview based on mystical gnosis. It is ubiquitous in the case reports. For example, van Lommel cites a typical case affirming evolution to the Omega Point:

I also saw where evolution is headed, what the ultimate goal is. I realized that this grand scheme not only includes me, but everything and everybody, every human being, every soul, every animal, every cell, the earth and every other planet, the universe, the cosmos, the Light. Everything is connected and everything is one.[38]

Similarly, Long cites Hafur's wisdom as, "We live in a 'plural unity' or 'oneness,'" and "Our reality is unity in plurality and plurality in unity." She also states that "everything is God."[39] All of this seems close to the view held by Baruch Spinoza, the Dutch phi-

losopher who believed that "there is only one substance, or independently existing thing, and that both God and the universe are
aspects of this substance."[40] While many seem eager to accept this
metaphysic, it lacks logical coherence and explanatory scope when it
comes to human experience.

Evaluation

In addressing the subjective heavenly experience of NDErs, there
is an appropriate biblical analogy found in apocalyptic literature.
Christians widely agree that the visions of Daniel, Isaiah, Ezekiel,
and John have a real basis in an otherworldly reality. Even so, there
are different interpretations of these visions amongst sincere believers. That is not to say that some interpretations aren't better than
others, but it does reveal that there is an agreed element of subjectivity in interpreting apocalyptic and visionary Scripture. While there
is usually a consensus view on the meaning of these visions, it is not
always written in stone, and prophecy often has a way of surprising us. It seems fair to argue that what people describe of heaven in
an NDE falls into this same general type of experience; and non-
Christian presuppositions held by the majority of people, such as
pluralism and universalism, will find mystical confirmation.

The central metaphysical premise of pantheism, that all is one,
is an unproven and counterintuitive assumption. In surveying Eastern thought, oneist pantheistic philosophers simply assume that
"being" (meaning "existing") is univocal and then offer arguments
for monism. If "being" is defined in such a way that it always means
exactly the same thing, then anything that "is" is necessarily the
same thing. In other words, oneists claim that everything exists in
the same way, so it shares the same essence. Eastern philosophers

equivocate on the verb "to be"—circular reasoning of the worst kind. However, if "being" is conceived as analogous and not necessarily the same kind of thing, then there can be more than one kind of "being" in the universe. For example, we commonly hold to the distinctions: material and immaterial. Thus, mind and body do not exist in the exact same way, and the mind lives on after the body dies. Monists simply assume their metaphysic, but there are strong reasons to doubt it.

In contrast, the Supernatural Worldview of the Bible is one of distinction. The concept of holiness means "set apart." The biblical worldview makes a Creator/Creation distinction (Genesis 1:1; John 1:1; Romans 1:18ff.), and the standard model of Big-Bang cosmology indicates that Creation was a supernatural event. For something to cause the universe, it must be distinct from it. Thus, monism is false. The Bible teaches that all men are created in God's image, but each has his own identity and moral responsibility. Monism has fundamental coherence problems as a system (which will be discussed further below).

What Is the Problem?

The shamanized NDEr might think that the greatest problem with the human race is that everyone has forgotten that they are god or a piece of god. The Western world was deceived by Christianity and doesn't realize that "all is one." Recall Hafur's NDE-derived statement, "Everything was me, without essential differences other than in earthly appearances."[41] Earthly appearances, including the notion of individualism, are a concept called "maya" in Hinduism. Maya interfaces between the material and immaterial and is believed to deceive man into thinking that he is an individual.[42] In Long's

NDE theology, even death is an illusion. Hafur offers, "Death is a metamorphosis of time—one more illusion born of our mental concepts."[43] Thus, expressed in Eastern terms, the problem is that man is deceived by maya—a product of his mind.

Evaluation

Traditions in Hinduism disagree as to what maya is, exactly. Some, like Sarvepalli Radhakrishnan, say it is the manifestation of god, whereas others, like Mysore Hiriyanna, understand the world and its distinctions as an illusory appearance of Brahman (ultimate reality) in the same way a rope appears to be a snake from a distance.[44] According to this view, separateness is a misperception. Due to ignorance, the mind perpetuates the illusion of individuality. However, upon analysis, this is nonsensical, because with monism, individual minds do not exist. But if one's mind is responsible for the illusion, then the particular mind held accountable is itself also an illusion. It's self defeating because misperceptions require a real perceiver, and nonexisting entities bear no responsibility. Thus, the mind cannot really be responsible for such a deception (or anything else, for that matter). It follows necessarily that the concept of maya is logically incoherent. It refutes itself. The analogical metaphysic based on a Creator/Creation distinction is much more satisfying than appeals to maya. Even so, there is an element of truth to the idea (2 Corinthians 4:4). Some people live in a worldview-derived illusion.

Philosophical materialists really are deceived by appearances. The dominant naturalist paradigm described in chapter 2 is an example. On the *Skeptiko* podcast, which covers NDEs and other paranormal topics, Alex Tsakiris frequently confronts atheists and skeptics with hard data and arguments for the soul, which they routinely dismiss and dodge. For instance, after presenting philosopher Robert Kuhn with veridical NDE cases, rather than accounting for the external confirmations, Kuhn responded incredulously:

> Look, I understand the view; it's just not something that I personally would put a lot of stock in, in terms of I don't base my belief or hope that there is something beyond the material brain. I don't base it on NDE. I mean, that's just full-stop. Could I be wrong? Sure. But I don't think so.[45]

Actually, Kuhn's interview revealed a great deal of ignorance concerning the veridical cases and the latest books by Long and van Lommel. The Christian can certainly empathize with Tsakiris here. On the other hand, Tsakiris thinks Christianity, specifically Christian exclusivity, is part of the problem. One thing naturalists and pagan supernaturalists agree on is their disdain for biblical Christianity.

During the *Skeptiko* interview with Gary Habermas, the two found many points of agreement, principally that naturalism is in big trouble evidentially. However, the offense of the cross came into focus when Tsakiris argued:

> But I also get the sense that there's a deep disenchantment with Christianity. This is borne out of statistics of people leaving the church in large numbers, and a lot of them aren't leaving the church and going—some of them are leaving the church and becoming Atheists. But a much, much greater number are leaving the church and finding their own spiritual truth. I think that's at the heart of what we're talking about here. If we can't talk about the near-death experience

and we can't deal with the data and say, you know what? This is highly suggestive of this point, Christianity isn't the only way. [46]

He firmly believes that NDEs suggest many paths to God. Habermas was winsome as ever and kept his composure while bringing the conversation back to *verifiable* evidence. This is where the autoscopic /transcendental distinction is so crucial. He pointed out:

By and large, the NDE evidential data is going to be this-worldly data. You know, your example was what mom was cooking for dinner. What happened in the car accident down the street? What happened with the tennis shoe on the roof of the hospital in the well-known tennis shoe cases? They're this-worldly. When that same guy says, "Then I went up through the clouds and I went to Heaven." And one person says, "I saw an angel." And one person says, "I saw Jesus," I don't have any criteria. At that point, I don't have any criteria to say that they met a person, even Jesus. [47]

Missing the point, Tsakiris replied that the Golden Rule is present in all spiritual traditions, and "it doesn't seem to be about exclusively Jesus, the Trinity, or any of the other fundamental doctrines in Christianity." [48] He denies the gospel for a belief in universalism and oneism. In this way, for him and other pluralists, Christianity is the problem.

Universal salvation is the majority conclusion derived from the transcendent component of the NDE. But should this really be so surprising? Given the subjective nature of the mystical portion, it's not too surprising, since the majority of the culture believes there are many paths to God. It seems probable that folks are imposing their theological preferences to the subjective part of the experience. Jeffrey Long states:

> The results of the NDERF [Near-Death Experience Research Foundation] study clearly indicate remarkable consistency among NDE case studies. This study finds that what people discovered during their near-death experience about God, love, afterlife, reason for our earthly existence, earthly hardships, forgiveness, and many other concepts is strikingly consistent across cultures, races, and creeds. Also, these discoveries are generally not what would have been expected from preexisting societal beliefs, religious teachings, or any other source of earthly knowledge.

There are obvious fallacies in this assertion. First, it assumes that all previous religious teachings are merely "earthly knowledge" as opposed to the supposedly novel revelations of NDErs. But Long's NDE theology, quoted extensively here, is demonstrably pantheistic monism, which falls into a well-known form of preexisting earthly knowledge. Whom does he think he is fooling? Far from unexpected, Long's beloved Hafur is trite. Her pithy one-liners remind one of the *Star Wars* character Yoda. In contrast, the biblical prophets spoke the very words of God when they prefaced their pronouncements with "thus sayeth the Lord," and Jesus indeed claimed to be God incarnate (John 8:58, 14:9). The transcendent ethics listed in chapter 2 and biblical prophecy stand far and above NDE revelations. Of course, many Christians have addressed these issues authoritatively.

When it comes to Christian apologists, they do not come more winsome than Ravi Zacharias, and it is also difficult to find one more qualified to speak on pantheism and the Eastern mindset. Zacharias grew up in India amidst the relativistic clamor of some 330 million Hindu gods, as well as pure monism. Christian missionaries in India are often amazed at the positive response they get. Whole crowds seem to accept the gospel message. Yet, they are later disappointed to learn that those they thought were converts simply added Jesus to their pantheon. But the Jesus described in the Bible did not allow for it (John 14:6). In the biblical worldview, truth is necessarily exclusive and antithetical to falsity. The law of noncontradiction is essential to rationality: Two contradictory statements cannot both be true in the same sense at the same time. However, pantheistic monism is plagued by logical contradictions.

Zacharias became a follower of Jesus at age seventeen and has dedicated himself to addressing this issue. Understandably, he is, above all, aware of the exclusive-truth claims of Christ and the troubling incoherence of Eastern thought:

You hear it a thousand times and more growing up in the East: "We all come through different routes and end up in the same place." But I say to you, God is not a place or an experience or a feeling.… All religions are not the same. All religions do not point to God. All religions do not say that all religions are the same. At the heart of every religion is an uncompromising commitment to a particular way of defining who God is or is not and accordingly, of defining life's purpose. Anyone who claims that all religions are the same betrays not only an ignorance of all religions but also a caricatured view of even the best-known ones. Every religion at its core is exclusive.[49]

In other words, you can argue that all world religions are wrong, but it is not possible for them to all be right. Accordingly, pluralists and universalists are necessarily arguing that all world religions are wrong, which seems to imply that their own belief systems are exclusively correct. That seems rather arrogant and elitist, and reveals the contradictory nature of pluralism.

Zacharias' critique applies equally to the faith expressed by many NDErs. Whether it is Hinduism or NDE monism, the gospel message presents a stumbling block. The real problem is that man is fallen and sinful and separated from God. This situation is not new. The Johannine writings employ thought-forms, which have affinities with pantheistic, monistic thought. In the early church, the fourth Gospel was suspected of gnostic tendencies. Not surprisingly, today, missionaries report that, upon a superficial reading, it is eagerly received by Hindus. Yet, John was using these thought-forms in such a way as to confront the mystical worldview.

In John's thought, the "Logos" is no longer a universal principle permeating the cosmos, but a man with an exclusive truth claim. According to Lesslie Newbigin, Church of Scotland missionary serving in the former Madras State (now Tamil Nadu), India, "I have found that Hindus who begin by welcoming the Fourth Gospel as the one that uses their language and speaks to their hearts end by being horrified when they understand what it is really saying."[50] While John's Gospel speaks their language, it is also the strongest discourse of the deity and exclusivity of Christ (John 1:1, 4:8–10, 8:57–59, 10:30–33, 14:6–7, 20:27–28).

What Is the Answer?

For the typical NDEr, the answer is ultimately enlightenment in the same manner as Eastern religion and New Age thought. If man would just clear his mind and meditate upon his true self, Atman, then he would realize that Atman is Brahman. Hafur's NDE wisdom is "that there is no God outside ourselves, but rather, God is in everything and everything is a part of God, as is life itself."[51] It is all about becoming one with the whole and, on the positive side, this usually entails living a peaceful and loving lifestyle. In Hafur's ideal NDE teaching, "Consciously living by love is the essence of life itself."[52] On the surface, a Christian might find this difficult to criticize, because it seemingly reflects Christ's wisdom (Mark 12:30–31). The NDE pantheist might say the answer is "love," or even cite the Golden Rule.

Evaluation

The pantheistic monist understands living by love in a different way from Christians. Jesus taught that love for God was first and as foundational to all else in life (Matthew 22:37). Hafur is speaking of love between human beings, not love for the God of the Bible, and sees it as a matter of self effort and commitment, not as a matter of faith. Superficially, it sounds good, but in pantheistic monism, "becoming one" involves the annihilation of the individual and absorption into the whole. What good is it to love people if they are really just an illusion? One can affirm the altruism and humility of the pantheistic monist while remaining critical of the worldview and theology. Even worse, given monism, the so-called problem of evil often leveled at Christianity is far more formidable.

Whereas the problem of evil is often used against Christianity, it seems much more caustic to the pantheistic monism advocated by NDErs. The pantheistic life force serves as a substitute for those who don't want to admit an autonomous Creator into their worldview. They exchange monism, karma, and fate for the sovereign, Holy

God. The benefit of this tactic is that it offers the benefits of a personal God but none of the accountability. As C. S. Lewis eloquently stated:

> When you are feeling fit and the sun is shining and you do not want to believe that the whole universe is a mere mechanical dance of atoms, it is nice to be able to think of this great mysterious Force rolling on through the centuries and carrying you on its crest. If, on the other hand, you want to do something rather shabby, the Life-Force, being only a blind force, with no morals and no mind, will never interfere with you like that troublesome God.[53]

But if God is just a life force and all is one, where did evil come from? Peter Jones puts it this way, "The One-ist utopia is always threatened, because, while All Is One, all is one disgusting mess, which the fantasy of altered states of consciousness will not change."[54] The existence of real evil contradicts oneism. Furthermore, if we are all part of God, how is it possible for anyone to make a mistake? If God is necessarily perfect, it is necessarily the case that mistakes are impossible. But we do err, and frequently at that. If individual minds do not exist, then they cannot be blamed. It follows that pantheism is false if human error exists. Thus, pantheism is false. Morals are similar.

Most people intuitively know that objective moral standards exist. For example, hardly anyone but the most conscience-seared relativist will argue against the assertion that "torturing babies for fun is always morally wrong." NDErs acknowledge this in the life-review accounts, and the resulting improved personalities are based on an *objective* assessment against moral absolutes. The objective standard implies a moral law, and that entails a moral lawgiver. Ultimate judgment is necessary for morality to be meaningful. Philosopher William Lane Craig has addressed this forcefully:

In a world without God, there can be no objective right and wrong, only our culturally and personally relative, subjective judgments. This means that it is impossible to condemn war, oppression, or crime as evil. Nor can one praise brotherhood, equality, and love as good. For in a universe without God, good and evil do not exist—there is only the bare valueless fact of existence, and there is no one to say you are right and I am wrong.[55]

While Craig is addressing the absurdity of life without God, this applies to God's ultimate justice as well. If the NDE worldview is true and everyone goes to heaven, does this mean that Adolf Hitler escaped justice by committing suicide and now enjoys heavenly bliss? The innocent victims of his brutality surely cry out that evil is real and justice is needed. Pantheistic NDErs show inconsistency when it comes to objective values, and their answer is insufficient. Even so, the life review common to many NDEs implies accountability.

The Life Review

The most troublesome aspects of NDE theology are the trivialization of evil and denial of sin's significance. Many NDErs describe a life review in which they relive past mistakes and even feel the pain of folks they hurt. They usually describe beings like angels who are present during this evaluation. For example, Long comments on the role of spiritual beings in the NDE:

A spiritual being sometimes accompanies the person who is having the life review…. Near death experiencers almost never describe feeling negatively judged by this spiritual being, no matter how unkind they were up to that point in their lives. Near death experiencers who reviewed many of their own prior cruel actions often express great relief that they were not negatively judged during their NDEs.[56]

A major deficiency in this line of thinking is that it has no place for ontological evil and ultimate justice. Also, the conclusions are unwarranted. Perhaps the spiritual being is merely a servant as represented in the Bible, and it is far too hasty to assume that Long's lenience implies a free ride. In fact, Scripture is quite clear that judgment is reserved for Christ alone: "The Father judges no one, but has given all judgment to the Son" (John 5:22; cf. John 17:1–2; 2 Timothy 4:1; 1 Peter 4:5; Revelation 20:12). The NDE is by definition merely a *near*-death experience. It is not wise to draw ultimate conclusions based on the transitory nature of the experience.

In close accord to Eastern religion, some NDErs speak in terms of karma: good and bad deeds weighed on a balance:

I could feel the good and bad emotions I made them go through. I was also capable of seeing that the better I made them feel, and the better the emotions they had because of me, [the more] credit (karma) [I would accumulate] and that the bad [emotions] would take some of it back…just like in a bank account, but here it was like a karma account to my knowledge.[57]

This is problematic in many ways. First, it presupposes standards by which to judge, but seems to make human emotions rather than objective moral truths the rule. As millions of counselors will certainly attest, emotions are very subjective and often misleading. Feelings simply do not determine reality. Next, karma as an explanation for evil and suffering is logically incoherent. In Eastern thought, it is based on the idea that all human suffering is based on a karmic debt from a past life. Through a series of incarnations, one can work off karmic debt and become one with the whole—nirvana or the Omega Point. But if everyone started out morally neutral, there would be no bad karma to get the process started—it's all dressed up with nowhere to go. Therefore, the biblical concept of a fall and separation from God more adequately explains evil and suffering.

Despite vain universalist hopes that no one is judged, the life review implies accountability for one's actions. Paul wrote of non-Christians:

They show that the work of the law is written on their hearts, while their conscience also bears witness, and their conflicting thoughts accuse or even excuse them on that day when, according to my gospel, God judges the secrets of men by Christ Jesus. (Romans 2:15–16)

Note that Paul says God judges their secrets. NDErs report learning new information about how *others* felt when they mistreated them. Van Lommel quotes a patient's description of the life review:

Not only did I perceive everything from my own viewpoint, but I also knew the thoughts of everyone involved in the event, as if I had their thoughts within me. This meant that I perceived not only what I had done or thought, but even in what way it had influenced others, as if I saw things with all-seeing eyes. And so, even your thoughts are apparently

not wiped out. Time and distance seemed not to exist. I was
in all places at the same time.[58]

While this is largely subjective, it is noteworthy that those who
describe this emphatic perception of others' emotions are often
shocked and dismayed by the impact of their actions. In other words,
they were formerly unaware of how they hurt others. This begs the
question of where the new information is coming from. Who or
what could possibly be in a position to not only record the NDErs'
actions and motives, but also of those affected? Those affected by
the NDEr are often still alive, so who is reading their minds to supply the data? Who or what would have an interest in educating the
NDEr about his or her own selfishness and lack of compassion? If it
is not a personal and moral God as judge, then who or what is keeping score? The biblical answer is that this sort of information is solely
the purveyance of God (1 Corinthians 2:11).

The life reviews describe a sense of guilt. The best explanation is that they *are* guilty in the sight of a holy God. These
brief accounts are incomplete and reveal they have not faced the
finality. Most NDE theology excludes judgment in hell from the
realm of possibility based on the idea that a diverse spectrum of
NDErs seem to experience heaven. But does this really follow? It
is simply assumed to be heaven, but it could easily be a middle
realm. Recall that Long's eleventh common element is a barrier
that the NDEr cannot cross. Could the barrier be reflective of
the "great chasm" described in Jesus' parable of Lazarus and the
rich man, "that those who would pass from here to you may
not be able, and none may cross from there to us" (Luke 16:2)?
This barrier and the brevity of the NDE speak to the incomplete
nature of the experience. It seems entirely possible that the posi-

tive experiences are not trips to heaven proper, rather to a temporary meeting place or "some type of sorting ground," as Maurice
Rawlings believes.[59] The euphoria could simply be inherent in the
state of disembodiment and, in many of the clinical cases, indicative of relief from chronic pain and disease. The atmosphere of
love suggests divine presence, but it doesn't necessarily preclude
later judgment beyond the barrier.

Negative NDEs

There are also many accounts of negative, even hellish, NDEs. Barbara Rommer determined that 17.7 percent of her study group had
"a less than positive experience."[60] She classifies four types: 1) misin-
terpreted positive NDEs; 2) the eternal void; 3) the hellish NDE; and
4) the frightening life review. She finds that such experiences, while
often frightening, are usually transformative and therefore "blessings
in disguise"—the title of her book. Some NDEs, like that of Bill
Wiese[61] and Howard Storm,[62] are near-hell experiences that result
in repentance and saving faith in Christ. Rawlings has suggested
that these memories are often repressed and thus underreported.[63]
Charles Garfield's interviews with terminal cancer patient NDErs
concluded: "Almost as many of the dying patients I interviewed
reported negative visions (demons and so forth) as reported blissful
experiences, while some reported both."[64] While van Lommel writes
that only 1 to 2 percent of NDEs are negative, he does admit, "The
exact number of people that experience such a frightening NDE is
unknown because they often keep quiet out of shame and guilt."[65]
Non-Christian researchers tend to emphasize the cases that support
pluralism while deemphasizing contrary data.

Conclusion

This chapter offered a summary and analysis of the near-death experience. It sought to illustrate the value of the veridical NDE for evidencing the immaterial soul. This evidence is far too important to ignore, and Christians should be able to handle the surrounding issues. It was argued that the transcendent component is subjective, and, in reflection of popular culture, it is often interpreted through a pluralistic lens. It was also argued that pantheistic monism (one-ism) is logically incoherent and necessarily false. Universalism is also unsatisfactory because it trivializes evil and discounts justice. The NDE is by definition an incomplete experience. Pastor and theologian Erwin Lutzer wrote:

> We cannot overstate the deception perpetuated by the "religion of the resuscitated," who report only the utopian idea that death leads to a higher degree of consciousness for all people regardless of their religion or beliefs. We must remember that all near-death reports are from those who might have died clinically but have not experienced biological or irreversible death. None has been resurrected. Whether the experience is positive or negative, it must always be evaluated by a more reliable authority.
>
> Personally, I am much more concerned about what I will experience after death than what I will experience when I am near death. It's not the transition but the destination that really counts. Thus, to discover what really lies on the other side, we must find a more credible map, a more certain authority than people who go only to the threshold of the life beyond and give us their reports.[66]

Because God knows who is saved and who is not, it seems likely that the best NDEs are the scary ones. Rather than an entitled sense of paranormal empowerment and self determination, hellish NDEs lead toward the gospel. Perhaps pantheistic NDErs do get a real glimpse of the afterlife. But what if part of the agony of hell is fully realizing what one is missing? In fact, many scholars see the flames of hell as a metaphor for being separated from God. Sean McDowell and Jonathan Morrow wrote, "It would be tempting, then, to think that hell may not be that bad after all since actual fire isn't there, but that would be a mistake because the reality is far worse than the symbol."[67] Without a taste of heaven, the contrast would lack punitive force. Accordingly, it is extremely shortsighted to draw universalist conclusions based on such partial data. It is much wiser to take Jesus at His word, trusting that He has the complete picture. He authenticated His view by returning from the dead after a *much* more extended period. Jesus taught, "If they do not hear Moses and the Prophets, neither will they be convinced if someone should rise from the dead" (Luke 16:31).

Notes

1. Kimberly Clark, "Clinical Interventions with Near-Death Experiencers," in Bruce Greyson and Charles P. Flynn, eds., *The Near-Death Experience: Problems, Prospects, Perspectives* (Springfield, IL: Charles C. Thomas, 1984) 243.

2. Ibid.

3. Gary R. Habermas and J. P. Moreland, *Beyond Death: Exploring the Evidence for Immortality* (Wheaton, IL: Crossway, 1998) 213.

4. IANDS, http://iands.org/publications/brochures.html (accessed 07/11/2012).

5. John Ankerberg and Robert Weldon, "Life After Death—Part 2," Ankerberg Theological Research Institute, http://www.johnankerberg.com/Articles/theological-dictionary/TD1004W4.htm (accessed 07/12/2012).

6. Robert Morey, *Death and the Afterlife* (Minneapolis, MN: Bethany, 1984) 258–266.

7. See: http://www.howardstorm.com/.

8. Jeffrey Long and Paul Perry, *Evidence of the Afterlife: The Science of Near-Death Experiences* (New York: HarperOne, 2011) 6–7.

9. Ibid., 46–52.

10. Ibid., 44.

11. Pim van Lommel, *Consciousness beyond Life: the Science of the Near-Death Experience* (New York: HarperOne, 2010).

12. Michael Sabom, *Recollections of Death: A Medical Investigation* (New York: Harper Collins, 1982) 14–23.

13. Michael Sabom, *Light & Death: One Doctor's Fascinating Account of Near-Death Experiences* (Grand Rapids, MI: Zondervan, 1998) Kindle edition, 2908.

14. Ibid., 2913–2914.

15. Ibid., 2918–2919.

16. Mario Beauregard and Denyse O'Leary, *The Spiritual Brain: A Neuroscientist's Case for the Existence of the Soul* (New York: HarperOne, 2007).

17. R. C. Sproul, *Now, That's a Good Question!* (Wheaton, IL: Tyndale, 1996) 300.

18. John Ankerberg and John Weldon, *The Facts on Near-Death Experiences* (Nashville: Ankerberg Theological Research Institute, 2009); Douglas R. Groothuis, *Deceived by the Light* (Eugene, OR: Harvest House, 1995); Robert Morey, *Death and the Afterlife* (Minneapolis, MN: Bethany, 1984); Maurice Rawlings, *Beyond Death's Door* (Nashville: Thomas Nelson, 2008).

19. Eben Alexander, "My Proof of Heaven: A Doctor's Experience with the Afterlife," *Newsweek,* October 15, 2012, 32.

20. Groothius, 29.

21. Millard J. Erickson, *Christian Theology*, 2nd ed. (Grand Rapids, MI: Baker, 1998) 1189.

22. William White, "2198 הָפַר" in *Theological Wordbook of the Old Testament*, eds. R. Laird Harris, Gleason L. Archer Jr., and Bruce K. Waltke (Chicago: Moody, 1999) electronic ed., 858.

23. James Swanson, *Dictionary of Biblical Languages with Semantic Domains: Greek New Testament* (Oak Harbor, WI: Logos Research Systems, 1997) electronic ed., DBLG 773, 1.

24. David E. Garland, "2 Corinthians," *The New American Commentary,* vol. 29, (Nashville: Broadman & Holman, 2001) 514.

25. Habermas and Moreland, 180.

26. Alex Tsakiris, "112. Christian Apologist Dr. Gary Habermas Skeptical of Near-Death Experience Spirituality," Skeptiko, http://www.skeptiko.com/112-gary-habermas-skeptical-of-near-death-experience-spirituality/ (accessed 07/14/12).

27. Alex Tsakiris, "About," Skeptiko, http://www.skeptiko.com/about-alex-tsakiris/ (accessed 07/14/12).

28. Alex Tsakiris, "169. Dr. Michael Heiser on Why Christians Are Skeptical of the Supernatural," Skeptiko, http://www.skeptiko.com/169-michael-heiser-why-christians-are-skeptical-of-supernatural/ (accessed 07/14/12).

29. Long and Perry, 158.

30. Moody discusses his séances at length in his biography here: Raymond Moody and Paul Perry, *Paranormal: My Life in Pursuit of the Afterlife* (New York: HarperOne, 2012); also see Kenneth Ring, *The Omega Project: Near-Death Experiences, UFO Encounters, and Mind at Large* (New York: William Morrow, 1992). Atwater's claims to be a psychic and spiritist are documented in Groothius, *Deceived*, 143.

31. P. M. H. Atwater, "Aftereffects Percentages," http://www.cinemind.com/atwater/resource/downloads/files/Aftereffects%20Percentages.pdf (accessed 07/14/12).

32. John Ankerberg and John Weldon, *The Facts on Life After Death* (Eugene, OR: Harvest House, 1992) 20.

33. Long and Perry, 158.

34. Jim Harold interview with P. M. H. Atwater, "NDEs—The Rest of the Story," Paranormal Podcast 283, May 6, 2013, 24:38–25:18.

35. Ibid, 25:46–26:57.

36. Watchman Nee, *The Latent Power of the Soul* (Christian Literature Crusade, 1980) 24.

37. Ibid., 113.

38. Van Lommel, 35.

39. Long and Perry, *Evidence*, 158.

40. D. B. Fletcher, "Monism" in Walter A. Elwell, *Evangelical Dictionary of Theology: 2nd ed.* (Grand Rapids, MI: Baker, 2001) 787.

41. Long and Perry, 159.

42. Norman L. Geisler and William D. Watkins, *Worlds Apart: A Handbook on World Views* (Grand Rapids, MI: Baker, 1989) 81.
43. Long and Perry, 159.
44. Sarvepali Radhakrishnan, *The Principal Upanishads,* 80, 82, 83; see: http://www.scribd.com/doc/129481965/The-Principal-Upanishads-by-S-Radhakrishnan; also Mysore Hiriyanna, *The Essentials of Indian Philosophy,* 158–59, https://archive.org/details/Mysore.Hiriyanna-The.Essentials.of.Indian.Philosophy.
45. Alex Tsakiris, "156. Closer to Truth Host, Dr. Robert Kuhn, Skeptical of Near-Death Experience Science," Skeptiko, http://www.skeptiko.com/156-robert-kuhn-skeptical-of-near-death-experience-science/ (accessed 07/16/12).
46. Alex Tsakiris, "112. Christian Apologist Dr. Gary Habermas Skeptical of Near-Death Experience Spirituality," Skeptiko, http://www.skeptiko.com/112-gary-habermas-skeptical-of-near-death-experience-spirituality/ (accessed 07/14/12).
47. Ibid.
48. Ibid.
49. Ravi Zacharias, *Jesus among Other Gods: The Absolute Claims of the Christian Message* (Nashville: W Publishing Group, 2002) 12.
50. Lesslie Newbigin, *Foolishness to the Greeks: The Gospel and Western Culture,* (Grand Rapids, MI: Eerdmans, 1986) Kindle edition, 90–91.
51. Long and Perry, 158.
52. Long and Perry, 159.
53. C. S. Lewis, *Mere Christianity* (New York: Macmillan, 1960) 35.
54. Peter Jones, *One or Two: Seeing a World of Difference* (Escondido, CA: Main Entry, 2010) Kindle edition, 2491–2492.
55. William Lane Craig, *Reasonable Faith: Christian Truth and Apologetics* (Wheaton, IL: Crossway, 1994) 61.

56. Long and Perry, 110.
57. Long and Perry, 111.
58. Pim van Lommel, "Continuity of Consciousness—Typical Elements of NDE," International Association for Near-Death Studies, http://iands.org/research/important-research-articles/43-dr-pim-van-lommel-md-continuity-of-consciousness.html?start=3 (accessed 07/18/12).
59. Maurice Rawlings, *Beyond Death's Door* (Nashville: Thomas Nelson, 2008) 92.
60. Barbara R. Rommer, *Blessing in Disguise: Another Side of the Near-Death Experience* (St. Paul, MN: Llewellyn, 2000) 24.
61. Bill Wiese, *23 Minutes in Hell* (Lake Mary, FL: Charisma, 2006).
62. "Saved From Hell: Rev. Howard Storm's Near-Death Experience," Near-Death.com, http://www.near-death.com/experiences/storm02.html (accessed 07/14/12).
63. Rawlings, 22, 66.
64. Robert Kastenbaum, *Between Life and Death* (New York: Springer, 1979) 55.
65. Van Lommel, *Consciousness*, 30.
66. Erwin W. Lutzer, *One Minute after You Die: A Preview of Your Final Destination* (Chicago: Moody, 1997) 27.
67. Sean McDowell and Jonathan Morrow, *Is God Just a Human Invention? And Seventeen Other Questions Raised by the New Atheists* (Grand Rapids, MI: Kregel, 2010) 162.

TELEPATHY, DREAMS, AND REMOTE VIEWING

I know a man in Christ who fourteen years ago was
caught up to the third heaven—whether in the body or
out of the body I do not know, God knows.
—2 CORINTHIANS 12:2

But as he considered these things, behold, an angel of
the Lord appeared to him in a dream, saying, "Joseph, son of
David, do not fear to take Mary as your wife, for that which is
conceived in her is from the Holy Spirit."
—MATTHEW 1:20

Is it possible for thoughts to be projected across vast distances? Can
someone leave his or her body and "see" things in a faraway land
or even the future? The Supernatural Worldview of the Bible has
always supported such ideas. While Western scientific orthodoxy
asserts that there are only five senses, there is surprising evidence
for more. If Watchmen Nee was correct about the latent power
of the soul, we would expect to find a growing body of evidence

for these abilities. This chapter will sample some of parapsychological literature, which contains overwhelming evidence for the existence of paranormal abilities labeled "telepathy" and "remote viewing" and their relationship to dreams. The next chapter will pick up where this one leaves off to explore precognition in more detail and examine how recent evidence supports Nee's prophetic warning.

Discussed within are well-documented, spontaneous cases, laboratory experiments, and, if applicable, biblical analogs. Spontaneous cases can either be personal and subjective or objective if they have external confirmation. Almost every family seems to have a personal, subjective experience like this one:

> *At 3:00 in the morning I awoke gasping for air and feeling a pain in my chest. After a few minutes, I calmed down but had a strange feeling that something bad had happened. As I tried to go back to sleep, the phone rang. It was my stepmother on the phone. She said, "I have terrible news. Your father had a massive stroke and is in intensive care at the hospital. You need to get down here right away; he may not live through the night."*

These kinds of stories are actually very common. The above is very close to what happened to me the night my father died. Most of these stories go unexamined, but nearly every family has at least one. While it is difficult to imagine an adequate explanation consistent with naturalistic materialism, an appeal to sheer coincidence is an option. Perhaps I suffer from an anxiety disorder or simply had a bad dream and my reaction was unrelated to my father's death. It would be appropriate to ask if this sort of episode (awakening in a panic) has happened before or if it is an ongoing condition. In my case, I believe it was really related to my father's death. While coincidence is an option, the cases you are about to read will convince you otherwise. Here is a compelling one with external but anecdotal confirmation from one of my readers, Cindy Nuara, a Bible-believing Christian:

> *I had a precognitive dream in the late '70s about the death of a coworker's son. I did not relate this dream to him, and unfortunately it came true a short time later. In the dream I was in a hospital waiting room with a few of my fellow employees. We were told that Robert's son had died during surgery of a gunshot wound to the abdomen. I remember being very sad at this news.*
>
> *I was off work that day and received a phone call from my assistant manager. I knew Robert had a six-year-old son, but I didn't know he also had a fourteen-year old son. That day when both parents were not home and his brother was babysitting, the six-year-old had a couple of friends over. He was able to reach the top of the closet by climbing on something and grabbed his father's rifle. When he came into the living room with it with it, his older brother grabbed the other end of it to wrestle it away from him. The child's finger happened to be on the trigger and the gun went off, shooting his older brother in the stomach. He died during surgery.[1]*

This defies coincidence in its timing and specificity, but it's impossible to prove because she didn't tell anyone before it happened. Even so, I believe her. I suggest that many folks are aware of similar cases, but seldom talk about them or consider their implications. Could this sort of precognition be the work of well-intended but imperfect ministering angels or is it a mysterious human ability like Nee's "soul power"? It is hard to say.

This chapter will examine telepathy, remote viewing, and dreams. These phenomena are often classified as "psi," a generic term used by parapsychologists. A textbook explains: "The Greek letter *psi* here is used to denote the unknown paranormal element in these experiences in much the same way as the letter x represents the unknown in an algebraic equation until its identity is determined."[2] Only cases of psi that meet certain rigorous criteria are considered. Appeals to coincidence can apply to anything, but in the cases shown within, such answers stretch credulity. Today's researchers are conducting repeatable controlled experiments that cannot be easily relegated to fraud or chance. The fact that many seemingly paranormal experiences can be explained away with "just-so" stories does not discredit the immense body of research. It only takes one genuine example of psi to overthrow the dominant materialism. George Hansen has argued:

> The existence of psi suggests that imagination and reality are not clearly separable. This is a disconcerting idea, but it must be explored if one wishes to understand the paranormal. The binary oppositions of internal-external, subjective-objective, fantasy-reality are fundamental to the Western worldview, and anything that proposes a blurring of them is dismissed as irrational. Yet psi engages both the mental and physical worlds, both the imagination and reality; there is an interface, an interaction.[3]

Truthfully, materialism is already dead, but the scientific community is very slow to change. Dean Radin writes, "Contrary to the assertions of some skeptics, the question is not whether there is any scientific evidence, but 'What does a proper evaluation of the evidence reveal?' and 'Has positive evidence been independently replicated?'"[4] Radin is actually a leading researcher in repeatable laboratory experimentation, but for each phenomenon, we first examine spontaneous examples from real-world experience. Real-life examples are the most obviously paranormal, too.

This is the dilemma for parapsychology: Spontaneous manifestations of psi are the most powerful and effective because they involve real, emotionally charged events often entailing life-and-death circumstances. Like the Skubish car accident (see chapter 1), they are not the sorts of things that translate well to the laboratory for repeatable experiment. Some have tried to emulate the intensity of real-world energy of spontaneous cases. A Hungarian physicist working at the Psychophysical Research Laboratories at Princeton, Zoltán Vassy, subjected himself to electric shocks to see if a receiver could telepathically pick up on it. In so doing, he probably managed to recreate a spontaneous situation. He set up a classical conditioning experiment in which a "viewer" would see a light, wait five seconds, and then press a button that delivered an electric shock to the other subject. This was repeated several times, so the "shockee" was trained to know that within five seconds of the light, a shock was coming. Electrodes were hooked up to measure skin conductance as a sign of arousal. Then the two subjects were separated so they could not see each other. Would the shockee be able to sense when the viewer was about to press the shock button? If psi is a real ability, you would expect this adaptive warning to occur. It did.

Vassy's research proved beyond a reasonable doubt that the shockee could telepathically sense when the shock was coming.[5] While these results have been duplicated,[6] the methodology isn't likely to catch on for obvious reasons (it hurts). In science, controlled laboratory-type experiments are preferred because the variables are minimized, the experiments can be duplicated, and the methodology is subject to peer review. From the work already done, it is reasonable to conclude that ESP-type phenomena have been proven for a long time. It is a worldview issue for those within the scientific community who cling religiously to reductive materialism in spite of the data. In Christianity, objections seem to rise from incredulity, appropriate fear, and willful avoidance of the data. Even so, the Bible is full of anomalous phenomena. Appropriate biblical evidence for analogous phenomena will be cited.

Telepathy

The term "telepathy" denotes extrasensory perception from one mind to another via an unknown pathway distinct from the five accepted senses. It comes from the Greek *tele* for "distant" and *pathos*, meaning "feeling." Watchman Nee wrote, "Telepathy—being communication between mind and mind otherwise than through the known channels of the senses—enables a person to use his own psychic force to ascertain another's thought without the need of being told."[7] In the case at the beginning of this book, Karen Nichols was able to telepathically sense that three-year-old Nick Skubish was alive and in desperate condition. Her confidence in this psi perception and the resulting determination stemming from it probably saved the boy's life. Karen believes that Nick had a near-death experience, which explained a brief interval when she could no longer telepathically sense him. This was later corroborated by the boy's statement at the hospital that he had visited heaven and had seen Jesus. While it is hard to prove spontaneous examples, they are the most common instances of telepathy. In fact, a University of Virginia psychiatrist, Ian Stevenson, reported that from 50 to 80 percent of telepathic communications occur during a serious crisis.[8] It makes perfect sense given the emotional intensity of such events.

J. B. Rhine, Hubert Pearce, and the Duke Parapsychology Lab

I recently completed course work at the Rhine Institute, the remnants of the famous Duke University Parapsychology lab. It was here that some of the most famous laboratory research on telepathy was done from 1929 to 1962 by J. B. Rhine with a deck of twenty-five ESP cards. The cards, called the Zener deck, contained five different symbols: a circle, a star, a square, wavy lines, and a cross. In a typical experiment, one person randomly chose a card and tried to mentally send its symbol to another person. The most frequently cited experiments were conducted from 1933 to 1934 with Hubert E. Pearce Jr., a Duke divinity student (and later pastor) who believed he inherited his mother's psychic abilities.

Pearce did these experiments with Rhine and his associate, J. G. Pratt. What follows is an excerpt from the paper on the Pearce-Pratt distance telepathy experiments from the *Journal of Parapsychology*:

At the time agreed upon, Pearce visited Pratt in his research room on the top floor of what is now the Social Science Building on the main Duke campus. The two men synchronized their watches and set an exact time for starting the test, allowing enough time for Pearce to cross the quadrangle to the Duke Library, where he occupied a cubicle in the stacks at the back of the building. From his window, Pratt could see Pearce enter the library.

Pratt then selected a pack of ESP cards from several packs always available in the room. He gave this pack of cards a number of dovetail shuffles and a final cut, keeping them facedown throughout. He then placed the pack on the right-hand side of the table at which he was sitting. In the center of the table was a closed book on which it had been agreed with Pearce that the card for each trial would be placed. At the minute set for starting the test, Pratt lifted the top card from the inverted deck, placed it facedown on the book, and allowed it to remain there for approximately a full minute. At the beginning of the next minute, this card was picked up with the left hand and laid, still facedown, on the left-hand side of the table, while with the right hand, Pratt picked up the next card and put it on the book. At the end of the second minute, this card was placed on top of the one on the left, and the next one was put on the book. In this way, at the rate of one card per minute, the entire pack of twenty-five cards went through the process of being isolated, one card at a time, on the book in the center of the table, where it was the target or stimulus object for that ESP trial.

In his cubicle in the library, Pearce attempted to identify the target cards, minute by minute, and recorded his responses in pencil. At the end of the run, there was, on most test days, a rest period of five minutes before a second run followed in exactly the same way. Pearce made a duplicate of his call record, signed one copy, and sealed it in an envelope for Rhine. The two sealed records were delivered personally to Rhine, most of the time before Pratt and Pearce compared their records and scored the number of successes. On a few occasions when Pratt and Pearce met and compared their unsealed duplicates before both of them had delivered their sealed records to Rhine, the data could not have been changed without collusion, as Pratt kept the results from the unsealed records, and any discrepancy between them and Rhine's results would have been noticed. In subseries D, Rhine was on hand to receive the duplicates as the two other men met immediately after each session for the checkup.[9]

Pearce's accuracy was 30 percent, scoring 558 hits when 370 were expected by chance, a full 10 percent above the expected 20 percent. The odds against this occurring by chance are ten thousand to one. At the time, many intellectuals and philosophers considered Rhine's work decisive in favor of psi. It was accepted to be proven. However, old paradigms do not fall so easily. Enter the debunkers…

Professor Charles Hansel, a caustic critic of Rhine's work, wrote *ESP, a Scientific Evaluation.*[10] Hansel claimed to have effectively discredited Rhine by devising scenarios in which Rhine's best subjects could have cheated. However, there was no actual evidence they had done so, and Rhine mentioned taking specific precautions to discourage it. The materialist camp considers this a decisive blow. It is one thing to devise a possible means of cheating, and another to prove cheating occurred. Nevertheless, materialist science still disregards Rhine's entire body of work because of Hansel's debunking efforts. This doesn't seem to be a viable option for intellectually honest theologians operating from a Supernatural Worldview, primarily due to the character witness of Rhine's star subject, Hubert Pearce.

Pearce appears to be an exceptional individual of strong character. Rhine had great confidence in Pearce's integrity. In his *Extra-Sensory Perception* (1934), Rhine wrote:

Pearce is a young Methodist ministerial student in the Duke School of Religion, very much devoted to his work, though fairly liberal in his theology. He is very sociable and approachable, and is much interested in people. There is also a pretty general artistic trend to his personality, expressing itself mainly in musical interest and production, but extending into other fields of art as well.

Pearce has not, himself, had any striking parapsychological experiences other than numerous "hunches" and "intuitions," but he reports that his mother and others of her family have had certain clairvoyant experiences. It was on learning from him of these experiences of his family that I asked him to try our clairvoyance tests with my assistant, Mr. Pratt.

All of Pearce's work has been carefully witnessed; but I wish to state in addition that I have fullest confidence in his honesty, although in this work the question of honesty arises in my mind with every one, preacher or no.[11]

Pearce went on to full-time pastoral ministry, and although he did not remain involved in parapsychology, he followed with interest. Interestingly, he received a letter many years later from skeptic Martin Gardner, asking if he was ready to confess to cheating due to the overwhelming data for telepathy—something Gardner could not countenance.

Pearce replied:

Dear Mr. Gardner:

Upon my return from a trip to Durham and Washington I found your interesting letter. I will have to admit that it is a new approach and I wish that I might have had it to send to Dr. Rhine. Of course, you realize that it isn't deserving of a respectable reply. There are a lot of things that might be said to express my opinion of it—and probably of you.

May I say simply that I am as much interested in the project now as I was when I was in the University and the longer I live the more I become convinced of its reality.

Those of us who have worked with Dr. Rhine have never once doubted his ability as a scientist and research director, his devotion to the Truth, his brilliance, or his integrity.

You are simply beating again the path that was beat by Experts in the 1930's.

The day will come when Dr. Rhine's name will be among the Immortals—and the name of his critics forgotten.

Sincerely,

Hubert E. Pearce [12]

Pearce seems to have lost his abilities as he grew older and could no longer score exceptionally high when retested in 1950. He was a career Methodist minister and was also known as a church builder.

Telepathy in the Bible

Telepathy is certainly found in Scripture. In the Bible, angels do not have to communicate through the five senses; they communicate directly into the mind, often in dreams. A few examples demonstrate this:

Then the angel of God said to me in the dream, "Jacob," and I said, "Here I am." (Genesis 31:11)

But as he was considering these things, behold, an angel of the Lord appeared to him in a dream, saying, "Joseph, son of David, do not be afraid to take Mary as your wife, for what has been conceived in her is from the Holy Spirit." (Matthew 1:20)

Now after they had gone away, behold, an angel of the Lord appeared in a dream to Joseph, saying, "Get up, take the child and his mother and flee to Egypt, and stay there until I tell you. For Herod is about to seek the child to destroy him." (Matthew 2:13)

Now after Herod had died, behold, an angel of the Lord appeared in a dream to Joseph in Egypt. (Matthew 2:19)

Jacob and Joseph both received messages from God through angels who visited their dreams. If an angel communicates directly into a dream, then it must be telepathy. Dreams are thoughts. This means the angel communicated directly into the thoughts of both Jacob and Joseph. Even more interesting is that if the angels interact within our dreams, then they must be able to hear our thoughts as well. It is also troublesome when considering fallen angels. If the holy ones communicate telepathically, then the fallen ones likely do, too, and perhaps they influence dreams as well? Dreams are very conducive to psi phenomena.

Dreams

In the ancient world, dreams were one of several ways people sought to predict the future and to make beneficial decisions. In some societies, people went to temples or holy places to sleep in order to have a dream that would show them the best decision to make. Sigmund Freud seemed to think the ego was trying to communicate truths that the conscious mind was hesitant to accept. He saw dreams as a form of wish fulfillment or attempts by the unconscious to resolve an internal conflict of some sort. That might have some truth to it, but it seems too reductionistic to handle psi phenomena. Psychologist Carl Jung's ideas about the collective unconscious and archetypes offer a more explanatory scope. Jung wrote:

> Another dream-determinant that deserves mention is telepathy. The authenticity of this phenomenon can no longer be disputed today. It is, of course, very simple to deny its existence without examining the evidence, but that is an unscientific procedure which is unworthy of notice. I have found by experience that telepathy does in fact influence dreams, as has been asserted since ancient times.[13]

If one allows that the dream state accesses a timeless dimension, then foreseeing future events in dreams is plausible. In fact, dreams are a well-known and documented avenue by which people have seen the future in advance. It is widely held to be true. In a recent survey of college psychology students, 21.7 percent reported to have precognitive dreams.[14] In a 1974 survey of three hundred students from the University of Virginia and seven hundred adult residents of Charlottesville, Virginia, 36 percent of respondents reported precognitive dreams.[15] Although the subject of precognition and its implications will be formally addressed in the next chapter, dreams of future events will be discussed here.

Abraham Lincoln's Dream

Because so many people have reported precognitive dreams, it follows that some of them are famous. Abraham Lincoln had an amazing dream just prior to his assassination that could have changed the course of history. He is documented to have said:

> About ten days ago, I retired very late. I had been up waiting for important dispatches from the front. I could not have been long in bed when I fell into a slumber, for I was weary. I soon began to dream. There seemed to be a death-like stillness about me. Then I heard subdued sobs, as if a number of people were weeping. I thought I left my bed and wandered downstairs. There the silence was broken by the same pitiful sobbing, but the mourners were invisible. I went from room to room; no living person was in sight, but the same mournful sounds of distress met me as I passed along. I saw light in all the rooms; every object was familiar to me; but where were all the people who were grieving as if their hearts would break? I was puzzled and alarmed. What could be the meaning of all this? Determined to find the cause of a state of things so mysterious and so shocking, I kept on until I arrived at the East Room, which I entered. There I met with a sickening surprise. Before me was a catafalque, on which rested a corpse wrapped in funeral vestments.

Around it were stationed soldiers who were acting as guards; and there was a throng of people, gazing mournfully upon the corpse, whose face was covered, others weeping pitifully. "Who is dead in the White House?" I demanded of one of the soldiers, "The President," was his answer; "he was killed by an assassin." Then came a loud burst of grief from the crowd, which woke me from my dream. I slept no more that night; and although it was only a dream, I have been strangely annoyed by it ever since.[16]

According to Ward Hill Lamon, a close friend of Lincoln who was present for the conversation, the president had personally related this dream to his wife and a few friends a mere three days before he was shot. It poses troubling questions. How might the course of history have been altered had he taken more caution? If a warning fails to save, was it from God? Interestingly, it is also a matter of record that Mrs. Ulysses S. Grant had persuaded her husband, General Grant, not to accompany Lincoln out on that same evening due to a premonition. It subsequently emerged that the general had also been an intended victim that night. Apparently, precognition saved Grant but not Lincoln. It seems that tragic events are often perceived ahead of time by someone.

The Aberfan Disaster

The Aberfan Disaster was a catastrophic collapse of a coal mining operation in the Welsh village of Aberfan. It was caused by water that built up in the rock and shale, resulting in a cataclysmic landslide onto the town below. Interestingly, Eryl Mai Jones, a ten-year-old

Welsh schoolgirl, told her mother about a dream she had the *previous* night. She dreamt that something black had covered her school. On October 21, 1966, the avalanche crushed everything in its way, killing 116 children and 28 adults, including part of the Pantglas School where Jones attended. Fortunately, an enterprising researcher was able to solicit and document data from the public at large with surprising results.

Aberfan Disaster, October 21, 1966[17]

J. C. Barker, an English psychiatrist, used the local press to poll the public concerning foreknowledge of the disaster. He got seventy-six letters in response, of which sixty merited investigations. People representing a wide range of ages from ten to seventy-three reported dreaming about the event. Women outnumbered men five to one. Many believed they had previous premonitions. The dreams varied from vague to very vivid. Of the sixty, eighteen were verified to have been reported before the disaster occurred. Sixteen told someone about their dreams (in most cases, a few people corroborated) and two wrote them down—one in a dream notebook and one mailed in a postmarked envelope dated September 18, 1966, a month before the tragedy.[18]

The time intervals spanned from six weeks to only hours before event. Rather than coming from locals who might have feared such a disaster, most of the examples were from people in other parts of the country who would have no reason to worry about it. It is hard to say if any lives were spared due to these premonitions, but it certainly seems possible, given the pervasive precognitions. Whether by divine agency or innate ability, examples like these suggest that time is much stranger than commonly assumed. Even more controversial, paranormal perceptions may be commonplace but underreported because of the naturalistic bias.

Maimonides Dream Laboratory Experiments

At the Maimonides Medical Center in Brooklyn, New York, a team of scientists consisting of Montague Ullman, Stanley Krippner, and Charles Honorton conducted some intriguing studies on ESP during dreams. They conducted thirteen formal ESP dream studies; eleven were designed to investigate telepathy and two were designed to test precognition. In the experiments, two subjects, a "receiver" and a "sender," stayed overnight in the sleep laboratory. In a special isolated sleep room, the receiver's eye movements and brainwaves were recorded as he or she slept. When the receiver's eye movements indicated REM sleep, the sender was signaled by one of the scientists to begin sending. The sender would then concentrate on a randomly chosen target picture, which no one knew about prior, trying to telepathically communicate it into the receiver's dream. At the end of REM sleep, the researchers awoke the receiver and asked him or her to describe any dreams he or she could recall. The same target, often a famous work of art, was retained through the night and all the dream reports were written down. Then a team of outside judges blindly rated the similarity of the dream reports to a series of control images including the target.

The resulting data shows a number of very striking matches between the dream transcripts and the randomized target pictures. In one example, a perfect score was achieved.[19] After reviewing the data, a Yale University psychologist, Irvin Child, concluded, "What is clear is that the tendency toward hits rather than misses cannot reasonably be ascribed to chance. There is some systematic—that is, nonrandom source—of anomalous resemblance of dreams to target."[20] A meta-analysis of the 450 Maimonides ESP trials found the overall success rate to be 63 percent, with a 95-percent confidence rate. The odds against chance were seventy-five million to one.[21] Similar findings were subsequently reported by other research teams.[22]

Remote Viewing

Remote viewing is another way of denoting clairvoyance, the ability to perceive out of sensory range. Sometimes this is connected to an out-of-body experience (OBE), but other times not. Parapsychologist Charles Tart recorded a remarkable instance of an OBE in a laboratory setting in which the subject was able to see something outside the range of access of the normal five senses:

On the first three laboratory nights, Miss Z reported that in spite of occasionally being "out," she hadn't been able to control her OBEs enough to be in position to see the target number (which was different each night). On the fourth night, at 5:57 a.m., there was a seven-minute period of somewhat ambiguous EEG activity, sometimes looking like stage 1, sometimes like brief waking states. Then Miss Z awakened and called out over the intercom that the target number was 25,132, which I wrote on the EEG recording. After she slept a few more minutes, I woke her so she could go to work, and this is what she reported regarding the previous awakening (Tart 1968, 17):

> I woke up; it was stifling in the room. Awake for about five minutes. I kept waking up and drifting off, having floating feelings over and over. I needed to go higher, because the number was lying down. Between 5:50 and 6:00 a.m., that did it…I wanted to go read the number in the next room, but I couldn't leave the room, open the door, or float through the door…. I couldn't turn on the air conditioner!

The number 25,132 was indeed the correct target number near the ceiling above her bed.[23]

This kind of evidence is rare. The fact that Miss Z reported the number was "lying down" rather than leaning against the wall as she expected (a detail verified by Tart) strongly suggests she somehow *saw* the card. What makes this especially compelling is that she couldn't have gotten up to see the numbers, because she was hooked up to an EEG machine; any physical movement would have disturbed the recordings of her brainwaves. The odds of guessing a five-digit number are one hundred thousand to one. Although the distinction is somewhat arbitrary, the term *remote viewing* was invented to distinguish it from clairvoyance. It has received a lot of attention due to its modern use by intelligence agencies.

Remote viewing was popularized following the declassification of documents related to the Stargate Project, a $20-million-dollar CIA research program trying to determine possible military application of psychic phenomena. Much of the research was done at Stanford Research Institute (SRI) by Russell Targ and Harold Puthoff, two former laser physicists, and Edwin C. May, a former nuclear physicist. The projects spanned from the 1970s until 1995, and were primarily handled by the CIA and Defense Intelligence Agency (DIA). Some believe remote-viewing programs still exist, but are now deeply classified black projects.

The star remote viewers of the SRI studies were Ingo Swann, Pat Price, and Joe McMoneagle. Swann, who died February 1, 2013, was an artist known for psychic abilities who wrote a book called *Natural ESP: The Esp Core and Its Raw Characteristics,* and another called *Penetration: The Question of Extraterrestrial and Human Telepathy* that discussed extraterrestrial life. The latter work suggests that Swann was contacted by nonhuman entities in the guise of space aliens, an idea explored in my former work, *Exo-Vaticana* with Thomas Horn. Swann came to the attention of Targ and Puthoff when he demonstrated his ability to intentionally change the readings of Superconducting Quantum Interference Device (SQUID), which was buried deep underneath the Stanford physics building and shielded from electromagnetic influence by several layers of thick armor. Swann remotely viewed the SQUID and drew accurate pictures of its interior. Even more, he was able to influence its sinusoidal output, which was normally a consistent and predictable sine wave. When Swann projected his consciousness toward it, the wave doubled in frequency. He was able to repeat it at will, and the wave returned to normal frequency when he stopped. This was documented by several technical experts and recorded by Russell Targ.[24] The successful experiments with Swann led to a visit from two employees of the CIA's Directorate of Science and Technology. Swann's demonstrable ability to view locations all over world is what purportedly got the project off the ground. The initial CIA-funded project was later renewed and expanded. A number of CIA officials, including John N. McMahon (later the CIA's deputy director), became strong supporters of the program. It is beyond question that significant evidence for psi drove the funding.

Pat Price was a retired police commissioner from California who had used his psychic abilities to solve crimes. While working for SRI, he was asked to investigate the kidnapping of Patricia Hearst, the teenaged newspaper heiress held hostage by the Symbionese Liberation Army in 1974. After a visit to the location of the kidnapping, Price correctly identified Donald DeFreeze out of forty mug shots. Also, he was able to lead police to the location of the car used in the crime.[25] Price is best known for his sketches of cranes and gantries retrieved by remotely viewing secret Soviet research at Semipalatinsk behind Soviet lines. His highly accurate sketches preceded the CIA intelligence photographs that confirmed them by many years.

Joe McMoneagle's most amazing results include the time he drew the locations of a CIA team while the agents were hiding hundreds of miles away at Lawrence Livermore Laboratories in the San Francisco area. He drew many of the laboratory buildings and structures in specific detail. Then the team moved to a nearby Windmill Farm, and McMoneagle drew the windmill structures and landscape with astounding accuracy. In 1984, McMoneagle was awarded a legion of merit for "producing crucial and vital intelligence unavailable from any other source."[26] This sort of evidence cannot simply be brushed aside, but very few people are aware of it to take it seriously. Even U.S. presidents have testified to the veracity of remote viewing.

President Jimmy Carter, in an interview with *GQ* magazine, revealed the use of psychics in parapsychological espionage directed against the USSR. He recounted a specific incident he was personally involved with that produced viable intelligence:

GQ: One of the promises you made in 1976 was that if you were elected, you would look into the reports from Roswell and see if there had been any cover-ups. Did you look into that?

Carter: Well, in a way. I became more aware of what our intelligence services were doing. There was only one instance that I'll talk about now. We had a plane go down in the Central African Republic—a twin-engine plane, small plane. And we couldn't find it. And so we oriented satellites that were going around the earth every ninety minutes to fly over that spot where we thought it might be and take photographs. We couldn't find it. So the director of the CIA came and told me that he had contacted a woman in California that claimed to have supernatural capabilities. And she went in a trance, and she wrote down latitudes and longitudes, and we sent our satellite over that latitude and longitude, and there was the plane.

GQ: That must have been surreal for you. You're the president of the United States, and you're getting intelligence information from a woman in a trance in California.

Carter: That's exactly right.[27]

Biblical Examples

In the Old Testament, Samuel was called a "seer," apparently because he was able to see what others could not, like the location of the lost donkeys of Saul:

Samuel answered Saul and said, "I am the seer. Go up ahead of me to the high place, and you will eat with me today; then I will send you away in the morning. I will tell you all that is on your mind. And as for your female donkeys that were lost three days ago, do not be concerned about them, because they have been found. For whom is all the desire of Israel? Is it not for you and for all the house of your father?" (1 Samuel 9:19–20, LEB)

It isn't clear that this entails remote viewing, but it seems like something akin. Samuel was gifted by Yahweh to serve as a spokesperson for God. It is essential to remember that the biblical prophets derived their authority from God. With that understood, Scripture does seem to imply that some people have these abilities.

In the book of 2 Kings, Naaman, the second in command to the king of Syria, suffered from leprosy. He heard about Elisha, the Lord's prophet, who could invoke Yahweh to heal the dreaded disease. When Naaman arrived at Elisha's house bearing great sums of money, a messenger instructed Naaman to bathe seven times in the River Jordan. Because of his immense pride he went away angry, refusing to wash in the muddy river waters. His servants convinced him to do so, and God healed him. Naaman declared, "There is no God in all the world except in Israel" (5:15). Although Elisha had refused a monetary gift from Naaman, the prophet's servant Gehazi secretly followed Naaman to ask for money.

Somehow, Elisha was able to follow Gehazi's wrongful actions and confront him with specific details on his return. "Then he said to him, 'Did not my heart go with you as the man turned from on his chariot to meet you? Is it time to take silver, clothes, olive orchards, vineyards, sheep, oxen, male slaves, and female slaves?'" (2 Kings 5:26). The passage gives the impression that Elisha *saw* exactly what went on out of his normal sensory purview. This gift was evidently a divinely ordained ability for a prophet.

The book of Revelation seems to be John's accounting of an OBE:

> After this I looked, and behold, a door standing open in heaven! And the first voice, which I had heard speaking to me like a trumpet, said, "Come up here, and I will show you what must take place after this." <u>At once I was in the Spirit</u>, and behold, a throne stood in heaven, with one seated on the throne. (Revelation 4:1–2, underline added)

This has been described as a "state in which the ordinary faculties of the flesh are suspended, and the inward senses opened."[28] In this altered state of consciousness, God brings a man's spirit into direct contact with the invisible spiritual world. According to biblical scholar Robert Thomas:

"In the spirit" is descriptive of the prophetic trance into which the prophet's spirit entered. This miraculous ecstatic state wrought by the Spirit of God was, to all intents and purposes, a complete translation from Patmos to heaven. All of the prophet's senses were operative: his ears heard, his eyes saw, and his emotions were as real as though his body was literally in heaven instead of remaining on Patmos.[29]

John seems to be describing an altered state of consciousness similar to remote viewing. Many evangelicals have a fear of mysticism, probably from its association with Roman Catholic monasticism. Even so, Acts 10:10 speaks of Peter "falling into a trance" while praying. This was not a nighttime dream, but an altered state of consciousness induced by prayer. Peter describes it as an ecstatic vision using the Greek term *ekstasis*. In the first century, the term generally denoted "a vision accompanied by an ecstatic psychological state."[30] While these examples certainly don't suggest it is wise to attempt remote viewing for one's own ends, they do demonstrate the existence of such phenomena is consistent with the Bible and a Supernatural Worldview. If one isn't careful, he or she could beckon an uninvited guest.

Why have Christians usually associated clairvoyance with demonization? Other than divinely inspired prophecy, the Bible doesn't tell us much. However, there is an instructive incident in Acts 16. On one of Paul's visits to the Jewish place of prayer, he and his cohorts were met by a slave girl who had the gift of second sight and earned money for her owners by giving readings. The text reads, "And it came to pass, as we went to prayer, a certain damsel possessed with a spirit of divination met us, which brought her masters much gain by soothsaying" (Acts 16:16). The girl's gift is attributed by Luke to a spirit of divination, *penuma pythona*, literally, "a spirit, a

Python." The background of this attribution reaches back into classical Greek mythology.

The Python was a legendary dragon serpent that guarded the temple and oracle of Apollo, located on the slope of Mt. Parnassus just north of the Gulf of Corinth. The giant serpent was supposed to have lived at the foot of Mt. Parnassus and to have eventually been killed by Apollo. The Latin scholar Gaius Julius Hyginus (64 BC–AD 17) elaborates:

> Apollo exacted vengeance for his mother. For he went to Parnassus and slew Python with his arrows. (Because of this deed he is called Pythian.) He put Python's bones in a cauldron, deposited them in his temple, and instituted funeral games for him which are called Pythian.[31]

Accordingly, the name is related to the site of Delphi *(Pythō),* the most important oracle in the classical Greek world, and is also associated with the putrid corpse of the serpent dragon stored in the cauldron (from the verb *pythein,* "to rot"). While the myth is well known, could it have any historical basis?

The historian Strabo (64 BC–AD 24) preserves a more ancient Greek historian, Ephorus' (400–330 BC), interpretation of the classical legend. While reading this account, it is essential to note that Ephorus had previously issued a complaint concerning those who mix mythology and history, a seeming inconsistency as he proceeds to do just that, as Strabo perplexingly comments:

> And that at this time Apollo, visiting the land, civilized the people by introducing cultivated fruits and cultured modes of life; and that when he set out from Athens to Delphi he

went by the road which the Athenians now take when they conduct the Pythias; and that when he arrived at the land of the Panopaeans he destroyed Tityus, a violent and lawless man who ruled there; and that the Parnassians joined him and informed him of another cruel man named Python and known as the Dragon, and that when Apollo shot at him with his arrows the Parnassians shouted "Hie Paean" to encourage him (the origin, Ephorus adds, of the singing of the Paean which has been handed down as a custom for armies just before the clash of battle); and that the tent of Python was burnt by the Delphians at that time, just as they still burn it to this day in remembrance of what took place at that time. But what could be more mythical than Apollo shooting with arrows and punishing Tityuses and Pythons, and travelling from Athens to Delphi and visiting the whole earth? But if Ephorus did not take these stories for myths, by what right did he call the mythological Themis a woman, and the mythological Dragon a human being—unless he wished to confound the two types, history and myth?[32]

This begs the question of whether Ephorus was demythologizing the Python legend or, more interestingly, if the serpent dragon actually took the form of a man. Reptilian shape shifters or something like the nachash? Etymologically, there appears a semantic development from the specific serpent dragon to an oracle inspiring spirit in general. A massive, tenth-century Byzantine encyclopedia of the ancient Mediterranean world known as the Suda defines the Python as a *daimonion mantikos*. The first word is the root of the modern term "demon," examined in detail in chapter 10, and the second, the Greek *mantikos*, is "prophetic, oracular, of or for a soothsayer," from the word "mantis," or "prophet"; literally, it means "one touched by divine madness."[33] In AD 60 or so when Luke wrote Acts, a person with "a spirit of the Python" was a demon-possessed person through whom a Python spirit spoke. This is corroborated by early writers like Pseudoclementine, Origen, and Jerome, who wrote of "Python-demons" inspiring pagan prophetic oracles.[34] Certainly, the practices of contemporary channelers and remote viewers do not significantly differ from the ancient world. Even so, perhaps it is pressing too hard to apply this text to clairvoyance across the board.

Conclusion

It might come as a surprise that some very conservative theologians allow for innate human abilities—along the lines of Watchman Nee's latent power of the soul—as an explanation for some forms of extra-sensory perception. A contemporary and friend of the celebrated evangelist D. L. Moody, Frederick Brotherton Meyer (1847–1929), was a Baptist pastor and evangelist during the heyday of the popular spiritualist movement of the nineteenth century. In a polemic against spiritualism, Meyer railed against the mediums, but conceded that psi abilities are not necessarily occult:

> Neither telepathy nor clairvoyance appears deserving of our censure. They are natural properties of the mind, and only reveal the wondrous faculties with which the Almighty has endowed us. If it is possible to send out circling waves of wireless telegraphy, which widen out as the rings from a stone cast into a pond Or lake, and can only be appreciated where the receiver and the transmitter are perfectly attuned,

so it is not difficult to believe that our minds are Constantly radiating motions and influences through our brains, which are perceived by sympathetic correspondence with other brains.[35]

Meyer allowed that telepathy and clairvoyance are human abilities endowed by the Creator. While dominant Western scientific consensus denies these abilities, the evidence for them is quite compelling and consistent with biblical revelation. While this may raise the hackles of a few critics, the biblical worldview has more in common with the findings of parapsychology than philosophical naturalism, and theologians have much to learn from the research. My conviction is that the Christian has nothing to fear from the pursuit of truth, even from unconventional sources.

Notes

1. Cindy Nuara, in personal email to author December 25, 2013.
2. Harvey J. Irwin and Caroline A. Watt, *An Introduction to Parapsychology*, 5th ed. (Jefferson, NC: McFarland, 2007) Kindle edition, 248–249.
3. George P. Hansen, *The Trickster and the Paranormal* (Bloomington, IN: Xlibris, 2001) Kindle edition, 7629–7632.
4. Dean Radin, *The Conscious Universe: The Scientific Truth of Psychic Phenomena*, (New York: HarperOne, 2009) 6.
5. Zoltan Vassy, "A Study of Telepathy by Classical Conditioning," *Journal of Parapsychology*, 68 (2004) 323–350.
6. Edwin C. May, Tamás Paulinyi, and Zoltán Vassy, "Anomalous Anticipatory Skin Conductance Response to Acoustic Stimuli: Experimental Results and Speculation about a Mechanism," *Journal of Alternative & Complementary Medicine*, 11, no. 4 (2005) 695–702.
7. Watchman Nee, *The Latent Power of the Soul* (Christian Literature Crusade, 1980) 20.
8. Ian Stevenson, *Telepathic Impressions* (Charlottesville, VA: University of Virginia, 1970) 2.
9. J. B. Rhine and J. G. Pratt, "Review of the Pearce-Pratt Distance Series of ESP Tests," *Journal of Parapsychology* 18 (1954):165–77.
10. Charles Edward and Mark Hansel, *ESP: A Scientific Evaluation* (New York: Scribner, 1966).
11. J. B. Rhine, *Extra-Sensory Perception* (1934) 73–74. Available online: http://www.sacred-texts.com/psi/esp/.
12. Sally Rhine Feather, "Hubert Pearce, an Extraordinary Case of Psychic Ability, by Warren Pearce and Sally Rhine Feather, Ph.D.," *Rhine Magazine*, October 8, 2013, http://rhinemagazine.wordpress. com/2013/10/08/hubert-pearce-an-extraordinary-case-of-psychic-

ability-by-warren-pearce-and-sally-rhine-feather-ph-d/ (accessed 01/24/13).

13. C. G. Jung, *The Practical Use of Dream Analysis* (1934) in *Dreams: From Volumes 4, 8, 12, and 16 of the Collected Works of C. G. Jung*, (Princeton, NJ: Princeton University, 2012) 47–48.

14. Alejandro Parra, *A Phenomenological Examination of Premonitions* (Buenos Aires, Argentina: Universidad Abierta Interamericana, 2013) 1.

15. John Palmer, "A Community Mail Survey of Psychic Experiences," *Journal for the American Society for Psychical Research*, 73 (July 1979) 228 (table 1).

16. Ward Hill Lamon, *Recollections of Abraham Lincoln 1847–1865* (Lincoln, NE: University of Nebraska Press, 1994) 116–117.

17. "Aberfan Disaster," http://www.alangeorge.co.uk/Images_A-H/Aberfan_Disaster.jpg.

18. J. C. Barker, "Premonitions of the Aberfan Disaster," *Journal of the Society for Psychical Research*, 44, 734 (December 1967) 171.

19. "Series F Second Erwin" scored eight hits and zero misses in the GESP trials in "Table 1 Summary of Maimonides Results."

20. Irvin Child, "Psychology and Anomalous Observations," *American Psychologist*, 40, 11 (November 1985) 1222.

21. Radin, 72.

22. S. J. Sherwood and C. A. Roe, "A Review of Dream ESP Studies Conducted Since the Maimonides Dream ESP Programme," *Journal of Consciousness Studies*, 10 (2003) 85–109.

23. Charles T. Tart, *The End of Materialism* (Oakland, CA: Fearless, 2012) Kindle edition, 3482–3491.

24. Russell Targ, *Limitless Mind* (Novato, CA: New World Library, 2004) 26.

25. Diane Hennacy Powell, *The ESP Enigma: The Scientific Case for*

Psychic Phenomena (New York: Bloomsbury, 2009) Kindle edition, 939–940.

26. Edwin C. May, "The American Institutes for Research Review of the Department of Defense's STAR GATE Program," *Journal of Parapsychology,* 60 (March 1996) 3–23.

27. Wil S. Hylton "The Gospel According to Jimmy," *GQ,* January 2005, http://www.gq.com/news-politics/newsmakers/200512/jimmy-carter-ted-kennedy-ufo-republicans?currentPage=2 (accessed 11/28/13).

28 F. J. A. Hort, *The Apocalypse of St. John* (London: Macmillan, 1908) 15.

29. Robert L. Thomas, *Revelation 1–7: An Exegetical Commentary* (Chicago: Moody, 1992) 338.

30. Johannes P. Louw and Eugene Albert Nida, *Greek-English Lexicon of the New Testament: Based on Semantic Domains* (New York: United Bible Societies, 1996) 444.

31. Hyginus, "Fabulae" Classical E Texts, http://www.theoi.com/Text/HyginusFabulae3.html#140, (accessed 05/02/13).

32. Strabo, ed., H. L. Jones, *The Geography of Strabo* (Medford, Cambridge MA: Harvard University Press; William Heinemann, 1924).

33. "Mantic," Online Etymology Dictionary, http://www.etymonline.com/index.php?term=mantic&allowed_in_frame=0 (accessed 05/02/13).

34. "Python," *Theological Dictionary of the New Testament,* vol. 6, eds. Gerhard Kittel, Geoffrey W. Bromiley, and Gerhard Friedrich (Grand Rapids, MI: Eerdmans, 1964) electronic edition, 920.

35. Frederick Brotherton Meyer, *The Modern Craze of Spiritualism* (Joseph Kreifels, 1919).

PRECOGNITION, THEOLOGY, AND WATCHMAN'S WARNING

> Satan is behind all these parapsychic researches. He is trying
> his best to use the latent energy of the soul to accomplish
> his goal. For this reason, all who develop their soul power
> cannot avoid being contacted and used by the evil spirit.
> —WATCHMAN NEE[1]

Do human beings have the power to "feel" the future? Is there
an unknown way that events in the future influence events in the
present? This chapter will sample some parapsychological literature that contains overwhelming evidence for the existence of
precognition. While human precognition seems limited, biblical
prophecy often spans hundreds of years, revealing a transcendent
source. Accordingly, this chapter examines precognition in light
of Christian theology and biblical revelation. Although humans
seem to vaguely anticipate short-term events, it will be suggested
that some phenomena suggest divine intervention or a source
from the spirit realm more than a human ability. Theism offers

unique solutions to parapsychological conundrums. It will be argued that an eternal first cause existing "all-timely" resolves the infinite regress problem in justifying time. This will be evidenced by specific fulfilled prophecy associated with the God of the Bible. Although often shunned by theologians, parapsychology offers unique evidences consistent with biblical theology. Finally, Watchman Nee's warning concerning an upsurge in psi abilities before the Tribulation will be examined.

History is full of examples of fulfilled prophecies and predictions, but they seldom win ardent skeptics to a Supernatural Worldview. They usually assert that the prophecy was written after the event or through some form of cheating. To be convincing, it is essential that the prediction precedes the fulfillment. Next, there needs to be a degree of specificity to the prediction that connects it to its fulfillment. It needs to be the sort of thing that is not likely to be guessed by chance. For example, to sit at an outdoor café and predict: "A person will walk around the corner in the next five minutes" is so general that it is trivial. One would reasonably expect this to occur merely by chance on a street corner. Better would be: "A lady wearing a red dress will walk around the corner in the next five minutes." The specificity of "a woman in a red dress" and a tight time range— "in the next five minutes"—narrows the field for a much more compelling example.

The chapter will also cite relevant laboratory work. Because spontaneous, real-world cases always introduce uncontrollable variables, they will always invite criticism from debunker-type skeptics. For example, given the illustration about predicting a red-clad woman walking around the corner, an enterprising psychic con artist could arrange for a confederate in a red dress to walk around at prearranged time. Of course, fraud happens, but debunkers can concoct a theory to explain away anything that seems paranormal. The laboratory data renders the debunking project much more challenging.

Precognition

In parapsychology, precognition (from the Latin *præ-*, "before," and *cognitio*, "acquiring knowledge") is a type of extrasensory perception in which some future event that cannot be deduced from normally known data is known in the present.[2] A premonition and a presentiment are information about the future that is perceived as a feeling or emotion.[3] Researcher J. Fraiser Nicol, a parapsychologist educated at Edinburgh University, Scotland, defined spontaneous precognition as *"knowledge* of a *future* event that could not be foretold from *(a)* the operation of the laws of nature or *(b)* inferred from *contemporary* information."[4] While history is replete with examples as far back as records exist, formal scientific study began in the nineteenth century.

The British Society for Psychical Research (SPR) pioneered the study of precognition as a scientific discipline. Most precognition cases are spontaneous (one-time) events that are extremely hard to subject to scientific scrutiny. They usually involve emotionally charged events like death and disaster, and for this reason they probably demonstrate a greater effect. One of the earliest recorded examples was investigated by Sir William Barrett, an Irish physicist and parapsychologist who helped found the SPR, who was, at the time, in the United States. He interviewed Army Capt. A. B. Mac-Gowan of the 12th U. S. Infantry concerning a precognitive experience while taking his boys to the theater in 1877. MacGowan's testimony reads:

In January, 1877, I was on leave of absence in Brooklyn, with my two boys, then on vacation from school. I promised the boys that I would take them to the theatre that night, and I engaged seats for us three. At the same time I had the opportunity to examine the interior of the theatre, and I went over it carefully, stage and all. These seats were engaged the previous day, but on the day of the proposed visit it seemed as if a voice within me was constantly saying, "Do not go to the theatre; take the boys back to school." I could not keep these words out of my mind; they grew stronger and stronger, and at noon I told my friends and the boys that we would not go to the theatre. My friends remonstrated with me, and said I was cruel to deprive the boys of a promised and unfamiliar pleasure to which they had looked forward, and I partly relented. But all the afternoon the words kept repeating themselves and impressing themselves upon me. That evening, less than an hour before the doors opened, I insisted on the boys going to New York with me, and spending the night at a hotel convenient to the railroad, by which we could start in the early morning. I felt ashamed of the feeling that impelled me to act thus, but there seemed no escape from it. That night the theatre was destroyed by fire with a loss of some 300 lives. Had I been present, from my previous examination of the building, I would certainly have taken my children over the stage, when the fire broke out, in order to escape by a private exit, and would just as certainly have been lost as were all those who trusted to it, for that passage, by an accident, could not be used. Had I gone my sister, who was present, but in another part of the house, would surely have been lost also, for we had arranged to go home together. As it was she left the building before the play finished and was at home when the fire began.

I have never had a presentiment before or since. I am not in the habit of changing my plans without good reasons, and on this occasion I did so only with the greatest reluctance. What was it that caused me, against my desire, to abandon the play after having secured the seats and carefully arranged for the pleasure?

August 27th, 1884. (Captain MacGowan stated to me that the voice was perfectly clear, "like someone talking inside me," it kept saying: "Take the boys home, take the boys home." And this from breakfast time till he took the boys away, shortly before the theatre opened. He never experienced anything like it before or since; never had any other hallucination. His sister has still got the tickets which he had bought and paid for. Three hundred and five people were burnt to death that night.—W. F. B.)[5]

The Brooklyn Theatre fire of December 5, 1876, killed three hundred and injured hundreds more. It is very well documented and easily verifiable.[6] Even more, MacGowan still possessed the unused theater tickets that he showed to Barrett to corroborate his story. It seems the mysterious voice prevented tragic circumstances, suggesting an odd synchronicity in that the evening play was *The Two Orphans* starring Harry S. Murdock and Kate Claxton.

A problem with using a case like this to suggest that humans have precognitive ability is that one cannot rule out agency by a third party. For instance, if one is a theist, it is natural to interpret the voice MacGowan heard as a divine warning from an angel (Psalm 34:7, 91:11). Like with Nick Skubish in chapter 1, it doesn't seem farfetched to suppose God had future plans for MacGowan and his sons. While parapsychologists might be quick to classify it as spontaneous precognition, MacGowan said he heard a voice. Investigators cannot rule out that he actually received a message from a third party of the spirit variety like an angel or even God Himself.

Precognition is interesting because it not only involves ESP, it implies something about the nature of time as well. Albert Einstein proved that time is not absolute and that it is actually different for different observers. For example, gravity dilates time, so it actually moves slower on the sun than on the earth. Even weirder is that acceleration affects time. This is where we get the thought experiment involving a space traveler who travels approaching light speed for one year and then returns to find that decades have passed on earth. In this way, one could return home thirty years older than a twin sibling, but given Einstein's general relativity, there doesn't seem to be a way to ever go back. It implies that time only flows in one direction. Recent evidence from parapsychology upsets the apple cart.

At a recent meeting of the Parapsychological Association in Viterbo, Italy, Jon Taylor presented a survey of the relevant literature, deriving some principles that seem to apply broadly.[7] First, it seems that precognition is the fundamental form of psychic functioning. In other words, it is a distinct perception rather than a general ability. Second, it is more likely to occur when the future event produces a strong emotional impact. Third, precognition is more likely to occur when the time interval is shorter. Fourth, belief in precognition has an impact on results in laboratory tests. Fifth, effects on random number generators (RNGs) may be due to precognition rather than psychokinesis: an idea that will be explored when we examine the Global Consciousness Project near the end of this chapter.

Laboratory Evidence: Presentiment

The presentiment work done by Dean Radin at the Institute of Noetic Sciences is probably some of the most compelling to date. He designed a computer screen interface that flashes emotionally charged images mixed with mundane ones and recorded people's emotional responses to a randomized series of pictures selected by computer using a random number generator from a pool of around seven hundred images. These images, from a standardized set used in psychological experiments, reflect different emotional states: calm, positive, negative (sometimes violent), and erotic. Thirty to forty trials are repeated in one sitting lasting around fifteen minutes. Obviously, the more graphic the image, the higher the expected response evokes.

To detect an emotional response, Radin measures skin-conductance level. When we are aroused, we always sweat a little, and the moisture increases electrical conductivity on the skin. This electrodermal activity is easily measured. Other indicators are heart rate, blood volume, blood oxygenation, respiration, pupil dilation, blink rate, and eye movement. A more advanced method using electroencephalography (EEG) and functional magnetic resonance imaging (FMRI) detection of brain activity has also been employed. These are all well accepted experimental indicators of arousal within psychology.

People consistently show an emotional response a few seconds or so *prior* to the evocative images. Even more interesting, the more intense images elicit a higher anticipatory response. Radin labels this the "presentiment effect," and believes the results to be evidence of retrocausation, another way of suggesting precognition, albeit reversed.

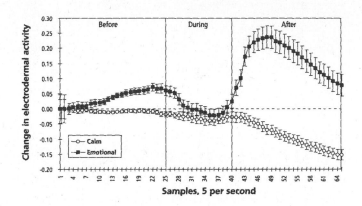

Notice arousal three seconds prior to evocative images.

The data on the graphic is from one set of experiments, but is a good general illustration of how the effect works. Consistently, people are aroused three seconds *before* an evocative image is displayed. Radin has conducted several different studies on it with consistent results. His overall odds ratio was 125,000 to 1 against chance in favor of a real, precognitive phenomenon.

Radin's results were replicated by Dick Bierman, a psychologist at the University of Amsterdam. He did a FMRI study on ten subjects that shows exactly what parts of the brain are firing in great detail. The amygdala (almond-shaped mass of gray matter associated with fear) activates consistently during the presentiment period and right-brain activity is enhanced. In women, he found a presentiment effect for both violent and ironic images, but with men, not too surprisingly, the effect was shown exclusively for the erotic content. His odds against change were fifty to one.[8] The presentiment data is the strongest to date that nearly all of us have some latent paranormal ability, an idea Watchman Nee arrived at from his reading of Genesis.

Probably the most controversial data in recent memory is the work released by parapsychologist Daryl Bem in 2012. The "feeling the future" experiments were designed to examine backward causation. Bem cleverly used well known areas of psychological research: 1) approach/avoidance; 2) effective priming; 3) habituation; and 4) facilitation of recall, but he cleverly reversed them so that the effect seemed to precede the cause. For example, Bem had people study vocabulary *after* being tested, and observed that the scores of those who studied *afterwards* improved with statistical significance. This suggests some sort of retrocausation, but reverse causation seems irrational because of our understanding that time only moves in one direction. As discussed above, our everyday assumptions might not reflect ultimate reality. Time might flow in more than one direction.

Precognition seems to work backwards and suggests retrocausation—the effect appears to precede the cause. While that sounds like nonsense, theoreticians speculate that if the time vector is reversed, the law of causation is maintained. In other words, it appears that way to us, but somehow, cause and effect are reversed in retrocognitive phenomenon.

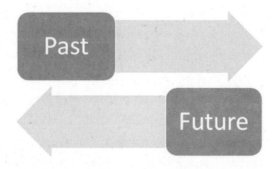

Top arrow represents normal causality, bottom arrow represents retrocausality.

The idea that time is not absolute is uncontroversial in science, but the idea that the human mind can access the future still is. It seems that if precognition is true, it implies that mind transcends space time. It means we are more than biological robots—and that is a great heresy in academia, but it should not be so in theology.

The methodology in this recent lab work is very strict, so it goes a long way toward establishing that something very interesting is going on. Dean Radin has a special web page presenting some of the latest scientific papers on psi available at: http://deanradin.com/evidence/evidence.htm. Even with overwhelmingly significant data, skeptics are inconsolable. For instance, a meta-analysis of twenty-six studies from 1978 to 2010 shows consistency across experimenters, laboratories, language groups, and detection methods. The analysis conceded the probability of obtaining the results by chance was $p < 2.7 \times 10^{-12}$ or 1 in 27,000,000,000,000. Even so, the authors qualified their assessment with this comment: "The cause of this anticipatory activity, which undoubtedly lies within the realm of natural physical processes (as opposed to supernatural or paranormal ones), remains to be determined."[9]

Radin replied:

The parenthetical portion of the last line of the abstract is rather peculiar. As I understand it, it was added by the authors due to the concerns of at least one referee, who was apparently worried that some may see this paper as supporting evidence for an anomaly that is far too similar to what people have reported through the ages as instances of precognition.[10]

In other words, the data is there, but the worldview is an obstacle. This research goes a long way toward demonstrating that Watchman

Nee was correct to believe that everyone has a little bit of psychic power—perhaps a remnant of mankind's pre-Fall status. It also has some very interesting implications for how we understand time.

Time Paradox

In his examination of precognition, parapsychologist John Randall addressed skeptics who assume that knowledge of the future is incompatible with science by charging, "In fact, orthodox science is very far from coherent."[11] Speaking to incompatibility between classical and quantum physics, he noted that no one has found a satisfying solution. First, he examined the Einsteinium block universe consisting of four-dimensional space time, but found that it ultimately implies determinism, which undermines rationality itself. He also noted that a major problem discovered by what he dubbed the "Cambridge School" of time philosophers based on their work at Cambridge University (J. M. E. McTaggart, C. D. Broad, and Adrian Dobbs) was that any second series of time designed to track a preceding one would, in turn, need a secondary timeline to track it, resulting in a vicious infinite regress.[12] While the Cambridge School used this to dismiss time as illusory, Randall found it wanting for obvious reasons: An infinite regress is irrational, and our experience of time appears to be real.

Of all the views surveyed by Randall, he was most favorable to the Christian theologian and theoretical physicist John Polkinghorne. While Polkinghorne's view allows that we live in a universe with a partially open future allowing free will for both ourselves and the Creator, he asserts the "free process defense" as an answer to why evil is allowed to exist in a theistic reality:

The well-known free will defence in relation to moral evil asserts that a world with a possibility of sinful people is better than one with perfectly programmed machines. The tale of human evil is such that one cannot make that assertion without a quiver, but I believe that it is true nevertheless. I have added to it the free-process defence, that a world allowed to make itself is better than a puppet theatre with a Cosmic Tyrant. I think that these two defences are opposite sides of the same coin, that our nature is inextricably linked with that of the physical world which has given us birth.[13]

Choices and ethical decisions presuppose a flow from past to future. Perhaps our experience of time in a series is designed by God to be instructional? I believe Polkinghorne's open view unnecessarily diminishes the sovereignty of God. It seems to me that classical theism solves the infinite regress derived by the Cambridge School by positing the Creator God as the ultimate temporal standard.

Omnitemporality

A British aeronautical engineer, John William Dunne, had a dream on May 7, 1902, about a catastrophic volcanic eruption. In the dream, he notified the French authorities that an eruption on a French-controlled island would result in four thousand casualties. The eruption of Mount Pelée in Martinique (a French Island near Puerto Rico) made the headlines of the newspaper the next day. However, Dunne saw that there were *forty* thousand deaths rather than *four* thousand. Intriguingly, he was off by a precise factor of ten. He hypothesized that he misread the future newspaper account of the tragedy in his precognitive dream. He wrote, "Clearly it must have come to my mind *because of the newspaper paragraph*."[14] He meant the one he saw *after* the dream. His dream had accessed details from his future reading of the paper.

Dunne began recording and studying his dreams in earnest. This led him to reevaluate the meaning and significance of dreams. He speculated that dreams are a blend of memories of past and future events. Of course, the most upsetting aspect of this idea is that it contradicts the accepted model of time as a series of events flowing only one way: into the future. This is our lower-case 'r' reality, but, what if, in REALITY, time is not like that at all? Dunne developed a multidimensional theory to account for time travel and published a widely read book in 1927 called *An Experiment with Time*.[15] Drawing upon Einstein and others, he concluded that the past, present, and future must all ultimately coexist. Dreams access this REALITY, but when we are awake, the limiting factor is human consciousness that arranges things in a past-to-future flow. We experience REALITY like a parade is viewed by the man on the street: float by float. In this way, temporal reality is relative to the observer.

A noted German theologian, Kurt E. Koch (1913–1987), was renowned as an expert on the occult and paranormal. A conservative Lutheran, he saw no inherent inconsistency between precognition, timelessness, and Christian theology. He explained:

One philosophical explanation of precognition would be the concept of timelessness. If past, present, and future all lie on one plane, there is no absolute before and after. In eternity, our concept of time ceases. Revelation 10:6 can be translated: "Time will be no more" (cf. AV [Authorized Version of KJV] "there should be time no longer").[16]

Because God transcends time, heaven is conceived to be atemporal. Thus, it can be argued that, while there are issues, there is no inherent contradiction between Dunn's theory of dream precognition and biblical theology. Although there is considerable debate concerning God's relationship to time, I suggest the term *omnitemporality*. "Omni" means "all" or "universal." "Temporal" means "timely," "related to," or "conditioned by" time. So "omnitemporality" means "all-timely." It is similar to timelessness, but more comprehensive.

Omnitemporality affirms that God is always in time in the same way He is thought to be everywhere according to omnipresence. According to the latter, God is not contained or restricted to any particular place, but rather He is present everywhere at once. In the same way, God is not contained or restricted to any particular time, but rather He is in every moment of time. The Bible implies this in passages like: "'I am the Alpha and the Omega,' says the Lord God, 'who is and who was and who is to come, the Almighty'"(Revelation 1:8). For the universe to be coherent, the buck must stop somewhere. An endless regress of causation is irrational. If anything exists at all, then something somewhere must be eternal and have the power of being within itself, properly known in theology as *aseity*.[17] Plato's term for this was the "unmoved mover."

The cosmological argument for the existence of God in chapter 2 goes a long way toward proving a transcendent Creator God. But how do we know the Bible is really a message from this transcendent Creator? The apocalyptic (revealed) word of biblical prophecy is the standard by which God asks seekers to examine Him: "For I am God, and there is no other; I am God, and there is none like me, declaring the end from the beginning and from ancient times things not yet done, saying, 'My counsel shall stand, and I will accomplish all my purpose'" (Isaiah 46:9–10). A minimal-facts argument from

Daniel's seventy-weeks prophecy (Daniel 9:24– 27) was offered in chapter 2, and this presentation will examine another lesser-known but extremely compelling example.

A Source Who Transcends Time

Biblical prophecies stand head and shoulders above the most compelling cases in the parapsychological literature. They span many generations, precluding mere human interest and implying a timeless source. Skeptics routinely charge that Bible prophecies were written after the fulfillment to give the impression of predictive prophecy. For example, liberal scholars always attempt to date the Gospels after the destruction of Jerusalem in AD 70 because Jesus predicted the Roman conquest (Mark 13:2; Matthew 24:2; Luke 19:44, 21:6). In fact, Luke includes uncanny detail, "But when you see Jerusalem surrounded by armies, then know that its desolation has come near" (Luke 21:20). Even though there are good reasons to believe it was written prior, critical scholars label it *vaticinia ex eventu* ("prophecy after the event"). New Testament scholar David Alan Black explains:

> It is difficult for them to accept such a prophecy prior to the event. However, we should be able to accept that Jesus had such prophetic gifts and that the statement in Luke 21:20 is a genuine prophecy of the future. If we accept this passage of Scripture as prophecy, we should have little difficulty in accepting an earlier date for the writing of Luke and Acts. At the conclusion of Acts Paul was still awaiting trial. Nero had not yet turned against the Christians as he did in a.d. 64. Luke wrote Acts at some time in the early sixties.[18]

Luke and Acts were written together, and Acts ends abruptly in the early AD sixties with Paul in Rome. It makes little sense that Luke would not have recorded the sacking of Jerusalem and capitalized on the apologetic value of Jesus' fulfilled prophecy for the first-century readers. Given the author's intent to persuade his contemporaries, there is no reason to presume a hermeneutic of suspicion. Astonishingly, the destruction of Jerusalem by the Romans was also predicted in one of the oldest books of the Torah.

Old Testament scholar Gleason Archer, from whom this discussion below was borrowed, states, "It is most significant that there are prophecies both in the Old Testament and the New Testament which were not fulfilled until a period after the composition of all 66 books of the Bible had been completed."[19] This is highly significant, because one can anchor the prediction's date to make a strong case for the supernatural. With the discovery of the Dead Sea Scrolls, it is now possible to prove that certain prophecies were written down hundreds of years prior to their fulfillment.

Leviticus 26:32–44, a book from the Torah estimated to date back to the fifteenth or thirteenth century BC, depending on when one dates the Exodus, contains a prediction that after the descendants of Abraham had taken possession of the Promised Land, they would fall into such apostasy that God would discipline them by bringing a conquering enemy to take them captive. This is well documented as the Babylonian Exile, which occurred between 605 and 536 BC. Leviticus 26:44 reads: "And in spite of this, when they are in the land of their enemies I will not reject them, and I will not abhor them to destroy them, to break my covenant with them, because I am Yahweh their God" (Leviticus 26:44). Indeed, the Israelites returned to the land when King Darius of Persia conquered the Babylonians and set them free. The prediction was very accurate, but hard to document due to the extreme antiquity of its fulfillment in the Babylonian captivity. No extant copy of Leviticus dates before 536 BC.

Interestingly, the same sort of warning appears again in Deuteronomy 28:36 with a different nuance: "Yahweh will bring you and your king whom you set up over you to a nation that you or your ancestors have not known, and there you will serve other gods of wood and stone" (Deuteronomy 28:36, LEB). A few lines down in the same chapter, we read: "Yahweh will raise up against you a nation from far off, from the end of the earth, attacking <u>as the eagle swoops down</u>, a nation <u>whose language you will not understand</u>" (Deuteronomy 28:49, LEB, underline added). It seems this passage predicts a second exile from Palestine, because, in this case, the invaders come from a region remote from the Middle East, speaking a non-Semitic language (as was the language of Babylon) and having an eagle for their military symbol. An *aquila*, or eagle, was the symbol used by ancient Rome as the standard of a Roman legion. A legionary known as an *aquilifer*, or eagle-bearer, carried this standard. Each legion carried one eagle. The prophetic eagle imagery strongly suggests the Roman invasion and sacking of Jerusalem by Titus Vespasian in AD 70—the only other time Jerusalem was sacked in history. In this case, one can easily prove the prophecy was written before the fulfillment.

Roman Aquila[20]

Dating from the second century BC and earlier, there are many fragments of Deuteronomy amongst the Dead Sea Scrolls preserved in the Qumran caves. Also, *Papyrus Rylands 458* is a copy of the Torah in a Greek version known as the Septuagint.[21] The manuscript has been assigned palaeographically to the second century BC and contains fragments of Leviticus chapter 28 quoted here. Because of this, no one can argue that this prophecy was written after its fulfillment in AD 70. Significant to the first-century association is verse 68: "And Yahweh shall bring you back to Egypt in ships by the route that I promised to you that 'You shall not see it again!' And you shall sell yourself there to your enemies as slaves and as female slaves, but there will not be a buyer" (Deuteronomy 28:68, LEB). Extrabiblical historians like Josephus, a first-century Jew working for the Romans, recorded that when Titus finally took Jerusalem, he sold the survivors in Alexandria, Egypt, the largest slave market in the Roman Empire. In *Wars of the Jews*, Josephus recorded, "He put them into bonds, and sent them to the Egyptian mines," and, "Now the number of those that were carried captive during this whole war was collected to be ninety-seven thousand."[22] But just as the prophecy detailed, the vast number of slaves glutted the market, and there were no bidders left to buy them. [23]All of the details of this prediction point so strongly to the events of AD 70 that it is reasonable to conclude the author of Deuteronomy (Moses) accurately recorded the future. Of course, Moses claimed God spoke the prophecy to him. Given its precision, this seems reasonable. The vast amount of time between prediction and fulfillment (more than 1,200 years) also suggests divine rather than human interest.

Interestingly, the Bible also records many precognitive dreams. A historical narrative dating back to Middle Kingdom of Egypt in the second millennium BC preserves the story of an Egyptian Pharaoh who had a dream of skinny cows that a Hebrew prisoner, Joseph, interpreted as future famine. This precognitive dream was said to be from God so that Joseph would be elevated to a position of authority (Genesis 41), and is what led Jacob and the patriarchs to Egypt. More interesting, God revealed the future to a hostile Pharaoh, and Joseph gained his favor by interpreting the dream. Another such example is King Nebuchadnezzar's dream in Daniel 2. In that a dream, a giant statue forecasted the great kingdoms of the world from Babylon to Persia to Greece to Rome, even detailing the split of the Roman Empire into the two legs: Byzantine and Western. God chose to reveal this prophecy through the dream of an arrogant, narcissistic, pagan king. Of course, it was interpreted by the Hebrew prophet Daniel, who did what none of the soothsayers and magicians could manage (Daniel 2:10). The point of interest is that, even in the Bible, God delivered real prophecies to unlikely, even hostile, agents like Pharaoh and Nebuchadnezzar.

Is Precognition Divinely Inspired?

If we accept that God exists omnitemporally and that dreams access this timeless state, it follows that God allows glimpses of the future for our benefit. Accordingly, when surveying the parapsychological literature replete with very well-documented cases of precognition, it seems fair to wonder if the source is ultimately divine. As shown in the section about telepathy, perhaps it was delivered by an angel. While many Christians recoil from all such discussion as an embrace of the occult, it seems wrongheaded to subscribe the preservation of life to malintent. Precognition seems to play a role in human survival.

W. E. Cox analyzed the number of tickets sold for twenty-eight passenger trains that crashed between 1950 and 1955. Interestingly,

the trains that crashed always had fewer people than similar trains on
the same day of the previous week. Taylor reports Cox's data:

> There is definite evidence that people can use intuition to
> avoid accidents. W. E. Cox (1956) carried out a survey of
> passenger statistics over a number of ears on the U.S. railway
> system. The survey shows that significantly fewer people
> travelled on trains at the time of accidents, compared with
> the number who travelled on comparable "control" days
> (e.g., 7 and 28 days) before the accidents.[24]

This sort of thing is probably much more common than any of
us imagine. How many times have you had a gut feeling not to take
a certain road or ride with an individual? How many times have you
decided to not participate in an activity that ended up turning bad?
While good judgment can explain some of it, it does not adequately
account for the premonitions and hunches that nearly everyone has
experienced. Because of the Western materialistic paradigm, not
enough research has been done. Nevertheless, I predict that as more
data comes in, this sort of thing will become well established. As a
general trend, people seem to instinctively avoid calamities.

This brings to mind the fact that there were fewer passengers
on the four planes involved in 9/11 than normally would have been
the case. Only 51 percent of the seats were occupied on American
Flight 11; 31 percent on United Flight 175; 20 percent on American
Flight 77; and 16 percent on United Flight 93. The aggregate occupancy was only 31 percent.[25] The average occupancy of flights in the
United States generally falls between 70 and 80 percent. Whereas
it has been suggested that this represents a government conspiracy,
it could be an example of human psi or the grace of God, or per-

haps *both*. As shown in the previous chapter, it is consistent with the Bible to believe in telepathic communication, especially from spirit entities.

Visions

This chapter has suggested that dreams induce an altered state of consciousness that accesses the all-timely—or omnitemporal—realm. As the Creator God's ultimate REALITY, He alone has full access to it and grants prophets dreams and visions according to His will. A vision differs from a dream in that it occurs in wakeful state. A Bible dictionary defines a vision as "experience in the life of a person whereby a special revelation from God was received."[26] Some visions are seen in the mind's eye, but others are described as prophetic oracles. A good example is the prophet Isaiah, who described Jesus of Nazareth in amazing detail centuries before He walked the earth. Many people have come to believe in the divine inspiration of Scripture because of this precognitive description:

> However, he was the one who lifted up our sicknesses,
> and he carried our pain,
> yet we ourselves assumed him stricken,
> struck down by God and afflicted.
> But he was pierced for our transgressions,
> crushed because of our iniquities;
> the chastisement for our peace was upon him,
> and by his wounds we were healed.
> All of us have wandered about like sheep;

we each have turned to his own way;
and Yahweh let fall on him
the iniquity of us all.[27]
(Isaiah 53:4–6, LEB)

Did Isaiah have a vision of Jesus dying on the cross for our sins? It would seem so. It is hard to imagine anyone but Jesus being pierced for our transgressions, and it is indisputable that this was written centuries prior, as the Great Isaiah Scroll found in Qumran has been paleographically dated to around 125 BC.[28] Liberal scholars date it during the Babylonian captivity in the 500 BC range. However, most conservative scholars agree the text was originally penned by Isaiah in the seventh century BC. All views precede Jesus's crucifixion by centuries. It also serves to draw an important distinction between biblical prophecy and psi. The vast time spans of the biblical prophecies stretch over many human lifetimes. This suggests they were really inspired by an eternal God whose interests transcend those of mortal humans.

The book of Daniel from which the minimal-facts argument was derived in chapter 2 is also instructive. The term "vision" in varying forms occurs approximately thirty times, denoting a mysterious revelation of future knowledge. Whether earthbound or through mystical ascension to heaven, apocalyptic visions serve as means to encourage God's people that the kingdom of God will certainly come. If one accepts the inspiration of Scripture, an apocalyptic vision should be interpreted as what the prophet actually saw, not merely a genre of symbolic literature. Daniel even expressed perplexity at some of his visions. Usually the symbolic images were interpreted to the visionary by an angel. In contrast, the parapsychological literature contains cases in which everyday folks are keyed in to a future event by what appears to be a visionary hallucination.

The Flixborough Disaster

The Flixborough disaster was an explosion at a chemical plant close to the village of Flixborough, England, on June 1, 1974. It killed twenty-eight people and seriously injured thirty-six. About five hours prior to the explosion, a woman living five miles away in Grimsby was watching television alone. She saw the word "Newsflash" on the screen accompanied by an announcement that an explosion had occurred at the Flixborough chemical plant about twenty miles away. The plant was not significant to her, and she didn't know anyone who worked there. However, when two friends (reliable witnesses) came over for lunch, she told them about the announcement, which they verified in subsequent interviews.[29] Just a few hours later, at 4.53 p.m., a massive explosion occurred when a bypass pipe ruptured unexpectedly. Of course, none of the television stations had actually broadcast a newsflash of any kind at noon. This case seems to involve some sort of visionary phenomenon.

Since there was no actual television report at noon, her perception of a television news report was the visionary medium by which the precognition was delivered. Could this vision have been telepathically sent by a divine agent? It is problematic to attribute this to God, because it did not save any lives—although it certainly could have. If only she had been able to prevent loss of life, it would have been heralded as a divinely inspired miracle. Even so, such a thing is entirely consistent. Even in the Bible, prophetic warnings were not heeded, as in the case of the prophets repeatedly warning Israel prior to invasion and Paul's choice to ignore a warning to proceed to Jerusalem, where he was arrested (Acts 21:10–14). It seems that precognitive warnings can change the future, but not necessarily so.

The point here is not to equate parapsychological cases to biblical prophecy and miracles, but rather to draw some parallels and explore Watchman Nee's hypothesis that all human beings have latent paranormal soul power. Radin's presentiment research suggests that nearly all of us have short-term premonitions on a regular basis whether we know it or not. Might this be the latent power of the soul? Nee's warning that men would be encouraged to develop this power for Satan's end-time purposes has recently come to pass.

Institute of Noetic Sciences (IONS) and Watchman Nee Revisited

Watchman Nee warned, "Satan is behind all these parapsychic researches. He is trying his best to use the latent energy of the soul to accomplish his goal. For this reason, all who develop their soul power cannot avoid being contacted and used by the evil spirit."[30] Unfortunately, even major, state-sponsored universities are working diligently toward those ends. The Division of Perceptual Studies (DOPS) at the University of Virginia's School of Medicine is actively studying ESP, poltergeists, near-death experiences, out-of-body experiences, and alleged memories of past lives.[31] Even more, Radford University in Virginia teaches a course on contacting the dead and provides a psychomanteum—a specially mirrored dark room—for doing so.[32] These research programs share a commitment to the oneist worldview.

IONS chief scientist, Dean Radin, in his books, *The Conscious Universe* and *Entangled Minds,* supports belief in Eastern spirituality and lends credence to modern forms of pantheistic monism. Evidence that the universe has an attribute like consciousness supports pantheism, and evidence that our minds connect at the quantum level lends credence to monism. In his latest book, *Supernormal: Science, Yoga, and the Evidence for Extraordinary Psychic Abilities*, Radin has virtually fulfilled Nee's prophecy. Many have connected pantheistic monism to quantum entanglement, and now Radin has taken the extra step to embrace yoga and Eastern meditation as means to developing these abilities. He weaves threads of yoga, meditation, and the data from Western psi experiments into a spiritual embroidery that not only seems to authenticate the existence of psi, but does so through the lens of monistic religion and suggests readers engage in Eastern meditation to develop psi ability.

According to a 2008 study, there are 15.8 million Americans who practice yoga, including many self-proclaimed Christians.[33] Twenty years ago, these numbers would have been unthinkable. Stefanie Syman, in her recent book, *The Subtle Body: The Story of Yoga in America,* wrote that yoga "is one of the first and most successful products of globalization, and it has augured a truly post-Christian, spiritually polyglot country."[34] Because there is compelling data that yoga and meditation do develop psi abilities,[35] this very well could be the fulfillment of Nee's end-time warning. Given the worldview implications of monism, it isn't too difficult to imagine that Satan could very well be behind it. Might psi abilities and deceptive miracles lead people to accept Eastern religion? In support, Nee cited Matthew 24:24; Revelation 13:2–5, 12–13; and 2 Thessalonians 2:8–10 as examples of deceptive Tribulation signs and wonders.

The Global Consciousness Project is also thought by many folks to be evidence for monism. Roger Nelson, as lead scientist working on the GCP, explains, "The Global Consciousness Project (GCP)… is, simply put, an effort to detect signs of a coalescing global consciousness."[36] They approvingly cite Teilhard de Chardin and present this work as evidence of the noosphere, a term coined to denote the numinous sphere of collective human thought. In my former work with coauthor Tom Horn on the book *Exo-Vaticana,* I explained Chardin's mystical Darwinian synthesis and its relation to the extraterrestrial disclosure movement, the technological singularity of transhumanism, and the popularization of pantheistic monism.[37] In making Chardin's vision a reality, the GCP has produced some tangible data that cannot be easily ignored.

The GCP is directed by Nelson, a psychologist who developed the organization from the controversial Princeton Engineering Anomalies Research Lab, from his home office in Princeton. The Institute of Noetic Sciences provides a logistical home for the GCP, which works through a series of computer-powered, random-number generators (RNG) placed at seventy different locations around the world. The project monitors the geographically distributed network of RNGs in order to identify anomalous outputs that correlate with widespread emotional responses to world events, or periods of focused attention by large numbers of people. The idea is that when major events cause the earth's people to come together, a form of psychokinesis causes anomalies of nonrandomness in the output of the RNGs. The GCP website explains:

When human consciousness becomes coherent and synchronized, the behavior of random systems may change. Quantum event based random number generators (RNGs) produce completely unpredictable sequences of zeroes and ones. But when a great event synchronizes the feelings of millions of people, our network of RNGs becomes subtly structured. The probability is less than one in a hundred million that the effect is due to chance. The evidence suggests an emerging noosphere, or the unifying field of consciousness described by sages in all cultures.[38]

Seemingly confirming the existence of the noosphere, the GCP has collected some interesting data. For example, during the 9/11 tragedy, they recorded highly significant deviations from expected randomness.[39] However, as mentioned previously, this is not necessarily due to psychokinesis acting on the RNGs. John Taylor proposed that "psi can be simplified to only two phenomena: precognition, which consists of a transfer of information from the brain in the future to the brain in the present; and telepathy, which consists of a transfer between two different brains."[40] Psychokinesis (PK) and precognition are often hard to distinguish in laboratory work. For example, if a test subject can predict dice throws, is it because PK is causing the dice to settle on the chosen numbers or is it because the subject had a precognition of how the dice would land? Similarly, Taylor suggests that rather than global consciousness, the GCP researchers could unconsciously be using precognition to sample the data at the right moment to pick up a specific, nonrandom sequence that appears to be PK-influenced data, but actually is an artifact of the selection process. While it is still a paranormal effect, it's local and doesn't imply that a global consciousness focusing on an event like 9/11 is responsible for the nonrandom results. The interesting data could just as well be due to the individual researcher's precognitions leading to a serendipitous sampling, negating the notion that there is such a thing as global consciousness. The evidence suggesting monism can be similarly challenged.

The GCP operates from a worldview that assumes nothing is external to nature. The data doesn't necessarily support monism, but the project interprets and presents it that way. However, one with a Supernatural Worldview can explain the same data in other terms. Perhaps the deviation from randomness demarks an outside influence? For instance, an external, nonhuman influence could be influencing the environment. Theistic philosophical arguments and evidences like answered prayer lend support. Thus, it seems fair to argue that the GCP assumes its conclusions by using this data to support global consciousness and oneism. It is circular reasoning. The same results could just as well be presented in support of the supernatural.

Of course, IONS is not the only organization with these goals. Others include the United Nations Spiritual Forum, the Parliament of the World's Religions, United Religions, the International Interfaith Center, the International Institute of Integral Human Sciences, the Peace Council, the Temple of Understanding, the World Conference on Religion and Peace, the World Congress of Faiths, the World Faiths Development Dialogue, the World Fellowship of Inter-Religious Dialogue, and the Millennium World Peace Summit of Religious and Spiritual Leaders. In truth, Oprah Winfrey may have done more to promote pagan spirituality than any one of them through her tremendous influence.

Psychiatrist Stanislav Grof, one of the founders of the field of transpersonal psychology, writes books on employing shamanistic techniques to awaken the divine within. Peter Jones comments:

Grof's workshops are no Sunday School. His shamanistic methods produce bizarre psychic phenomena, such as visions of divine light, encounters with various blissful and wrathful deities, communication with spirit guides and superhuman entities, contact with shamanic power animals, direct apprehension of universal symbols, and episodes of religious and creative inspiration.[41]

Grof was featured in the film *Entheogen: Awakening the Divine Within*, a 2007 documentary about rediscovering an enchanted cosmos in the modern world.[42] There are a plethora of gurus and shamans from the Westernized Deepak Chopra and Eckhart Tolle across the ocean to the Dalai Lama in Tibet promising to help the average person to develop psi powers and tune into the global consciousness. Today, *oneism* rules the religious landscape.

Conclusion

I am dismayed that pantheistic monism is the dominant religious idea associated with parapsychology, and this is probably due to a lack of thoughtful interaction by Christian theologians more than any inherent consistency with Eastern thought. Reality is stranger than commonly assumed, and Christians should be eager to acknowledge it. Precognition and psi are very consistent with the Supernatural Worldview presented in the Bible. From floating axe heads (2 Kings 6:6) to walking on water (Matthew 14:29), the Bible is chock full of weird anomalies and miracles.

Unfortunately, many Christian apologists tend to paint with broad brush strokes, labeling all paranormal phenomena to be occult. Even though the Bible is full of precognitive dreams, an academic apologetics source defines precognition as "the occult belief that one can possess the power to peer into the future."[43] While caution is in order, there is an all-too-common tendency to demonize what one does not understand. I find it intriguing that Watchman Nee anticipated parapsychological research, writing, "To the practitioners of this science these many miraculous phenomena are quite natural. To us believers they are even more natural. For we know they are merely the consequences of the releasing of the latent power of the soul."[44]

As Christians, we also need to recognize that, other than profession-als like Ingo Swann, most of the subjects in these cases and experi-ments are just regular folks. They are not practicing the occult arts or worshipping the devil, yet they seem to have accurate precognitive dreams and premonitions that anticipate the future. It seems that this sort of thing really is much more common than our Western sci-entific paradigm has led us to believe. It also lends credence to Nee's idea of latent soul power and, as a result, to his end-times warning.

Notes

1. Watchman Nee, *The Latent Power of the Soul* (Christian Literature Crusade, 1980) 22.
2. "Precognition," Glossary, Parapsychological Association, http://archived.parapsych.org/glossary_l_r.html#p (accessed 12/04/13).
3. Ibid., "Premonition."
4. J. Fraiser Nicol, "Apparent Spontaneous Precognition: A Historical Review," *Journal of Parapsychology,* vol. 1, no. 2 (Spring 1961) 26.
5. W. F. Barrett, "Premonition," *Journal of the Society for Psychical Research*, vol. 1, 1884–1885.
6. See: http://www.history.com/this-day-in-history/hundreds-die-in-brooklyn-theater-fire.
7. Jon Taylor (Spain), *The Nature of Precognition,* presented at the 2013 conference in Viterbo, Italy, http://www.parapsych.org/section/45/2013_convention.aspx.
8. Dean Radin, *The Conscious Universe: The Scientific Truth of Psychic Phenomena*, (New York: HarperOne, 2009) 123.
9. Meta-analysis of presentiment experiments published in *Frontiers in Perception Science* by Northwestern University neuroscientist Julia Mossbridge, University of Padova psychologist Patrizio Tressoldi, and University of California Irvine statistician Jessica Utts.
10. Dean Radin, "Presentiment Update," http://deanradin.blogspot.com/2012/10/presentiment-update.html.
11. John L. Randall, "Physics, Philosophy and Precognition: Some Reflections," *Journal of the Society for Psychical Research,* 63, 853 (10/98) 1.
12. Ibid., 3.
13. John Polkinghorne, *Belief in God in an Age of Science* (New Haven, CT: Yale Nota Bene, 2003) 14.

14. J. W. Dunn, *An Experiment With Time* (London: A. & C. Black, 1929) 37.

15. Free download here: https://archive.org/details/ AnExperimentWithTime.

16. Kurt E. Koch, *Occult ABC: Exposing Occult Practices and Ideologies* (Grand Rapids, MI: Kregel, 1978) Kindle edition, 625–626.

17. R. C. Sproul, *Not a Chance: The Myth of Chance in Modern Science and Cosmology* (Grand Rapids, MI: Baker, 1994) electronic edition, 181.

18. Thomas D. Lea and David Alan Black, *The New Testament: Its Background and Message*, 2nd ed. (Nashville, TN: Broadman & Holman, 2003) 284.

19. Gleason Leonard Archer, *A Survey of Old Testament Introduction*, 3rd. ed. (Chicago: Moody, 1998) 564.

20. "Roman Aquila.jpg," http://en.wikipedia.org/wiki/File:Roman_ aquila.jpg.

21. See http://www.katapi.org.uk/BibleMSS/P957.htm.

22. Flavius Josephus and William Whiston, *The Works of Josephus: Complete and Unabridged* (Peabody: Hendrickson, 1996, c1987) Wars 6.420.

23. Archer, 566.

24. W. E. Cox, "Precognition: An Analysis," II, *Journal of the American Society for Psychical Research,* 50, 99–109. Cited in Jon Taylor, "Memory and Precognition," *Journal of Scientific Exploration,* vol. 21, no. 3, 2007, 553–571.

25. "Flights," 9-11 Research, http://911research.wtc7.net/sept11/ analysis/bodycount.html#flights (accessed 12/04/13).

26. James Newell, "Vision," ed. Chad Brand, et al., *Holman Illustrated Bible Dictionary* (Nashville, TN: Holman, 2003) 1654.

27. W. Hall Harris III, Elliot Ritzema, Rick Brannan, Douglas Mangum,

John Dunham, Jeffrey A. Reimer, and Micah Wierenga, eds., *The Lexham English Bible* (Bellingham, WA: Lexham Press, 2012).

28. "The Great Isaiah Scroll," The Digital Dead Sea Scrolls, http://dss. collections.imj.org.il/isaiah (accessed 12/04/13).

29. K. M. T. Hearne, "An Ostensible Precognition of the 1974 Flixborough Disaster," *Journal of the Society for Psychical Research*, 51, 790 (1982) 210–13.

30. Nee, 22.

31. Jake Flanagin, "There Is a Paranormal Activity Lab at University of Virginia: Respected Scientists Are Lending Credibility to Parapsychological Research," *The Atlantic*, February 10, 2014, http://www.theatlantic.com/health/archive/2014/02/there-is-a-paranormal-activity-lab-at-university-of-virginia/283584/ (accessed 02/11/14).

32. Orlando Salinas, "Radford University Offering Independent Study Course in Communicating with the Dead," *WDBJ7*, October 17, 2012, http://articles.wdbj7.com/2012-10-17/radford-university_34532864 (accessed 02/11/14).

33. "Yoga Journal Releases 2008 'Yoga in America' Market Study," *Yogajournal*, http://www.yogajournal.com/advertise/press_releases/10 (accessed 01/30/14).

34. Stefanie Syman, *The Subtle Body: The Story of Yoga in America* (New York: Farrar, Straus and Giroux, 2010) 9.

35. Two recent studies connect Eastern meditation to an increase in psi ability: S. M. Roney-Dougal, J. Solfvin, J. Fox, "An Exploration of the Degree of Meditation Attainment in Relation to Psychic Awareness with Tibetan Buddhists," *Journal of Scientific Exploration*, 2008; 22(2):161–178; and S. M. Roney-Dougal, J. Solfvin, "Exploring the Relationship between Tibetan Meditation Attainment and Precognition," *Journal of Scientific Exploration*, 2011; 25(1):29–46.

36. Roger Nelson, "Gathering of Global Mind," Global Consciousness Project, http://noosphere.princeton.edu/story.html (accessed 01/30/14).

37. Chardin's system was explained in chapter 19 of Cris Putnam and Thomas Horn, *Exo-Vaticana: Petrus Romanus, Project L.u.c.i.f.e.r. and the Vatican's Astonishing Plan for the Arrival of an Alien Savior* (Crane, MO: Defender, 2013) 521.

38. Global Consciousness Project, http://noosphere.princeton.edu/index.html (accessed 1/30/14).

39. Global Consciousness Project, "Formal Analysis, September 11, 2001," http://noosphere.princeton.edu/911formal.html (accessed 01/30/14).

40. Jon Taylor, "About Me," Parapsychological Association, http://www.parapsych.org/users/jontaylor/profile.aspx (accessed 02/15/14).

41. Peter Jones, *One or Two: Seeing a World of Difference* (Escondido, CA: Main Entry Editions, 2010) Kindle edition, 2072–2079.

42. *Entheogen: Awakening the Divine Within*, IMDB, http://www.imdb.com/title/tt1549781/?ref_=nm_flmg_slf_5 (accessed 01/30/14).

43. Larry A. Nichols, George A. Mather, and Alvin J. Schmidt, *Encyclopedic Dictionary of Cults, Sects, and World Religions* (Grand Rapids, MI: Zondervan, 2006) 434.

44. Nee, 20.

APPARITIONS, HAUNTINGS, AND POLTERGEISTS

So long as the stories multiply in various lands, and so few are
positively explained away, it is bad method to ignore them.
—WILLIAM JAMES, PHILOSOPHER AND PSYCHOLOGIST[1]

Ghosts are most definitely real. At least, *some* ghosts are.
—JOHN WARWICK MONTGOMERY, LUTHERAN THEOLOGIAN[2]

It seems like everybody knows someone who has seen a ghost, and
nearly every family has a ghost story somewhere in its past. Looking as far back into antiquity as written records allow, ghost stories
have always been popular. The next chapter examines the ancient
material, but this one will define terms, present a few modern
cases, examine parapsychological hypotheses, and critique a few
popular Christian apologetic treatments. I believe my fellow apologists have made some cogent points, but all too often they paint
broad brushstrokes relegating all ghost accounts to nonsense or

demons. I contend that rigorous intellectual honesty demands a more open-minded evaluation than popular Christian treatments. But I am indebted to other scholars. The seminal apologist John Warwick Montgomery's book, *Powers and Principalities: A New Look at the World of the Occult* (1973), was an important formative work in my education. Montgomery, a towering figure in evidential apologetics and a bastion of Christian orthodoxy, did not believe everything called "occult" was either nonsense or demonic. His scholarly approach led me to agree it is unsound to assert that all ghosts are demonic. I think the reader might agree that the Skubish case presented in the beginning of the book strongly supports that contention. Christine Skubish's apparition saved her son Nick's life, and, as a result of that case's notoriety, Nick is now a confessing Christian. It strains credulity to assign those events to demons.

Apparitions

Apparitions seem to be disincarnate humans, and are what most people mean by the term "ghost." The term "apparition" comes from the Latin word *apparere* ("to appear"), and, in its most literal sense, means merely an appearance or "out-of-place" perception, as opposed to something real and tangible. In parapsychology, the term denotes "an abnormal or paranormal appearance or perception, which cannot be explained by any mundane objective cause."[3] If we disallow pathology, it is an objectively existing, disembodied, conscious intelligence. Consequently, a true apparition should exhibit interactive intellect and personality. Although there are reports of living persons seen outside of their bodies, most apparitions are believed to be deceased humans and are thought to support the survival hypothesis—the idea that death is transitional rather than absolute.

Paranormal investigators and parapsychologists are, for the most part, convinced that apparitions are real, but have varying hypotheses on what they might actually be. Classically, they are thought to be disembodied spirits of the dead, the actual life force (or soul) of a human being trapped in or visiting the physical world. Of course, naturalists assume they are hallucinations brought on by mental illness or intoxication. But those pseudo skeptics are seldom well versed in the evidence and typically employ circular reasoning from naturalistic presuppositions. More interesting theories postulate ghosts to be energy manifestations or even quantum entanglement, like the Quantum Theory of Ghosts developed by Dr. Max Bruin, which states that ghosts are "an impression upon the subatomic weave of the universe, created via strong emotion of a sentient observer."[4] While it sounds sophisticated, it seems impossible to prove.

According to popular mediums and paranormal television programs, ghosts are allegedly trapped in an in-between state, not able to "cross over" because they have "unfinished business." For example, Hans Holzer, the popular author of *The Supernatural*, believes that ghosts are trapped in a state between two parallel worlds: the one we experience in life and the "Other Side."[5] He denies any sort of ultimate justice or hell and asserts that everyone experiences heaven. Of course this is appealing, but it seems inherently unjust, with Adolf Hitler enjoying the same afterlife as my grandmother. The popular ghost theory is not very convincing, either. Think about it: Who dies with everything in perfect order? If unfinished business is to blame for not being able to cross over, it seems like everyone would be trapped. Even so, a transitory, immaterial state explains both subjective (mental) and objective (physical) aspects. In other words, a ghost may take on an observable physical appearance, like a figure of an old man or a floating orb of light, but also may be in the witnesses' mind through some form of telepathy. There are myriad interesting possibilities, and no one can be completely certain, but compelling evidence supports a real phenomenon. Complicating matters is the likelihood of multiple phenomena that are all vaguely attributed to ghosts. We aren't likely to sort it out this side of eternity.

In researching this book, I studied paranormal investigation with parapsychologist Loyd Auerbach at the Rhine Institute. Although I have never been ghost hunting, I'm registered as a trained investigator with the Office of Paranormal Investigations (OPI).[6] As a regular on *Coast to Coast AM,* various popular paranormal media, and serious scholarly scientific work, Auerbach has a sober, scientific approach. His website, The Paranormal Network, features more academic content than the typical ghost-hunter fare.[7] As a critic of the popular television shows, he bemoans their sloppy methodology and neglect of the clients' needs. Rather than sensationalizing, he genuinely tries to help folks resolve paranormal manifestations. While not a Christian, he definitely has a Supernatural Worldview. Even though we disagree on some very important issues like the existence of demons, I found him to be intellectually honest, rigorously scientific, and worthy of my respect. On the subject of apparitions, Auerbach's definition is one of the best:

> Apparitions are conscious, thinking beings existing after the death of their bodies and capable of some form of communication with the living. People who have seen ghosts have not reported them to be like white-sheeted, cloudy figures, nor are they green, hot-dog-gobbling figures. True apparitions are often more startling than what is in old ghost sto-

ries. Ghosts look like people, like you and me. Sometimes they may be a bit fuzzy around the edges—sort of an out-of-focus image, or a bit on the see-through side. Those are exceptions. In general, reported apparitions are in 3-D and look like solid citizens. Apparitions usually run from the tops of the head to just around the knees, with the feet missing.[8]

Think about the implications of the last sentence and you will get a feel for Auerbach's style of teaching. Why would the apparitions' feet be missing? The answer makes a lot of sense if you think like an archeologist. It is generally believed that ghosts from many centuries ago are "walking" on ancient streets a few feet under the ones existing today. If so, it makes sense that they appear cut off at the knees. In this way, Auerbach was an intriguing teacher who really made me think outside the box. For instance, he would ask us to consider things like: Where do ghosts' clothes come from? Is there a special mall for spirits? Do ghosts need reading glasses? How about their voices when they speak? Considering that when we speak, our lungs push air through our vocal chords that vibrate, producing sound waves in the air, how does a translucent, immaterial being speak? It seems the best answer is some sort of telepathy. So, what in the world adequately explains electronic voice phenomena (EVP)? It must be nonphysical, psychic energy somehow transferring to physical energy. In this way, this class of paranormal manifestations supports the psi hypothesis and the idea that mind is more fundamental than matter—an idea theologians should readily affirm.

Joshua P. Warren also presents a scientific assessment of ghosts. Authoring thirteen books on paranormal topics as well as making many network television appearances, he has amassed quite a lot of data.[9] While his endorsement of occult methods gives me pause, he has some well-reasoned ideas. Interestingly, he believes spirits reside in the mental realm, the same as that of consciousness, an idea consistent with Cartesian mind-body dualism. Concerning ghosts, Warren states, "They may primarily reside in the same dimension as that of our minds. Understanding how and why they manifest relies on both understanding that realm, and determining what conditions in our physical realm bring those two dimensions temporarily closer."[10] In an intriguing way, this invokes substance dualism, the philosophical relationship between mind and matter, and in particular the relationship between consciousness and the brain. Nearly all conservative, Bible-believing Christians adopt some form of substance dualism (body/soul), so this is an acceptable hypothesis as far as it goes. Please note that I am not endorsing the beliefs of any parapsychologist or paranormal researcher in total. The intent is to explore their thinking, offer analysis, and assess how it might confirm or deny a Supernatural Worldview. Other investigators think such apparitions are merely subjective.

Some parapsychologists define an apparition as "an experience—usually visual but sometimes in other sense-modalities—in which there appears to be present a person or animal (deceased or living) and even inanimate objects."[11] Accordingly, an alternative hypothesis is that such sightings are only hallucinations—a false perception. Simply put, one senses something that is not really "out there," but only in the mind, a purely subjective mental experience. A scientific definition is "a percept-like experience having the full force and impact of an actual perception."[12] Of course, a naturalistic worldview will dictate hallucination while a Supernatural Worldview will allow for either, depending on the evidence. Interestingly, there seems to be some truth to both, being that it could be manifested in the mental realm but at the same time experienced objectively—even by multiple witnesses.

There are three basic categories into which "ghost" phenomena can be categorized: apparitions, hauntings, and poltergeists. Theoretically, they are distinct, but real-world cases suggest they can overlap and manifest simultaneously. What makes an interesting study for parapsychologists is how they align with the main categories of psi phenomenon. Auerbach notes, "Interestingly, each can be connected to one of the main categories of parapsychology: hauntings to ESP, poltergeists to PK (psychokinesis), and apparitions to Survival (after death)."[13] While I don't always agree with Auerbach's conclusions, this chapter is a mere introduction to these complicated topics. Its objective is to present the evidence while challenging the easy dismissal and demonization coming from my Christian brothers and sisters. As with the Skubish case that introduced the book, there are some very compelling examples that for all intents and purposes exclude demonic causation. That all cases are nonsense is easily discredited.

Cases with more than one witness reporting the same apparition falsify the hallucination hypothesis. In the Skubish case, the highway patrolman said three people reported the apparition. People don't normally share hallucinations. If they do, then it suggests a very interesting paranormal cause! While the two hypotheses (paranormal, hallucination) seem contradictory, it is possible that the actual phenomenon could be a combination of both. In other words, there is an objective paranormal source causing the hallucination. For example, an apparition could be a telepathically induced hallucination. In fact, it is often unclear how to draw a distinction between the two possibilities. One of the best ways is to look for a veridical element in the perception. (Veridical simply means it has corroborative, real-world evidence.)

A famous apparition account with veridical evidence involved a traveling salesman known as "Mr. F. G." During a 1876 business trip, he was lodging in a St. Joseph, Missouri, hotel. At about noon, he was sitting and smoking a cigar while working on his sales orders. Peculiarly, he sensed he was not alone. When he looked up, seated at the table across from him, he saw his sister, a tragic cholera casualty who had died at the young of age eighteen back in 1867. While skeptics hastily label such a case as "grief-inspired hallucination," the astonishing details preserved in a letter dated January 11, 1888, to the Society for Psychical Research (SPR) suggest otherwise. Today, the letter is famously known as *The Case of the Scratch on the Cheek.* Mr. F. G. wrote:

I had not been thinking of my late sister, or in any manner reflecting on the past. The hour was high noon, and the sun was shining cheerfully into my room. While busily smoking a cigar, and writing out my orders, I suddenly became conscious that someone was sitting on my left, with one arm resting on the table. Quick as a flash I turned and distinctly saw the form of my dead sister, and for a brief second or so I looked her squarely in the face; and so sure was I that it was she, that I sprang forward in delight, calling her by name, and, as I did so, the apparition instantly vanished. Naturally I was startled and dumbfounded, almost doubting my senses; but the cigar in my mouth, and pen in hand, with the ink still moist on my letter, I satisfied myself I had not been dreaming and was wide awake. I was near enough to touch her, had it been a physical possibility, and noted her features, expression, and details of dress &c. She appeared as if alive. Her eyes looked kindly and perfectly natural into mine. Her skin was so life-like that I could see the glow or moisture on its surface, and, on the whole, there was no change in her appearance, otherwise than when alive.

Now comes the most remarkable *confirmation* of my statement, which cannot be doubted by those who know what I state actually occurred. This visitation, or whatever you may call it, so impressed me that I took the next train home, and in the presence of my parents and others I related what had occurred. My father, a man of rare good sense and very practical, was inclined to ridicule me, as he saw how earnestly I believed what I stated; but he, too, was amazed when later on I told them of a bright red line or *scratch* on the right-hand side of my sister's face, which I distinctly had seen. When I mentioned this, my mother rose trembling to her feet and nearly fainted away, and as soon as she sufficiently recovered her self-possession with tears streaming down her face, she exclaimed that I had indeed seen my sister, as no living mortal but herself was aware of that scratch, which she had accidentally made while doing some little act of kindness after my sister's death. She said she well remembered how pained she was to think she should have, unintentionally, marred the features of her dead daughter, and that unknown to all, how she had carefully obliterated all traces of the slight scratch with the aid of powder &c., and that she had never mentioned it to a human being, from that day to this. In proof, neither my father nor any of our family had detected it, and positively were unaware of the incident, yet I saw the scratch *as bright as if just made.* So strangely impressed was my mother that even after she had retired to rest, she got up and dressed, came to me and told me *she knew* at least that I had seen my sister. A few weeks later my mother died, happy in her belief she would rejoin her favourite daughter in a better world.[14]

In the SPR report, this account is followed up with a signed letter from the man's father, allegedly a prominent St. Louis business-
man, and is also signed by his brother confirming the conversation
with his mother before her death. The father confirmed the story,
writing:

DEAR F.,—Yours of 16th inst. is received. In reply to your
questions relating to your having seen our Annie, while at St.
Joseph, Mo., I will state that I well remember the statement
you made to family on your return home. I remember your
stating how she looked in ordinary home dress, and particularly about the scratch (or red spot) on her face, which
you could not account for, but which was fully explained by
your mother. The spot was made while adjusting something
about her head while in the casket, and covered with powder. All who heard you relate the phenomenal sight thought
it was true. You well know how sceptical I am about things
which reason cannot explain.

Affectionately,

(Signed) H. G. (father).

I was present at the time and indorse the above.

(Signed) K. G. (brother). [15]

Now that is a good ghost story—almost *too good*. The literary
quality of the story is on par with masterpieces by Edgar Allen Poe
or Charles Dickens. Taken at face value, it seems to confirm life after
death, that ghosts really are surviving human spirits. More interesting, the subsequent death of the mother suggests that this apparition
had a purpose. The mother was the only person who could confirm

the scratch on the cheek, suggesting that the ghost was aware of the mother's soon demise. Because only God could possess such information, this could reveal His infinite grace. Of course, we have no way to verify that the persons writing the letters are really telling the truth, albeit the author of the article, Myers, was a reputable psychologist who founded the SPR. If one were in a position to know, the veridical nature of the mother's testimony would strongly favor this as an authentic apparition rather than a hallucination. However, with this sort of anecdotal evidence, fair-minded skepticism is in order.

Hauntings

Most folks assume that "haunting" refers to what an apparition who frequents a location is doing. One might say, "A spooky ghost is *haunting* the old museum." However, in modern research, the word "haunting" has come to denote a distinct type of paranormal phenomenon. In contrast to intelligent apparitions, hauntings display neither personality nor intelligence and seem to be like a recording or an imprint of an emotionally charged past event. I have often wondered if Abel's blood crying to God from the ground (Genesis 4:1) is a reference to the haunting phenomenon and not a simple metaphor. Hauntings are distinguished from proper apparitions by communication. If an entity is responsive to questions, then it is an apparition, but a lack of interaction is not conclusive either way. Often, hauntings are described as repetitive loops of events, and careful observation will reveal the repetition. For example, spectral soldiers have been seen charging up the same hill at Gettysburg over and over. The battle charge plays in a loop and has continued to be reported for decades. Because they are oblivious to human witnesses, true hauntings appear to be as harmless as video recordings. Of the three, the scariest and most dangerous are poltergeists.

Poltergeists

The term "poltergeist" comes from the German words *poltern* ("to make sound") and *geist* ("spirit") and literally translates as, "noisy ghost." They appear often in cultural folklore as troublesome spirits who haunt a particular person instead of a specific location. Classically, the term has been defined as a type of haunting associated with physical disturbances such as loud noises, violence, and destruction of property. Poltergeists seem to be capable of scratching, pinching, biting, hitting, and tripping people. Accordingly, they should be classified as an extremely dangerous and unpredictable paranormal phenomenon. They are nothing to play around with.

From a parapsychological point of view, the term has come to denote something completely different from a human ghost. As above, the distinguishing factors are the physical phenomena, like opening and closing doors, unexplained movement of objects, levitation of objects, unexplained knocks and noises, the appearance and/or disappearance of objects, unusual performance with electrical appliances, and unexplained temperature changes, as well as combinations of all the above. Parapsychologists typically posit poltergeist activity to be caused by the subconscious mind of a living agent. Normally, the agent is someone experiencing psychological stress or emotional trauma. This was labeled "recurrent spontaneous psychokinesis," or RSPK, by the famed parapsychologist Dr. William G. Roll, who specialized in these cases, writing a seminal book,

The Poltergeist, in 1972. A giant in the field, Roll studied at Oxford University, where he did parapsychology research for eight years. He wrote his master's thesis on "Theory and Experiment in Psychical Research" and served as president of the Oxford University Society for Psychical Research. After moving to America, he often appeared on the television show *Unsolved Mysteries* as an expert on apparitions, poltergeists, and hauntings.

The RSPK hypothesis asserts that people, often adolescents, who generally reside in the affected environment are manifesting psychokinetic effects as way of venting emotional angst. Through some unknown mechanism, the subconscious wreaks havoc on the environment by moving objects, slamming doors, and making noises, giving the illusory impression of a noisy ghost. Auerbach amusingly quips, "Think of the poltergeist scenario as a sort of telekinetic temper tantrum."[16] While RSPK has explanatory scope for much of the phenomenon, I think it is open to challenge. I believe it is only partially correct. It could be some of both, as in a spirit using a human's psychic energy. In fact, these cases powerfully support Watchman Nee's hypothesis that malevolent spirits harness human psychic energy to fuel their paranormal manifestations. Recalling Nee's prophetic analysis:

> Because of the development of the soul's latent force, wonders are increasing nowadays. Of these wonders, many are highly supernatural and miraculous. Yet all these are only the manifestations of the latent power of the soul. Though I am no prophet, I have read books on prophecy. I learn that hereafter soul's latent power will have greater manifestations. For in the last days the enemy will seize upon man's psychic force to fulfill his work. If he succeeds in seizing this power, he will be able to do great wonders.[17]

If Nee is correct, one can readily see how a scientifically trained parapsychologist would conclude that such physical effects were only from a human agent when, in reality, a surreptitious spirit being is exploiting the person's psychic force to promote fear and chaos. This idea will be developed in chapter 10, where an example of poltergeist phenomenon suggests demonic causation. For now, let's turn to modern ghost cases that don't appear to be malevolent, but rather benevolent.

Godly Ghosts?

Clive Staples Lewis (1898–1963), popularly known as C. S. Lewis, was an academic, novelist, poet, medievalist, literary critic, theologian, and Christian apologist. Holding teaching positions at Oxford and Cambridge, he is best known for his fictional writings: *The Screwtape Letters*, *The Chronicles of Narnia*, and *The Space Trilogy*, and for his nonfiction Christian apologetics, such as *Mere Christianity*, *Miracles*, and *The Problem of Pain*. He was single for most of his life—that is, other than his brief marriage to Joy Davidman Gresham, an American writer of Jewish ancestry who converted from atheism to Christianity. Very soon after they married, she was diagnosed with terminal bone cancer. The couple enjoyed a brief romantic respite in Greece during a remission, but Joy died a few years later, in 1960. Devastated, Lewis dealt with his grief through writing.

Lewis worked through his heartache and honored his wife in *A Grief Observed*. It is written in such raw and passionate prose that the publisher originally released it under the pseudonym N. W. Clerk. Only after Lewis' demise was the true author revealed. He transparently discussed his loss of faith and struggle to regain it. Many Christians were shocked that he accused God of being a "Cosmic Sadist."[18] Even more readers were incredulous that he believed his deceased wife visited him as a disincarnate intelligence or pure mind—for all intents and purposes, a ghost. Lewis referred to her as "H" for Helen:

> I said, several notebooks ago, that even if I got what seemed like an assurance of H.'s presence, I wouldn't believe it. Easier said than done. Even now, though, I won't treat anything of that sort as evidence. It's the quality of last night's experience—not what it proves but what it was—that makes it worth putting down. It was quite incredibly unemotional. Just the impression of her mind momentarily facing my own. Mind, not "soul" as we tend to think of soul. Certainly the reverse of what is called "soulful." Not at all like a rapturous reunion of lovers. Much more like getting a telephone call or a wire from her about some practical arrangement. Not that there was any "message"—just intelligence and attention. No sense of joy or sorrow. No love even, in our ordinary sense. No un-love. I had never in any mood imagined the dead as being so—well, so business-like. Yet there was an extreme and cheerful intimacy. An intimacy that had not passed through the senses or the emotions at all.[19]

What astonished Lewis was that the sense of her presence did not occur in an emotionally charged state, but in a detached, clinical manner. That fact should give serious pause to one who would hastily ascribe his experience to extreme bereavement. Thinking critically as ever, Lewis soberly considered the hypothesis that she was a product of his unconscious mind:

If this was a throw-up from my unconscious, then my unconscious must be a far more interesting region than the depth psychologists have led me to expect. For one thing, it is apparently much less primitive than my consciousness.[20]

Interestingly, this is a common theme coming from near-death experiencers as well; they describe what they see and feel as "ultra-vivid" and as "more real than real." Lewis described his wife's presence as a "pure intelligence," characterizing it as:

Above all, solid. Utterly reliable. Firm. There is no nonsense about the dead. When I say "intellect," I include will. Attention is an act of will. Intelligence in action is will *par excellence*. What seemed to meet me was full of resolution.[21]

This event reinvigorated Lewis' faith and inspired to him get on with life. Given his scrupulous transparency throughout the book, it seems unfair to write the visitation off as a figment of his grief-worn imagination. Surely, Bible believers don't prefer a naturalistic explanation? Can Christian theology accommodate this disembodied intelligence at face value? I not only believe it can but, even more, if we are to be taken seriously by the culture at large, we must offer coherent answers from a Supernatural Worldview.

Two years after his wife's death, Lewis began to have heart problems. Deteriorating, he fell into a long coma. Interestingly, his wife had promised on her deathbed to come for him upon his own demise:

Once very near the end I said, "If you can—if it is allowed—come to me when I too am on my death bed." "Allowed!"

she said. "Heaven would have a job to hold me; and as for Hell, I'd break it into bits." She knew she was speaking a kind of mythological language, with even an element of comedy in it. There was a twinkle as well as a tear in her eye. But there was no myth and no joke about the will, deeper than any feeling, that flashed through her.

Was Lewis with Joy while in the coma? It is impossible to say, but he shocked his doctors by unexpectedly snapping out of the coma. He quipped, "I was unexpectedly revived from a long coma and perhaps the almost continuous prayers of my friends did it—but it would have been a luxuriously easy passage and one almost regrets having the door shut in one's face."[22] After the brief respite, Lewis died one week before his sixty-fifth birthday, on Friday, November 22, 1963—the same day on which John F. Kennedy was assassinated and Aldous Huxley died. It is not known if Joy kept her promise to meet him upon his demise, but I expect so. Interestingly, Lewis made an apparitional appearance of his own.

Apparently, Lewis himself paid a postmortem call on a depressed colleague in need. His friend, John Bertram Phillips, or J. B. Phillips, was an English Bible scholar, translator, author, and clergyman. While working as a minister for the Church of the Good Shepherd in London during the Second World War, he noticed that the youth did not well understand the King James Version. In response, he took on the arduous endeavor of translating the New Testament into modern English from the original Greek text. However, without a ghostly visitation it never would have been accomplished.

In his book, *The Newborn Christian*, Phillips stated that C. S. Lewis' apparition appeared to him in a moment of great need. It seems Phillips was prone to depression and had all but given up his ambitious translation project. Out of nowhere, Lewis bodily appeared in his home unfettered by the surely locked doors. Phillips wrote:

> A few days after [Lewis'] death, while I was watching televi-
> sion, he "appeared" sitting in a chair within a few feet of me.
> He was ruddier in complexion than ever, grinning all over
> his face and, as the old-fashioned saying has it, positively
> glowing with health. The interesting thing to me was that
> I had not been thinking about him at all.... He was just
> there—"large as life and twice as natural."[23]

Lewis made one brief statement—"J. B., it's not as hard as you think!"[24]—and vanished. The after-death visitation not only con-firmed that death was not the end for Phillips, it encouraged his ministry.

At the time of the initial visit, Phillips was unaware of Lewis' death because the assassination of JFK had dominated the news. Subsequently, he confirmed that Lewis had passed the previous day, but his grief was consumed by the wonderment concerning his col-league's appearance. Lewis appeared once more two weeks later and repeated the same message. As a result, hope became assurance. *It wasn't as hard as he thought.* Phillips' depression waned, allowing him to complete the Bible translation for which he is still famous: *The New Testament in Modern English.*[25] Here again, we have a ghost story from an influential Christian that was not only harmless, it was redemptive. This is hard to reconcile with many Christian authors' generalizations about apparitions. Let's turn to another modern account involving a pastor.

Kurt E. Koch (1913–1987), noted German theologian, minister, and evangelist, received a doctor of theology degree at Tubingen

University and specialized in ministry to those involved in the occult. Authoring over one hundred books, he is a renowned expert on the occult and paranormal, and he specialized in counseling those suffering from demonic affliction. His ministry took him to more than sixty-five countries on five continents. He characteristically took a hard line against spiritualist practices, but conceded, "There are genuine ghosts."[26] Of course, he cited the biblical examples like 1 Samuel 28 addressed in the next chapter, but he also recounted contemporary accounts.

Koch defined a ghost as a "shadowy reappearance of a deceased person in the place where he formerly lived."[27] His many works on paranormal phenomena cataloged hundreds of cases, most consisting of testimony from other pastors and missionaries. Here is an example that, taken at face value, seriously challenges the prevailing evangelical consensus about apparitions:

A Protestant minister had a remarkable experience, while he was preparing his sermon, one Saturday evening. Suddenly the door opened and his deceased predecessor, whom he was able to recognize from a photograph, came into his study. The pastor was startled by this extraordinary visitation and did not know if he was suffering from a hallucination, or if the vision was something real. The dead pastor spoke to him. He complained that he could find no rest in the world beyond. The pastor asked him whether he could help him in some way. The ghost replied that the reason he could not find rest was because of a sordid matter concerning a bequest. He would not be free from his torment until the wrong had been put right. He told his amazed colleague that, together with his church council, he had made an unjust decision about a will. As a result, several of his church members had lost an inheritance they should have received from America. The ghost asked the pastor to come with him to take the relevant file from the filing cabinet. The ghost led the way to the record office and found the relevant file among a pile of papers. Taking the papers, the ghost explained the circumstances to the pastor. Then the phantom disappeared. The pastor immediately took steps to put the matter right, and went to visit the elderly former members of the church council. A meeting of the present council was called, and the decision in question was rescinded and the matter put right. From that time on, the ghost never again appeared in the minister's house, although for years strange footsteps and other phenomena had been observed there.

I realize this story raises difficult theological problems. Is it really possible at all that a man who is dead can come back from the life beyond to put right something he has done wrong here? Our understanding of the Bible's teaching would normally make us say *no*. On the other hand, this remarkable experience allowed a family to gain their rightful inheritance.[28]

These accounts challenge the most common Christian answer to the question of human ghosts. Along with those from Lewis and Phillips, this pastor's account scarcely makes sense if one believes that human apparitions are impossible. It is a mistake to deny their reality. Koch spent a great deal of time as a missionary in Africa. In a book about his experience with the Zulus he wrote:

Poltergeists or ghosts are seen on many continents, but such sightings are often judged differently. Rationalists, with their limited field of vision, ridicule such happenings as being unreal. Others regard it all as a joke. Non-Christian psychiatrists see the source of such occurrences as only being in the mind of mentally disturbed people, having no real existence in the world. All these explanations have little to do with such phenomena. There is no doubt that such spirits actually do exist objectively, and are bound to persons and places, as well as in the deluded ideas of paranoid people.[29]

Koch did not start out a wide-eyed believer in such things, but became convinced by hard evidence when he came face to face with case after case during his missionary work. There really does seem to be a remarkable difference between the West and the majority world when it comes to supernatural phenomena. Once-skeptical missionaries have radical worldview shifts after leaving their home countries. As the West is becoming increasingly pagan—an idea well documented by Peter Jones[30] and James Herrick[31]—this will need to be rethought.

Critiquing the Demonic Imposter Hypothesis

Most often, Christian authors either write off ghosts as nonsense or they assert that demons are masquerading as humans. A representative example comes from the book *The Truth behind Ghosts, Mediums, and Psychic Phenomena* by Christian apologist Dr. Ron Rhodes:

One might get the idea that I dismiss all alleged paranormal encounters as either fraudulent, a misinterpretation of the data, sheer subjectivism ("I feel like I'm being watched"), or the result of awakening from deep sleep. This is not the case. Though alleged ghost encounters can be explained in this way, people sometimes genuinely encounter a spirit entity— though not a dead human. Some people encounter demonic spirits who may mimic dead people in order to deceive the living (see 1 John 4:1; 1 Timothy 4:1–3).[32]

Of course, Rhodes may indeed be correct for some cases, but his blanket statement goes too far. The first cited proof text admonishes one to test the spirits to see if they are of God. The test is easy enough: "By this you know the Spirit of God: every spirit that confesses that Jesus Christ has come in the flesh is from God" (1 John 4:2). While I do not doubt that demons can impersonate the deceased, the prescription assumes that they may be tested to determine their status (godly, ungodly). Why bother to test if the answer is already an absolute given? That alone falsifies such a sweeping generalization.

More so, the above cases involving C. S. Lewis and Koch's pastor friend apparently pass the test. Surely the apologist would not have us conclude that demons are interested in justice concerning a rightful inheritance? Or that J. B. Phillips was demonically inspired to make the New Testament more accessible to young people? Or that Lewis' faith was encouraged by a demon impersonating his wife? The second proof text begs the question in that it doesn't apply unless one already assumes the supernatural apparitions are demonic. I am extremely concerned that Christians are offering unsatisfying (and sometimes false) answers to a world hungry for truth.

Apparitions are commonly believed to be deceased human beings who are trapped at a certain location or unable to cross over due to some sort of unfinished business. There seems to be some sort of intense emotional connection, and sometimes the spirit is alleged to be unaware of his or her death. This "soul-in-transition" belief presents interesting challenges to the biblical model. However, there is no reason to accept popular ghost theory. One is not required to accept that all ghosts are trapped spirits. There do seem to be apparitions that appear briefly by divine appointment. While the stock evangelical answer has been that ghosts are demonic impersonations, this inference is based more on incredulity than biblical theology.

In *Seeing Ghosts through God's Eyes,* Mark Hunnemann defines a ghost as "a disembodied spirit who is trapped in our dimension."[33] Hunnemann offers an excellent critique of popular ghost theory as seen on paranormal television shows like *Ghost Hunters.*

I can readily agree with Hunnemann's argument that we don't see trapped human souls in Scripture:

> Not once, from the dawn of human history with Adam and Eve, to Job and Abraham, and ultimately with the close of the New Testament, is there a single biblical affirmation of a soul that is trapped in our dimension. That bears repeating: if we define ghosts as human souls that are trapped on Earth, then ghosts are never affirmed as existing in either the Old or New Testament! That is a bold claim, and one that would sink the ghost ship if you put any stock in the Bible as being the inspired Word of God.[34]

However, this argument from silence is not terribly compelling. The Bible doesn't mention chimpanzees, but we know they exist. The biggest problem for this way of reasoning is that Scripture never teaches that demons pretend to be human spirits, either.

Hunnemann concludes that all ghosts are necessarily demons. He offers this rationale, "Given the sheer quantity of ghosts that are said to exist in America, many Christians would have to be ghosts."[35] From this assumption, he argues, "It necessarily implies that our

Father is an absentee Parent, who thus is breaking His promise never to leave us or forsake us: The Trinity dwells within believers through the agency of the Holy Spirit (John 14:23, 26)."[36] While I agree that God is not going to abandon a blood-bought believer in Christ, Hunnemann neglects to handle degenerate people involved in violent and evil supernaturalism. He presumes that for any of the apparitions to be human, it requires including Christians—an idea hardly in evidence. This suggests several questions.

First, why should we accept that the number of ghosts requires Christian inclusion? He does not provide the number of paranormal apparitions or its source. His assessment seems to be derived from watching paranormal television shows. Because those shows are in the entertainment business, it is safe to assume that all is not as it appears. Parapsychologists like my instructor Loyd Auerbach bemoan their methodology and don't take them seriously. Second, why suppose an "all-or-nothing" state of affairs? Some apparitions could be damned humans and others demons (fallen angels)...or the term "demon" might actually include humans. Third, the history of the United States reaches farther back into antiquity than commonly assumed. Did Hunnemann consider the millions of pre-Americans who died here? The Puritan theologian Cotton Mather wrote that "a People of God settled in those, which were once the Devil's Territories."[37] The ritual burial mounds in the Northeast led John Keel in *The Mothman Prophecies* and Peter Levenda in *Sinister Forces* (Book One) to conclude those areas are haunted by a variety of entities. I agree with a great deal of *Seeing Ghosts through God's Eyes,* but this argument from numbers is not compelling. Unfortunately, much of the book rests on it.

Human apparitions are messy to explain, so it is easy to proclaim that everyone goes instantly to either heaven or hell and write off the rest as demonic. However, not only does the biblical data not demand this notion, but some passages count strongly against it—and there are compelling counterexamples throughout history from reliable Christian witnesses. Although the Bible teaches that those who follow Jesus go to heaven (2 Corinthians 5:8; Philippians 1:23), it doesn't say much about the intermediate state of the unbeliever. In case I am misunderstood, I am not questioning whether God decides one's eternal destiny, but the claimed knowledge of the timing. Scripture teaches, "And as it is appointed unto men once to die, but after this the judgment" (Hebrews 9:27). However, "after" is not very specific. Does this mean that everyone *immediately* enters heaven or hell?

Scripture teaches that the dead will rise from their graves to be judged by Jesus Christ. In the Old Testament, the preacher of Ecclesiastes forecasted the ultimate day of reckoning: "I said in my heart, God will judge the righteous and the wicked, for there is a time for every matter and for every work" (Ecclesiastes 3:17). Furthermore, Isaiah 26:19 predicts the resurrection of the dead, and Daniel 12:2 places final judgment *after* the bodily resurrection. In the New Testament, many passages indicate this appointed time of judgment (Matthew 7:23; Hebrews 10:27; Philippians 2:11), but the final verdict occurs at the Great White Throne Judgment after Jesus' return (Revelation 20:11–15). Paul also indicates that the appointed time is post-Second Coming: "Therefore judge nothing before the time, until the Lord come, who both will bring to light the hidden things of darkness, and will make manifest the counsels of the hearts: and then shall every man have praise of God" (1 Corinthians 4:5, underline added). Even the demons cast out by Jesus were aware of this appointed time: "And, behold, they [the demons] cried out, saying, What have we to do with thee, Jesus, thou Son of God? art thou come hither to torment us before the time?" (Matthew 8:29, underline added). This implies that the demons enjoy a degree of freedom until the appointed time.

What about the human dead who reject the offer of salvation

given by Jesus? Many English translations oversimplify the biblical data. Scripture does not indicate the fastidious schedule that is often presumed.

Examining the ProofTexts

In most evangelical ghost apologetics, the instantaneous postmortem timetable is simply assumed without argument. However, historically, the intermediate state was vigorously debated by those who believe in soul sleep. Psychopannychy is the idea that the dead sleep in the earth until Christ returns to judge them. According to the *Evangelical Dictionary of Theology*, "It is not a heresy in the narrower sense, due to the paucity of Scripture teaching on the intermediate state, but it may be called a doctrinal aberration."[38] While I am not suggesting the soul sleep doctrine is true, the admission concerning the "paucity of Scripture teaching" suggests thoughtfulness rather than absolutism. For example, two scholars I respect—John Ankerberg and John Weldon—argue that Scripture absolutely precludes human apparitions: "The alleged spirits of the dead cannot be the human dead, for Scripture tells us that the unsaved dead are confined and unable to reach the living, and the saved dead are with Christ (2 Pet 2:9; Luke 16:19–31; Acts 1:25; 2 Cor. 5:8; Phil. 1:23)."[39]

But do those Scriptures necessarily lead to those conclusions? Let's examine the proof texts cited.

2 Peter 2:9

The passage that best addresses the state of the unsaved dead reads, "then the Lord knows how to rescue the godly from trials, and to keep the unrighteous under punishment until the day of judgment"

(2 Peter 2:9, underline added). The verb "keep" is rendered from the Greek *tereo*, meaning "to cause a state to continue—'to cause to continue, to retain, to keep.'"[40] But what if God sovereignly decrees some to roam the earth in a disembodied, invisible state until the final judgment? Not only does this passage suggest that the unsaved are treated differently at death, this retaining until the Day of Judgment does necessarily demand quarantine from the living. We're not told *where* the damned are kept until judgment, albeit the assumption is hades. However, hades and hell (the lake of fire) are not synonymous.

Luke 16:29

An inference from the parable of the rich man and Lazarus suggests the quarantine—specifically, when Jesus tells the rich man: "And besides all this, between us and you a great chasm has been fixed, in order that those who would pass from here to you may not be able, and none may cross from there to us" (Luke 16:26). Two observations imply that this passage does not do the work demonic exclusivity assigns to it. First, this is a chasm between Lazarus in Abraham's bosom and the rich man in hades. New Testament scholar Craig Keener explains: "In the later Jewish literature we meet with divisions within sheol for the wicked and the righteous, in which each experiences a foretaste of his final destiny (Enoch 22:1–14). This idea appears to underlie the imagery of the parable of the rich man and Lazarus in Luke 16:19–31."[41] It is not between the living and the dead, but between sections in hades (both seen as temporary holding areas in first-century Jewish thought). Also, the rich man is not completely isolated, for he can see Lazarus.

Second, theological principalization from parables properly centers on the final point and not internal details. Scholars emphasize,

"The story parables function as a means of *calling forth a response* on the part of the hearer."[42] This parable is likely a fictional vehicle. According to biblical scholar Leon Morris, "Many see it as an adaptation of a popular folk-tale, perhaps originating in Egypt, which contrasted the eternal fates of a bad rich man and a virtuous poor man."[43] Deriving dogma from within is tenuous at best. Jesus' point that if people do not repent in response to Moses and the prophets, then they will not repent if someone should rise from the dead (Luke 16:31) is forecasting the future—Jesus' resurrection. While death seals one's ultimate destiny, the parable hints at His own resurrection and the Jews' unbelief more than setting metaphysical boundaries concerning the underworld.

Acts 1:25

This passage is set when the apostles are about to vote on who will "take the place in this ministry and apostleship from which Judas turned aside to go to <u>his own place</u>" (Acts 1:25, underline added). It is difficult to precisely determine what was meant by "his own place," but it probably meant "to go where he belongs." While most of us have a good idea of what it implies, an idiom doesn't do the work required to form dogma.

2 Corinthians 5:8 and Philippians 1:23

"Yes, we are of good courage, and we would rather be away from the body and at home with the Lord." (2 Corinthians 5:8)

"I am hard pressed between the two. My desire is to depart and be with Christ, for that is far better." (Philippians 1:23)

While providing awesome assurance for believers, these passages say nothing about the state of unbelievers or the boundaries of the spiritual realm. This exhausts the proof texts supplied by Ankerberg and Weldon for why dead cannot appear to the living, and they are found wanting.

Conclusion

This chapter has suggested that the typical evangelical apologists' absolutism concerning ghosts is unwarranted and misplaced. Cases involving influential Christians who do not fit the demonic impersonator hypothesis were cited. Furthermore, the biblical support used to suggest an immediate afterlife sequestering of unbelievers was judged to be less than persuasive. The Old Testament in its original Hebrew has much more to say than most English translations reveal, and the next chapter will unpack some shocking biblical evidence that is masked by most all English translations. Even if one dismisses the findings of parapsychology, I believe that human apparitions were an integral part of the worldview of the Hebrew Bible and even of Jesus of Nazareth Himself. If so, it behooves Christians to amend their worldview accordingly, rather than presuming Enlightenment skepticism.

Notes

1. *Proceedings: Society for Psychical Research* (Google books, 1897) http://books.google.com/books?id=o0jYAAAAIAAJ&dq=So+lo ng+as+the+stories+multiply%E2%80%A6+and+so+few+are+pos itively+explained+away,+it+is+bad+method+to+ignore+them.&s ource=gbs_navlinks_s.

2. John Warwick Montgomery, *Principalities and Powers: The World of the Occult*, (Minneapolis, MN: Bethany Fellowship, 1973) 137.

3. "Apparition," *Encylopedia of Occultism & Paprapsychology*, vol. 1, 5th ed., ed. Gordon Melton (Detroit: Gale Group, 2001) 63.

4. Andrew Black, *The Quantum Theory of Ghosts*, The Mask of Reason blog: http://maskofreason.wordpress.com/the-book-of-mysteries/ theories/quantum-theory-of-ghosts/.

5. Hans Holzer, *The Supernatural: Explaining the Unexplained* (Franklin Lakes, NJ: New Page, 2003) 112.

6. Office of Paranormal Investigations (OPI), http://mindreader.com/ info/the-office-of-paranormal-investigations-opi/.

7. See: http://mindreader.com/.

8. Loyd Auerbach. *Hauntings and Poltergeists: A Ghost Hunter's Guide* (Berkeley, CA: Ronin, 2004) Kindle edition, 430–434.

9. See: http://www.joshuapwarren.com/film.html.

10. Marie D. Jones, *PSIence: How New Discoveries in Quantum Physics and New Science May Explain the Existence of Paranormal Phenomena* (Franklin Lakes, NJ: New Page, 2007) Kindle edition, 53–54.

11. Michael A. Thalbourne, *A Glossary of Terms Used in Parapsychology* (Charlottesville, VA: Puente, 2004).

12. Peter D. Slade and Richard P. Bentall, *Sensory Deception: A Scientific Analysis of Hallucination* (Baltimore, MD: Johns Hopkins University Press, 1988) 24.

13. Auerbach, 58–61.

14. F. W. H. Myers, "On Recognised Apparitions Occurring More Than a Year After Death," *Proceedings Society for Psychical Research,* vol. 6, no. 17 (London: Trench Trubner, 1889–1890) 18. Viewable here: http://books.google.com/books?id=LBIrAAAAYAAJ&pg=PA18&vq =#v=onepage&q&f=false.

15. Ibid., 19–20.

16. Ibid., 72–77.

17. Watchman Nee, *The Latent Power of the Soul,* (Christian Fellowship Publishers, 1980) Kindle edition, 632–636.

18. C. S. Lewis, *A Grief Observed* (New York: HarperOne, 2009) 50.

19. Ibid., 85–86.

20. Ibid., 86.

21. Ibid., 87.

22. Joseph Pearce, *C. S. Lewis and the Catholic Church* (San Francisco: Ignatius, 2003) http://books.google.com/books?id=sastgl2e7 w0C&lpg=PT60&ots=MisWiCXjjd&dq=CS%20Lewis%20 Coma&pg=PT60#v=onepage&q=CS%20Lewis%20Coma&f=false.

23. J. B. Phillips, *The Newborn Christian: 114 Readings from J. B. Phillips.*, 1st Macmillan paperbacks ed. (New York: Macmillan, 1984) 214.

24. Marie A. Conn, *C .S. Lewis and Human Suffering: Light among the Shadows* (Mahwah, NJ: Hidden Spring, 2008) 1.

25. J. B. Phillips, *The New Testament in Modern English,* available online here: http://www.ccel.org/bible/phillips/JBPNT.htm.

26. Kurt E. Koch, *Occult ABC: Exposing Occult Practices and Ideologies* (Grand Rapids, MI: Kregel, 1986) 77.

27. Ibid., 77.

28. Ibid., 78.

29. Kurt Koch, *God among the Zulus* (Gmünd-Lindach Germany, Bibel- und Schriftenmission, 2001) 65.

30. Peter Jones, *Spirit Wars: Pagan Revival in Christian America* (Mukilteo, WA: Winepress, 1997).

31. James A. Herrick, *The Making of the New Spirituality: The Eclipse of the Western Religious Tradition* (Downers Grove, IL: IVP Books, 2004).

32. Ron Rhodes, *The Truth Behind Ghosts, Mediums, and Psychic Phenomena* (Eugene, OR: Harvest House, 2006) 71.

33. Mark Hunnemann, *Seeing Ghosts through God's Eyes* (Lake Placid, NY: Aviva, 2010) Kindle edition, 1928.

34. Ibid., 1936–1940.

35. Ibid., 1130–1131.

36. Ibid., 1214–1217.

37. Cotton Mather, *The Wonders of the Invisible World*, 13.

38. Walter A. Elwell, *Evangelical Dictionary of Theology: Second Edition* (Grand Rapids, MI: Baker, 2001) 1130.

39. John Ankerberg and. John Weldon, "Life After Death—Part 2" JASWIKI, http://www.jashow.org/wiki/index.php?title=Life_After_ Death_-_Part_2 (accessed 08/16/13).

40. 13.32 *tereo* in Johannes P. Louw and Eugene Albert Nida, vol. 1, *Greek-English Lexicon of the New Testament: Based on Semantic Domains*, electronic ed. of the 2nd edition. (New York: United Bible Societies, 1996) 152.

41. D. K. Innes, "Sheol," ed. D. R. W. Wood, et al., *New Bible Dictionary* (Leicester, England; Downers Grove, IL: InterVarsity, 1996) 1092.

42. Gordon D. Fee and Douglas K. Stuart, *How to Read the Bible for All Its Worth*, 3rd ed. (Grand Rapids, MI: Zondervan, 1993) 152.

43. Leon Morris, *Luke: An Introduction and Commentary*, *Tyndale New Testament Commentaries*, vol. 3 (Downers Grove, IL: InterVarsity, 1988) 269.

MEDIUMS, GHOSTS, FAMILIAR SPIRITS, AND THE SUPERNATURAL WORLDVIEW

Some can be sent to the living from the dead,
just as in the opposite direction divine Scripture testifies
that Paul was snatched from the living into paradise.
Samuel the prophet, although dead, predicted future events
to King Saul, who was alive...

—AUGUSTINE[1]

Scripture presents at least one human ghost in absolutely objective terms: the apparition of Samuel that appeared to King Saul. The book of 1 Samuel is set in Israel during the transition from the formative period of the judges to the renowned Davidic monarchy. Beginning with Samuel's birth, the book describes his role as a judge and prophet over Israel. Although it may not be obvious from some passages, God did not prefer Israel to have a human king. In Deuteronomy 33:5, the Lord had become Israel's king. He preferred that the nation remain a theocracy, but due to disobedience, it wasn't practical. God's desire seems clear when He lamented to Samuel, "For they have not rejected you, but they have rejected me from being king over them" (1 Samuel 8:7b). Israel's desire for a human king was a rejection of God.

When the people pleaded for a king, the Lord instructed Samuel to anoint Saul as Israel's first king. Unfortunately, human sin has a way of making something that seems good an obstacle to God's best. So it is not too surprising that while King Saul started well, he ended poorly. By the time we reach chapter 28's famous account of the medium at Endor, Saul had been rejected by God, having painted himself into a corner with his jealousy of David, whom God had chosen as Saul's replacement. If that wasn't enough, the Philistine armies were circling like vultures.

Out of God's favor and facing overwhelming odds from the approaching Philistine invasion, Saul decided that the only one who could guide him was the prophet who had originally crowned him king: Samuel. However, Saul had a small problem in that Samuel was deceased (1 Samuel 28:3). Contacting the dead was forbidden by God, and Saul himself had purged the mediums and necromancers from the land. Desperate, Saul utilized the underground market for the black arts: "So Saul said to his servants, 'Search for me a woman who is a medium so that I may go to her and inquire of her.' His servants said to him, 'Look there is a woman who is a medium in Endor'" (1 Samuel 28:7, LEB).

A strictly literal rendering of the Hebrew text is much more informative than "woman who is a medium." The term "medium" in English likely brings to mind for most readers a swindling gypsy preying on the bereaved, or perhaps the Long Island Medium or John Edward of recent television fame for other readers. However, this three-thousand-year-old narrative traverses a vast historical, cultural, and linguistic chasm between the reader's context and the author's. The ancient Israelites had a deeply Supernatural Worldview. They didn't doubt that real mediums could contact the spirit realm.

Mediums in the Old Testament

Saul had purged all the mediums from the land because the Mosaic Law ascribed the death penalty to mediums and necromancers. Interestingly, the Hebrew text preserves a distinction lost in most English translations. The English Standard Version gives the impression that the text is exclusively addressing human beings who engage in these forbidden activities: "A man or a woman who is a medium or a necromancer shall surely be put to death. They shall be stoned with stones; their blood shall be upon them" (Leviticus 20:27).

However, in the original language, the terms "medium" and "necromancer" don't refer only to humans, but also to humans associated with spirits. The more accurate rendering of the Hebrew found in Lexham English Bible is helpful: "And a man or a woman, if a spirit of the dead *[ob]* or a spirit of divination *[yiddeoni]* is in them, they shall surely be put to death; they shall stone them with stones—their blood is on them" (Leviticus 20:27, LEB).

This translation is a huge improvement toward understanding what being a medium in the Old Testament entailed. Where most English Bibles read "who is a medium," the Hebrew transliterated "*ki yiyeh b a-hem 'ob*" literally means, "if is in them a spirit of the dead." The far-reaching implications will be explored below. Paramount, the text disallows an easy escape. Bible believers cannot remain consistent while relegating mediums and spirits to the domain of superstitious nonsense. God is delivering His law—the covenant stipulations for Israel—for a practice carrying the death penalty. This is very serious business.

God would not institute law for offenses that could not be committed. Why would He prescribe such a harsh punishment for the impossible? If one takes God seriously, then familiar spirits are real and communicating with the dead is possible. The ill-advised alternative is that God trades in absurdity. Unfortunately, well-meaning translators have insulated English Bible readers from the reality of God's Word. To further illustrate this point, examine a passage from 2 Kings concerning King Manasseh, who was infamous for his deep entanglement in black magic, in two modern translations, the English Standard Version and Today's New International Version:

"And he burned his son as an offering and used fortune-telling and omens and dealt with mediums *[ob]* and with necromancers *[yiddeoni]*. He did much evil in the sight of the Lord, provoking him to anger" (2 Kings 21:6, ESV).

"He sacrificed his own son in the fire, practiced divination, sought omens, and consulted mediums *['ob]* and spiritists *[yiddeoni]*. He did much evil in the eyes of the LORD, arousing his anger" (2 Kings 21:6, TNIV).

These translations are somewhat sanitized because it is far more likely that original author meant for the reader to understand that he "dealt with ghosts and familiar spirits," not merely human mediums and human necromancers/spiritists. A medium is "someone with a spirit of the dead," but this 2 Kings passage only uses the term *'ob*. It implies that Manasseh interacted with actual spirits for divination. Flavius Josephus explained the Jewish belief that, "For this sort of necromantic women that bring up the souls of the dead, do by them foretell future events to such as desire them."[2] Later, the King James translators rendered it "dealt with familiar spirits and wizards," reflecting a more Supernatural Worldview than some modern versions.

Are the 'Ob Human Ghosts?

Interestingly, higher-critical biblical scholars writing for the Anchor Yale Biblical Commentary series, Mordechai Cogan and Hayim

Tadmor, readily acknowledge that the term medium means "one who has a spirit":

> The terms "ghosts" (ŏb) and "spirits" *(yiddĕ* ōnî) refer to the practice of necromancy, and from Leviticus 20:27, it is clear that they are distinct from the mediums who conjure them. It has been shown by Hoffner that *'ŏb* is an ancient term, attested in most Near Eastern languages, for a "ritual pit" through which mortals communicated with the chthonic deities of the underworld.[3]

The idea of the ritual pit in which ghosts and underworld spirits could be contacted is seen in Isaiah's prophecy of a coming siege on Jerusalem. The city is personified by the name Ariel and addressed personally in the oracle: "Then you shall be low; you shall speak from the earth, and your words will be low, from dust. And your voice will be from the earth, like a ghost, and your word will whisper from the dust" (Isaiah 29:4, LEB).

It preserves a reference to the ghosts whispering from the earth and reflects the writer's knowledge of the practice used by the medium of Endor when she summoned Samuel from a ritual pit in the ground.

Rephaim as Human Ghosts

The term "rephaim" is often misunderstood. Some are confused because the Pentateuch mentions a clan of giants known as "Rephaim" and miss the correct meaning of the prophets. Scholars agree the term has two uses: It denoted deceased humans in the poetic oracles and giants in the historical texts. According to Willem

VanGemeren, "Interestingly, all these examples occur in poetic con-texts, while references to the ethnic Rephaim are found exclusively in historical narrative passages."[4] For example, Isaiah 14:9–10 describes disembodied souls as "rephaim" or "shades" meaning "ghosts of the dead" or "the dead inhabitants of the netherworld" called *sheol.*[5] Isaiah wrote, "Sheol below is getting excited over you, to meet you when you come; it arouses <u>the dead spirits</u> for you, all of the lead-ers of the earth. It raises all of the kings of the nations from their thrones" (Isaiah 14:9, LEB, underline added). It is used in this way three times in Isaiah (14:9, 26:14, 26:19) and three times in Proverbs (2:18, 9:18, 21:16), as well as in Psalm 88:10 and Job 26:5. Accord-ing to Wheaton College Hebrew professor, John Walton:

> The dead were not viewed as completely separated from the living. Their spirit could be summoned back (e.g., 1 Sam. 29:11–20). The emphasis here is the powerlessness of the shades on the living, in contrast to the royal power they used to wield. "Spirits" or "shades" are the same as the Ugaritic *rapium,* who represent the departed Canaanite ancestors. They parallel "the dead" (Isa. 26:14) and are at times benefi-cent spirits, like Samuel, invoked to visit and aid.[6]

The context clearly implies them to be deceased human beings, as the rephaim are associated with Sheol and the Hebrew term for "death."

Interestingly, the rabbinic commentator Malbim or Rabbi Meir Leib ben Yehiel Michal (1808–1879) explained that one could only contact the dead by means of an *'ob* for one year after death. This idea derived from the belief that the soul consists of two compo-nents: one tied to the physical body and the other not. He wrote:

For the soul delegated from above departs immediately as death takes place, returning to the God who gave it. The primitive soul, however, that is connected to the body, does not depart prior to the bodies decomposition in the grave. As long as the body is not decomposed, the '*ob* has the power to rule over the primitive soul and to divine the future by consulting it with the aid of sorcery.[7]

The primitive soul distinction could be equivalent to the idea of a separate soul and spirit, hinted at in the New Testament as explained in chapter 3 on Watchman Nee's tripartism.

The Ghost of Samuel

In 1 Samuel 28, the Hebrew translated "medium" uses two words, *balat 'ob*. It strictly renders "owner of a spirit of the dead." The issue explored above was, "What exactly is an '*ob*?" Is it a nonhuman spirit associated with the realm of the dead, or is it the spirit of a dead human? Scholars are divided, but the latter is favored. It seems to serve a dual purpose for underworld spirits as well as for deceased humans. Jewish scholar Jacob Bazak's survey of the rabbinic and tal-mudic literature supports translating it as "ghost."[8] If the consensus understanding of '*ob*, "spirit of the dead" is correct, then the Hebrew text implies that humans *can* have a spirit of the dead associated with them. I realize that, for many Christians, this is controversial, but the original language text strongly implies it. It also implies that a great deal of evangelical writings about the afterlife and demonology are drastically oversimplified, if not wholly incorrect.

Because translators have shielded English Bible students from the meaning of the text for so long, these ideas seem novel, but they are indeed much closer to the ancient inspired author's intended meaning. For its superior accuracy in rendering the Hebrew text, the Lexham English Bible is employed for the narrative of Samuel's ghost. Let's turn now to the account:

> So Saul disguised himself and put on other clothes, and he went with two of his men. And they came to the woman by night and he said, "Please consult a spirit for me through the ritual pit, and bring up for me the one whom I tell you." But the woman said to him, "Look, you know what Saul did, how he exterminated the mediums and the soothsayers from the land! Why are you setting a trap for my life to kill me?" Then Saul swore to her by Yahweh, "As Yahweh lives, you will not be punished for this thing." So the woman asked, "Whom shall I bring up for you?" He said, "Bring up Samuel for me." When the woman saw Samuel, she cried out with a loud voice, and the woman said to Saul, "Why did you deceive me? You are Saul!" The king said to her, "Do not be afraid! What do you see?" And the woman said to Saul, "I see a god coming up from the ground!" Then he said to her, "What is his appearance?" She said, "An old man is coming up, and he is wrapped in a robe." Then Saul realized that it was Samuel, and he knelt with his face to the ground and bowed down.
>
> Then Samuel said to Saul, "Why have you disturbed me by bringing me up?" And Saul said, "I am in distress! For the Philistines are about to make war against me, but God has turned away from me, and he does not answer me any more, not by the prophets or by the dreams. So I called to

you to let me know what I should do." Then Samuel said, "Why do you ask me, since Yahweh has turned away from you and has become your enemy? Yahweh has done to you just as he spoke by my hand! Yahweh has torn the kingdom from your hand and has given it to your neighbor, to David. Because you did not obey Yahweh and did not carry out the fierce anger of his wrath against Amalek, therefore Yahweh has done this thing to you today. And Yahweh will also give Israel with you into the hands of the Philistines, and tomorrow you and your sons will be with me, and Yahweh will also give the army of Israel into the hand of the Philistines." Then Saul immediately fell prostrate to the ground, and he was very afraid because of the words of Samuel; there was no more strength in him, for he had not eaten food all day and all night. (1 Samuel 28:8–20)

For most evangelicals, this story is uncomfortable. But we shouldn't be afraid of what the Bible really contains. We can draw seven controversial conclusions from this narrative.

First, Scripture presents this as real history and relates Samuel's ghost in objective terms. The appearance of Samuel in his disembodied state gives biblical support to the fact that disembodied spirits—even of believers—can appear to believers. Accordingly, a consistent biblical worldview must have room to accommodate the possibility of human apparitions, even though they are uncommon and counterfeit prone.

Second, ghosts retain the physical characteristics and clothing they are associated with. Samuel was recognized by his characteristic robe (1 Samuel 28:14).

Third, Samuel lived in the underworld of the dead, but he knew what was happening on earth among the living. When Saul stated his reason for summoning the prophet, Samuel's reply revealed a thorough grasp of the situation. We must allow that the dead have knowledge of the living. The book of Hebrews implies this: "Therefore, since we are surrounded by so great a cloud of witnesses, let us also lay aside every weight, and sin which clings so closely, and let us run with endurance the race that is set before us" (Hebrews 12:1). Theologian Wayne Grudem explains that "the fact that the author encourages us to run the race of life with perseverance because we are surrounded by this great cloud of witnesses…suggests that those who have died and gone before have some awareness of what is going on in the earth."[9]

Fourth, Samuel knew Saul was facing a Philistine invasion and stated that Saul and his sons would die the next day in battle. This prophecy came to pass. While this may have been revealed by God, it is also possible that the afterlife is atemporal; spirits may have some access to the past, present, and future.

Fifth, the account takes mediums seriously, as if there really are spirits being contacted, but against the law of God. Mediums are "possessors of a spirit of the dead." To reiterate the discussion above concerning the law: *God does not trade in absurdities*. While the Old Testament laws were for the ancient Israelites, God's character does not change. Contacting the dead was seen by God as religious unfaithfulness and forbidden in the strongest terms (cf. Deuteronomy 18). Even though the field today is demonstrably replete with con artists, we should not be quick to dismiss everything as fakery. The Supernatural Worldview must allow for the possibility that some mediums really do contact the dead and that the dead can communicate to the living.

Sixth, the medium described Samuel's apparition as a "god." This reflects the Lexham's commitment to literal translation. Samuel's ghost is called an "elohim"—the very same term used of Yahweh throughout the Old Testament. How can a human ghost be an elohim? Although one will not likely learn about it in Sunday school, the Hebrew Bible sustains that there are many elohim, good and evil, in addition to Yahweh. In a groundbreaking paper presented to the Evangelical Theological Society, Dr. Michael Heiser argued, "The deceased Samuel who appears to Saul is an *elohim*. While this might seem strange to us, the notion that the departed dead were 'gods' is quite in concert with ancient Canaanite thinking."[10] While the Canaanites were Israel's enemies, they were also their neighbors and they shared common vocabulary. Accordingly, studies of Ugaritic literature have garnered many new insights into the Hebrew Bible and ancient worldview. It seems scholars have too narrowly defined the term.

A biblical word study reveals that "elohim" is used of Yahweh (more than two thousand times), gods of the divine council (Psalm 82, 89, 58:11; Deuteronomy 32:8–9, 43), demons (Deuteronomy 32:17), human ghosts (1 Samuel 28:13), and angels (Genesis 35:7). This scope demands a reconsideration of the typical rendering as "God" or "gods." Heiser argues the thing these entities all have in common is that "they all inhabit the non-human realm. That is, they are by nature not part of the world of humankind, a world of embodiment by nature."[11] In other words, "elohim" is not so much an ontological classification as a metaphysical one. Heiser calls it a "place of residence" term. Samuel's ghost was an elohim because he came from the spirit realm. This makes good sense.

Seventh, the demonic imposter hypothesis is revealed to be eisegesis (imposing one's presuppositions on the text) of the worst sort. When interpreting Scripture, one should first seek the original author's intention for his original readers. Samuel is portrayed

in the text as a real human spirit. He is even upset that he has been
brought up. There is not a hint that he is an imposter. His communication is consistent with God's pronouncements against Saul,
and the prophecy concerning his imminent demise comes to pass.
Better yet, ancient Jewish literature reveals how the Hebrew readers
interpreted it.

The ancient Greek translation of the Hebrew Bible known as
the Septuagint preserves the Jews' understanding that it was the real
Samuel: "Saul died due to his evil acts, in which he had acted wickedly against God, against the word of the Lord, since he had not kept
it; for Saul had inquired by the one who speaks from the belly to seek
advice, and Samuel the prophet had answered him" (1 Chronicles
10:13, LES).[12] Furthermore, the apocryphal book of Sirach, written in
Hebrew between 200 and 175 BC, speaks of Samuel as rising from
the grave: "Even when he lay buried, his guidance was sought; he
made known to the king his fate, And from the grave he raised his
voice as a prophet, to put an end to wickedness" (Sirach 46:20, NAB).
Josephus understood it literally too, writing, "To this his sad end did
Saul come, according to the prophecy of Samuel."[13] These sources
preserve the Israelite understanding that it was actually Samuel. This
was unanimously held until the second century AD.

Incredulous Christians have long postulated a demon impersonating Samuel. An early example, Tertullian, was driven by his need to
refute the Simonian cult that was practicing necromancy:

> At this very time, even, the heretical dupes of this same Simon
> (Magus) are so much elated by the extravagant pretensions
> of their art, that they undertake to bring up from Hades
> the souls of the prophets themselves. And I suppose that
> they can do so under cover of a lying wonder. For, indeed,

it was no less than this that was anciently permitted to the Pythonic (or ventriloquistic) spirit—even to represent the soul of Samuel, when Saul consulted the dead, after (losing the living) God. God forbid, however, that we should suppose that the soul of any saint, much less of a prophet, can be dragged out of (its resting-place in Hades) by a demon.[14]

Although a Python spirit (discussed in chapter 6) was a creative supernatural alternative, Tertullian's interpretation seems rather obviously imposed onto the text by a contemporary issue. His view did not come by seeking the original inspired author's intention. In biblical studies, this is known as eisegesis or imposing a personal bias. Because Christians find it uncomfortable, this text inspires eisegesis like few others. Other famous examples include Martin Luther, who proffered "the devil's ghost," and John Calvin, who said that "it was not the real Samuel, but a spectre."[15] Calvin meant an evil spirit or demon.

What about the fact that Samuel came up from the ground?

Sheol, the Abode of the Dead

Modern Christians are often confused by the Old Testament afterlife paradigm. They think Samuel should have been in heaven, not coming up out of a pit.[16] Actually, the idea of the dead going to heaven is not taught in the Old Testament. The ancient Hebrews believed that the deceased, good and bad, went to the underworld called "sheol." Upon death, they descended to "the pit" (Isaiah 14:15), the place of the spirits of the dead. Job described God's mastery of the extreme ends of creation in these terms: "The spirits of the dead tremble below the waters and their inhabitants. Sheol is naked before him, and there is no covering for Abaddon" (Job 26:5–6, LEB).

Scholars derive that sheol was divided into two sections, one known as Abraham's Bosom and the other Abaddon, the realm of the damned, separated by a great chasm. Jesus' parable about Lazarus and the rich man seems to reflect this ancient underworld geography. Jesus indicated that the rich man being punished in Hades could still see Lazarus and Abraham: "And in Hades he lifted up his eyes as he was in torment and saw Abraham from a distance, and Lazarus at his side" (Luke 16:23). For this to be possible, Abraham must be in Hades too but in a cooler climate. However, the paradigm changes after the Gospels conclude. It was Jesus' atoning sacrifice on the cross that made it possible for sinful humans to enter God's presence.

His death, burial, and resurrection marked the afterlife turning point. Peter wrote that Jesus, after dying on the cross, went down and preached in Tartarus (2 Peter 2:4), the deepest part of Hades, to the angels who sinned during the days of Noah:

> For Christ also suffered once for sins, the just for the unjust, in order that he could bring you to God, being put to death in the flesh, but made alive in the spirit, in which also he went and proclaimed to the spirits in prison, who were formerly disobedient, when the patience of God waited in the days of Noah, while an ark was being constructed, in which a few—that is, eight souls—were rescued through water. (1 Peter 3:18–20)

After this, Christ ascended, leading the believers to heaven. A cryptic reference by Paul in Ephesians 4:8–9 (citing Psalm 68:18) could speak to their release from the underworld: "Therefore it says,

'Ascending on high he led captivity captive; he gave gifts to men.' Now 'he ascended,' what is it, except that he also descended to the lower regions of the earth?" (Ephesians 4:8–9, LEB).

It seems that today, the realm of the wicked dead is the same as in the Old Testament sheol, but the cross changed everything—allowing believers to enter God's presence—if they put their faith in Jesus' death and resurrection (Romans 10:9). Let's now turn to the New Testament.

New Testament

The New Testament affirms the worldview of the Old and carries it forward a few steps. Belief in human apparitions was a part of Jesus' disciples' worldview. In the account of Jesus walking on water after the feeding of the five thousand, Mark (6:45–51) and Matthew (14:22–33) both record that Jesus was mistaken for a ghost. When the disciples saw Jesus walking on the water of Galilee at night, they cried, "It's a ghost!" Naturally, Jesus calmly answered, "Be of good cheer; it is I; be not afraid" (Matthew14:27). Interestingly, this would have been an opportune time to disabuse His superstitious disciples of their ghost belief, but He didn't bother. If it was an important truth, then why not? Jesus' silence doesn't necessarily mean that ghosts are human spirits, but it does lean that way.

The term employed for "ghost" in Matthew 14, "phantasm," is unique to this account. The verb *phantazo*, meaning "to bring to manifestation," is often used in the sense "to appear" for supernatural phenomena; used as a noun, it literally means "apparition" or "ghost." We can look to Greek literature from around the time of the Gospels to see how Mark and Matthew were using it. Lucian of

Samosata (120–AD 200) was the author of more than eighty known manuscripts and is considered the supreme Ancient Greek satirist. His *Philopseudes* ("Lover of Lies") is a story within a story, which includes the original version of *The Sorcerer's Apprentice* adapted into a poem by Goethe in 1797 and later Disney's *Fantasia* (1940).

Written shortly after the New Testament, around AD 150, Tychiades as the narrator is visiting the house of a sick and elderly friend, Eucrates, where he has an argument about the reality of the supernatural. Several internal narrators then tell Tychiades various tales intended to convince him that supernatural phenomena are real. In this exchange, we see the term in question used in the same way as in the Gospels:

> Eucrates pointed to me. "We were only trying," he said, "to convince this man of adamant that there are such things as supernatural beings and ghosts, and that the spirits of the dead walk the earth and manifest themselves to whomsoever they will." Moved by the august presence of Arignotus, I blushed, and hung my head. "Ah, but, Eucrates," said he, "perhaps all that Tychiades means is, that a spirit only walks if its owner met with a violent end, if he was strangled, for instance, or beheaded or crucified, and not if he died a natural death. If that is what he means, there is great justice in his contention." "No, no," says Dinomachus, "he maintains that there is absolutely no such thing as an apparition." "What is this I hear?" asked Arignotus, scowling upon me; "you deny the existence of the supernatural, when there is scarcely a man who has not seen some evidence of it?"[17]

This passage is valuable for two reasons. First, this ancient story demonstrates that the debate between the naturalist and the supernaturalist is not a product of modernity. Second, the Greek term *phantasma* used by the Gospel authors is also used here for the spirits of the dead, establishing the way the term was widely understood by readers of that time.

Jesus Believed in Ghosts

Jesus had another opportunity to correct the disciples' belief in ghosts that is even more telling. After He was crucified, the last thing the disciples were expecting was to see Him. However, Luke records that He appeared unexpectedly in their midst:

> And while they were saying these things, he himself stood there among them. But they were startled and became terrified, and thought they <u>had seen a ghost</u>. And he said to them, "Why are you frightened? And for what reason do doubts arise in your hearts? Look at my hands and my feet, that I am I myself! Touch me and see, because <u>a ghost does not have flesh and bones</u>, as you see that I have." And when he had said this, he showed them his hands and his feet. (Luke 24:36–40, LEB, underline added)

The passage is compelling, both because it is the second time the disciples made this mistake and also for what Jesus did say rather than what He did not say. Eric James observed, "Had Jesus rebuked or corrected them the first time, off the record, then surely the second time around He would have even more harshly, or made it excruciatingly clear that ghosts aren't real."[18] Not only did Jesus *not* correct their belief in ghosts, He made a point of distinguishing Himself from a ghost based on its attributes: "a ghost does not have flesh and bones." He implies that ghosts exist, but that He is not one because He has flesh and bones. This wouldn't make sense if ghosts do not exist. Jesus strongly implies that ghosts are real entities.

When Jesus died on the cross, some dead folks actually rose from their graves and walked around Jerusalem: "And the graves were opened; and many bodies of the saints which slept arose, And came out of the graves after his resurrection, and went into the holy city, and appeared unto many" (Matthew 27:52–53). This event doesn't fit tidily into our theological boxes either. Although some have cited it as a ghost story, they are in error. This passage describes physical bodily resurrection rather than apparitions. Even so, it seriously challenges the Western worldview and has become a stumbling block for otherwise believing scholars.[19]

The Transfiguration a Gateway between Realms?

Jesus knew that He came to earth to die for the sins of men. When He tried discussing His impending death with Peter, James, and John, they gave Him no support. Peter urged Him not to go through with it, angering Jesus with his words (Matthew 16:21–23). Shortly after that, in an amazing supernatural event known as the Transfiguration—a link between worlds—allowed Moses and Elijah to come and speak with Him about His impending death:

> As he was praying, the appearance of his face changed, and his clothes became as bright as a flash of lightning. Two men, Moses and Elijah, appeared in glorious splendor, talking with Jesus. They spoke about his departure, which he was about to bring to fulfillment at Jerusalem. (Luke 9:29–31)

While this reveals that Jesus was God incarnate in all His glory, it includes two apparitions of biblical prophets. It also shows that it is possible for them to return to the land of living if God allows.

Are the Dead Watching?

Interestingly, both Moses and Elijah knew what was happening on earth even though they had been deceased for centuries. They each knew that Jesus was about to bring the era of the law and prophets to fulfillment in Jerusalem. Under the Old Testament paradigm, they lived in Paradise with all the other righteous dead. Yet they knew what was happening on earth. This implies that they were able to observe the events on earth. Can they see earth, or is the information broadcast in heaven? I don't know. But many Christians believe that Hebrews 12:1 teaches that the righteous dead have observational access to what occurs here. The verse implies that we should behave because we are under observation: "Therefore, since we also have such a great cloud of witnesses surrounding us, putting aside every weight and the sin that so easily ensnares us, let us run with patient endurance the race that has been set before us" (Hebrews 12:1).

Another example comes from heaven itself. It doesn't give the story of a righteous dead person returning to earth. Instead, it tells of the righteous dead praying in heaven. John saw them there:

When he opened the fifth seal, I saw under the altar the souls of those who had been slain because of the word of God and the testimony they had maintained. They called out in a loud voice: "How long, holy and true Lord, will you not judge and avenge our blood from those who live on the earth?" (Revelation 6:9–11, LEB)

Somehow, the martyrs knew they had not been avenged on earth. They lived in the presence of God, but knew what was happening on earth. Their blood had not been avenged, and they prayed for God to avenge it. This implies that they were not only observing, but were growing weary of waiting. Nevertheless, they were told to wait until the right time and that justice would come in God's timing. These examples should be enough to conclude the righteous dead have knowledge of the happenings on earth. What we do not know much about is the state of the damned. Demons and the damned are the subject of the next chapter.

Conclusion

This chapter examined the Hebrew text of 1 Samuel 28 amongst others dealing with mediums and spirits and demonstrated that English translations mask the deeper implications of inspired Word. It was argued that human ghosts are presented as real entities and that God's laws against mediums and necromancy only make sense in light of these being real possibilities. God would not bother to institute such serious penalties for impossible acts. Furthermore, the Gospels reveal that the disciples certainly believed in ghosts and strongly imply that Jesus did, too. It seems that expediency and tradition have a tendency to demythologize the Supernatural Worldview of the Bible.

Notes

1. Augustine, "The Care to Be Taken for the Dead," 15.18, in John R. Franke, *Joshua, Judges, Ruth, 1–2 Samuel, Ancient Christian Commentary on Scripture OT 4* (Downers Grove, IL: InterVarsity, 2005) 323.

2. Flavius Josephus and William Whiston, *The Works of Josephus: Complete and Unabridged* (Peabody: Hendrickson, 1996, c1987), Ant. 6.330.

3. Mordechai Cogan and Hayim Tadmor, *II Kings: A New Translation with Introduction and Commentary*, includes index (New Haven; London: Yale University Press, 2008) 267.

4. Willem VanGemeren, *New International Dictionary of Old Testament Theology & Exegesis* (Grand Rapids, MI: Zondervan, 1998) 3:1176.

5. William White, "2198 הָפַר" in *Theological Wordbook of the Old Testament*, ed. R. Laird Harris, Gleason L. Archer, Jr., and Bruce K. Waltke, electronic ed. (Chicago: Moody, 1999) 858.

6. John H Walton, *Zondervan Illustrated Bible Backgrounds Commentary (Old Testament)* vol. 4: *Isaiah, Jeremiah, Lamentations, Ezekiel, Daniel* (Grand Rapids, MI: Zondervan, 2009) 72.

7. Malbim "on 1 Samuel 28:13" cited in Jacob Bazak, *Judaism and Psychical Phenomena: A Study of Extrasensory Perception in Biblical, Talmudic, and Rabbinical Literature in the Light of Contemporary Parapsychological Research* (New York: Garrett, 1971) 84–85.

8. Ibid., 83.

9. Wayne A. Grudem, *Systematic Theology: An Introduction to Biblical Doctrine* (Leicester, England; Grand Rapids, MI: InterVarsity Press; Zondervan, 1994) 820.

10. Michael Heiser, "What Is an Elohim?" Paper presented at the Evangelical Theological Society Meeting, 2010, www.

thedivinecouncil.com/WhatisareanelohimETS2010.pdf (accessed 10/12/13) 8.

11. Ibid., 11.

12. Rick Brannan, Ken M. Penner, Israel Loken, Michael Aubrey, and Isaiah Hoogendyk, eds., *The Lexham English Septuagint* (Bellingham, WA: Logos Bible Software, 2012).

13. Flavius Josephus and William Whiston, *The Works of Josephus: Complete and Unabridged*, (Peabody: Hendrickson, 1996) Ant 6.378.

14. Tertullian, *A Treatise on the Soul*, Chapter 57:335–337, http://www. tertullian.org/anf/anf03/anf03-22.htm#P3065_1109150.

15. John Peter Lange, Philip Schaff, David Erdmann, et al., *A Commentary on the Holy Scriptures: 1 & 2 Samuel* (Bellingham, WA: Logos, 2008) 335.

16. Jack Zavada, "What Does the Bible Say About Ghosts?" About.com Christianity, http://christianity.about.com/od/whatdoesthebiblesay/a/Ghosts-In-The-Bible.htm (accessed 10/16/13).

17. Samosata Lucian, "Philopseudes" in *Works of Lucian of Samosata,* vol. 3., translated by H. W. Fowler and F. G. Fowler. Available Project Gutenberg: http://www.gutenberg.org/ebooks/6829.

18. Eric James, *Are Ghosts Biblical?* (Mustang, OK: Tate, 2013) Kindle edition, 30.

19. In his scholarly apologetic, *The Resurrection of Jesus: A New Historiographical Approach,* Michael Licona PhD suggested that this might be apocalyptic symbolism resulting in a firestorm of controversy that led to his dismissal from the North American Mission Board of the Southern Baptist Convention.

SATAN, DEMONS, AND THE GHOST HYPOTHESIS

Now the Spirit expressly says that in later times some
will depart from the faith by devoting themselves to
deceitful spirits and teachings of demons.
—1 TIMOTHY 4:1

One of my schools is the Bible Institute of Los Angeles, now
known as BIOLA University, where I earned a certification in
Christian apologetics.[1] A few years back, the *BIOLA* magazine ran
a very interesting article called "Exorcizing Our Demons." I was
surprised to read that Dr. Daniel B. Wallace (1974, BIOLA)—
one of the top New Testament scholars, Greek textbook authors,
and professors at Dallas Theological Seminary—was asked to
perform a house blessing/exorcism that became overtly supernatural. A wealthy Christian homeowner had reported poltergeist
phenomena that began when his elderly father moved in, and
he asked Wallace to bless the house. As Wallace and a colleague
prayed through the rooms, objects began to move with no apparent cause. The *BIOLA* article reads:

"It was small objects, like magnets on the refrigerator flying clear across the room. It was really remarkable," said Wallace, who once doubted that demonic activity occurs today. He's now writing a book arguing that many evangelicals have become unbiblically antisupernatural.[2]

Wallace no longer doubts the Supernatural Worldview, and this impressed me, because it's not often that a big name like Wallace (from a cessationist seminary like Dallas) will openly speak about such activity. I wrote Dr. Wallace, and he personally confirmed the above to be accurate, except for the part about the book, entitled *Who's Afraid of the Holy Spirit?*, which was already written. Not only that, he also confirmed the overt poltergeist activity to me personally:

Cris, it has been awhile but I can say this regarding the items that flew in the house. There was an elderly gentleman living there who was dying. His son owned the home. It's a very large home, and the father was upstairs in the "mother-in-law apartment." Besides the father and son, the son's wife and one baby lived in the house. No teenagers. Husband and wife in their 40s at the time. When the items flew, we were in the kitchen—about the farthest place from the mother-in-law apartment (which was on the third floor, I believe).[3]

I had him asked about teenagers and who else lived there because most parapsychologists try to explain poltergeist-type activity as psychokinesis from a living agent present in the haunted location. Usually a teenager is the culprit, and poltergeist activity is labeled RSPK (recurrent spontaneous psychokinesis), which sounds scientific but explains very little. However, because there were no typical

RSPK agents present, this case excludes it and strongly supports the demonic hypothesis for this activity, as the objects were flying across the room in response to Wallace's blessing the house. Thus, demons are immaterial beings who can affect the physical world, perhaps even reading and implanting ideas in our minds (Luke 8:27–29; Mark 9:22) and empowering false religions and some psychic phenomena. The demonic is all but dismissed under the delusion of scientism as per Carl Sagan's *The Demon-Haunted World: Science as a Candle in the Dark*,[4] and is still controversial amongst purported believers, as 59 percent of professing American *Christians* do not believe Satan is real.[5] The greatest trick the devil ever pulled, indeed.

Is the Trickster Really Satan?

Recalling the "trickster" mentioned by parapsychologist George Hansen (discussed in chapter 3): "The paranormal encompasses everything from levitating monks to ESP, from spirits to cattle mutilations—an incredible and unsavory hodgepodge. The mix seems incoherent. But the trickster makes sense of it."[6] Hansen believes that paranormal events, the manifestation of strange creatures, UFO sightings, and ghosts occur when the society is in transition. Most interestingly, he forecast that during the transition, "Charismatic leaders may arise who demonstrate paranormal powers, attracting followers, and challenging the legitimacy of the establishment."[7] Pope Francis is seen by prophecy scholars as matching the description, and my former volume, *Petrus Romanus,* details how he satisfies a nine-hundred-year-old prophecy pointing toward the False Prophet or second beast in the biblical Apocalypse (Revelation 13:11). Pope Francis is confirming this identity by asserting universal salvation:

"The Lord has redeemed all of us, all of us, with the Blood of Christ: all of us, not just Catholics. Everyone! 'Father, the atheists?' Even the atheists. Everyone!"[8] Of course, the idea that atheists are redeemed is contrary to the teaching of Jesus (Matthew 7:13–14) and the New Testament in general (Galatians 2:16; Hebrews 11:6). Whether or not Pope Francis is *the* False Prophet remains to be seen, but it is indisputable that he is *a* false prophet. We've seen plenty of evidence for the transition—the paranormal paradigm shift—but who is the trickster?

In mythology, folklore, and religious studies, a trickster is a god, goddess, spirit, man, woman, or anthropomorphic animal that plays tricks that defy the rules and conventional behavior. Often this deceptive behavior is cast as heroic. Brer Rabbit from American folklore and Bugs Bunny from Warner Brothers Cartoons are the tricksters from a purely literary standpoint. Popular folklore posits the trickster as a high-ranking angel indulging in some off-the-clock fun. On the CW network's television show *Supernatural,* there was a villain known as "The Trickster" appearing in seasons 2, 3, and 5. In the show, the Trickster was revealed in to be the archangel Gabriel, who allegedly used the Trickster persona to indulge certain personal desires. Gabriel was killed by Lucifer, but he managed to leave a video that eventually helped the two brothers to defeat Lucifer. Who says the age of myth is dead?

While it isn't possible to say with any authority whether or not the trickster is objectively real, Scripture does seem to offer a few hints. Satan is said to blind the minds of unbelievers (2 Corinthians 4:4); his mission is to deceive (2 Thessalonians 2:9) and to disguise himself as "an angel of light" (2 Corinthians 11:4). Hansen also sees sexual perversion as a trickster attribute: "There is another component of the trickster constellation—sexuality. I have not addressed the sexual imagination, but it is a powerful force. So here we have the trickster elements of deception, sex, and psi, which are all closely associated with the imagination."[9] Of course, Satan and demons are associated with sexual temptation (1 Corinthians 7:5; Jude 6–7).

The devil is a trickster in that he lures and entices with promises of great success and fantastic pleasure, but, in the end, the results never truly satisfy. Peter Jones writes, "The paranormal world of the occult is real, and practitioners have regularly spoken of the cruelty with which they are treated by demonic powers."[10] He then cites Helena Blavatsky, founder of the occult Theosophical Society, who late in life wrote to an old friend and declared: "I would gladly return, be Russian, be Christian, be Orthodox. I yearn for it. But there is no returning; I am in chains, I am not my own."[11] This is an astonishing admission of enslavement coming from such an infamous occultist. While such deceptive entrapments are consistent with the trickster archetype, it is still hard to make a definite identification. Nevertheless, Hansen's inferences about the trickster making sense of the paranormal do loosely fit the biblical data about Satan and demons and, even more so, match the end-time parapsychological agenda forecast by Watchman Nee that people "who develop their soul power cannot avoid being contacted and used by the evil spirit."[12] Chapter 7 provided compelling evidence that someone like the trickster is enticing people through yoga, meditation, and pantheistic monism. Did Watchman Nee anticipate this so well in the early 1930s, or was his warning divinely inspired? One way or the other, it is coming to pass. But let us now examine the identity of the adversary. Christian tradition holds that Satan was once a powerful archangel named Lucifer who was the worship leader in heaven.

Did Lucifer Become Satan or
Did Satan Become Lucifer?

Speaking of delusions of grandeur, the grandest of all is attributed to Lucifer: "How art thou fallen from heaven, O Lucifer, son of the morning! how art thou cut down to the ground, which didst weaken the nations!" (Isaiah 14:12, KJV). More up-to-date translations render this: "How you have fallen from heaven, morning star, son of dawn! You are cut down to the ground, conqueror of nations!" (Isaiah 14:12, LEB). The ESV refers to the being in question as "morning star, son of Dawn," and most scholars agree the description is a reference to the planet Venus rather than to a proper name like "Lucifer." According to David Lowe, "Justin Martyr was the first early church father to connect Isaiah 14:12 to Satan falling from heaven."[13] Lowe's *Deconstructing Lucifer* is a fair but controversial treatment of this topic, but I part ways a bit, allowing for the traditional interpretation to apply with a few caveats.

The popular name for the devil, Lucifer, is a Latin translation derived from the Hebrew phrase *helel ben-shachar* in Isaiah 14:12. While on the surface the phrase speaks to the king of Babylon, it has been interpreted to speak about varying entities. However, there is still a good case for the traditional understanding of it as the devil or Satan—that is, if one is willing to say that Satan became Lucifer rather than the converse. I argue this based on his claim to divinity and his fall and destruction that parallel the account in Revelation. In its original context, scholars agree that this phrase is related to Ugaritic mythology concerning Baal and Athtar.[14] While Isaiah could be simply borrowing from local mythology for an illustration, it seems as if the prophet sees through the king of Babylon to the wicked spiritual power behind him. As explained later under the heading "The Divine Council," Psalm 82 and the book of Daniel suggest that earthly kingdoms have cosmic overlords (Daniel 10:13, 20), a paradigm that fits nicely with the beast of Revelation who is similarly empowered by the great red dragon identified as Satan (Revelation 12:9; 13:2).

In Ugaritic lore, this usurper is argued to be Athtar, who was referred to as Venus (morning star), who seeks to displace Baal.[15] Other scholars relate this passage to an ancient Babylonian or Hebrew star myth, similar to the Greek legend of Phaethon.[16] Even so, one can imagine that, in a cosmic sense, all of these myths stem from a common netherworld event. The New Testament is clear that angels rebelled (Matthew 25:41; Revelation 12:9) and that the earth is currently under the power of a usurper (2 Corinthians 4:4; 1 John 5:19). While the king of Babylon could hardly hope to "ascend to heaven above the stars of God," it certainly speaks to his extreme hubris. C. S. Lewis famously said, "It was through pride that the devil became the devil: Pride leads to every other vice: it is the complete anti-God state of mind."[17] *Helel Ben-Shachar's* frustrated divine ambition harks back to the account of a war in heaven in Revelation 12:7–17 in which Satan is thrown to earth, suggesting commonality with "the man who made the Earth tremble" (Isaiah 14:16). When Satan tempted Jesus, he offered Him all the "kingdoms of the world and their glory" with only one requirement: "if you will fall down and worship me" (Mathew 4:8–9). This is quite consistent with the taunt song in Isaiah 14.

During the intertestamental period, the angels' fall associated with the morning star was subsequently associated explicitly with the name "Satan," as seen the second Book of Enoch (29:4; 31:4). This early Jewish association suggests some influence on the New Testament authors. Accordingly, the association of the Latin title "Lucifer"

with Satan continued with the church fathers, because he is represented as being "cast down from heaven" (Revelation 12:7–10; cf.
Luke 10:18). For example, Origen wrote, "Again, we are taught as
follows by the prophet Isaiah regarding another opposing power. The
prophet says, 'How is Lucifer, who used to arise in the morning, fallen
from heaven!'"[18] Origen also wrote of the devil, "This opinion, however, is held by most, that the devil was an angel, and that, having
become an apostate, he induced as many of the angels as possible
to fall away with himself, and these up to the present time are called
his angels."[19] Thus, prior to the Vulgate, scholars were applying the
name "Lucifer" to Satan and associating him with the angelic apostasy legend. But this was all well after the biblical texts were written,
It seems there is an arguable but weak historical case for applying the
term "Lucifer"—as loosely derived from *Helel Ben-Shachar*—to the
adversary found in the New Testament. If there is any valid connection at all, then *Satan became Lucifer* as a Christian construct. The
legend about the archangel Lucifer becoming Satan is only a Roman
Catholic fairy tale.

The Origin of Demons

While it is relatively clear in the New Testament that Satan is a rebel
archangel adversarial to Christ and humanity (Matthew 25:41;
1 Peter 5:8; Revelation 12:9), the origins of his brood are less clear.
For a thorough treatment of the subject of Satan, I recommend David
Lowe's work, *Deconstructing Lucifer.*[20] Even though I do not necessarily agree with all of his conclusions, Lowe takes on the difficult issues
that too many overlook. The original Greek term *daimon* from which
we render "demon" in the New Testament had a wide range of mean-

THE SUPERNATURAL WORLDVIEW

ing. In fact, in popular Koine Greek, the word commonly referred to human ghosts. According to a leading scholarly lexicon, "So far as concerns popular belief and its animistic basis we may simply say that demons are fundamentally the spirits of the departed."[21] This is rooted deep in antiquity as Hesiodus of Ascra (c. 700 BC), the oldest Greek poet to emerge as a tangible figure, called the souls of the departed *daimones*.[22] This is generally consistent with Jewish beliefs.

In the Hebrew Bible, the spirits of the dead consulted in witchcraft are called *elohim*, as seen in the invocation of the witch of Endor, who marveled: "I saw gods *(elohim)* ascending out of the earth" (1 Samuel 28:13). What we want to know is what the New Testament authors meant when they used the Greek term *daimon*. The problem is that because we have very little data on the origin of demons and evil spirits in the Bible, we just do not know with any certainty. Theologian Millard Erickson conceded, "The Bible has little to say about how evil angels came to have their current moral character and even less about their origin."[23]

Furthermore, there could be truth in more than one theory. There is no reason they all must be the same. Some of these entities could have started out as humans and others angels. Thomas Horn lists seven possibilities held by various scholars: 1) Spirits of a pre-Adamic race; 2) Otherworldly beings (extraterrestrials, as unpacked in our cowritten book, *Exo-Vaticana*); 3) Offspring of angels and women (the nephilim-origin hypothesis); 4) Spirits of deceased wicked men; 5) Fallen angels; 6) Several of the above; 7) None of the above (demythologization). Of the seven, I fall under the broad area of number six, concerning which Horn wrote:

> The proponents of this hypothesis believe a singular concept for the origin of "demons" is a mistake, that in fact

what is routinely considered "the demonic realm" could be made up of several of the explanations above, and that this might demonstrate the hierarchy of demons as outlined in the book of Ephesians. In this view, "fallen angels" would rank above the "spirits of Nephilim" and so on, with each being part of the army of darkness. Just as privates in the United States military serve under sergeants who serve under majors, Satan's forces consist of wicked spirits *(poneria:* the mass of common demon soldiers comprising Satan's hordes) under rulers of darkness *(kosmokrators:* martial spirits that influence or administer the affairs of earthly governments) and powers *(exousia:* high-ranking officials whose modes of operation are primarily battlefield ops). Above these are principalities or archons *(arche:* brigadier generals over the divisions of Satan's hosts). Satan, who reigns as supreme commander and king, is the "prince of the powers of the air." (Ephesians 2:2)[24]

There seem to be a variety of evil spirits at work, and too many unknowns plague our knowledge. As discussed previously, we live amongst a widespread resurgence in occult practices, including witchcraft and magic. More disturbingly, satanic cults have arisen, resulting in ritual murders by conscience-seared adults and misguided teenagers. The reality of demonization no longer seems fanciful, but it is probably still too often explained away by mental illness. Many Americans are falling prey to devices of deceitful supernatural entities, mainly through ignorance. The most advanced books of demonic magic, spiritism, and witchcraft are readily available to anyone on the Internet. The flood of supernaturalism in America is beyond the control of law-enforcement agencies and organized churches, but it is not beyond the sovereignty of God. I hope to expand your worldview in preparation for what many believe to be an unprecedented rise in demonic activity prior to the return of Christ. Before moving into speculative territory regarding their origins, I want to clarify what we can be confident in.

Seven Biblical Propositions on Demons

First, a controversy is explored and then seven more definite propositions are listed. In the past, I have argued in a manner learned from my mentor and Bible teacher Chuck Missler that demons and fallen angels are not necessarily the same thing.[25] While I agree in principle, the meaning of the term "demon" is the very thing we are defining. After studying Greek, it now seems to me that the Christian scholars are deferring to the Greek term *daimon* rather than drawing conclusions from the New Testament alone. If we understand the term "demon" in a manner consistent with its early Greek use, as well as in later Christian developments, it could arguably be understood to encompass all evil spirits aligned with Satan. In this way, one could preserve the important distinctions made by Missler but argue that although all fallen angels are demons, not all demons are fallen angels. Of course, Missler's arguments are directed toward the controversy over the nephilim and the identity of the "sons of God" in Genesis 6. I have addressed that debate ad nauseum and see no need to argue it here. The Supernatural Worldview unequivocally supports that the "sons of God" are spirit entities.

The reason for most of the push-back in the nephilim discussion is that it points to fallen angels procreating with human women. Many people refuse to allow this as a possibility, I suppose because it is too scary. It also begs the question about the physicality of angels and demons. This is where I believe we must allow that not every entity labeled "demon" is the same sort of being. Missler points out that holy angels seem to manifest human bodies at will, but demons seek to control the bodies of others. This is well supported by biblical texts, as Missler points out: "Angels can materialize, take people by the hand (Genesis 19:16), eat meals with mankind (Genesis 18:7, 8), and indulge in combat (2 Kings 19:35). Some have even entertained angels unawares (Hebrews 13:2)."[26] But what about cases in which evil spirits or demons seem to manifest physically? The following case is borrowed from my former work with Tom Horn, *Exo-Vaticana:*

In the early 1950s, Dr. [Lester] Sumrall was in Manila building a church, which today is known as the Cathedral of Praise. On May 12, 1953, the *Daily Mirror* in Manila published a startling story under the headline, "Police Medic Explodes Biting Demons Yarn," in which a most unusual story unfolded of law enforcers and medical examiners being mystified by an inmate whose body continuously bore deep teeth marks. The frightened girl claimed that two beings were appearing and biting her. One of the devils was big and dark with long hair all over his head, chest, and arms. He had fangs like a dog and large, sharp eyes, and his feet were at least three times larger than normal. He was dressed in a black robe with what appeared to be a hood on the back. His voice was deep, with a tunnel-like echo. The second being was squatty, maybe thirty inches tall, and it was also dark, hairy, and deformed. As the witnesses watched, the girl's facial expressions would suddenly change, and she would begin glancing about, as if she was seeing something the others could not. (What she was seeing was dubbed "The Thing" by the press.) Then the girl would start screaming and struggling against an invisible force, before collapsing, half-conscious, into the arms of the prison staff member holding her. At that moment, there would be teeth marks wet with saliva marking her body. Dr. Mariano B. Lara, then chief medical examiner of the Manila Police Department and a university professor of pathology and legal medicine, was convinced of the genuineness of the possession and exorcism and provided his own description, recounted in this excerpt from the official medical report filed at the prison:

> I find it difficult and near impossible to accept anything of a supernatural character.... Equipped with a magnifying lens and an unbelieving mind about this biting phenomena, I scrutinized carefully the exposed parts of her [Clarita Villanueva's] body, the arms, hands, and neck, to find out whether they had the biting impressions. I saw the reddish human-like bite marks on the arms.... At that very instant, this girl in a semi-trance loudly screamed repeatedly.... I saw, with my unbelieving eyes, the clear marks or impressions of human-like teeth from both the upper and lower jaws. It was a little moist in the area bitten on the dorsal aspect of the left hand, and the teeth impressions were mostly from the form of the front or incisor teeth. Seeing these with my unbelieving eyes, yet I could not

understand nor explain how they were produced as her hand had all the time been held away from the reach of her mouth.…

In full possession of her normal mind, I asked her (Clarita Villanueva) who was causing her to suffer from the bites. She answered that there are two who are alternately biting her; one big, black, hairy human-like fellow, very tall, with two sharp eyes, two sharp canine teeth, long beard like a Hindu, hairy extremities and chest, wearing a black garment, with a little whitish piece on the back resembling a hood. His feet are about three times the size of normal feet. The other fellow is a very small one about two or three feet tall allegedly also black, hairy and ugly.[27]

After first hearing the report on the radio then reading the newspaper story the next day, Dr. Sumrall, who believed the girl was demon possessed, grew convicted that the Lord wanted him to procure permission from prison authorities to pray for the prostitute's deliverance. Through his church architect, who was a friend of the mayor of Manila, he received the okay to visit with the chief medical advisor of the police department, Dr. Mariano Lara. While talking with the doctor inside the prison morgue, Lara acknowledged to Sumrall that something beyond his professional knowledge was happening and that he was actually afraid of "The Thing" after witnessing the bite marks appear before his own eyes. With Lara's approval, Sumrall was allowed to pray for the girl while observers watched. She was very resistant, cursing him in English (which she could not speak), screaming, and fighting every moment to get away. The first day of prayer failed to provide healing, and Sumrall believed he needed to fast and pray for another day. That evening, the newspaper published his picture on the front page, three columns wide, with the headline, "The Thing Defies Pastor."[28] The next day would be different. Following a spiritual battle reminiscent of an Old Testament prophet challenging the followers of Baal, and with repentance of her sins and acceptance of Jesus as Savior, the girl was delivered, yet, that was not the end of the story. Sumrall explains what happened next:

> As I was leaving I told Clarita that I was sure these devils would return. "After I am gone," I said, "they will come. Then you must demand them to leave without my being present. You must say, 'Go, in Jesus' name,' and they will obey." With this I left the compound.
>
> We asked the newsmen not to write about the morning's events, but they said they were obliged to. The story had run for two weeks and it must be concluded. Since the Methodist Church is the oldest Protestant denomination in the islands, they presumed I was a Methodist, and it was in the papers that way. They did not know how to write of such an experience; therefore, some of what they said was not correct. But I feel mostly responsible for this, as I gave them no interview and left the city to get away from publicity.

The devils did return to attack Clarita, and a
strange thing happened when she called on them to
leave. *She was engaged in a mortal struggle and went
into a coma, her fists clenched. The doctor pried her
hands open and to his astonishment, there lay some
long, black, coarse hair. Dr. Lara placed this hair in
an envelope and put it in a guarded place. Under the
microscope he found that the hair was not from any
part of the human body. The doctor has no answer to
this mystery—how an invisible being, presumably a
devil, could have lost hair by a visible being pulling it
out.*[29] (emphasis added)

The notion of physical material like hair having been
pulled from a wraithlike demon opens the fascinating
proposal that ultraterrestrial beings (call them angels,
demons, or aliens) can migrate back and forth between
different realities and take forms that are both material and
immaterial.[30]

Furthermore, we cited medieval cases of incubi and succubi
demons that were documented by Ludovico Sinistrari to be very real
physical manifestations.[31] Cases aside, it is not very precisely clear as
to what level demons are physical; some seem to be and others do
not, but this ambiguity most likely implies that a variety of entities
fall under the broad category of "demon." Even though it is an esoteric and thorny area of inquiry, I found seven propositions concerning demons that I believe to be biblically solid.

First, the Bible is clear that demons are powerful personal
beings who dominate that non-Christian world (2 Corinthians 4:4;

Ephesians 2:2; John 14:30; and 1 John 5:19). According to Dr. Larry
Richards in *Every Angel in the Bible:*

> The Gospels use personal pronouns when reporting dia-
> logues with demons (see Luke 8:27–30); individual demons
> apparently have personal names, and groups of demons
> have "team" names (see Luke 8:30). Demons can commu-
> nicate and hold conversations (see Luke 4:22–26; 8:28–30).
> Demons also have intelligence (see Mark 1:23, 24; Luke
> 4:34; 8:28), emotions (see Luke 8:28), and a will (see Mark
> 1:27; Luke 4:35, 36).[32]

While liberals castigate the demonic as some sort of metaphor,
the Bible clearly teaches a personal superhuman opposition to God
active in the world that we should not so glibly underestimate.

Second, demons seek to control, deceive, and destroy people,
especially believers—sometimes physically but largely through the
thought life (Matthew 4:1 ff.; John 8:44; 2 Corinthians 2:11, 11:14;
Ephesians 6:11; 2 Thessalonians 2:9; Hebrews 2:14; and 1 Peter
5:8). According to Richards:

> Demons have the ability to control, or to influence, human
> beings. The Gospels report incidents in which demons
> caused mental derangement, including full-fledged insanity
> (see Luke 8:27–29) and suicidal mania (see Mark 9:22). The
> Gospels also report that demons cause a variety of physi-
> cal disabilities. These include muteness (see Matt. 9:32, 33;
> Mark 9:17–29), blindness (see Matt. 12:11), deformities
> (see Luke 13:11–17), and severe seizures (see Matt. 17:15–
> 18; Luke 9:39).[33]

These are not myths and metaphors, but hostile personal beings bent on harming humans.

Third, demons seem to be dependent on human sin and derive their power from it (Ephesians 4:7; 1 Corinthians 7:5; and 2 Corinthians 4:4). This idea works remarkably well with Watchman Nee's end-time warning of a rise in psychic phenomena because oneism appeals to mankind's pride by suggesting evolution toward divinity. Jones puts it this way: "The ultimate pagan declaration is 'Man becomes God,' but the Christian declaration is: 'God became Man.'"[34]

Fourth, demons are not divine but rather created (Psalm 82:7 and Colossians 1:16).

Fifth, demons are morally perverted evil beings that are at least partially representative of rebellious angels (Genesis 6:1–5; Psalm 82; 2 Peter 2:4; and Jude 6). While this accounts for some entities, it is not necessarily comprehensive. Richards concludes:

> Demons are called "evil spirits" (see Luke 7:31). The Greek word for evil, *pone-ros,* indicates an active, virulent wickedness that expresses itself in doing harm to others. Demons are also called "unclean spirits" (see Matt. 10:1; Mark 1:23), which also has a moral connotation.[35]

Sixth, although we face an imminent conflict (Revelation 12:9), demons have been defeated by the cross (Colossians 2:15).

Seventh, demons will ultimately be judged and destroyed (Matthew 25:41; Revelation 12:9, 20:10). I am confident in these seven assertions along with their implications and encourage the reader to study the listed passages.

The Divine Council

Semitics expert Dr. Michael Heiser calls this the "Deuteronomy 32 Worldview," a theological construct based on the oldest manuscript's reading of verse 8. This is one concept that is much clearer in the original languages than English translations, and the translation used makes all the difference. Where one reads in the King James Version, "according to the number of the children of Israel," in the Dead Sea Scrolls [DSS] as well as the Greek Septuagint, this verse is translated, "according to the number of the sons of God," which is a clear reference to angels (Deuteronomy 32:8, ESV [the ESV translation used the DSS reading]).

The passage is teaching that the number of the nations is proportional to the number of the *bene ha elohim*, the "sons of God" mentioned in Genesis 6:2 and Job 1:6, among other passages. This is a more logical reading, because at no time in history was mankind divided in reference to the number of Israelites, a Masoretic text/KJV-derived idea that doesn't add up. Of the seventy nations in the Genesis 10 table, certain "sons of God" or "powers and principalities" are associated with specific geographic areas and people groups. In ancient Judaism, it was understood that the dispersal at the Tower of Babel entailed not only the confusion of the languages, but Yahweh's disinheriting of the other nations. In order to display distinction, Deuteronomy 32:9 indicates that He chose Israel as His own. This explains why God was so concerned that His people stood out as pure and holy. It explains the exact rules and God's frustration with them. Israel was an example. Although revealed in the New Testament as a "mystery," God's plan was always to reconcile the nations through the Messiah (Ephesians 3:6). However, the foreign gods still exact a rebellious influence. The territorial nature of these powers is supported by Scripture.

In the book of Daniel, the angel Gabriel reports to Daniel that he was delayed twenty-one days due to a battle with the "prince of the kingdom of Persia," and was only able to escape when Israel's champion, the archangel Michael, came to assist (Daniel 10:13–14). Even more, he reports that once he is done battling the Persian spirit, he must then fight the "prince of Greece." What immediately comes to mind is that at the time of Daniel's writing, the Persian Empire was in control of most of the world, but it was soon to be conquered by Alexander the Great of Greece. What we have in Daniel is a peek behind the curtain of an extradimensional battle, which finds its analog in our material world. It seems the purveyors of the control system have their own rivalries. The prophet Isaiah foretells the future judgment of these so-called gods: "On that day the Lord will punish the host of heaven, in heaven, and the kings of the earth, on the earth" (Isaiah 24:21). This is also seen in the Psalms.

With this background in mind, I suggest reading Psalm 82, where you will read that Yahweh was not pleased with the way these spirits—referred to as "gods" with a little "g"—misgoverned and abused their people. The same passage supporting the division according to the number of the sons of God also identifies them as devils (Deuteronomy 32:17). In fact, God says that because of their manipulation and deceitfulness, they are doomed to "die like men" (Psalm 82:7). Thus interpreting Psalm 82 to argue that the "gods" are human men violates the context. After all, men sentenced to "die like men" is hardly a meaningful punishment. Furthermore, Psalm 89:5–7 locates this assembly "in the heaven" (v. 6) and clarifies the deeper meaning behind the "sons of the mighty" as *bene ha elohim*, "sons of God," which always refers to heavenly beings. Other passages that mention the divine council include the following: 1 Kings 22:10–23; Isaiah 6:1–8 and 40:1–11; Psalms 29:1–2, 58:1, 89:5–8, 103:20–21, and

148:2; Job 1:6–12, 2:1–7, and 15:8; Jeremiah 23:18; and Daniel 7:9–10 and 10:13–14, 20–21. (If you would like to learn more concerning the Old Testament background, I suggest visiting Dr. Heiser's website at http://www.thedivinecouncil.com/, and I recommend his book, *The Myth That Is True*.[36])

With Heiser's "Deuteronomy 32 Worldview" in mind, the Hebrew background to Paul's discussions of rulers, powers, and principalities comes into clearer focus (Ephesians 3:10, 6:12; Colossians 1:16, 2:15). As demonstrated prior, it is most likely true that more than one sort of entity falls under the broad category of "demon." Perhaps these fallen "sons of God"—labeled little-'g' gods—are one and the same as the rulers *(archons)*, but what about the more commonplace evil spirits *(poneron pneumaton)* encountered in the Gospels and Acts (Matthew 12:45; Luke 7:21, 8:2; Acts 19:12–16)? The "ghost hypothesis" may account for some of these entities.

The Ghost Hypothesis, Johann Blumhardt, and Gottliebin Dittus

Although I give it some emphasis in this chapter, I am not saying that the human ghost theory of demonic origins is a fact, but rather that one should allow for it. As the fourth in Horn's list of seven, he wrote:

This teaching, still popular with a fragment of modern theologians, seems to have its origin in early Greek mythology. The Homeric gods, who were but supernatural men, were both good and evil. The hypothesis was that the good and powerful spirits of good men rose to assume places of deity after experiencing physical death, while the evil spirits of deceased, evil men were gods, doomed to roam the Earth and its interior. At death, their spirits remained in an eternal limbo, unable to perish, yet incapable of attaining heaven. Besides Greeks, the ancient Jewish historians, Philo and Josephus, held similar views, as did many of the early Church fathers.[37]

Could some demons be human ghosts? The theory actually has a lot of explanatory scope, especially for the demonic rationale for taking up residence in someone's body. Maybe the demons want back what they once had? One of the cases that led me to seriously investigate this line of thinking was that of Johann Christoph Blumhardt and Gottliebin Dittus, a nineteenth-century German account examined here in detail with links to further resources.

The modern state of affairs—a rise in all that is demonic—brings fresh new relevance to *Blumhardt's Battle: A Conflict with Satan,* a book published 1970 but based on a nineteenth-century report to the Lutheran Synod by Johann Christoph Blumhardt, a pastor in the little town of Möttlingen, Germany. His pastoral career was one of conventional preaching and ministering until, in 1842, one of his parishioners, a young woman named Gottlieben Dittus, was afflicted by a severe nervous disorder and whose household was visited with strange psychic phenomena. He records a fantastic account of spiritual warfare that, if accepted, will expand the horizons of one's Supernatural Worldview.

If there ever was a desperate case of demonization, it was that of Dittus, whose youthful involvement with folk magic caused a frightful attachment by various kinds of evil spirits. This twenty-eight-year-old woman from a good Christian home was incapacitated by kidney disease and was recuperating in an apartment with her brother and sisters with relatives in Möttlingen. Shortly thereafter, in February of 1840, sinister, poltergeist-like phenomena were seen and heard many witnesses. Pastor Blumhardt noted that Dittus' brother and sister had reported that from the first day poltergeist phenomena ensued, unexplained noises were heard about the house and Dittus was even struck unconscious while trying to pray.

As a result, her personality quickly transformed for the worse, and she behaved dangerously. Psychological torments and physical afflictions, including bleeding and convulsions, drove her to the brink of suicide. In fact, she tried to hang herself from a tree but the scarf broke. By all appearances, she was beyond human aid.

Thus, Blumhardt was led to enter into direct conflict with the powers of darkness on her behalf. He concluded that the case was like those reported in the New Testament as demonization. After two months of pastoral care and reverent hesitation, confessing that he had no knowledge or power that could help, he and the young girl prayed to Jesus together for her deliverance. In the battle that ensued, he learned much about the weapons of spiritual warfare and discovered a few things he wasn't expecting.

The whole neighborhood became aware of the haunting. Interestingly, one of the principal evil spirits involved was allegedly that of a deceased woman known previously to Pastor Blumhardt. Concerning hearing about a ghost in the house, he wrote:

At that time, Gottliebin saw with special frequency the figure of a woman of this town (who had died two years earlier), holding a dead child in her arms. Gottliebin carefully kept her name secret and did not tell it to me until later.[38]

The girl's torment escalated and the paranormal activity was so well attested that it began to attract tourists to the home. The pastor figured out the identity of the alleged ghost as one of his parishioners who had recently passed away. Blumhardt recalled that, prior to her passing, the woman had been plagued with a guilty conscience and confessed some serious sins to him on her death bed.

Blumhardt confronted the ghost directly:

"Don't you rest in the grave?"

"No."

"Why not?"

"That is the reward for my deeds."

"Didn't you," I continued, silently supposing that it was that person, "confess all of your sins to me?"

"No, I murdered two children and buried them in the field."

"Don't you know of any help now? Can't you pray?"

"I cannot pray."

"Don't you know Jesus Who forgives sins?"

"I can't stand to hear that Name."

"Are you alone?"

"No."

"Who is with you?"

The voice answered with hesitation, then with a rush, "The worst of all."[39]

According to the pastor's report, the conversation revealed that the woman believed herself bound to the devil for participating in magic. She now possessed the body of Gottliebin Dittus by satanic mandate. She had tried to leave her body seven times already, but was compelled to reenter by her diabolic overlords. Numerous demons were expelled from the young girl, and the pastor's account makes Hollywood's *The Exorcist* seem comparatively like a kinder-garten's story time. To fully appreciate the depth of the spiritual war-fare involved, I recommend that you follow the footnoted link and read the entire story.[40] What I find troublingly curious is the idea that human ghosts not only haunt human beings, but may actually inhabit and influence humans in the way classic demons do. Could some demons be disincarnate human spirits?

Astonishingly, Blumhardt records evil spirits actually seeking redemption, an idea foreign to conventional evangelical theology (cf. Hebrews 9:27). It seems inconsistent with many theological truths, especially divine election, foreknowledge, and predestination (Ephesians 1:5, 11). Even so, in this account, the evil spirit conveys truth not expected from a ruse, even applauding the pastor for not veering away from Scripture and prayer as his sole means of deliverance. Blumhardt reported:

> The first demon with which I dared to deal was, as far as I remember, the woman through whom the whole thing got started. She showed herself again in Gottliebin and cried with a firm and decided voice that she wanted to belong to the Savior and not to the devil. Then she said how much had been changed in the world of spirits through these battles up to now. She said that my good fortune had been that I had remained solely with the Word of God and prayer. If I had tried anything else and even taken refuge in secretly working means, as they were frequently used among the common people, and to which the demons had tempted me, I would have been lost…. Then she begged and implored me that I might pray for her so that she would get completely free from the power of the devil into which she had come nearly

ignorantly through idolatry, sympathy, and magic; and to pray that she might find a place of rest somewhere.[41]

Blumhardt recorded conversation where the spirit begged to take refuge in his home, which he wisely refused, Finally, he agreed the spirit could go to the church if it remained invisible and under the condition that Jesus allowed it. As Blumhardt assisted many human spirits to a place of rest, he was keenly aware of the questionable theological implications and wisely refused to derive doctrine from his experience:

> In this fashion it continued for a while. Whatever spirit was given a resting place, did not return again.... I do want to add to this that neither the dogma of purgatory nor the dogma of prayer for the dead are confirmed by the above in any way. The latter is so dangerous that I do want to warn every man of it in all seriousness. The most devastating effects from the unseen world can be the consequence of it.

After a full two years of struggle, Blumhardt finally saw Dittus fully restored to a physically and spiritually free, psychologically sane, normal existence. She was so reliable that Blumhardt went on to employ her as a nanny for his own children. Jesus' victory in the demonized girl immediately triggered a revival that transformed the entire village of Möttlingen, attracting spiritual seekers from all over Germany. This included the inexplicable conversions of hardened skeptics, miraculous healings, and radical transformations of life and character. Lifelong enemies reconciled, dysfunctional marriages were saved, and there was an all-around outpouring of evangelistic zeal. The fruit resulting from the described spiritual warfare was undeniably virtuous and served to further the gospel. One can read more of the details in *The Awakening: One Man's Battle with Darkness* by Friedrich Zuendel, which is available as a free ebook from Plough publishers at the endnoted URL.[42] The reason this story was cited is because this resulting good fruit seems to authenticate it, and Pastor Blumhardt makes for such a credible witness.

Johann Christoph Blumhardt[43]

Johann Blumhardt is regarded by many as the father of German pietism, and his son Christoph F. Blumhardt (1842–1919) influenced a whole generation of Europeans, including Dietrich Bonhoeffer, Emil Brunner, Oscar Cullmann, and Karl Barth. While it is never advisable to derive theology exclusively from anecdotes or personal experience, what are we to do with this account, given Blumhardt's impeccable Christian character and the resulting spiritual fruit? It is tempting to dismiss the claims of the spirits as lies and subterfuge, but a close reading of Blumhardt's narrative does not support it. Scripture warns of ultimate judgment for those who reject the gospel, but it is relatively quiet concerning the interval between death and the final judgment after the return of Christ (Revelation 20:11–15). Are there any passages that lend support to hauntings by human spirits? According to scholars, there is more support than one might first imagine.

Biblical Scholarship and the Ghost Hypothesis

Biblical scholar Peter G. Bolt's essay on "Jesus, the Daimons, and the Dead," an entire chapter in the feast of academic weirdness, *The Unseen World: Christian Reflections on Angels, Demons and the Heavenly Realm*,[44] argued that the original readers of Mark's Gospel would have believed the demons confronted and cast out by Christ to be deceased human spirits. The writer argues that unlike today, when almost none of us would think of interpreting the word "daimon" to mean the spirit of a deceased person, a first-century audience would have simply assumed it to mean a human ghost.

He cites numerous examples in the Greco-Roman literature from before, during, and after the New Testament period and demonstrates how the view fits well when interpreting passages involving daimons throughout Scripture. The exorcisms in the book of Mark are then analyzed from this viewpoint to show us what the implications would have been if the audience had indeed viewed daimons as the spirits of deceased humans. The ramifications are extensive, to say the least, if Dr. Bolt's thesis is indeed correct.

While it is popular amongst evangelicals to label "ghosts" as "demons," this reverses the roles. In this case, demons are ghosts of deceased humans. Is this a heretical notion or a possibility one should consider? I think the latter, because, as Bolt cogently argued, the literature from the New Testament period consistently allows for it. For example, in his First Apology (chapter 18), the second-century Christian apologist Justin Martyr makes an argument for the immortality of the soul that reflects the view that the term "demons" includes the souls of the deceased:

> For let even necromancy, and the divinations you practise by immaculate children, and the evoking of departed human souls, and those who are called among the magi, Dream-senders and Assistant-spirits (Familiars), and all that is done by those who are skilled in such matters—let these persuade you that even after death souls are in a state of sensation; and those who are seized and cast about by the spirits of the dead, whom all call daemoniacs or madmen.[45]

In a similar way, the Alexandrian Jewish scholar Philo uses "demon" to refer to the spirit of a man's deceased wife:

> Therefore, looking on Silanus as a bore, who only wished to check the impetuosity and indulgence of his appetites, and discarding all recollection of and regard for his deceased wife, he treacherously put her father to death, who was also his own father-in-law.[46]

Isn't it rather odd that the Greek *tois daimosi tes apothanouses gunaikos* is translated as "his deceased wife," omitting the term *daimon?* The Greek view was somewhat different than the Latin.

In Latin Christianity, the fallen angel view was promoted and assumed dominance. Around AD 200, Tertullian, a scholar from Carthage in North Africa, wrote in his *Apology:*

We are instructed, moreover, by our sacred books how from certain angels, who fell of their own free-will, there sprang a more wicked demon-brood, condemned of God along with the authors of their race, and that chief we have referred to. It will for the present be enough, however, that some account is given of their work. Their great business is the ruin of mankind.[47]

He associated some with the named pagan gods, but included a variety of evil spirits. He named the diseases that demons caused and then pretended to cure under the guise of healing spirits. Tertullian believed that demons used the ghost explanation as a ruse so that "that men may not readily believe that all souls remove to Hades, and that they may overthrow faith in the resurrection and the judgment."[48] Thus, he was an early proponent of the most popular view seen today, that fallen angels account for all demonic phenomena and the other theories are merely their lies. It is a hard construct to argue against, because any evidence against it simply becomes part of the conspiracy. Even so, many ancient Jews still believed that deceased humans (or human hybrids) could become evil demons afflicting the living.

The view concerning demonic origins held by most first-century Jews was derivative of the Book of Enoch's account that the spirits of the hybrid giants were damned to be earthbound (1 Enoch 15:8–10). The text *Legends of the Jews* well summarizes this still-popular belief:

Giants begotten by flesh and spirits will be called evil spirits on earth, and on the earth will be their dwelling-place. Evil spirits proceed from their bodies, because they are created from above, and from the holy watchers is their beginning and primal origin; they will be evil spirits on earth, and evil spirits they will be named. And the spirits of heaven have their dwelling in heaven, but the spirits of the earth, which were born upon the earth, have their dwelling on the earth. And the spirits of the giants will devour, oppress, destroy, attack, do battle, and cause destruction on the earth, and work affliction. They will take no kind of food, nor will they thirst, and they will be invisible. And these spirits will rise up against the children of men and against the women, because they have proceeded from them. Since the days of murder and destruction and the death of the giants, when the spirits went forth from the soul of their flesh, in order to destroy without incurring judgment—thus will they destroy until the day when the great consummation of the great world be consummated.[49]

Even so, we've seen that many of the early church fathers held a variety of opinions. As a nephilim believer, the Jewish historian Flavius Josephus describes widely practiced healing techniques allegedly passed down from King Solomon to cure mental disorders and expel demons—implying human spirits. As evidence, he cites a case in which one of his associates, Eleazar, performed such a healing in front the emperor and his court by these means:

God also enabled him to learn that skill which expels demons, which is a science useful and sanative to men. He composed such incantations also by which distempers are alleviated. And he left behind him the manner of using exorcisms, by which they drive away demons, so that they never return, and this method of cure is of great force unto this day; for I have seen a certain man of my own country whose name was Eleazar, releasing people that were demoniacal in the presence of Vespasian, and his sons, and his captains, and the whole multitude of his soldiers. The manner of the cure was this: He put a ring that had a root of one of those sorts mentioned by Solomon to the nostrils of the demoniac, after which he drew out the demon through his nostrils; and when the man fell down immediately, he abjured him to return into him no more, making still mention of Solomon, and reciting the incantations which he composed. And when Eleazar would persuade and demonstrate to the spectators that he had such a power, he set a little way off a cup or basin full of water, and commanded the demon, as he went out of the man, to overturn it, and thereby to let the spectators know that he had left the man; and when this was done, the skill and wisdom of Solomon was shown very manifestly; for which reason it is, that all men may know the vastness of Solomon's abilities, and how he was beloved of God, and that the extraordinary virtues of every kind with which this king was endowed may not be unknown to any people under the sun; for this reason, I say, it is that we have proceeded to speak so largely of these matters.[50]

These early accounts establish that deceased humans' activity in the spirit realm was surely a part of the worldview of the New Testament authors. Their silence seems instructive, because it was such a popular idea that a direct prohibition would have been appropriate. We never question the widely understood meaning of other Greek terms; why should we exclude a prevailing meaning for "demon" without a specific biblical rationale?

This history has led many theologians prior to Peter Bolt to also understand human ghosts as part of the demonic realm. Alexander

Campbell (1788–1866) was a Scots-Irish immigrant who became an ordained minister in the United States and joined a reform effort historically known as the Restoration Movement. It resulted in the development of nondenominational Christian churches, which stressed reliance on Scripture and few essentials. This excerpt from Campbell's 1841 "Address on Demonology" makes a compelling case for human origins:

> We have, from a careful survey of the history of the term *demon,* concluded that *the demons of Paganism, Judaism, and Christianity were the ghosts of dead men.* But we build not only upon the definition of the term, nor on its philological history; but upon the following seven pillars: 1. All the Pagan authors of note, whose works have survived the wreck of ages, affirm the opinion that demons were the spirits or ghosts of dead men. From Hesiod down to the more polished Celsus, their historians, poets, and philosophers occasionally express this opinion. 2. The Jewish historians, Josephus and Philo, also avow this conviction. Josephus says, "Demons are the spirits of wicked men, who enter into living men and destroy them, unless they are so happy as to meet with speedy relief." Philo says, "The souls of dead men are called demons." 3. The Christian Fathers, Justin Martyr, Ireneus, Origen, &c. depose to the same effect. Justin, when arguing for a future state, alleges, "Those who are seized and tormented by the souls of the dead, whom all call demons, and madmen." Lardner, after examining with the most laborious care the works of these, and all the Fathers of the first two centuries, says, "The notion of demons, or the souls of dead men, having power over living men, was *universally* prevalent among the heathen of these times, and believed by many

Christians." 4. The Evangelists and Apostles of Jesus Christ so understood the matter. As this is a very important, and of itself a sufficient pillar on which to rest our edifice, we shall be at more pains to illustrate and enforce it. We shall first state the philological law or canon of criticism, on the generality and truth of which all our dictionaries, grammars, and translations are formed. *Every word not specially explained or defined in a particular sense, by any standard writer of any particular age and country, is to be taken and applied in the current or commonly received signification of that country and age in which the writer lived and wrote.* If this canon of translation and of criticism be denied, then we affirm there is no value in dictionaries, nor in the acquisition of ancient languages in which any book may be written; nor is there any confidence in any translation of any ancient work, sacred or profane: for they are all made upon the assumption of the truth of this law. We have then only to ask first for the current signification of this term *demon* in Judea at the Christian era; and, in the second place, Did the inspired writers ever give any special definition of it? We have already found an answer to the first in the Greeks and Jews of the apostolic age—also, in the preceding and subsequent age. We have heard Josephus, Philo, Lucian, Justin, and Lardner, from whose writings and affirmations we are expressly told what the universal acceptation of the term was in Judea and in those times; and in the second place, the Apostles and our Lord, as already said, use this word in various forms 75 times, and on no occasion give any hint of a special, private, or peculiar interpretation of it; which was not their method when they used a term either not generally understood, or understood in a special sense. Does any one ask the meaning of the word Messiah, prophet, priest, elder, deacon, presbytery, altar, sacrifice, sabbath, circumcision, &c. &c.? We refer him to the current signification of these words among the Jews and Greeks of that age. Why, then, should any one except the term *demon* from the universal law? Are we not, therefore, sustained by the highest and most authoritative decision of that literary tribunal by whose rules and decrees all works sacred and profane are translated from a dead to a living tongue? We are, then, fully authorized to say that the demons of the New Testament were the spirits of dead men.[51]

Campbell's complete essay is compelling and included as appendix 1. I do not claim this is fact, but rather offer it as a possibility in light of the sweeping popularity of ghost hunting and all things paranormal.

Conclusion

The overarching thesis of this chapter is that those who claim to believe the Bible must be open to the possibilities it implies, no matter how unsettling. The Supernatural Worldview is one of distinctions. We do not assume all is one. The demonic realm is likely populated by a variety of different entities. The ghost hypothesis is well supported in ancient sources and offers a persuasive rationale for why some demons are obsessed with entering and controlling the bodies of humans. Accordingly, the next chapter will address spiritual warfare.

Notes

1. http://www.biola.edu/academics/sas/apologetics/certificate/.
2. Holly Pivec, "Exorcising Our Demons, Many Evangelicals Are Too Skeptical of the Demonic," *BIOLA* Magazine, Winter 2006, http://magazine.biola.edu/article/06-winter/exorcising-our-demons/ (accessed 01/29/14).
3. July 26, 2013 personal Facebook message from Wallace to Putnam.
4. Carl Sagan and Ann Druyan, *The Demon-Haunted World: Science as a Candle in the Dark* (New York: Ballantine, 1997).
5. "Most American Christians Do Not Believe that Satan or the Holy Spirit Exist," Barna Group, April 10, 2009, http://www.barna.org/barna-update/article/12-faithspirituality/260-most-american-christians-do-not-believe-that-satan-or-the-holy-spirit-exis (accessed 04/30/13).
6. George P. Hansen, "The Trickster and the Paranormal: Overview," http://www.tricksterbook.com/ (accessed 09/04/13).
7. George P. Hansen, *The Trickster and the Paranormal* (Bloomington, IN: Xlibris, 2001) Kindle edition, 2033–2034.
8. Pope Francis' sermon quoted in article: "Pope Francis Says Atheists Who Do Good Are Redeemed, Not Just Catholics," *Huffington Post*, May 22, 2013, http://www.huffingtonpost.com/2013/05/22/pope-francis-good-atheists_n_3320757.html (accessed 02/18/14).
9. Hansen, *Trickster*, 7816–7818.
10. Peter Jones, *One or Two: Seeing a World of Difference* (Escondido, CA: Main Entry Editions, 2010) Kindle edition, 3283.
11. Walter Leaf, *A Modern Priestess of Isis* (London: Longmans, Green & Co., 1895) 219. As cited in Jones, 3420–3421.
12. Watchman Nee, *The Latent Power of the Soul* (Christian Fellowship Publishers, 1980) 22.
13. David W. Lowe, *Deconstructing Lucifer: Reexamining the Ancient*

Origins of the Fallen Angel of Light (David W. Lowe, 2011) 55.

14. Michael S. Heiser, "The Mythological Provenance of Is. XVIV 12–15: A Reconsideration of the Ugaritic Material," *Vestus Testamentum* LI, 3, (2001): 356–357.

15. Ibid., 356–357.

16. Kaufmann Kohler, "Lucifer," http://www.jewishencyclopedia.com/ view.jsp?artid=612&letter=L (accessed 03/05/11).

17. C. S. Lewis, *Mere Christianity* (NY: Harper Collins, 2001) 122.

18. Origen, "Origen de Principiis," book 1, chapter 5, as quoted in: Alexander Roberts, James Donaldson, and A. Cleveland Coxe, *The Ante-Nicene Fathers Vol. IV: Translations of the Writings of the Fathers Down to A.D. 325* (Oak Harbor, WI: Logos Research Systems, 1997) 259.

19. Ibid., book 1, preface, 6.

20. Lowe.

21. "Daimon," vol. 2, *Theological Dictionary of the New Testament*, eds. Gerhard Kittel, Geoffrey W. Bromiley, and Gerhard Friedrich (Grand Rapids, MI: Eerdmans, 1964) electronic edition, 6.

22. Hesiodus, *Opera et Die*, 121.

23. Millard J. Erickson, *Christian Theology*, 2nd ed. (Grand Rapids, MI: Baker, 1998) 471.

24. Thomas R. Horn, ed., *God's Ghostbusters: Vampires? Ghosts? Aliens? Werewolves? Creatures of the Night Beware!* (Crane, MO: Defender, 2011), Kindle edition, 712–719.

25. Chuck Missler, "The Realm of Angels," KHouse, http://www. khouse.org/articles/2012/1044/ (accessed 1/27/2014). Also see Youtube: http://www.youtube.com/watch?v=2ti9HGEftmE. Note that I agree with his distinctions and that most theologies are grossly oversimplified; my point here is that in classical Greek, the term *daimon* could handle the biblical angels as well as the NT demons. Thus, we might preserve the coherence of most demonologies while

still making Missler's distinctions. Fallen angels might be demons, but not all demons were once angels.

26. Ibid.
27. Joseph Jacobs, "The Truth behind *The Exorcist*," TAT Journal 12 (1981), http://www.searchwithin.org/journal/tat_journal-12.html#1 (accessed 1/14/13).
28. Viewable here: "Demons: The Answer Book," *Anchor Distributors*, http://www.anchordistributors.com/ProductInfo1.aspx?item=13214 (accessed 1/14/13).
29. Ibid.
30. Thomas Horn and Cris Putnam, *Exo-Vaticana: Petrus Romanus, Project Lucifer, and the Vatican's Astonishing Exo-Theological Plan for the Arrival of an Alien Savior* (Crane, MO: Defender, 2013) 134–37.
31. Ludovico Sinistrari, *De Daemonialitate et Incubis et Succubis (Demoniality; or, Incubi and Succubi),* from the original 1680 Latin manuscript translated into English (Paris, I. Liseux, 1872) 53. The 1879 English translation of the book is available in full and free online in scanned format by the *California Digital Library* here: http://archive.org/details/demonialityorinc00sinirich (accessed 12/04/12).
32. Larry Richards, *Every Angel in the Bible* (Nashville: Thomas Nelson, 1997) 248.
33. Ibid., 249.
34. Jones, 3665–3666.
35. Richards, 248.
36. Not sure when it is to be published: http://michaelsheiser.com/TheNakedBible/2012/01/mikes-divine-council-book-draft-completed/.
37. Horn, *God's Ghostbusters*, 666–670.
38. Ibid.
39. Ibid.

40 Ibid.

41. Ibid.

42. Free download here: http://www.plough.com/en/ebooks/a/
awakening.

43. http://www.elk-wue.de/fileadmin/mediapool/elkwue/johann_
christoph_blumhardt_5616.jpg.

44. Peter G. Bolt, "Jesus, the Daimons and the Dead," *The Unseen
World: Christian Reflections on Angels, Demons and the Heavenly
Realm,* A. N. S. Lane, ed. (Carlisle, Cumbria: Paternoster Press,
1996) 75–102.

45. Justin Martyr, "First Apology" (18) in Alexander Roberts, James
Donaldson, and A. Cleveland Coxe, *The Ante-Nicene Fathers—Vol.
I: Translations of the Writings of the Fathers Down to A.D. 325, The
Apostolic Fathers with Justin Martyr and Irenaeus* (Oak Harbor, WI:
Logos Research Systems, 1997) 169.

46. Philo of Alexandria, *On The Embassy to Gaius* (65) in Charles Duke
Yonge, *The Works of Philo: Complete and Unabridged* (Peabody:
Hendrickson, 1996, c1993) 763.

47. Tertullian, "Apology 22" in *The Ante-Nicene Fathers Vol. III:
Translations of the Writings of the Fathers Down to A.D. 325, Latin
Christianity: Its Founder, Tertullian.* (Oak Harbor, WI: Logos
Research Systems, 1997) 36.

48. Ibid., 233.

49. Louis Ginzberg, Henrietta Szold, and Paul Radin, *Legends of the Jews,*
2nd ed. (Philadelphia: Jewish Publication Society, 2003) 120.

50. Flavius Josephus and William Whiston, *The Works of Josephus:
Complete and Unabridged* (Peabody: Hendrickson, 1987).

51. Alexander Campbell, "Demonology: An Address Delivered to the
Popular Lecture Club, Nashville, Tennessee, March 10, 1841,"
Millennial Harbinger (October 1841) 457–480.

SPIRITUAL WARFARE, JUVENILE PROPHETS OF BAAL, AND THE ZOMBIE APOCALYPSE

Be sober-minded; be watchful.
Your adversary the devil prowls around like a roaring lion,
seeking someone to devour.
—1 PETER 5:8, ESV

So they called out with a loud voice, and they cut
themselves with swords and with spears as was their
custom, until the blood poured out over them.
—1 KINGS 18:28, LEB

The inspiration for this book comes from the fact that I accepted
the gospel as a direct result of my experience with occult phenomena and demonic attack. During the process of coming to faith,
I was nearly led to suicide more than once. In a sense, God used
the demons to "sift me like wheat" (Luke 22:31), and I ended up
at the foot of the cross, eventually becoming an active member
of a church—which would have been the last place I would have
chosen as a younger man. I take no pride in my past mistakes
other than to boast in weakness (2 Corinthians 12:9), because it

magnifies His grace and to point out the truths of Scripture, like the sin list in 1 Corinthians 6:9–11, which ends, "And some of you were these things" (1 Corinthians 6:11a, underline added). Whereas I assumed Christians were judgmental hypocrites, I discovered in Scripture that Jesus did not come for the righteous, but to save sinners (1 Timothy 1:15). In view of that, true Christians acknowledge they are sinners too, in need of a Savior.

As a new believer, I was helped greatly by theologian Neil Anderson's book on spiritual warfare: *The Bondage Breaker*.[1] Within that work, he contends, "Freedom from spiritual conflicts and bondage is not a power encounter; it's a truth encounter."[2] The truth on which one stands is the gospel: "If you confess with your mouth that Jesus is Lord and believe in your heart that God raised him from the dead, you will be saved" (Romans 10:9). One should place no confidence in his or her own authority; those who do risk ending up like the sons of Sceva in Acts 19. Still yet, one needs not fear because Colossians 2:15 and Luke 11:21–22 reveal that Satan is a defeated foe. Thus, he and his demons gain their power through sin, fear, and ignorance. While they can hinder, they have no real authority over a Christian. Andersen argues from Ephesians 2:5–6 that believers are seated with Christ at the right hand of God, and through Him we have authority over the demons. He lists four qualifications for believers who confront these powers: 1) Belief, which is essential; 2) Humility, which is confidence properly placed because we can do nothing without Christ; 3) Boldness, which is having courage (2 Timothy 1:7); and 4) Dependence, in that our authority is in God's calling to kingdom ministry. These entities have no authority over those in Christ.

My theological training and biblical studies have carried me a long way. I have always believed that C. S. Lewis' depiction of demonic activity in the *Screwtape Letters* has much to commend it. Often, in hindsight, I can see where I have been led astray through subtle appeals to my sinful proclivities. It is interesting that James describes sinful desire in terms of "lured and enticed" (James 1:14), which sounds like the demons are sport fishing. Spiritual warfare is very real and ongoing in my life. I urge extreme caution when handling the topics in this book, and in retrospect, I do not recommend that anyone study parapsychology to the level I did. I urge prayerful caution before researching these areas.

Ephesians 6:11–17 is important enough to print the whole passage out here from the *Lexham English Bible* to give you some variety in translation for personal study:

> Put on the full armor of God, so that you may be able to stand against the stratagems of the devil, because our struggle is not against blood and flesh, but against the rulers, against the authorities, against the world rulers of this darkness, against the spiritual forces of wickedness in the heavenly places. Because of this, take up the full armor of God, in order that you may be able to resist in the evil day, and having done everything, to stand. Stand therefore, girding your waist with truth, and putting on the breastplate of righteousness, and binding shoes under your feet with the preparation of the good news of peace, in everything taking up the shield of faith, with which you are able to quench all the flaming arrows of the evil one, and receive the helmet of salvation, and the sword of the Spirit, which is the word of God.

The spiritual armor described by Paul is especially noteworthy in that we do not find special rituals or esoteric prayers for casting out demons; rather, we see the helmet of salvation, which the Christian always has on, and the breastplate of righteousness, which is our obedience and holiness. The gospel of peace, the shield of faith, and the belt of truth speak to our thought life. Finally, we see the sword of the spirit, which is God's Word one can study and memorize to use when challenged. In other words, the more you know and live by the truth, the more impenetrable your spiritual armor and the more effective your attack. This supports the assertion that spiritual warfare occurs largely in the realm of ideas and beliefs.

As far as interpreting this passage accurately, I can say with confidence that I have studied a dozen or so well-recommended scholars, and have completed a seminary course on spiritual warfare. As a result, in the scholarly realm, I recommend Clinton Arnold's *Powers of Darkness: Principalities and Powers in Paul's Letters.*[3] On the popular level, and especially for new believers, I wholeheartedly endorse the new book, *The Full Armor of God: Defending Your Life from Satan's Schemes* by Larry Richards:[4]

Richards' book is very powerful for anyone seeking personal freedom and clarity in these matters. It is also fresh off the press, so a brief encapsulation seems worthwhile. Many have noted that Paul's list is defensive other than one item: the sword of the spirit, which is offensive. It is also notable that the single offensive weapon is also the only piece of equipment that is specially defined "which is the word of God" (v. 17). Richards argues that the reason is found in the rest of Ephesians: "The reason is that each piece of armor has already been thoroughly discussed in his letter."[5] He divides the text of Ephesians into sections accordingly: the helmet of salvation (Ephesians 1:1–23); the shield of faith (Ephesians 2:1–10); the sandals of peace (Ephesians 2:11–4:16); the breastplate of righteousness (Ephesians 4:17–5:7); and the belt of truth (Ephesians 5:8–6:9). In this way, the passage serves as summary and encapsulation of the entire letter, which was to equip the Ephesian church to stand firm amongst one of the most well-known occult cities in the ancient world.[6] It explains why the emphasis is defensive, and Richards clarifies a few areas for me after years of study.

Modus Operandi Demonicus

Demons operate in the realm of ideas and seem to telepathically insert ideas and thoughts into one's thinking. That sounds controversial, but I really cannot think of a better way to describe it than *telepathically.* This is one of the reasons I wrote this book; the church tends to ignore this reality (see chapter 6). From personal experience as well as study, I surmise that the demonic strategy centers on one's thinking, especially one's besetting sins, and it usually proceeds to entice, tempt, frustrate, and finally accuse. For example, if eating candy was the proclivity one was battling, spiritual warfare might go along these lines: Once you have been "enticed" by seeing an attractive piece of candy, you are "tempted" as suggestions about how good the candy is are brought to mind and perhaps a memory of previously enjoying the same candy is recalled. I label the next stage "frustrate," because even when one gives in to temptation and bites the candy, it never satisfies, and it seems to me the demons love to dangle the promised yearning just out of reach. The final stage is the demonic specialty: to "accuse." In Hebrew, the term "Satan" means "accuser," and the figure in the first chapters of Job showcases this role. In the New Testament, Peter makes this point crystal clear as well with: "Be sober; be on the alert. Your adversary the devil walks around like a roaring lion, looking for someone to devour" (1 Peter 5:8, LEB). This verse stands in marked opposition to the amillennialists (a majority of denominational churches) who claim that we are in the millennium of Revelation 20 because that would require Satan to be bound (Revelation 20:3). Nothing could be farther from the truth; believers need to be spiritually vigilant, watching for attacks from the devil, their great opponent. The term "adversary" implies a prosecutorial role like the accuser in Revelation 12:10 and supports my argument that the war in heaven described in that chapter has not yet resolved. Other passages support the tempter/accuser role (Job 1:9–12; Matthew 4:1–11; Mark 1:12–13; Luke 4:1–13, 22:31; 2 Corinthians 2:11). The last verse reads: "so that we would not be outwitted by Satan; for we are not ignorant of his designs" (2 Corinthians 2:11). His designs are the *modus operandi* under discussion: entice, tempt, frustrate, and accuse. Thus, once you have eaten the candy, the demons are going to harp on how useless and weak you are for doing exactly what they were just suggesting. It's a lie (cf. Romans 8:1).

Let me offer a few caveats. First, we have a sin nature that is fully capable of leading us to sin without demonic assistance. I am not arguing that we can pin all of our mistakes on demons, but some are clearly more destructive and demonic than others. Others may be ambiguous. Next, while the greatest defense is personal purity, no believer is yet perfected, thus every Christian must face this in his or her spiritual life to one degree or another. Imputed righteousness is an essential doctrine. Even the apostle Paul struggled (Romans 7:15). Richards' book offers some new clarity on this matter.

Righteousness: Imputed or Realized?

Because everyone is a sinner, I have long assumed that the "breastplate of righteousness" in our spiritual armor necessarily referred to what is theologically termed "imputed righteousness." This is the idea that upon accepting the gospel, one's sin guilt is applied to Christ on the cross, one's debt is paid, and by divine imputation, one stands in a sinless position before God the Father. An academic source defines it:

> The Bible teaches that no person naturally possesses the standard of righteousness demanded by God (Ps 130:3; Is 64:6; Rom 3:10). Yet, in his gracious plan of salvation, God himself supplies the righteousness to satisfy his holy character (Is 45:24; 54:17; Hos 10:12). That is, as a person accepts by faith the work of Christ in satisfying the demands of God's Law, God imputes or reckons Christ's righteousness to the believer.[7]

Thus, when the Father looks upon a dirty, rotten sinner like me, he sees the character of Jesus Christ (e.g., Romans 8 states there is no condemnation for those in Christ). This extravagant grace has always baffled me. Although positional righteousness is an essential truth, it fails to adequately fill the role of defensive armor.

Richards lists four types of righteousness seen in Scripture: 1) comparative; 2) perfect; 3) imputed; and 4) realized. It is to this fourth and often overlooked form that Paul is most likely referring to in Ephesians 6. Richards writes:

> It is true that imputed righteousness is a dominant theme in the New Testament revelation. But God intends those to whom He credits righteousness on the basis of Jesus' cross to live righteous lives here and now. This fourth kind of righteousness is realized righteousness, a life lived in harmony

with God's will—here in this dark world, now in the present time.[8]

Initially, as an unbeliever, my supernatural experiences drove me to search for truth, and that search led me to the gospel. From there, I have struggled to fight the old nature and have grown well beyond what I would have once thought possible. The mere desire to obey God and to live the Christian life is, in and of itself, evidence that one has moved from darkness to light, death to life (1 John 1:7–10 and 3:10–23). Still, I acknowledge the best defense against demonic accusation and attack is *realized* righteousness. Interestingly, this is the truth that Samuel hammered home to King Saul:

> Then Samuel said, "Is there as much delight for Yahweh in burnt offerings and sacrifices as there is in obeying Yahweh? Look! To obey is better than sacrifice; to give heed than the fat of rams. For rebellion is like the sin of divination; arrogance is like iniquity and idolatry. Because you have rejected the word of Yahweh, he has rejected you from being king!" (1 Samuel 15:22–23, LEB)

I think it is safe to say that when facing accusation, obedience (realized) is better than sacrifice (imputed). This is the sort of thing those of us who grew up steeped in the paganized culture struggle with.

I expect there are thousands more like me (and my new friend Nick Skubish from chapter 1) who are searching for the true explanation of supernatural phenomena they have encountered who are in similar positions. Is the church prepared to give good answers concerning their experiences? In my experience, the average Christian isn't prepared to handle these areas carefully, and we need to study and prepare for the ongoing rise in all things paranormal.

A Plea for Caution

God's moral character does not change. He is immutable. Thus, His feelings concerning particular actions also remain consistent. The following rationale is why so many Christian teachers have steered clear of parapsychology, even though many of its terms and ideas are more consistent with the Supernatural Worldview of the Bible than secularized science. In the Hebrew Bible, God describes communicating with dead humans as an *abomination*. In a list of forbidden practices Yahweh included: "one who consults a spirit of the dead, or spiritist, or one who inquires of the dead" (Deuteronomy 18:11, LEB). The last forbidden practice "one who inquires of the dead" in the ESV and the LEB translation seems to be a minor attempt at communication.

It has a prefixed Hebrew conjunction, *wa*, that can mean either "and," "but," or "or". Most translators render "or," implying that each prohibited practice was distinctly forbidden due to its own offensiveness. It communicates the idea that it wasn't necessary for all of the listed acts to be committed in order to offend God. The prefixed verb *darash* is used as a participle, making it a noun grammatically: "one who inquires" or "a person who inquires." It denotes simple communication:

> **1875.** *darash* (205a); a prim. root; *to resort to, seek*:—ask(1), avenge(1), calls(1), care(1), cares(3), comes the reckoning(1), consult(2), consulted by them at all(1), demand(1),

inquire(33), inquired(5), inquirer(1), investigate(3), investigated(1), looks(2), making inquiry(1), questioned(1), require(7), required(1), requires(1), resort(3), search(6), searched(1), searched carefully(1), searches(2), seek(53), seek after(1), seeking(2), seeks(3), sought(18), studied(1), study(1), surely require(1).[9]

From its use, one can see that *darash* doesn't necessarily imply an overt occult magical practice but very minimal contact. The text lists charmers and necromancers right alongside of simply "seeking" a dead human. Thus, any attempt to contact the dead seems to violate this biblical prohibition.

Demonic Transference?

A scholar I respect, Dr. Arnold Fruchtenbaum, warns that demonic transference can occur "even when one has never directly practiced the occult, simply having contact with it by observing it or merely being present as it is practiced can result in demonic transference."[10] He cites the passage from Mark 5, in which a legion of demons from one man transfers to a herd of two thousand pigs and causes them to commit suicide. The pigs were innocent bystanders, but a lake full of swine suicide was nevertheless what occurred. However, the text says the demons asked Jesus for permission before they could enter the pigs. Perhaps Fruchtenbaum pushes too hard, because the two thousand pigs were killed to free one human (Mark 5:15). The farmers of the area were upset because Jesus affected their profit margins to save a demonized man that they did not think much of. Imagine Jesus destroying a store full of new tablet computers while saving a meth-addicted derelict, and you get an accurate sense of the situation. As a result, the farmers asked Jesus to leave. Craig Keener explains, "The opposition to Jesus arises from both economic causes—the loss of a large herd of swine—and certain Greek conceptions of dangerous wonderworking magicians, whom most people feared."[11] Jesus put one sinful and unattractive man above the capital-generating herd of swine and the farmer's profit margins. The context works against the transference warning, because the demons might have taken the pig farmers rather than the pigs, but they did not. It is not likely that Jesus would have allowed the transference to humans. For these reasons, I have a hard time with Fruchtenbaum using this text in a way to cause fear of demonic transference from passively observing the occult. It is a misuse of the text.

A More Cogent Caution

In addition, Fruchtenbaum more cogently points out that Paul argues that one can easily become partaker of the demonic merely by experimentation or being present in non-Christian religious contexts:

> No, I imply that what pagans sacrifice they offer to demons and not to God. I do not want you to be participants with demons. You cannot drink the cup of the Lord and the cup of demons. You cannot partake of the table of the Lord and the table of demons. (1 Corinthians 10:20–21)

This could occur while visiting a Buddhist temple as a tourist, or perhaps by simply observing an Islamic prayer service. This has real application, because in a multicultural society it is nearly impossible to avoid coming into contact with pagan worship practices. Dr. Sydney Page writes:

> It seems that Paul believed the worship of pagan gods put one in contact with maleficent forces and Christians were not immune to the baneful influences of such forces. He does not indicate what might happen to Christians who disobeyed his warnings, but he evidently believed that they would be exposed to some sort of danger.[12]

This text seems more applicable because it is about people and religions we still face today. It seems fair to argue that paranormal investigations might fall within this category as well. In truth, everyone faces these situations at one time or another. What about a military or prison chaplain whose job description forces him to address all faiths?

Even though many have pressed too hard warning against the occult, they do so with good motives. The point is that a very mild form of contact with the dead (or occult practice) still makes participation in much of parapsychological research troublesome. Indeed, if one seeks the deceased's ear, asks for the deceased's blessing, protection, or healing or, within paranormal investigation, asks the deceased to speak into a recorder, no matter how innocent one's intent, it is *inquiring of a dead human*. Worse yet, it is morally assigned to be the most offensive type of act possible: *toe-bah*, Hebrew for "an abomination" (Deuteronomy 18:11–12). It seems that any contact with the dead qualifies. Some think praying to Christian saints changes the moral status, but another passage counts against that idea.

When it comes to this sort of act, Yahweh does not distinguish between saints and pagans. Saul was condemned for seeking the holy prophet Samuel's postmortem advice. The Septuagint is clear that this was an abomination:

> Saul died due to his evil acts, in which he had acted wickedly against God, against the word of the Lord, since he had not kept it; for Saul had inquired by the one who speaks from the belly to seek advice, and Samuel the prophet had answered him. (1 Chronicles 10:13, LES)

The one who speaks from the belly is a spirit medium with a familiar, which was examined in chapter 9. But the consultation with a holy prophet was also condemned. That fact should invoke sober reconsideration from those who pray to saints. No matter how ancient, a human tradition should not openly defy Yahweh's inspired word. Praying to/with dead humans does just that. I realize the intent is not sorcerous, but what does God lack that requires one to seek the attention of a human saint? Is God not enough? It seems to imply the need to ask another...is that faithful to God?

It also seems idolatrous for a logical reason: How can a deceased human hear the prayers of thousands of petitioners simultaneously? A popular saint likely has worldwide followers seeking his blessing, healing, or protection. But only God is omniscient and omnipresent! Deceased humans don't have the ability to hear thousands of folks to answer their many and diverse prayers. Even if this hasn't occurred to the petitioner, by default they are necessarily assigning divine attributes to a deceased human. That seems blasphemous... doesn't it?

Why Do American Kids Behave Like
the Prophets of Baal?

"So they called out with a loud voice, and they cut themselves with swords and with spears as was their custom, until the blood poured out over them" (1 Kings 18:28, LEB). In this passage, the prophets of the hostile Canaanite god Baal were faced with escalating challenges from Yahweh's prophet Elijah, but Baal wasn't meeting the challenge. In order to intensify their calls to him, they cut themselves and injured their own bodies. Self-mutilation, bloodletting, and human sacrifice are common aspects of demonic spirituality. It has been speculated that extreme practices of "mortification of the flesh" may be used to obtain altered states of consciousness to achieve spiritual experiences or visions. In Africa and Australia, indigenous people sometimes use genital mutilation on youth of both sexes that is intentionally painful, including circumcision, subincision, clitoridectomy, piercing, or infibulation. Self harm is common in Roman Catholic orders like Opus Dei, Sufism, and Shi'a Islam, Buddhism, and Hinduism. More recently, *The Church of Body Modification* believes that by manipulating their bodies using painful techniques, they can reinforce the bond between their body and soul, and become more spiritually aware. This unfortunate group adopted rites of passage from many traditions to accomplish their painful goals, including Hindu, Buddhist, and shamanic methods of seeking altered states of consciousness.[13] Most rational people cringe at such ideas.

It seems necessary to point out that our land is so transparently demonic that small schoolkids are unwittingly seduced into bloodletting *themselves*. Although it's ongoing, we currently have several generations of it, and it unabashedly grows worse. Attending public school through the 1970s and '80s, I had never heard of "self harm" as a mental health issue, but today it is estimated that up to 6 percent of American youth hurt themselves *intentionally*. A recent *Boston Globe* article reads:

> Some secretly slice their thighs with scissors. Others repeatedly scratch their wrists until they draw blood. And there are those who chronically punch themselves. For many who wince at a paper cut, the thought of picking up a knife, and intentionally slicing a thigh or arm, seems unimaginable.
>
> But mental health specialists say they are increasingly encountering young patients, including children, who cut, punch, burn, and find other ways to hurt themselves in a desperate attempt to cope with stress, anxiety, and depression.
>
> It's difficult to pinpoint just how widespread the behavior of self-injury is. It's not tracked by health officials, and rates of self-harm revealed through research vary widely. Estimates of prevalence in the general US population range from about 2 to 6 percent, while findings among high school students have pegged it much higher, between 13 and 25 percent. A recent study found that roughly 15 percent of college students surveyed admitted engaging in the behavior at some point in their lives.[14]

Because my wife, a trained biblical counselor working within the confines of a secular boarding school for teenage girls with problematic emotions and addictions, confronts this behavior on a regular basis, I have a personal connection. She estimates that on any given day, at least half of the enrolled students are self harmers. Why do these "well-to-do" young girls want to harm themselves? It seems so obviously demonic.

These behaviors are fueled by satanically motivated media. The black metal band *Slayer* performs a song, "Spill the Blood":

> Come walk with me through endless time
> See what has been and what the future sees
> Share the wisdom of the old world that has passed
> Step in a life that's yet to be born
> You spill the blood
> Eternal soul
> I'll show you sights that you would not believe
> Experience pleasures thought unobtained
> At one with evil that has ruled before
> Now smell the stench of immortality
> You spill the blood
> Eternal soul
> Spill your blood, let it run on to me
> Take my hand and let go of your life
> Close your eyes and see what is me
> Raise the chalice, embrace for evermore
> You've spilt the blood
> I'll have your soul.[15]

As part of my personal ministry, I volunteer in a local state prison that processes young men aged eighteen to twenty-three. The chaplain, trained at a Baptist seminary, must accommodate all religious claims, from Rastafarianism and Native American spirituality to overt witchcraft, satanism, and neo-paganism. In my small groups, I regularly hear about inmates who practice Satan worship and sport tattoos that say so. As I travel around the country speaking at prophecy conferences and teaching at churches, I listen to what the locals have to say, and the message is monolithically: "We are now a pagan culture and demonic activity is on the rise." American society is getting increasingly dangerous as well. As one example of many, the following is a personal email from a recently retired career prison counselor from Florida, Johnnee Kieslich, who was an eyewitness to the increase in violence, self harm, and demonic spirituality over the last few decades:

> I worked as a School Counselor for over nine years (from the mid 80's to the mid 90's). In March of 1995, I started work as a Psychological Specialist at Florida State Prison (where John Arthur Spenkelink and Ted Bundy were executed) and then moved to an inpatient psychiatric unit for Close Management inmates at Union Correctional Institution (U.C.I.) from October 1998 until I retired November of 2011. The inpatient unit housed the highest security graded individuals who also had mental health requirements nevertheless. Most of my experience was in a unit called The Transitional Care Unit (TCU) and I also did some time with the Crisis Stabilization Unit (CSU). Both units were not supposed to house inmates on a permanent basis as theoretically we were preparing the inmates to reintegrate in the outpatient units in the prison system. The practical reality was there were many who repeatedly were admitted, discharged and readmitted and there were many who were never able to be discharged to a lower level of mental health care and stayed in inpatient care permanently.
>
> Regarding the demonic manifestations, I don't have dramatic individual cases like Russ Dizdar (a pastor/author who specializes in the occult). However, I can tell you that

the manifestations of demonization became much more pronounced after approximately 2001–2002 for some reason. These manifestations revealed themselves in multiple personalities, voice and personality alterations, episodes of extreme-violence and/or detachment, extreme self-injurious behavior by head banging, self-inflicted lacerations, suicidal behavior included and not limited to hanging, jumping off sinks on top of their heads, and extreme forms of self-neglect, etc., oppositional behavior which intensified with the progression of time. I can tell you that early in my tenure at the inpatient unit it was not uncommon for me to be on the unit while an officer (note, just one or perhaps two) was organizing and arranging the inmates for line like grade school unshackled waiting for access to the dayroom beyond the locked and monitored wing doors where I presented group and performed individual sessions in and around the "dayroom." The dangerousness of the this procedure, called in the vernacular "pulling the inmates" on the unit by Security increased dramatically from 2001 on until the time I left.

Several officers were severely beaten and hurt and "civilians" were hurt also not to mention other inmates. Tragically one officer had his eye put out and he died shortly thereafter. Many officers were stabbed by a variety of weapons, usually inmate made and transported to the unit by other inmates. Toward the end of my tenure each inmate was "pulled" individually for group or one to one individual sessions by a strictly mandated protocol where a team of security personnel was present and the inmate was usually shackled hand and foot per State of Florida security guidelines depending

on status. Even with this procedure inmate on officer violence was common. By this time I was not allowed on the
wing and I was under "guard" waiting for the inmates outside the locked dayroom waiting for my cue to enter the
dayroom only after a full security cadre could watch every
development in the dayroom. Finally, officers had to stay
in the dayroom for proximity access. I can tell you that the
increase in self-inflicted injury, (usually self-inflicted lacerations) was dramatic, such that it was costing Florida and
The Department of Corrections much and ever increasing
money for required blood transfusions to keep the inmates
alive, not to mention the extreme cost of hospitalizations
and dramatic medical interventions. These interventions did
not always work as inmates did often die of these episodes.
There were many interventions and "think tanks" that dealt
with the purpose of decreasing this particular inmate behavior as it was so dangerous and costly.

Officially the Department or State did not consider
the spiritual reality as the increase in inmate violence and
oppositional behavior was seen as an outgrowth of gang
affiliation, drug use and involvement or an increase in overall criminal milieu for which Florida is regretfully famous.
Much of what these self-injurious or other-injurious inmates
were seen as manipulating the system for self enhancement
in some aspect. I spoke with inmates who slipped in and out
of extremely variant and opposite personalities. It was clear
that some of these personalities were much more dangerous to be around, with biting and spitting a distinct possibility. We had episodes of inmates biting noses and ears
off of other inmates while shackled! The emotional stress

for staff and inmates is hard to emphasize enough. With bizarre and strange behavior and speech patterns there was always an "alert" status or emergency response mindset. Everybody watched everybody else for safety. Things could explode spontaneously, with many a "psychotic" episode which I felt had a demonic source which was definitely contagious and could expand to most of the other inmates on the wing or even the unit. It felt like it was difficult to stay on top of ongoing developments. As a side note, I learned about "astral projection" as a means of mind/body or out of body travel from an inmate! He felt it was his secret coping mechanism! Being the bright man I was I started to look into the demonic/spiritual aspects of life. Inmate artwork degenerated into an even harder more evil variety with obvious occultic references. Many inmates openly worshiped Satan and or demonic entities and others openly had conversations with internal and external voices. Inmates often spoke of visual "hallucinations" of these entities, many times receiving commands to hurt others/self. Laughter was of the labile or in the vernacular maniacal type.[16]

I hear testimony like the above all over the country, and you are probably aware of many such cases yourself. Those on the front lines of law enforcement, mental health, and the schools know it all too well. The paranormal paradigm shift is getting scary.

A Foreboding Prophecy

Scholars who interpret the book of Revelation as mostly a prophecy concerning the future believe that soon Satan will be active on earth like never before. There has been debate concerning the timing of this passage: "And the great dragon was thrown down, the ancient serpent, who is called the devil and Satan, who deceives the whole world. He was thrown down to the earth, and his angels were thrown down with him" (Revelation 12:9). His purging from heaven inspires a hymn (Revelation 10–12). Because the chapter refers to Jesus' birth and death (Revelation 12:5–6), many have argued that Satan was thrown down by the atonement of the cross. However, there are serious problems with that view. Any claimed fulfillment of Satan's expulsion (like the cross) must satisfy the conditions of the hymn sung in response. Biblical scholar Robert Thomas has pointed out:

> To refer it to the present era would mean that the accusing work of Satan is over, according to the next line of the hymn. This can hardly be. The removal of Satan from heaven is in conjunction with the victory of Michael in heaven, not with the cross of Christ. The victory of the brethren through the blood of the Lamb mentioned in v. 11 covers a period preceding that victory of Michael. Only a referral of the kingdom to the future satisfies the proleptic perspective of the singers of this song. The kingdom of God on earth has not arrived at this point in the book's chronological progression, because Satan has further work to carry out on earth. The song looks forward to the consummation that has not yet occurred in actuality, though it has in principle.[17]

Few would contend that Satan is no longer our accuser. If he isn't accusing, then why does Jesus need to stand as our intercessor (Romans 8:34 and Hebrews 7:25)? Another respected scholar, Alan Johnson, commented, "When the battle grows fiercer and darker

for the church, it is but the sign of the last futile attempt of the
dragon to exercise his power before the kingdom of Christ comes
(v. 12)."[18] Indeed, the battle is fiercer and darker for the church now
than perhaps ever before. Once Christian America is now imposing legal sanctions and fines for holding to Christian values, leading
many to expect violence to be next. Homosexual activists have called
for anti-Christian violence, including church bombings and both
the castration and even murder of Christians in the US.[19] The latest global findings from the Pew Research Center reveal that overall
restrictions have reached a six-year high, and Christians are harassed
in more countries than any other religious group.[20] The attrition of
Christians in the Middle East, Indonesia, and Africa daily escalates.
In Syria, they are calling it Christian *annihilation!*[21]

Thus, interpreting Satan's relegation to earth as a Tribulation
event is not only a valid interpretation, it is the most consistent with
the total context of the New Testament and ongoing developments.
This means that "woe to the earth and to the sea, because the devil
has come down to you, having great anger, because he knows that he
has little time!" (Revelation 12:12) is an impending event. Indeed,
many of us born in the 1960s onward will likely live to experience it.
Consistent with the 1960s turning point established by most scholars, Catholic exorcist Malachi Martin wrote of an onslaught of possession cases beginning in that era rising to epidemic levels:

> Even in such difficult circumstances, however, the incidence
> of Exorcism has been on a steady rise. There has been a 750
> percent increase in the number of Exorcisms performed
> between the early 1960s and the mid-1970s. Over the same
> period, there has been an alarming increase in the number of
> requested Possessions—that is, cases in which the Possessed

formally request Satan to possess them—in comparison to the cases of incurred Possessions, which result from other sorts of activities of the Possessed that facilitate Possession.

Each year, some 800 to 1,300 major Exorcisms, and some thousands of minor Exorcisms are performed. For experts in the field, this is a sobering barometer of the increase in known cases of Possession. But it is still more sobering to realize how many more cases of Possession cannot be addressed at all. The thousands of letters I receive from people who are desperate for help—Catholic, Protestant, Evangelical, and unchurched—are eloquent, anguished, and a steadily mounting testimony to the crisis.[22]

More recent Catholic articles, written after Martin's demise, indicate that this trend has since increased. For example, a priest named Fr. John Zuhlsdorf wrote in early 2013, "What I am hearing is that there is a sharp increase over the last four years or so in manifestations of demonic activity. I want to impress something on you: this is no joke."[23] Recent events offer evidential support.

As this book goes to press, several stories involving overt demonization are going viral. In Gary, Indiana, the Ammons case has incredible official documentation. Department of Child Services (DCS) family case manager Valerie Washington and registered nurse Willie Lee Walker were both eyewitnesses to an extraordinary paranormal event. They saw a demonized nine-year-old boy glide backwards up a wall and across the ceiling, flip over his grandmother, Rosa Campbell, and land on his feet. All the while, he was holding his grandmother's hand. This sounds like a scene right out of Hollywood horror film, but here it is in an official state document:

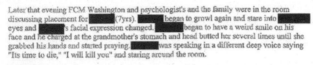

Later that evening FCM Washington and psychologist's and the family were in the room discussing placement for ▮▮▮▮(7yrs). ▮▮▮▮began to growl again and stare into ▮▮▮▮ eyes and ▮▮▮'s facial expression changed. ▮▮▮▮began to have a weird smile on his face and he charged at the grandmother's stomach and head butted her several times until she grabbed his hands and started praying. ▮▮▮▮was speaking in a different deep voice saying "Its time to die," "I will kill you" and staring around the room.

▮▮▮▮had the weird grin on his face and began to walk backwards while the grandmother was holding his hand and he walked up the wall backwards while holding the grandmother's hand and he never let go. He flipped over and landed on his feet in front of the grandmother and sat down in the chair. A few minutes later he looked up as if he was back to himself.

FCM Washington and psychologists left the room immediately and went to the attending doctor, Dr. Richardson, and told him what was just witnessed in the Ammons family room.

Dr. Richardson did not believe it so he asked if the child can perform this act again, the psychologist stated I doubt it seriously, this kid was not himself when he did that. Dr. Richardson, FCM Washington, and the psychologist went back to the room to ask ▮▮▮▮if he can walk up the wall again? ▮▮▮▮stated "I did not walk up a wall. I cannot walk up a wall". When he tried to walk up the wall again he could not get his balance nor place his feet properly to walk up the wall.

The children were removed from the mother's care to ensure their safety.

Official DCS Report, State of Indiana[24]

When I started this book, the rise in demonic activity was a speculation. As it goes to print, it's a certainty. On February 16, 2014, the Associated Press reported, "Pa. woman admits Craigslist killing, 22 other satanic murders."[25] New cases like that are added to my list daily; it is unprecedented. This paragraph's last endnote will provide links to a multitude of news stories supporting the idea that demons are increasingly active. For example, a 2012 article at *Christian News*, "Extreme Demonic Manifestations on the Rise Worldwide," states:

The reports have been alarming for many, who wonder what possessed these individuals to behave in such a depraved and barbaric manner. While there is talk that the events are a precursor to a "zombie apocalypse," others are convinced that demonic activity is taking place and are pointing to Biblical accounts as parallels.

For instance, in Luke 8, a naked demon-possessed man came out to see Jesus, similar to the attack that happened in Miami. Matthew 17 also speaks of a boy that was oppressed of the devil, who would often throw himself into the fire and water.

"Satan and his legion of demons are possessing human beings in these end times," said one man. "What you're seeing is people who've opened up the door to these demons, and you're seeing a manifestation of demons unprecedented."

"This is a sure sign that the God Almighty's great judgment is right around the corner," wrote an online commentator, who identifies himself as Elijah. "The fact that there are so many similar stories, and becoming increasingly more and more common, is a definite sign that Hell has literally broken loose upon the earth."[26]

Based on my volunteer work, recent events, and the available media data, I think one can generalize that such demonization is increasing worldwide. I am not saying it is valid to make scientific sociological assertions from anecdotal accounts, but when I encounter so many people saying the same sorts of things, I feel confident that this sort of testimony is characteristic. Russ Dizdar, author of *The Black Awakening*,[27] is a pastor who specializes in the occult. I emailed Russ for his opinion on recent events and he replied:

Yes I believe the supernatural…especially the dark side of it has ramped up in a massive way over the last 35 years…and I do believe what we have seen and researched and heard in the last three decades is merely a scratch of what's to come. I say this on these levels:

1. My 35 years in the field of evangelism, counseling, and dealing with demonized people—there are just so many. The issues of "sleep paralysis," voices in the head, new rituals, astral projection, channeling, and crazed, supernaturally driven killings are all growing.

2. My 30 years of work targeting the "underground"… satanic ritual abuse, the covens, and the organized side of what is so hidden. The sheer number of victims in many nations now is staggering: 40 million and now four generations of them.

3. The growth of the New Age movement worldwide… to infect 1 billion-plus.

4. The growth of old occultism like Aleister Crowley's work worldwide, secret societies, and clubs.

5. The exponential growth of cults and sects (like Mormonism's 14 million, Scientology, Moonies etc.)

6. The volumes of books from the New Age to very deep, dark-side works read by hundreds of millions.

7. The global gatherings in 2012 continue…convergences and rituals continue.

8. The reopening of ancient ritual sites, nephilim sites worldwide.

Cris, ultimately it's the biblical prophecy that unveils the massive ramping up to the point of a worldwide quest that infects politics, economics, and the military (Revelation 12 explains it is the dragon who seeks to lead the world world astray). Biblical prophecy gives us the heads up and the cutting edge to know what the enemy is bringing. And it paints a picture of unprecedented, unequaled, and globally gripping satanic/demonic powers infecting and manifesting beyond anything in all of history.[28]

I believe Pastor Dizdar is correct. Some of the articles listed in the prior endnote discussing cannibalism and acts of depraved, zombie-like carnage are so horrible it seems incomprehensible that people would do these things on their own. Former Evangelical Theological Society president, Clinton Arnold, has argued:

Purely naturalistic explanations are not adequate for describing many forms of evil in the world. Although the impact of sin on the human soul explains much of the proliferation of evil, some situations are still so abhorrent or inexplicable that they suggest a demonic origin. The horrors of an Auschwitz or of a mother roasting her own child to death imply a powerful force leading humanity to destruction.[29]

Conclusion

As demons replace once-Christianized power structures in this country, crimes are getting uglier, mass shootings are becoming more common, and things will probably get much worse. In closing, the warning issued by Tom Horn and Defender Publishing a few years back in *God's Ghostbusters* is prescient and worth repeating:

Although the Bible warns against inviting such supernaturalism into one's life via fascination with the occult, the revival of ancient paganism and the experiences being drawn from them are especially seductive curiosities today. Sociologists understand that the public's demand for pop-media material such as we started this chapter discussing—*Twilight, New Moon, Eclipse, Ghost Hunters, Paranormal State, Psychic Kids: Children of the Paranormal*, Animal Planet's

The Haunted, and more—may be evidence of something far deeper than today's entertainment fads; it could be indicative of a new preferred spirituality, an informal consensus toward a post-New Testament theological condition, which, unfortunately, has been helped as much by Gospel-depleted modern churches as anything else. As such, it may not be unreasonable to believe today's culture is rapidly approaching a prophetic end-times conflict known to Christians as "Armageddon": a time in which the demonic influences behind the gods and idols of *Twilight, The Vampire Diaries, True Blood*, and Harry Potter actually go to war with Jesus Christ. "The LORD will be terrible unto them: for he will famish all the gods of the earth" says Zephaniah 2:11 of this time. "The LORD of hosts, the God of Israel, saith; 'Behold, I will punish the…gods'" (Jeremiah 46:25). Human followers of the pagan deities will join this conflict, calling upon their idols (Revelation 9:20) to convene their powers against the Christian God, uniting with "the spirits of devils working miracles, which go forth unto the kings of the earth… to gather them to the battle of that great day…[to] a place called in the Hebrew tongue Armageddon [Megiddo]" (Revelation 16:13–14, 16). If the world's current fascination with creatures of the night—from demons and werewolves to vampires and ghosts—is indicative of this timeframe, a deal with the devil has been struck by society and every man, woman, boy, and girl had better quickly choose whose side they are on…because things may be about to get ugly.[30]

Given events since his book's publication, I don't believe Horn was beating the drum of sensationalism. The warning was vatic and deserves attention. Furthermore, its fulfillment supports the contention that as culture becomes increasingly pagan, it increasingly bears demonic fruit. The final chapter will review the worldview questions of chapter 2, discuss a simple way to expose and refute the pagan worldview dominating the culture, and then offer interviews with a couple of folks who have a resilient Supernatural Worldview.

Notes

1. Neil T. Anderson, *The Bondage Breaker: Overcoming Negative Thoughts, Irrational Feelings, Habitual Sins* (Grand Rapids, MI: Harvest House, 2006).
2. Ibid., 3.
3. Clinton E. Arnold, *Powers of Darkness: Principalities and Powers in Paul's Letters* (Downers Grove, IL: IVP Academic, 1992).
4. Larry Richards, *The Full Armor of God: Defending Your Life from Satan's Schemes* (Minneapolis: Chosen, 2013).
5. Ibid., 131.
6. Ephesus was famous for its temple of Artemis and magical practice; e.g., Acts 19:21–41.
7. Walter A. Elwell and Barry J. Beitzel, *Baker Encyclopedia of the Bible* (Grand Rapids, MI: Baker, 1988) 1025.
8. Richards, 100.
9. Robert L. Thomas, *New American Standard Hebrew-Aramaic and Greek Dictionaries,* updated edition (Anaheim, CA: Foundation, 1998).
10. Arnold Fruchtenbaum, *Demonology: the Doctrine of Demons* (Ariel Ministries Digital Press, date) www.ariel.org/mbstoc/mbs082t.pdf) 35–36.
11. Craig S. Keener, *The IVP Bible Background Commentary: New Testament* (Downers Grove, IL: InterVarsity, 1993) Luke 8:34–37.
12. Sydney H. T. Page, *Powers of Evil: A Biblical Study of Satan and Demons* (Grand Rapids, MI: Baker, 1995) 225.
13. Church of Body Modification, http://uscobm.com/ (accessed 01/27/14).
14. Kay Lazar, "Facing the Puzzling Urge to Injure," *Boston Globe,* March 11, 2013, http://www.bostonglobe.com/lifestyle/health-

wellness/2013/03/10/self-injury-behavior-appears-increasing-puzzling-researchers/NrgLQ3ftZZbEoGyqGkzzEN/story.html (accessed 01/29/14).

15. Jeffrey John Hanneman, "Spill the Blood," track 10, *South of Heaven*, http://www.metrolyrics.com/spill-the-blood-lyrics-slayer.html (accessed 01/30/14).

16. Personal email from Johnnee Kieslich to Cris Putnam, Friday, August 9, 2013, 2:18:56 PM.

17. Robert L. Thomas, *Revelation 8–22: An Exegetical Commentary* (Chicago: Moody, 1995) 133.

18. Alan F. Johnson, "Revelation," *The Expositor's Bible Commentary, Volume 12: Hebrews Through Revelation*, ed. Frank E. Gaebelein (Grand Rapids, MI: Zondervan, 1981) 517.

19. See http://christianpersecutioninamerica.com/ for developments, but characteristic of the vitriol is this: Matt Barber, "Blogging Gays Urge Murder, Castration of Christians," *Charisma News,* December 5, 2013, http://www.charismanews.com/opinion/clarion-call/42019-blogging-gays-urge-murder-castration-of-christians (accessed 01/30/14).

20. Katherine Burgess, "Pew: Religious Hostility Reaches Six-Year High Worldwide," *Christianity Today,* January 14, 2014, http://www.christianitytoday.com/gleanings/2014/january/pew-religious-hostility-reaches-six-year-high-worldwide.html (accessed 01/30/14). Also see: http://www.catholicnewsagency.com/news/reports-of-christian-martyrdom-nearly-doubled-in-2013/?utm_source=feedburner&utm_medium=feed&utm_campaign=Feed%3A+catholicnewsagency%2Fdailynews+%28CNA+Daily+News%29&utm_term=daily+news.

21. Alyssa Farah, "Christian Persecution? No. Annihilation!" *World Net Daily,* January 27, 2014, http://www.wnd.com/2014/01/christian-persecution-no-annihilation/ (accessed 01/29/14).

22. Malachi Martin, *Hostage to the Devil: The Possession and Exorcism of Five Living Americans* (New York: HarperOne, 1992) xviii.

23. John Zuhlsdorf , "Tulsa Day 2—Conference," *Fr. Zs Blog*, January 28, 2013, http://wdtprs.com/blog/2013/01/tulsa-day-2-conference/ (accessed 01/29/14).

24. Official State of Indiana DCS Report: https://www.documentcloud. org/documents/1004899-intake-officers-report.html.

25. The Associated Press, "Pa. Woman Admits Craigslist killing, 22 Other Satanic Murders," February 16, 2014, http://www.wjla.com/ articles/2014/02/pa-woman-admits-craigslist-killing-22-other-satanic-murders-100274.html#ixzz2tWs5KfWf (accessed 02/19/14).

26. Heather Clark, "Extreme Demonic Manifestations on the Rise Worldwide," *Christian News,* June 5, 2012, http://christiannews. net/2012/06/05/extreme-demonic-manifestations-on-the-rise-worldwide/ (accessed 01/27/14).

    Many recent articles and TV news reports point to a rise in demonic activity worldwide:

    This Youtube compilation contains recent footage from many local news stations: "An Epidemic of Demonic Possession!" (2014), https://www.youtube.com/ watch?feature=player_embedded&v=0jomaMctRT8.

    Rebecca Kent, "Victim of Miami Zombie Attack Ronald Poppo Speaks for the First Time after Having Face Bitten Off, Says 'Go Heat,'" *TNT Magazine* June 13, 2012, http://www.tntmagazine. com/news/world/victim-of-miami-zombie-attack-ronald-poppo-speaks-for-the-first-time-after-having-face-bitten-off-says-go-heat (accessed 01/29/14).

    Quinton Sturgis, "Zombie Attack Count Reaches 34 after Arm Biting in Florida," *Skew News*, June 13, 2012, http://skewnews.com/ zombie-attack-count-34/#.UumfZ7SoKOc (accessed 01/29/14).

Brad Plumer, "Why Are Mass Shootings Becoming More Common?" *Washington Post,* December 14, 2012, http://www. washingtonpost.com/blogs/wonkblog/wp/2012/12/14/why-are-mass-shootings-becoming-more-frequent/ (accessed 01/29/14).

Alan Hall, "Cannibal Who Ate Head of Former Lover Proposes to Satan-Worshipping Vampire Girlfriend Behind Bars of Psychiatric Unit," MailOnline, February 2, 2012, http://www.dailymail.co.uk/ news/article-2094724/Cannibal-ate-girlfriend-finds-love-vampire-bars-psychiatric-unit.html#ixzz1lMoY6tbB (accessed 01/29/14).

Lydia Warren, "Police and Medical Staff Document America's Real-Life Possession: Official Reports Claim Boy, Nine, Walked Backwards Up Hospital Wall and Police Captain Was Too Scared to Enter Family's 'Haunted' House," MailOnline January 27, 2014, http://www.dailymail.co.uk/news/article-2546850/Children-possessed-200-demons-levitated-walked-backwards-walls-hospital-staff.html (accessed 01/28/14).

Erica Ritz, "The 'Full-Fledged Witchcraft and Demonic Glorification' in a Grammy Performance That Has Glenn Beck Saying 'It's Not Going to End Well,'" *The Blaze,* January 28, 2014, http://www.theblaze.com/stories/2014/01/28/the-full-fledged-witchraft-and-demonic-glorification-in-a-grammy-performance-that-has-glenn-beck-saying-its-not-going-to-end-well/ (accessed 01/29/14).

Laura Collins, "Exclusive Video—Inside the 'Portal to Hell': Relative Gives Investigators Tour of Haunted Indiana Home Where 'Possessed' Children Were 'Chanting Satanically' and Saw 'Ugly, Black Monster,'" MailOnline January 28, 2014, http://www. dailymail.co.uk/news/article-2547224/EXCLUSIVE-A-portal-hell-Police-chief-priest-examined-possessed-children-haunted-Indiana-home-official-reports-saying-no-hoax.html (accessed 01/8/14).

Natalina, "Grade School Student Threatens to Sacrifice Her Classmates to Satan," *Extraordinary Intelligence*, May 12, 2013, http://extraordinaryintelligence.com/grade-school-student-threatens-to-sacrifice-her-classmates-to-satan-says-shes-in-the-illuminati/ (accessed 01/28/14).

Natalina, "Actor Kills Mother with Sword: Possible Freemason Connection," *Extraordinary Intelligence*, November 24, 2010, http://extraordinaryintelligence.com/actor-kills-mother-with-sword-possible-freemason-connection/ (accessed 01/29/14).

Jason Howerton, "A Real-Life Demon Possession Is Being Reported in Indiana—The Details Are Almost Too Horrifying to Believe," *The Blaze* January 27, 2014, http://www.theblaze.com/stories/2014/01/27/a-real-life-demon-possession-is-being-reported-in-indiana-the-details-are-almost-too-horrifying-to-believe/ (accessed 01/28/14).

Anna Hodgekiss, "The Disturbing Rise in SELF-HARM Selfies: Teenagers Are Posting Gruesome Images Online 'Because They Have No One to Turn To,'" MailOnline, January 22, 2014, http://www.dailymail.co.uk/health/article-2544055/The-disturbing-rise-SELF-HARM-selfies-Teenagers-posting-gruesome-images-online-no-one-turn-to.html (accessed 01/29/14).

Rachael Rettner, "The Kids Aren't All Right. Self-Harming On the Rise," NBC News, September 12, 2010, http://www.nbcnews.com/id/39100605/ns/health-childrens_health/t/kids-arent-all-right-self-harming-rise/ (accessed 01/29/14).

Billy Hallowell, "Police Shoot Dead a Wild Naked Man With 'Superhuman Strength' After He Allegedly Violently Assaulted Countless Victims," *The Blaze*, February 6, 2014, http://www.theblaze.com/stories/2014/02/06/police-shoot-dead-a-wild-naked-man-after-he-allegedly-violently-assaulted-countless-victims/ (accessed 02/19/14).

Faith Karimi, "Police: Maryland Mom Kills 2 of Her Children During Attempted Exorcism," *CNN*, January 19, 2014, http://www.cnn.com/2014/01/19/justice/maryland-exorcism-deaths/ (accessed 01/29/14).

Lee Moran, "Baby Burned to Death in Satanic Ritual after Chilean Cult Leader Says Infant Is the Antichrist," *New York Daily News*, Friday, April 26, 2013, http://www.nydailynews.com/news/crime/baby-burned-death-satanic-ritual-article-1.1328050#ixzz2rqIvx2hM (accessed 01/29/14).

Associated Press, "Texas Man Accused of Carving Pentagram into Son," *USA Today*, December 12, 2012, http://www.usatoday.com/story/news/nation/2012/12/12/pentagram-carved-on-boy/1765061/ (accessed 01/29/14).

"Two Suspects Charged in Brutal Killing of Teen Found in Clear Lake Area Apartment," ABC 13 Eyewitness News, February 10, 2014, http://abclocal.go.com/ktrk/story?section=news%2Flocal&id=9426359 , (accessed 02/19/14). Note that: "Reyes confessed to killing Cervantes so his friend 'could sell his soul to the devil.'"

"Satan Worshipper Killed and Skinned His Mother on 'Unholy day' that Demands for a Ritual Human Sacrifice," MailOnline, July 13, 2013, http://www.dailymail.co.uk/news/article-2368737/Satan-worshiper-gets-life-prison-killing-skinning-mother-day-calling-human-sacrifice.html#ixzz2rqKLnDDf (accessed 01/29/14).

27. Book available here: http://www.lulu.com/us/en/shop/russ-dizdar/the-black-awakening-rise-of-the-satanic-super-soldiers-and-the-coming-chaos/paperback/product-5965594.html. Free course on *The Black Awakening*: http://www.theblackawakening.com/page30.html.

28. Russ Dizdar in personal email response dated February 11, 2014, to author Cris Putnam.

29. Clinton E. Arnold, "Can We Still Believe in Demons Today," in
The Apologetics Study Bible: Real Questions, Straight Answers, Stronger Faith, ed. Ted Cabal, et al. (Nashville: Holman, 2007) 1475.

30. Thomas Horn, et. al, *God's Ghostbusters* (Crane MO: Defender, 2011) Kindle edition, 751–766.

THE SUPERNATURAL WORLDVIEW OF THE BIBLE

The natural person does not accept the things of the
Spirit of God, for they are folly to him, and he is not able to
understand them because they are spiritually discerned.
—1 CORINTHIANS 2:14

The existence of an idea consists in being perceived.
—BISHOP GEORGE BERKELEY

In Colossians 2:8, the apostle Paul issued a warning, "See to it
that no one takes you captive by philosophy and empty deceit,
according to human tradition, according to the elemental spirits
of the world, and not according to Christ." I hope that by now the
reader understands those "elemental spirits" to be real supernatural beings and not worldly principles. The significance of Paul's
ancient admonition is readily seen in the modern marketplace of
ideas where biblical faith is increasingly marginalized. Belief in
the supernatural is routinely ridiculed and dismissed as superstition, but supernatural phenomena are increasingly manifesting.

As we come full circle, recall the worldview questions: (1) What is really real? (2) What is the nature of external reality, the world around us? (3) What is a human being? (4) What happens to a person after death? (5) Why is it possible to know anything at all? (6) How do we know what is right and wrong? (7) What is the meaning of human history?[1] Are your answers informed by the Creator or the created? Has this book changed how you answer any of them? If so, your worldview has changed.

Also review a few of the controversial propositions made within: God exists. Supernatural entities exist. Time had a beginning. Time is not absolute but relative to the observer. Reality is real regardless of human opinion. The Bible contains many proven, accurate prophecies. There is a remarkable increase in all things paranormal. The immaterial is as real as the material. ESP is a reality. Dreams sometimes forecast the future. Psychokinesis is real. The past might somehow influence the future. Apparitions are real. Poltergeists could be demons. Poltergeists could be recurring spontaneous psychokinesis. Some ghosts are discarnate humans. Evil, nonhuman adversaries are manipulating and steering history toward their own malevolent ends. Some demons could be human spirits. There is an increase in demonic activity. There is an increase in Christian persecution. The Tribulation and return of Jesus Christ could happen soon. All of these issues have been discussed within. Might you now respond differently to those controversial statements than before you read this far? If so, then your worldview has probably been changed. My hope is that after reading this far, one's opinions in regard to these propositions and worldview questions have been broadened and refined by the evidence and arguments presented within.

As documented in the previous chapter, America is currently experiencing a massive influx of demonic activity. We live in a spiritual war zone and, according to biblical prophecy, it only gets worse until Christ returns. Understanding "the world" or *kosmos* as the evil satanic system opposed to God and the church is particularly enlightening to one's worldview (Romans 12:2 and 1 John 5:19). In *The Adversary: The Christian Versus Demon Activity,* Mark Bubeck exposits 1 John 2:16 as the idea "that the world contains much in its system that is an extension, a larger expression, of man's depraved inner nature."[2] This reflects the American consumer culture so perfectly. Think about advertising in which idolatry and covetousness are routinely promoted as virtues. We are constantly bombarded with messages like: "You deserve the best," "Newer is better," and "You can be the envy of the neighborhood."

Accordingly, it is not hard to find areas of my own life still in captivity to the world system. As one of the first generations that grew up with pop-culture, mass-media propaganda, I am painfully aware that the world aggressively programs us to extol its values. Bubeck argues: "Governments, television, educational systems, the press, music, literature, art, interaction with the people in our work and leisure, and virtually everything in our society can bring the world's pressure to tempt us to step out of God's will."[3] It is deeply entrenched, and I believe that much of modern evangelicalism has been snared by the pagan culture. It seems that God uniquely placed one scholar in an observational position to clearly see what has happened to America over the last few decades.

The Gnostic Empire Strikes Back and Spirit Wars

Dr. Peter R. Jones holds an MDiv from Gordon-Conwell Theological Seminary, a ThM from Harvard Divinity School, and a PhD from Princeton Theological Seminary. He grew up in Liverpool, England, and was a childhood friend of Beatles' superstar John Lennon. He moved to the United States in the early 1960s and then took a teaching position in France in 1964. For seventeen years, he was professor of New Testament in Aix-en-Provence France at the Faculté de Théologie Réformée. While in France, he taught and published scholarly materials in his field. Because of these two decades, he was insulated from the social changes in America from the mid 1960s through the 1980s, a period that profoundly altered American spirituality.

In 1991, he returned to the United States and was shocked to find the Christian U.S. he had first known twenty years prior had been replaced by a radically different country steeped in anti-Christian ideas. He noticed that, despite secularism, most people were still very religious; it was just that they had adopted a different, non-Christian religion. Noticing remarkable parallels to early gnosticism, he wrote his first book on the subject, *The Gnostic Empire Strikes Back* (1992), a historical overview of gnosticism with an analysis of its parallels to New Age spirituality. After being vigorously criticized by neognostics, he adapted his course somewhat using the broader category of paganism in his next work, *Spirit Wars: Pagan Revival in Christian America* (1997) (cited in chapter 3). Also note that Dr. Jones was interviewed on the *FutureQuake* radio show/podcast February 2, 2009.[4]

Because terms like "paganism" and "gnosticism" have had particular schools of thought and can be identified in various specific ways throughout history, critics responding to Jones had a relatively easy time casting his work in such a way as to make it seem historically in error, mean spirited, and philosophically overblown. While he can defend his previous assertions admirably, he has simplified the approach in order to put first things (the gospel) first rather than being mired down in details regarding gnostic and pagan terminology and history. The solution comes from Paul's letter to the Romans.

The defining issue is the creature/creator distinction from exegesis of "who exchanged the truth of God for the lie, and worshiped and served the creature rather than the Creator, who is blessed forever. Amen" (Romans 1:25, NKJV, underline added). Although many use the indefinite article "a," it is argued by many competent scholars that the definite article "the" is the best translation so that the text juxtaposes "the lie" to "the Creator."[5] The lie is pantheistic monism, or "all is one," which entails the universe evolved. Remarkably, "pagan," or *paganus,* comes from the Latin word meaning "of the earth" and originally denoted rural folk.[6] From Paul's apposition in Romans 1:25, Jones observed that there are really only two religious perspectives, "oneism" (worship of creation) and "twoism" (worship of the creator). Jones explains:

> One-ism believes that "all is one" and shares the same essential nature. Theologians use the term "consubstantiality." As you probably know, "con" means "with" in Latin, and you know what "substantial" means—"substance" or "essence." In One-ism, everything shares the same essence. In a word, everything is a piece of the divine.[7]

Because I was ostensibly unaware of Jones' body of work until after I had written most of this book, I was encouraged to read that we came to many of the same conclusions regarding monism or "oneism." Although it is associated with the East, it is now (as explained in chapter 3) the dominant religious idea in the West and is deeply entrenched in the literature of parapsychology and near-death experience research. Oneism or pantheistic monism makes no distinction between the creature and the creator because they are one and the same. This is called an *esoteric* religion. Jones writes, "Applied to religion, esoteric means a quest for the divine within the self. The higher self or the deeper subconscious is the source of spiritual experience. So you go within to discover ultimate truth."[8] This sort of thinking is why Shirley MacLaine was comfortable saying "I am god" in her five-hour ABC TV miniseries and New-Age classic, *Out on a Limb*.[9] Chapter 5 on the NDE endeavored to address and refute some of the popular monistic—*oneist*—theology. In this case, it is best to start with a firm grasp of the truth.

The second religious idea contrasts oneism by making the creature/creator distinction through "worship and service of the Creator" (e.g., Romans 1:25). Jones explains:

Two-ism believes that while all of creation shares a certain essence (everything apart from God is created), the Creator of nature, namely God, is a completely different being, whose will determines the nature and function of all created things.[10]

Paul wrote of Jesus:

Who is the image of the invisible God, the firstborn over all creation, because all things in the heavens and on the earth were created by him, things visible and things invisible, whether thrones or dominions or rulers or powers, all things were created through him and for him, and he himself is before all things, and in him all things are held together. (Colossians 1:15–17, LEB, underline added)

Jones also calls this an *exoteric* religion writing, "Applied to religion, exoteric means a quest for a divinity that stands outside the self and outside human reality."[11] Whereas oneism looks within, twoism is revealed to man by God.

This also helps to explain the etymology of the term "supernatural," which derives from medieval Latin *supernaturalis,* "above or beyond nature, divine," from the Latin *super* ("above") plus *natura* ("nature"). Without a creator/creation distinction, everything is a part of nature, and supernaturalism is excluded by definition. However, according to the Bible, there are two kinds of reality: the divine eternal and created temporal. We worship the Creator. Thus, the Supernatural Worldview is what Jones labels *twoism.* Taking this simplified approach, Dr. Jones has written two extremely important books for twenty-first century Christians (I believe these works should be read by all American Christians): *Gospel Truth/Pagan Lies* (1999)—a work appropriate for teens and adults—and a more exhaustive treatment, *One or Two: Seeing a World of Difference* (2010).

Jones is now director of truthXchange (www.truthxchange.com), a nonprofit organization dedicated to helping Christians understand the rise of neopagan spirituality. In addition to his work with truthXchange, he teaches at Westminster Seminary California as adjunct professor of New Testament, as well as being a Scholar in Residence. He has written *The Gnostic Empire Strikes Back* (1992), *Spirit Wars* (1997), *Gospel Truth/Pagan Lies* (1999), *Capturing the Pagan Mind* (2003), *Cracking DaVinci's Code* (2004, coauthor, James Garlow), *Stolen Identity* (2006), *The God of Sex* (2006), and *One or Two* (2010). He has also edited an extremely important compendium volume, *On Global Wizardry* (2010), from which Dr. Michael Heiser's material on Old Testament divination was extensively cited within chapter 9. Jones' work in worldview apologetics is extremely important given the paradigm shift we are now experiencing.

Twoism is foundational to the gospel, which brings the hope of the restoration of everything God created. The gospel is centered on the most important supernatural event in history: the Resurrection of Jesus the Messiah. This is the central truth claim of biblical Christianity and upon it all else rests. Paul wrote, "And if Christ has not been raised, then our preaching is in vain and your faith is in vain" (1 Corinthians 15:14). Because it is so very important, I hope that every Christian would master the minimal-facts argument for Jesus' Resurrection.

The Minimal Facts Case for Jesus' Resurrection

When presenting the historical case for the Resurrection, the best approach is to stick to the matter at hand. In this case, less is more. For that reason, I prefer the minimal-facts approach employed by Gary Habermas, Mike Licona, and William Lane Craig. An excellent resource that goes into greater detail is *The Case for the Resurrection of Jesus* by Habermas and Licona. The minimal-facts approach entails arguing from evidence that the majority of scholars, even ardent skeptics, already accept. This works in evangelism as well, because the aim is to present the gospel, not the entirety of Christian doctrine. For instance, a skeptic can easily derail the conversation by bringing up alleged contradictions in the Bible or issues surrounding Noah's Flood. Don't get distracted. We are not arguing for inerrancy or the Flood, so it is best to direct the focus back to the historical facts about Jesus that demand an adequate explanation.

Because the data employed is so strongly supported by evidence, we systematically build a case that it is not easily dismissed. Five facts are employed. Four are nearly unanimously accepted, and the fifth, while compelling, is not quite as universally accepted. The four facts that nearly all scholars concede are: 1) Jesus did indeed die by crucifixion; 2) The disciples truly believed He rose from the dead; 3) The skeptic Paul experienced an uncharacteristic conversion; and 4) The skeptic James also experienced an unlikely conversion. The fifth fact is the empty tomb.

The first fact is attested to in all four Gospels plus five ancient secular sources: Josephus, Tacitus, Lucian, Mara Bar-Serapion, and the Talmud.[12] With this much corroboration, even John Dominic Crossan of the radically liberal Jesus Seminar allows this as a historical fact.[13] The second fact is that the disciples believed it happened. The fact is simply their sincere belief. This can be evidenced from nine independent sources in three categories: first, Paul's testimony about the disciples in 1 Corinthians 15:10–11; second, the oral traditions of the early church like the creed cited in 1 Corinthians 15:3–8; and third is the written tradition, as in the Gospels and writings of the apostolic fathers Clement and Polycarp. Furthermore, that they sincerely believed it is evidenced by their willingness to suffer and die. This is attested to in seven ancient sources: Acts, Clement of Rome, Polycarp, Ignatius, Dionysius of Corinth, Tertullian, and Origen.[14] Whereas people die for untruths all the time, they do not do so knowingly. The disciples had firsthand knowledge, unlike a modern-day suicide bomber believing from blind faith. The firsthand perspective puts the disciples' willingness to die in a different category.

The third fact centers on Paul, a devout Jew and highly trained Pharisee, who admits to killing and persecuting Christians. His unlikely conversion is evidenced by personal testimony in his letters to the churches in Corinth (1 Corinthians 15:9–10), Galatia (Galatians 1:12–16, 22, 23), and Philippi (Phillipians 3:6–7). He had nothing to gain and everything to lose by converting. This is powerfully enhanced by multiple attestations to his suffering and martyrdom for his belief. In addition to his own word and Luke's record in Acts, his stalwart stand for the message is recorded by Clement of Rome, Polycarp, Tertullian, and in quotations by Dionysius of Corinth and Origen found in the writing of Eusebius.[15] In like manner, the fourth fact concerns the brother of Jesus, James. He was initially dubious to his brother's messianic claims. The Gospel of Mark makes this plenty clear: "And when his family heard it, they went out to seize him, for they were saying, 'He is out of his mind'" (Mark 3:21). His subsequent conversion is evidenced by the creed in 1 Corinthians 15:7, which records the appearance to him by Jesus, and also by Paul and Luke's identification of James as the head of the Jerusalem church. His subsequent martyrdom recorded by Josephus and Eusebius makes for an airtight case.[16] The conversion of hostile skeptics is not easily dismissed.

While more contested than the preceding four, the empty tomb is certainly the most reasonable inference from the historical data. Probably the strongest argument is the Jerusalem factor. It stands to reason that the church would have never had a chance to flourish being so close to the burial site if the tomb had contained Jesus' body. The hostile Jews and Romans would have certainly produced the body had there been one available. Additionally, the fact that the Jews accused the disciples of stealing the body amounts to an admission for the empty tomb (Matthew 28:12–13). This is also recorded in extrabiblical writings by Justin Martyr and Tertullian, who were early apologists.[17] Finally, the fact that women are listed as the discoverers of the empty tomb speaks to veracity. The testimony of women was not highly valued by the patriarchal society, and this would be damaging to their claim. Thus, it is an unlikely fabrication.[18] The empty tomb is a reasonable reality.

It is not too hard for a skeptic to dispute each fact individually, but a rival theory has to account for all five facts. Most alternate theories only account for a few of the facts and are exposed by their failures. For example, if a skeptic says the disciples stole the body, then fact two stating that they sincerely believed it is not accounted for. Why would Paul and James then convert? Since no rival theories coherently account for all of the facts without appearing *ad hoc*, it follows that Jesus' bodily Resurrection is the most plausible explanation.

If you would like to see this minimal-facts case in action, there are several debates posted online: Gary Habermas vs. Anthony Flew,[19] Mike Licona vs. Greg Cavin,[20] and William Lane Craig vs. John Shelby Spong.[21] All of them are very informative and you will benefit from hearing some of Christianity's best and brightest scholars defending the faith.

Speaking of influential scholars with a Supernatural Worldview, another is Dr. Ray Boeche, whom I interviewed along with Natalina, creator of the Extraordinary Intelligence website (www.extraordinaryintelligence.com). Although we don't agree on all the specifics, I believe both to have a rigorous Supernatural Worldview.

Rev. Ray Boeche ThD

Founder and former director of the Fortean Research Center in Lincoln, Nebraska, Ray Boeche has been involved in the study of unexplained phenomena since 1965. He served as Nebraska state director for the Mutual UFO Network, on the board of advisors for Citizens Against UFO Secrecy, and in various capacities with numerous other organizations around the world involved in the study of unexplained phenomena.

He is also recognized for his extensive work in the areas of animal mutilations, out-of-place animal sightings, Midwestern Bigfoot reports, the Men-in-Black phenomenon, and occult religions and philosophies. Retained by the University of Nebraska as a consultant to organize and present research papers at two major international conferences on the unexplained in 1982 and 1983, he has published numerous articles, as well as two collections of writings: *An Anthology of the Unexplained* and *The Complete Annals of the Journal of the Fortean Research Center.*[22] Boeche is well known as one of the primary investigators of the 1980 Bentwaters (UK) UFO incident.

A graphic artist and book designer, Boeche holds a BA from Peru State College, a ThM from St. Mark's School of Divinity, and a ThD from St. Paul Theological College. Ordained since 1991, he serves as pastor for adult ministries and education at a large, Midwestern church. I first heard Boeche on the *Future Quake* radio show, billed: "Pastor and noted paranormal investigator Ray Boeche unveils evidence from eyewitnesses of government sponsored occult activities and spirit contact."[23] He was speaking about the Collins Elite and US government interest in UFOs and NASA rocket scientist Jack Parson's dark supernaturalism. As a pastor, former Mutual UFO Network (MUFON)[24] and paranormal investigator, he is a natural choice to be interviewed for this book.

CRIS: Have you ever been pressed on being a paranormal investigator? Some Christians seem to think it is inappropriate to even investigate hauntings or ghost phenomena, almost like attending a séance or playing with an Ouija board. For example, it seems to me that collecting Electronic Voice Phenomena (EVP) constitutes an attempt to communicate, which I believe is forbidden, so I wouldn't do it myself. The line is a little murky, admittedly. How do you justify being a Christian paranormal investigator?

RAY: This comes up on a fairly regular basis. I'm always reminded of Romans 14 when attacked by other Christians. While I don't want to violate scriptural principles and put a stumbling block in their path, I also think we must guard against allowing the "weaker brother" to become a tyrant ruling over us.

Let me start by saying I share your view of actively engaging in things like collecting EVPs. I believe that meaningful, substantive research and investigation can be accomplished without engaging in everything involved. I view it in much the same way as understanding it's possible to research and investigate alcoholism, drug addiction, or prostitution without slamming down a twelve-pack of beer, smoking crack, or visiting brothels.

In my view, if the ultimate point of research on any topic is to discover truth—as opposed to trying to catch a cheap thrill or satisfy idle curiosity—then eventually you are going to come face to face with God, the source of all truth.

Science and (Christian) theology are both seeking Ultimate Truth: science through the study of the created world, theology by seeking knowledge of the Creator both from general and special revelation (nature and Scripture).

While paradoxes may exist at times in the evidence uncovered by the opposing approaches, we know that God is immutable, sovereign, and never contradicts Himself, so we simply seek for more knowledge that may shed light on the paradox, or grant that we, as finite beings, cannot grasp the totality of the mind of the infinite God, and thus some things remain hidden until such time as God may choose to reveal them to us.

I believe this is a legitimate area for Christians to research (without joining in activities which amount to necromancy). After all, who better than people indwelt by God's Holy Spirit (who is promised to "lead us into all truth") to apply that truth to examining these troubling, anomalous events from the position of God's Absolute Truth?

CRIS: Do you believe in the existence of a sixth sense or psi? Please give us your thoughts on that as well as any experiences you have had that steered your opinion one way or another. Perhaps you might speak to three: ESP, psychokinesis, precognition (including precognitive dreams)?

RAY: There is great tension between conservative theologians who affirm the absolute authority and infallibility of Scripture on this subject. Some look to Jesus' words in Matthew 11:11 ("Truly I say to you, among those born of women there has not arisen *anyone* greater than John the Baptist!") and say that since John didn't exhibit any psi abilities, and he was the greatest human ever born, these abilities can't be natural.

But I see no evidence in Scripture that John the Baptiser was the strongest, fastest, most agile man who ever lived, nor that he had greater senses of sight, hearing, touch, and taste than any other human ever born.

Based on years of study, and the results of reputable researchers who have delved into this subject, I feel confident that many faculties such as ESP, psychokinesis, psychometry, and remote viewing are very much human faculties with which some people are gifted, while others lack or have completely neglected these abilities.

Some humans have absolute pitch, others are tone-deaf. Some humans have IQs that exceed measurement, others are severely intellectually challenged. Sprinters have disproportionate numbers of fast-twitch muscle cells, while long-distance runners have more slow-twitch muscle cells. I believe psi abilities are much like this.

The late physicist David Bohm, in his work, "Wholeness and the Implicate Order," began to express the groundwork for a concept which—applied to some situations—would seem to make allowance for the possibility to, in essence, peer into the past. This could offer an explanation for the ability of some people to sense past events (certain types of occurrences which are commonly referred to as hauntings).

True precognition, I believe, must be causally limited to glimpses of the future provided to particular individuals by God. As the Godhead (Father, Son, and Holy Spirit) is the only truly transcendent being in existence (that is, existing outside of the space-time continuum), as well as fully immanent within His creation, and ultimately sovereign, only God can possibly provide glimpses of true future events.

Thus, true precognition by its very nature must be attributed to specific revelation made by an omniscient, omnipresent, omnipotent, transcendent, and immanent being, and God is the only one who fits that description.

CRIS: While we know from Scripture that God is the source of prophetic dreams and visions, we also see that demon-possessed people emulate similar phenomena (Acts 16:16). Does this necessarily imply that all such non-Christian phenomena are demonic? It seems to me that perhaps some human beings have a natural ESP ability in the same way that some are extremely gifted in music.

RAY: A partial answer to this is essentially given above. You are correct in postulating that some human beings are naturally gifted with abilities of this nature. I would add that we fall into error when we, as Christians, immediately consign something we don't understand—which could have a natural explanation—to the realm of the demonic or satanic.

If we could travel back in time to 1690 Salem, Massachessetts, with a supply of aspirin tablets, antibiotics, and vitamin supplements, we could cure many diseases and save countless lives. But we would also most likely fall victim to charges of witchcraft and deviltry, because no one at the time, no matter how intellectually astute, would be able to believe that the various powders, liquids, and tablets we were dispensing were all natural substances and quite manmade.

As the late Arthur C. Clarke said, "Any sufficiently advanced technology is indistinguishable from magic." Just because we don't currently understand something doesn't make it demonic.

CRIS: Do you think near-death experiences are evidence for the immaterial human soul? Please indicate if you have had one or know anyone who has, and your level of interest—books you've read as well.

RAY: I'm not sure if NDEs are evidence for the existence of the soul or not. It is certainly a possibility. I have over the years read most of the major literature: the books of Dr. Raymond Moody, Kenneth Ring, Pim van Lommel's excellent study from the Netherlands,

Elisabeth Kübler-Ross, Dr. Maurice Rawlings' accounts of negative NDEs, as well as many other scholarly journal articles and popular pieces.

I've never had an NDE, but personally know two people who have: one a committed Christian, the other an unbeliever. Both were strengthened in their own views by their experiences.

Experience is always subjective, and so impossible to use as a sure, unchanging standard by which to judge the truth of those events. Only Scripture gives us the sure footing of truth, and it is certainly not expansive on the subject.

I find it an interesting subject, but I'm content to agree with Paul in 2 Corinthians 5:8, that I'd "prefer rather to be absent from the body and to be at home with the Lord."

CRIS: Do you believe out-of-body experiences are possible?

RAY: 2 Corinthians 12:2 seems to indicate they may be: "I know a man in Christ who fourteen years ago—whether in the body I do not know, or out of the body I do not know, God knows—such a man was caught up to the third heaven."

I find no scriptural evidence to support OBEs as something which we can control, or in which we should engage, but also no direct prohibition against it. Yet, 1 Corinthians 10 seems to lay out some applicable standards by which we can judge, summed up nicely in verse 23: "All things are lawful, but not all things are profitable. All things are lawful, but not all things edify."

Rightly or wrongly, I'm distinguishing between remote-viewing experimentation and the "classic" OBEs of astral projection as described by Robert Monroe and Celia Green, among others.

CRIS: Have you ever seen an apparition or experienced poltergeist?

RAY: I have never had either experience, although I have been involved in the investigation of many such occurrences.

CRIS: Do you think poltergeist phenomena could be recurring spontaneous psychokinesis from a person present on the scene?

RAY: I find that to be the most likely explanation in most poltergeist occurrences. Sometimes events may unfold in a way that seem less clear cut, but while not discounting the possibility of demonic activity, I think the more likely explanation is that put forward by two of the leading psychologists/parapsychologists in the world, Nandor Fodor in the 1930s, bolstered by the work of Dr. William Roll in the 1960s and '70s. Dr. Roll, whom I had the privilege of meeting with several times, was the director of the Psychical Research Foundation in Durham, North Carolina. He began by reviewing 116 documented poltergeist reports dating over four centuries and covering one hundred countries. In the process, Roll found a distinct pattern in such cases in which he labeled "recurrent spontaneous psychokinesis" or RSPK. Roll discovered that poltergeist activity was centered on a focal point, most often a child or teenager who was unknowingly expressing their anger without the fear of repercussions.

CRIS: Is it possible that some ghosts are really spirits of dead humans?

RAY: Tough question! Theoretically, I see no reason why God— being the Sovereign Creator and Sustainer of the universe—might not allow the spirit of someone's Aunty Tilly to go back and give them an encouraging or comforting word.

But does He or would He allow it often enough to account for all legitimate ghost sightings?

For those who contend that all ghosts are satanic and demonic counterfeits, they must ask themselves this question: If there are no real ghosts, why would Satan counterfeit something that doesn't exist? How many counterfeiters decide to print and distribute thirty-dollar bills?

The account of Saul and the witch or medium of Endor in 1 Samuel 28 certainly seems to be a legitimate encounter between Saul and Samuel's actual spirit.

When Matthew 17 describes the Transfiguration of Christ, the spirits of Moses and Elijah (who was still alive at least ten years after he was taken up in the heavenly chariot; see 2 Chronicles 21:12–15 and whom we can legitimately infer dies as every man does) are both there.

When Jesus walks on the water (Matthew 14:22–33; Mark 6:45–52; and John 6:16–21), Matthew and Mark both record that the disciples thought Jesus was a spirit or ghost.

When Jesus appeared to the disciples in the upper room after the resurrection, Luke 24:37 says that the disciples thought they were seeing a spirit or ghost.

The evidence seems to indicate that ghosts were something understood by the writers of Scripture to be the real spirits of deceased persons.

Perhaps that was one of the reasons the Holy Spirit prompted John to write: "Beloved, do not believe every spirit, but test the spirits to see whether they are from God!" in 1 John 4:1.

CRIS: I have suggested that while believers go to heaven, it is possible that because final judgment has been reserved until Christ's return

(1 Corinthians 4:5; Matthew 8:29; Revelation 20:11 ff.) and this might explain the presence of human spirits wandering the earth. I am interested if you think this is sound.

RAY: I believe that is a logical deduction from the available scriptural evidence God has given us.

CRIS: If so, how do you reconcile this with Jesus' parable concerning Lazarus and the rich man (Luke 16:9–31)?

RAY: I am very committed to the inspired, inerrant, infallible nature of Holy Scripture. I say that because of the possibility I'm about to raise, which some will look at as a wild liberal cop-out.

Consider this: Were Jesus' parables all accounts of actual, historical events, or were some or all of them illustrations told to make a point which has lasting, universal significance to all humanity?

Is the truth revealed to us about God's will and expectations and grace for, and toward, us in the parable of the prodigal son, or the good Samaritan, the master and the servants, the bridesmaids and their lamps, or Lazarus and the rich man any less true if they were illustrations rather than factual accounts of actual events?

I think the point of the Lazarus and the rich man parable is that even a supernatural event such as the reappearance of the rich man to his brothers won't change their hearts…that can only be the work of the Holy Spirit, and if the law and the prophets haven't opened their eyes, a visit from a ghost wouldn't either.

CRIS: Have you ever had an experience you think might been with an angel?

RAY: No.

CRIS: Do you believe God's holy angels are active in the world today?

RAY: Absolutely!

CRIS: Do you agree that most angelology and demonology is drastically oversimplified? If so, have you given much thought into different sorts of spirits?

If you're referring to the concepts of angelology based on Jewish Midrashic, Talmudic, and rabbinic tradition, or the medieval ranks, choirs, or orders of angels (seraphim, cherubim, thrones, dominions, virtues, powers, principalities, archangels, angels) and then the corresponding attempts to create a taxonomy of demons (7.5 million, more or less, according to Jewish Talmudic scholars), then I think we veer too far into the realm of speculation and human tradition.

Angels are literally "messengers" used by God to do His will and bidding. Demons, as contemporary Christianity generally speaks of them, are evil spirits who seek to tempt, distract, and usurp God's place in the life of humans.

Beyond the clear words of Scripture regarding the reality of spiritual forces opposed to God and the admonitions about how to conduct spiritual warfare, I find the centuries of speculation fascinating, but not very helpful when it comes down to helping the demonically oppressed or possessed individual overcome these forces through the power of Christ.

I find the oversimplification useful in pragmatic terms when helping people. After years of working with the demonically oppressed, the only certainty I have is that Christ dwelling in the believer is more powerful than Satan and all his diabolical cohorts combined. The war is won; we're just mopping up!

CRIS: I mean the demonology we find in most of the systematic theology textbooks we encounter in a seminary.

RAY: In terms of the majority of systematic theology texts, in my opinion these topics *are* oversimplified in terms of merely being briefly and broadly outlined. That's fine for a cursory examination of the subject, but in terms of being part of a "systematic" theology—in other words, how our knowledge of God provided through His revealed Word functions as a coherent whole—then most treatments are woefully inadequate. If a system of theological thought merely acknowledges that these beings exist, but fails to explain that the Sovereign God may, in order to accomplish His perfect (yet hidden) will for our lives, allow these beings to interact with us, these topics are grossly oversimplified.

Many, if not most, theologians and pastors have nothing more than an abstract notion of the existence of these beings, particularly demons, and are ill-equipped should they have occasion to deal with someone afflicted by them. And that is little comfort to the person seeking help.

CRIS: Are demons necessarily fallen angels? Could some demons be the spirits of the nephilim, as Jewish legend portrays (1 Enoch 15:8–12)?

RAY: Certainly. But aren't the Nephilim so closely connected with fallen angels, particularly the Watchers (egregoroi) and Semjaza as their leader, as to make the distinction slight at best?

And since 1 Enoch only mentions two hundred rebel angels coming down to breed the Nephilim, and Jubilees states that God allowed 10 percent of the Nephilims' spirits to stick around after the

Flood as demons, I think at best this would only account for a portion of the total number of demons.

Again, I find this fascinating to speculate about, but when you're dealing with (as I have been for the last couple of months) three women—unknown to each other—who are being sexually assaulted by invisible spiritual entities who cease their activity only at the name of Christ, how important is the distinction?

CRIS: Do you think poltergeist phenomena could be demonic?

RAY: That certainly remains a possibility, but with some of the really exciting research into psychokinesis carried out by Dr. Berthold Schwarz, J. B. Rhine, the PEAR (Princeton Engineering Anomalies Research) experiments, and the work done regarding the abilities of Nina Sergeyevna Kulagina in the former Soviet Union, for instance, as well as others, and the continuing investigation into both macro- and micro-psychokinesis (including some PK experiments aboard the International Space Station) it seems more likely—in those cases in which emotionally disturbed adolescents are the center of the activity—that spontaneous PK may be responsible.

The other aspect is that classic poltergeist activity seldom, if ever, seems to involve any sort of communication in which Christian belief is questioned or derided.

CRIS: Could some NDEs be a ruse to promote universalism?

RAY: I wanted to make a smart-aleck comment about mainline denominations doing a pretty good job of that all by themselves, but that wouldn't be kind. So never mind.

Yes, I think that could well be the case.

My standard rule of thumb in "testing the spirits" (literal or figurative) is to determine whether the concept being promoted attacks Christian thought and practice, as given by the Holy Spirit in Scripture.

As Christians, we can disagree all day long about, for instance, the nature of baptism and the Lord's Supper, arguing each varying position from Scripture. But the fundamental fact that Jesus commanded baptism and instructed us to continue the Lord's Supper is something we both agree on.

When we start to see attacks on the inspired nature and truth of Scripture; God's personal, transcendent and immanent nature; humanity's sinful condition and our need of a redeemer; denial of the deity, virgin birth and resurrection of Christ; and yet not a single objection against any other spiritual system (NDEs fit nicely into a framework of karmic cycles, reincarnation, etc.), we can be fairly certain we are observing a spiritual ruse in progress.

CRIS: Have you ever encountered a demon?

RAY: Yes, on more than one occasion.

CRIS: Have you ever performed an exorcism?

RAY: Several.

CRIS: Is it possible for any of these spirits to manifest a physical body?

RAY: A fascinating question, and one I've been pondering for the last twenty-plus years, particularly in relation to alien abduction phenomena. I believe the answer is yes, but I have nothing except anecdotal evidence to put forward as proof. There have been instances of incubi and succubi who seem to have manifested in physical, tangible form. There is also the Tibetan Buddhist concept of a tulpa, which is allegedly a physical form willed into existence by the power of thought alone.

CRIS: Could they be behind the alien abduction phenomenon or at least some aspect of it?

RAY: Absolutely. Logically, I am unable to deny the possible existence of physical alien life elsewhere in the universe.

However, the conduct of the so-called aliens with whom individuals have had contact, particularly in instances where contact has been repeated over long periods of time, seems to indicate a failure of the "testing of spirits" as I outlined above.

CRIS: Are you familiar with the case involving Johann Christoph Blumhardt in Möttlingen, Germany, who indicated some evil spirits-possessing folks were deceased humans who led evil lives?

RAY: Blumhardt's story is fascinating, but in assessing his views of what he experienced, I am compelled to go back to Scripture and judge Blumhardt's experiences against God's unchanging truth.

Hebrews 9:27, "And just as it is appointed for people to die once—and after this, judgment," seems to argue against the instances where Blumhardt calls the spirits of deceased people to repentance and frees Gottlieben from them.

The previously discussed parable of Lazarus and the rich man would seem to argue against this as well. Had the rich man been capable of repentance after death, it seems that he would certainly avail himself of it, yet it is not even discussed.

Second Corinthians 6:2b, "Behold, now is 'the acceptable time,'

414   Cris Putnam

behold, now is 'the day of salvation,'" certainly doesn't seem to hold out hope for anyone to "just wait until you're dead, and it will still be fine."

And if one raises the argument that these spirits just had a lapse of faith, or had minimalized their faith to the point they weren't able to quite get into the Lord's presence, then that begs the question of how much faith is enough to guarantee salvation?

If we believe Ephesians 2:1–10: "And you were dead in your trespasses and sins, in which you formerly walked according to the course of this world, according to the prince of the power of the air, of the spirit that is now working in the sons of disobedience. Among them we too all formerly lived in the lusts of our flesh, indulging the desires of the flesh and of the mind, and were by nature children of wrath, even as the rest. But God, being rich in mercy, because of His great love with which He loved us, even when we were dead in our transgressions, made us alive together with Christ (by grace you have been saved), and raised us up with Him, and seated us with Him in the heavenly *places* in Christ Jesus, so that in the ages to come He might show the surpassing riches of His grace in kindness toward us in Christ Jesus. For by grace you have been saved through faith; and that not of yourselves, *it is* the gift of God; not as a result of works, so that no one may boast. For we are His workmanship, created in Christ Jesus for good works, which God prepared beforehand so that we would walk in them," then our salvation is all the work of God, and "by grace [we] have been saved through faith; and that not of [ourselves], *it is* the gift of God; not as a result of works, so that no one may boast."

Romans 8:28–39 gives us our position in Christ, and the Holy Spirit through Paul speaks of our condition as redeemed children of God through Christ in the past tense:

"And we know that God causes all things to work together for good to those who love God, to those who are called according to *His* purpose. For **those whom He foreknew,** He also **predestined** *to become* **conformed** to the image of His Son, so that He would be the firstborn among many brethren; and these whom **He predestined,** He also **called**; and these whom He **called,** He also **justified**; and these whom He **justified,** He also **glorified.**

"What then shall we say to these things? If God *is* for us, who *is* against us? He who did not spare His own Son, but delivered Him over for us all, how will He not also with Him freely give us all things? Who will bring a charge against God's elect? God is the one who justifies; who is the one who condemns? Christ Jesus is He who died, yes, rather who was raised, who is at the right hand of God, who also intercedes for us. Who will separate us from the love of Christ? Will tribulation, or distress, or persecution, or famine, or nakedness, or peril, or sword? Just as it is written,

"For Your sake we are being put to death all day long; We were considered as sheep to be slaughtered.

"But in all these things we overwhelmingly conquer through Him who loved us. For I am convinced that neither death, nor life, nor angels, nor principalities, nor things present, nor things to come, nor powers, nor height, nor depth, nor any other created thing, will be able to separate us from the love of God, which is in Christ Jesus our Lord."

Jesus Himself said in John 6:44, "No one can come to Me unless the Father who sent Me draws him; and I will raise him up on the last day." And then in John 10:27–29, "My sheep hear My voice, and I know them, and they follow Me; and I give eternal life to them, and they will never perish; and no one will snatch them out of My hand. My Father, who has given *them* to Me, is greater than all; and no one is able to snatch *them* out of the Father's hand. I and the Father are one."

If Blumhardt is correct, where does that leave Jesus' promise of security to all those the Father has called?

CRIS: Could these evil, possessing spirits be the souls of unregenerate humans god has consigned to wander the earth?

RAY: Possibly, but then Blumhardt would not be able to "evangelize" them as he describes, nor would the spirits of believers still be waiting to compensate in some manner for their sins.

CRIS: For the record, I believe Scripture is very clear that believers were chosen by God before the world was created and that salvation is by divine fiat rather than anything that we do (Romans 8:29; Ephesians 1:5, 11). This excludes the possibility that a deceased person might have a second chance at salvation and excludes the existence of purgatory. Even if some deceased people become evil spirits on the earth, this must be a stage of punishment that will lead to eternal damnation, *not a second chance.*

Natalina from ExtraordinaryIntelligence.com

Natalina was born and raised in North Dakota. She's a writer, podcaster, musician (playing viola and singing), jewelry designer, is happily married, and is a proud mommy to a cat named Solomon. Ever since she was a little girl, Natalina has been drawn to the supernatural. As the granddaughter of a Lutheran minister, she struggled to find her spiritual identity. Although she had tremendous love and respect for her grandfather and his beliefs, she was unable to find the answers inside the church for her burning questions about the unseen realm of the supernatural, thus she gradually drew away from her Lutheran roots and gravitated more toward New Age philosophies.

In an effort to learn more about the "unexplained," Natalina started the website Extraordinary Intelligence. She explored all things paranormal, New Age, and occult related. It took her down some strange and dangerous roads. It wasn't until a profound encounter with God that she was able to shake free from her obsession with the New Age, and she became a believer in Jesus Christ. Since that time, she has changed the focus of her website from glorifying the New Age to exposing it, and she approaches all topics through a biblical lens. Natalina is a good friend, and I am in debt to her for the hours she spent proofreading this book.

CRIS: Please share how you moved from a New Age/paranormal worldview to a biblical worldview.

NATALINA: The things that would fall into the "paranormal" world-view always fascinated me. UFOs, aliens, ghosts, and all things occult were a source of constant fascination for me, as far back as I can remember.

Throughout my life, I'd fluctuated between considering myself a Christian (lukewarm at best) to being agnostic (a nice catchall that basically meant I was noncommittal). Essentially, I was always questioning and ever seeking. In 2009, I endeavored to open up that search to a wider audience by launching my website, Extraordinary Intelligence. The initial plan was for this site to explore all things supernatural and "unexplained." I covered topics from hauntings to abductions and everything in between.

As time went on, I found myself embracing an odd hybrid of ancient alien theory and New Age spiritualism. I was open to the idea of humanity being sprung from extraterrestrials in some way, yet I believed that there was a cosmic life force that we could all tap into. Basically, my belief system became a smorgasbord of philosophies, a mish-mash of various forms of spiritualism that fed my need to be a part of something bigger, without having to devote myself to a specific worldview. Often, my Lutheran upbringing would snap me out of this schizophrenic mindset. I'd feel my heart being tugged by memories of my grandfather (a Lutheran pastor) who warned against dabbling in the occult. Yet, I'd become so convinced that the world was one of supernatural wonder and mystery, I simply couldn't reconcile it with what I'd learned about Christianity.

After being married for a few years, my husband was diagnosed with multiple sclerosis. I was furious at God (who I claimed not to believe in) for allowing this to happen to such a good man. My rebellion kicked up a few notches, and suddenly I found myself fully immersed in the New Age. I wanted New Age healing. I wanted to embrace this peaceful philosophy of Oneness and Light and Love. That's how it was packaged, and I bought it.

As tends to happen, the more immersed I became in the New Age, the darker the material became. In time, I found myself surrounded by self-professed Luciferians and atheists. When I was in the midst of these folks, it fed this insatiable urge I had to rebel. Throughout this experience, my mindset became darker and my judgment was clouded. I found myself in the grip of indescribable panic attacks on a regular basis, which forced me deeper into my quest for a New Age type of balance. It was a vicious cycle. The saddest part is that I left my husband in the dust at this time. He was alone to deal with his diagnosis while I wallowed in the darkness of my own self-pity and self-loathing. My anxiety rose higher as my moral compass became virtually nonexistent.

Eventually, my husband confronted me about my behavior. He was very upset, and I thank God that he didn't leave me. Instead, he rallied what little common sense I had left and urged me to put these bad people behind me. I did. Our marriage got back on track and it provided me some comfort. However, that sense of rebellion was suddenly replaced by crushing guilt for how I'd been behaving. Again, my anxiety spiraled out of control to the point where I was medicated and counseled by a number of doctors. I felt like I was doomed to a life of crippling fear.

One night, I was listening to the radio and for the first time heard L. A. Marzulli discuss "Ancient Prophetic Texts." Once I realized he was talking about the Bible, I became intrigued. I wanted to know more. I found that what he was saying made sense, and for the first time since I was a little girl, I honestly considered that MAYBE there was some truth to the Bible. I started to research some of the topics that Mr. Marzulli discussed, but I wasn't ready yet to let go of my New Age quest for Oneness. Not yet.

I'll never forget the night that I was pulled out of my stupor. I was alone in my office, sitting at my computer. I was researching some random websites to write some random article, and I felt that fear grip me yet again. That familiar sense of creeping dread took hold, and I found myself in the midst of the worst panic attack of my life. I was shaking, sweating, and crying. I became convinced I was having a heart attack. All the while, my hand was clicking away at the mouse as if I was on autopilot. I wasn't paying attention to what I was clicking on. I finally gathered enough composure to look up at my computer screen.

What greeted my eyes was a white screen with black text. The text said:

Be anxious for nothing, but in everything by prayer and supplication with thanksgiving let your requests be made known to God. And the peace of God, which surpasses all comprehension, will guard your hearts and your minds in Christ Jesus. (Philippians 4:6–7)

You could have knocked me over with a feather. I stared at that screen and pondered… "Could those words be for me?" Surely not. Who was I? Yet, I felt in my mind and heart that this was no mere fluke. This was God Almighty…and He was talking to me, low as I was. I laid my head on the desk and asked Him for confirmation. In that moment, all fear, anxiety, darkness and pain lifted, and I experienced that peace that surpassed comprehension. I felt free. I gave my heart to Jesus in that instant, and promised to follow Him all the days of my life.

Looking back, I see that I wasn't merely depressed or anxious. I was tormented. Through my disobedience and dabbling, I had opened myself to dark influences who were driving me further into despair, while urging me to seek any path except the path that would set me free.

I recognize that not everyone has such a profound moment of revelation that brings them into the Light of Jesus. When the Lord revealed Himself to me through His Word, I now believe He had a number of reasons for doing so in the manner that He did. I think that my heart had been opened just enough by listening to L. A. Marzulli and allowing for the possibility of biblical truth. That crack was enough to make me receptive to hearing God's call. Also, I am convinced that my calling is to reach out to people who are stuck in situations similar to what I once was.

God's supernatural presence in that moment of revelation was sufficient to convince me not only that He is real, but that there is a supernatural dimension that exists and works and moves even today. Having experienced the supernatural now from both the darkness and the Light, I felt motivated to take that message to my readers on Extraordinary Intelligence. One needn't disregard the fact that we live in a supernatural world in order to be a Christian. Quite the contrary, the Bible itself is a supernatural book full of wonders beyond our comprehension! It also warns us about the darkness and evil forces operating in this world, which are also supernatural in nature.

The focus of my website and my life changed dramatically. I was no longer spending my energy dabbling and dwelling in the darkness of the New Age and the Occult. I was now devoted to exposing it.

CRIS: What does my title, *Supernatural Worldview*, mean to you?

NATALINA: "Supernatural" is one of those words that scares Christians. I have found that the instant implication is one of spiritualism and paranormal intrigue. To me, a Supernatural Worldview is right in line with the Bible. In fact, if you cannot embrace the supernatural aspects of Scripture, then you may as well disregard the gospel outright, because it is a supernatural story of epic proportions! A Supernatural Worldview is one that acknowledges the existence of the nonphysical realm and embraces the concept that there are forces operating just beyond our everyday perception, and sometimes these supernatural forces are manifest in ways that we can see in this realm (UFOs, "ghosts", etc.). In a biblical sense, it means to accept that from Creation to Revelation, the Bible is nothing if not a book that outlines the supernatural history of the mankind and the universe, and a supernatural revelation of things to come. When one espouses a Supernatural Worldview, it allows for the acceptance that there is not always a physical explanation for events that take place in our world.

CRIS: Do you believe the occult is mainstream today? Are you aware of more secretive darker elements?

NATALINA: I think the occult is more mainstream today, but in a much more insidious way than it has been in generations past. For example, if we look at rise of spiritualism in the mid 1800s, we see that séances and conjuring were becoming more and more prevalent, and even fashionable. The Fox Sisters (http://www.historynet.com/the-fox-sisters-spiritualisms-unlikely-founders.htm) were a great example of how the interest in paranormal events started to become the norm in parlors across the United States. But it was blatant. Those who were interested knew precisely what they were getting themselves into. Fast forward to the '60s and '70s…another time in American history when occultism came into fashion. Here we saw New Age philosophies taking center stage through Transcendental Meditation and other Eastern practices. There was no secret that these practices were steeped in spiritualism and metaphysics.

Today, we are bombarded with occultism of a more sinister sort. This New Age of occultism shrouds itself largely in entertainment. Children are being indoctrinated into esoteric philosophies through books and television, such as the Harry Potter series, *Percy Jackson and the Olympians*, Disney Channel shows like *The Wizards of Waverly Place,* and Nickelodeon shows like *House of Anubis*. All of these things are presented as lighthearted fun but display a dark occultism that I believe is a dangerous gateway for young people. Adult programming isn't much better, with popular shows like *True*

Blood and occult-themed movies. Certainly there has always been occultism in the entertainment industry, but I think today it permeates all aspects of pop culture and manages to present itself in an innocuous way, making these dark practices seem not so dark at all, and in some cases desirable.

I believe that this is by design. I think there is a concerted effort to draw people away from biblical Christianity, and into the arms of mysticism and magic. Ghost hunting programs are the norm now. Watching a team of paranormal investigators speaking directly to spirits and in some cases trying to conjure them is no longer a fringe affair, relegated to quiet living rooms and elite social gatherings; but rather it has become something so innocuous as to be taken for granted as part of daily life. Visiting a medium is no longer something one must do in secret. Television shows like *Long Island Medium* and *Crossing Over with John Edwards* are celebrated as uplifting family programs.

I do believe there is a dark group behind all of this. I use the term "Illuminati" not in the strictest sense of the word, as some people do, but more as a catch-all term for those elite members of the establishment that control the media and the government. I think they work in tandem to achieve certain ends. The ultimate goal is control. People are easier to control when they don't hold allegiance to a higher power. Christians are generally difficult to sway, because we KNOW about the powers and principalities mentioned in Ephesians 6:12. We are instantly skeptical of things that are counter to the values presented in Scripture. BUT…if they can use the media and entertainment industries to influence kids and young adults to steer away from the "rigidity" of Christianity, and open their minds to the sorts of things that make them susceptible to suggestion, they become quite pliable. Yes, there is a dark group that exists in the shadows. We can call them the "powers that be." And for those of us who embrace a Supernatural Worldview, we know that there are darker powers still that pull the strings of those elite men and women, whether they realize it or not.

CRIS: Do you recognize elements of your old worldview within certain "Christian" churches?

NATALINA: Today's churches are rife with New Age practices. It took me exactly one Sunday after my coming to Christ to figure that out. I attended what appeared to be a mainstream Midwestern Presbyterian church, and was greeted by a female pastor who used a Tibetan "singing bowl" to signify the beginning of services. She spent the majority of her sermon talking about finding "inner peace" (without scriptural references), and ended the sermon with an invitation to walk the "prayer (meditation) labyrinth." Another church I attended invited members to participate in "Holy Yoga." These are just a couple of examples. Beyond that, we find that many of the famous prosperity preachers are engaging in a practice nicknamed "Name it and claim it." The idea being that God has given us the ability to command certain things into reality simply by using positive affirmations and repetitive prayers that border on incantation. This is no different than the practice I used to swear by (although it was 100-percent ineffective) known in popular literature as "The Law of Attraction" and in more New Agey circles as "manifesting your own reality." We find this idea most prominently in best sellers like *The Secret* and in hit documentaries like *What the Bleep Do We Know?* The concept is simple and uses the burgeoning science of quantum physics as its biggest selling point and claim to legitimacy. In essence, because our world is merely an illusion, we can create our own reality. If we want something badly enough and we focus our energy on that object or outcome, we can make it happen, simply by believing it. This of course removes any need for a Creator, because it puts the task of creation into the hands of all of us. You want some money? Visualize yourself as wealthy and it shall be yours. How is this any different than what the prosperity gospel preaches? If we believe hard enough in our own abundance, we WILL receive what we believe. You see? God becomes irrelevant. At best, He is relegated to an impotent figure bound by His duty to fulfill all of our worldly desires.

CRIS: Do you believe in the existence of a sixth sense or psi? Please give us your thoughts on that as well as any experiences you have had that steered your opinion one way or another.

NATALINA: I think that the VAST majority of those who claim to exhibit extrasensory powers are charlatans. Take Uri Gellar, for example. This famous mentalist who has had a presence in pop culture since the '70s has been proven time and time again to be a fraud, yet he is consistently presented as the best example of psychokinetic powers. For this reason, I am highly skeptical of 95 percent of people who claim to have such abilities. The other 5 percent of cases that appear to display abilities that defy conventional science are a little trickier to define.

Things like ESP, clairvoyance, psychic phenomena and the like— in my mind—when genuine are likely manifestations of deceiving spirits. Often, one finds psychics will defer to "spirit guides" or helpers from "the other side." Clearly this practice is unbiblical.

Psychokinesis is trickier, because I've never seen it displayed in a way that is convincing. Again, if it IS possible, I think it is likely the work of sinister forces working behind the scenes. I do not think the

Cris Putnam

practitioner is always aware that this is the case, but it is likely that at some point in their life, they opened themselves up to influences of the demonic realm, and these forces aid them in portraying humans as potentially so powerful that they have no need for a Creator God, because, again, the power is in the hands of man.

Now, sometimes I do think it may come down to a matter of semantics. For example, I do believe that God gives some people revelations. If this revelation comes in the form of a dream, it could technically be referred to as a precognitive dream, I suppose. If the revelation comes in the form of a vision, some might call the person who receives the vision a psychic. But I think that God-given revelations are set apart by the fact that the one who receives it KNOWS without doubt what the source of the revelation was. I also believe in the gifts of the Holy Spirit being operational even today. Again, these gifts may manifest in completely supernatural ways that could be described as extrasensory, but always with the understanding that the power did NOT come from inside the human's own potential, but as a gift from God Almighty.

Remote viewing is another area that is strange. I think there may be enough evidence via government experimentation and private practice to suggest that such a thing is possible on some level. But again, we seem to always find that those who practice such things do so outside the assistance of God. It always comes down to the promotion of human potential that is latent within every being. I think this is the very point that Satan and his minions are trying to make us believe—human beings can operate in marvelous ways based upon their own will. After all, isn't that the very lie that was told at the beginning of time in the Garden? "Ye shall be as gods."

"Let every soul be subject unto the higher powers. For there is no power but of God: the powers that be are ordained of God" (Romans 13:1).

CRIS: Could this be latent "soul power," which was lost in the Fall (Genesis 3)?

NATALINA: I know very little about the concept of "soul power" beyond a cursory understanding that it is a reference to gifts that Adam had prior to sin coming into the world. I have considered that perhaps there is something to the idea that human beings DO have latent abilities within us that we're simply not meant to tap into, and that perhaps dark forces can manipulate these abilities. Is it possible that Satan can convince us to go against the will of God and use these abilities to undermine God? It is possible.

CRIS: Do you think near-death experiences are evidence for the immaterial human soul?

NATALINA: It seems that I've become quite the skeptic in my old age. The NDE is something that I once found fascinating, and I now find it troubling. Mostly, I find that those who claim to have experienced such an event tend not to check out when compared with Scripture. The popular book *Heaven Is for Real* is one that can be found in the household of nearly every Christian, it seems. Reportedly the true story of a little boy who went to heaven and came back, it is presented as a story of hope and encouragement. There have been many discernment ministries who've picked this story apart, but I take an even simpler approach. The three-year-old boy, Colton, describes heaven as a place where everyone has wings and halos. He talks about sitting on the lap of Jesus and petting a rainbow. To me, this smacks of the kind of imagery that kids are taught in Sunday school about how heaven is. It speaks to the naiveté of a child who has cartoonish ideas of what paradise would be like. Thus, if he did have some kind of vision, it seems to me it was probably something that was induced by his subconscious and manifested in exactly what you'd expect a little boy to dream up about heaven. I'm not convinced.

It seems to me that most NDEs reveal information that is outside of scriptural support. Further, I have to wonder why the Lord would choose to show things to modern men that He withheld from his disciples and are never described in biblical stories. When Paul was caught up into the third heaven, he was not permitted to speak of what he saw there (2 Corinthians 12:1–9). In fact, he describes the things that he witnessed as "not lawful for a man to utter."

CRIS: Do you believe out-of-body experiences are possible? Have you experienced one?

NATALINA: I believe that out-of-body experiences are possible to a certain extent. I think there is biblical precedent to show that some people in history have been taken out of their physical form. I think that Paul's visit to the third heaven could be looked at as an out-of-body experience. In the cases that are biblical, we find that they are always involuntary.

Astral projection is quite different. In this case, the practitioner is willingly trying to leave the body. This is dangerous and should NEVER be practiced. The reason is obvious. If you are capable of letting your spirit or soul travel outside of the body, you are leaving yourself open to be infiltrated by demonic forces. It's like laying out a welcome mat: "I'm not home right now but come on in and make yourself comfy!"

I tried a few times in the past to astral project. In only one case did anything unusual happen. I found myself drifting away…sort of like I was falling asleep…but then I was truly falling. The best way

I can describe it would be like I was falling through space at very high speeds. I could physically feel the g-forces on my face. In my mind, it was almost as though stars were rushing past me. The best visual I can give you is what it looks like in *Star Wars* when traveling at warp speed or hyperspace. Throughout the entire ordeal (I have no idea how much time actually passed), there was a deafening buzzing in my ears that got louder and louder. I was terrified. My heart was racing, and suddenly all I could think about was making it stop. I remember my teeth hurt. When I snapped back into reality, my teeth and jaw were aching as though they'd been subjected to tremendous pressure. My head hurt like it had been caught in a vice. I never tried it again.

CRIS: Have you ever seen an apparition or experienced a poltergeist?

NATALINA: A little over ten years ago, before I was married, I lived in a house with three other girls. It was a very old house that was owned by the parents of one of my roommates. It was built around the turn of the century. The house consisted of a main floor, an upstairs with two rooms (basically an attic with a landing), and a basement. I got one of the upstairs rooms.

The whole house was creepy and had on oppressive "vibe." When exploring the basement just after we moved in, we discovered a hidden room behind the furnace. Opening the door, we saw a small room with a dirt floor and a shovel in the corner. "This is where the dead bodies are kept," I joked to my roommates. They didn't think it was funny.

After living there for a short time, things began…happening. There were footsteps on the stairs and in the halls. The hardwood floor would echo and creak with the footfalls of an unseen visitor.

The television turned itself off, lights flickered. All of these things were explained away in our minds as products of an old house with bad wiring and a settling foundation.

One afternoon, I was in the shower in the basement bathroom. No one else was home, and all of the doors were locked. I thought I heard some commotion outside, so I turned off the water to listen more closely. "Hello?" I shouted. No answer. Hearing things again. Then as I stepped out of the shower to grab a towel, I heard it again. This time it was the distinct sound of footsteps on the floor right above me, which would have been in the kitchen.

I shouted again and the stepping stopped. I decided it must be one of the roomies, and went about my business. Once I emerged from the bathroom, I heard a man talking upstairs. At this point I was very alarmed. Grabbing the only weapon I could find (an unfortunately small screwdriver), I walked toward the stairs. As I approached, I heard the footsteps coming closer to the top of the stairs. This is the point in horror movies where you yell at the screen, "Don't go up there! Don't investigate! It isn't worth it!" You convince yourself that in the same situation, you would not do the same thing.

So there I was, at the bottom of the stairs, micro screwdriver in hand, and I thought to myself, "I really think I need to investigate this." So there you go. I began to scale the stairs that were comprised of two levels. Half way up they took a turn, so that when you were on the bottom level, you were unable to see the top. As I slowly crept up the steps, I continued to hear walking. Then, just as I was about to take the turn and face my intruder, I heard the front door slam shut. I ran the rest of the way up the stairs and was greeted by no one. There was no way possible that whoever had been walking in the kitchen would have been able to make it to the front door that fast, let alone without making any noise during the retreat.

Needless to say, I was very unsettled by this incident. I started to feel extremely uneasy as I lay in bed at night. The house seemed to come alive while everyone was sleeping. I blamed my fear on irrational paranoia and hypersensitivity. But I never really relaxed.

Sometime later, I was installing some bookshelves in my room. I heard a whisper of what sounded like my name coming from behind me. I quickly whipped around to see the source of the whisper. No one was there. I hesitantly turned back to the task at hand, and instantly heard the whisper again. This time I realized it was coming from the direction of the closet. Once again, I decided to investigate, so I slowly crept toward the closet. I stuck my head inside and looked around, this time I heard the whisper again, only it wasn't my name. It was saying, "Nancy." Clear as a bell.

I ran out of my room and shouted down the stairs for someone…anyone…to come up and hear this. I could still hear the voice coming from my room, louder now, and more insistent. Everyone was either gone or in bed. No one could help me. I slept on the couch that night, one eye open in fearful expectation of some specter that never arrived.

It is important to note that at this time I fully believed that ghosts were the spirits of dead people. I really had no concept that they might be anything else.

When I told my best friend (who also lived in the house) about what I had experienced, she had the same opinion and suggested that we go to the city library and research the history of the house. Fortunately for us, the library kept a very extensive series of records regarding the old homes in the area. We looked up the address of the place where we were living, and discovered something very odd. Since 1920, no one had owned the home for more than two years before selling it.

Prior to 1920, there had been only one owner. We'll call him John Larson. His wife…Nancy. Apparently Nancy had died in that house.

I moved out of the house not long after that, and new roommates moved in. One of them was a fellow named George, who moved into the basement. One day, he was in a very foul mood, and confronted my best friend, who occupied the room right above his bed. He scolded her for being up until 4:00 a.m. moving furniture around. She'd gone to sleep at 12:00 a.m.

So, this scenario solidified in my mind that hauntings HAD to be the result of dead people who were trapped in the place where they'd died. Really…wouldn't you?

I now believe that these spirits are liars, and their goal is to take us off track spiritually. I find it perfectly plausible that there was a demonic force that had taken residence in that house, and that it intentionally misled us into believing that "Nancy" was still present.

A really interesting passage of Scripture shows how this is possible in vivid detail:

"The LORD said, 'Who will entice Ahab king of Israel to go up and fall at Ramoth-gilead?' And one said this while another said that. Then a spirit came forward and stood before the LORD and said, 'I will entice him.' And the LORD said to him, 'How?' He said, 'I will go and be a deceiving spirit in the mouth of all his prophets.' Then He said, 'You are to entice him and prevail also. Go and do so'" (2 Chronicles 18:19–21).

Now, this isn't specifically referring to a haunting per se, but it shows how there is a spiritual realm that is devoted to lying and misleading humans into doing or believing incorrect things.

And really…there is no better explanation than this:

"But the Spirit explicitly says that in later times some will fall away from the faith, paying attention to deceitful spirits and doctrines of demons" (1 Timothy 4:1).

CRIS: Do you think poltergeist phenomena could be recurring spontaneous psychokinesis from a person present on the scene?

NATALINA: One school of thought about poltergeist is that it is different than what is observed at a normal "haunting," in that it seems to revolve around a singular individual. Generally, it seems this is an adolescent, often a girl. The prevailing thought is that the poltergeist activity may be a psychokinetic response to the already heightened emotional and hormonal state of the adolescent.

If one accepts that psychokinesis is possible, then the question is whether or not one can manifest psychokinetic phenomena without really trying. Most cases of poltergeist activity surround a specific family inside their own residence. Generally, the entire family presumes they are under some kind of attack. This would imply that IF an individual family member is the source of the activity, they do not know that they are responsible.

So, a few things need to happen. One, we will need to suppose psychokinesis is possible. Next, we need to identify the source of this ability. I tend to believe that if it is a real phenomenon, it likely isn't something that our Creator intended for us to tap into...certainly not in our fallen state (using the "soul power" concept). Thus, even if the poltergeist activity is the result of a latent ability found within an otherwise normal individual, it still tracks back to a demonic influence, whether it is manifesting through the use of a power inside a human, or of its own power, as can be presumed in other types of "hauntings."

CRIS: Is it possible that some ghosts are really spirits of dead humans?

[Some scholars have suggested that while believers go to heaven, it is possible that because final judgment has been reserved until Christ's return (1 Corinthians 4:5; Matthew 8:29; Revelation 20:11) and this might explain the presence of human spirits wandering the earth.]

NATALINA: I've heard some propose the theory that ghosts may actually be dead humans doomed to walk the earth until the final judgment. I've also heard some explain that the ghostly "spirits" that we see are actually those souls trapped in the "outer darkness" mentioned in Scripture. To me, I find both scenarios a little difficult to wrap my head around. Second Corinthians 5:8 says that to be absent from the body means to be at home with the Lord. Now, does this allow for the possibility that those who are not saved might be wandering in some earth-bound state until judgment? Is it possible that they may remain bound to the home where they lived in a suspended state? I found a really interesting passage in Job that seems to refute this:

As the cloud disappears and vanishes away, so he who goes down to the grave does not come up. HE SHALL NEVER RETURN TO HIS HOUSE, Nor shall his place know him anymore. (Job 7:9–10, emphasis added)

I tend to hold to the belief that hauntings are not earth-bound human spirits, but are demonic in nature.

CRIS: Have you ever had an experience you think might been with an angel?

NATALINA: I cannot say for certain whether or not I've had an encounter with an angel, but I can think of one instance that stands out in my mind as a possible angelic encounter. I was out on a nature hike with a friend. We were climbing on some rather treacherous rocks that rose above an area of a river with dangerous rushing rapids. Were one to fall that water, I cannot imagine that it would be possible to survive. The rapids rushed over large and jagged rocks, and in that area it is possible to see tree trunks being torn apart as they hit the chaotic water.

As I was climbing the rocks, I happened to step on one that was very loose and I lost my balance. I began to fall backwards. Had I fallen all of the way, there would have been nothing to stop me from falling directly into the water. As my momentum was headed backward, I said a quick prayer, and suddenly I was thrust forward so that I fell to my knees and was able to grab a rock for support. It was almost as though an unseen hand pushed me from behind. My trajectory was such that the momentum of my fall would have been almost impossible to reverse, yet somehow I reversed course and fell forward. I had the impression in that moment that it may have been angelic intervention that stopped my fall.

Psalm 91:9–11: "For He shall give His angels charge over you, to keep you in all your ways. They shall bear you up in their hands, lest you dash your foot against a stone."

CRIS: Do you believe God's holy angels are active in the world today? Have you seen one?

NATALINA: I believe that holy angels are here today and always, watching us and helping us. There are many instances in Scripture that show this to be true.

CRIS: Do you think there is an ongoing rise in paranormal activity? What leads you to this conclusion?

NATALINA: In my research, it certainly does seem that there may be an increase in paranormal activity…or at least an increased interest in it. In fact, it may be less that there are more paranormal events happening, but that there is a heightened interest in such phenomena and less reluctance to keep it private when one has a paranormal encounter. This probably has to do with how mainstream paranormal investigation has become.

For example, it is true that reports of hauntings and UFO encounters appear to have increased over the years, but it is impossible to say whether this is because the events are happening more frequently, or if it is simply that more people are willing to report the events when they occur.

With that said, I do see a possible scenario here. I think it is possible that with the rising increase of interest and general acceptance of paranormal research and investigation, people have become more open to seek these experiences out. When one becomes open to seeking these experiences, it is only a matter of time before they start consulting with a medium, an Ouija board, or some other form of conjuring. I think it is possible that a rise in this type of reaching out by humans is leading to an increase in the experiences. Maybe we are opening more doors, or putting out more invitations to these dark forces.

CRIS: If so, do you think this is indicative of the soon return of Christ?

NATALINA: For me, it is less the increase of paranormal activity that seems to point to the soon return of Christ, but more the increase in acceptance of this activity. I DO believe that the UFO phenomenon is on the rise and has a direct correlation to the great deception mentioned in Scripture. "And for this cause God shall send them strong delusion, that they should believe a lie" (2 Thessalonians 2:11). This strong delusion or great deception seems very likely to be related to a supernatural type of event that will emerge with the goal of countering the Word of the Bible.

A U.K. survey showed that more people in Britain believe in UFOs/aliens than those that believe in God. According to the report:

- 52 percent believe UFO evidence has been covered up because widespread knowledge of their existence would threaten government stability.
- 44 percent believe in God.[25]

It is important to note that of those who proclaim to believe in God, it is not necessarily the Judeo/Christian God that they believe in, thus the percentage of Christians who believe in God in Britain is likely considerably less than the survey bears out.

I think that the trajectory seems to hold that the gulf between those percentages continues to get wider and wider. Hollywood seems bent on tickling people's fantasies of benevolent aliens in films like *Avatar*, while television is determined to convince people that we're merely the offspring of *Ancient Aliens*. If this trend continues, and I see no reason to believe that it won't, it seems plausible and actually quite likely that the concept of extraterrestrials will contribute largely to that great deception mentioned in biblical prophecy. It is interesting to see how my beliefs have evolved. Initially, I presumed that ETs were physical beings from other planets. That made sense to my worldview. Later, as I embraced a New Age philosophy, I was convinced that ETs were spiritual beings of light and love…a benevolent force that was meant to help mankind evolve. I continue to believe that ETs are supernatural in nature, but I no longer hold that they have our best interests at heart. I believe they are part of those powers and principalities that we're warned to guard ourselves against. And I believe that they will play a large role in end-times events. Again, I point to 1 Timothy 4:1.

CRIS: Thanks to Ray Boeche and Natalina for taking the time to offer their thoughts. Finally, a metaphysical position is offered for consideration.

A Rigorously Supernatural Worldview

A Christ follower needs to cultivate a command of what he or she believes (theology) and why he or she believes it (philosophy). Accordingly, to answer the worldview question about what is real, one must enter a *metaphysical* discussion. Metaphysics deals with underlying principles or theories that form the basis the knowledge. In philosophy, it is the specialty area concerned with the nature of reality, existence, time, and space. The prefix "meta" means "beyond" or "transcending," so it is often thought of as "beyond physics" as in that which is out of the reach of physical science. This final section suggests a controversial but comprehensive metaphysical way of viewing the world.

What I am suggesting is a metaphysic which deals with *objective* reality. The term "objective" is somewhat loaded. It is often used to mean being free of prejudice or bias or perhaps simply as "based on facts" rather than opinions. Philosophers often use the term in a technical sense to denote something *existing independent of an individual mind or perception*. For example, the statement, "a triangle has three sides" is objectively true.

Subjectivity is its opposite. It is used popularly for bias or a state of mind that is based on feelings and opinions rather than facts and evidence. In philosophy, it is employed to denote something that *exists only in one's mind* and not independently of it. For instance, the statement, "I like orange creamsicles" is an example of a subjective truth. Many critics assume that metaphysical idealism (that everything is fundamentally mental) implies everything is subjective, but this is not necessary if one believes in God. Because it is very easy to misunderstand the metaphysic I am advocating, I cannot emphasize enough that the idealism presented here is completely *objective*.

Like worldviews, everyone has a metaphysical position, whether they know it or not. Most people never bother to give it much thought. Western culture has come to accept the scientific materialist metaphysic—everything is matter—as the pinnacle of rational objectivity and belief in the supernatural as purely subjective. Author Derek Gilbert, cohost of the *Peering into Darkness* podcast, once commented, "I often hear Christians trying to explain away strange events with natural explanations when a supernatural one seems more appropriate; as biblical Christians the supernatural should be our default position."[26] This can be explained in terms of Christians having a different plausibility structure. A theologian explains:

The boundary between this community and the society for which the Bible is not determinative is marked by the paradigm shift that is traditionally called conversion. However this conversion may occur—and it can occur in many different ways—those who belong to this community inhabit a different plausibility structure from that of their contemporaries. Things that are myths or illusions for others are real for them.[27]

What is plausible for believers is not for the materialist. The biblical worldview elevates the immaterial over the material. Unfortunately, many well-meaning Christians still think like materialists. It is completely understandable because we are bombarded with scientism. Scientism is the idea that the only path to true knowledge is science. Although garden-variety atheists will still bludgeon you with it, *it is nonsense.*

Indeed, scientism is self-refuting because scientific knowledge is based on repeatable experimental data, and the statement that "truth is only available from science" is not a product of the scientific method. Thus, it commits suicide by not meeting its own standard. In fact, the next time a skeptic uses that line on you, ask him if he knows what he is thinking at the moment. Press him on it. and when he answers yes, tell him he has just arrived at true knowledge apart from science. If he answers no, then ask him why anyone should believe anything he says since he is not even aware of his own thoughts. Science is wonderful as far as it goes, but it is far from exhaustive.

Scientism, naturalism, and physicalism are all branches from reductive materialist root. These secular "isms" are exactly the sort of things the apostle Paul was warning the Colossians about when he wrote: "See to it that no one takes you captive by philosophy and empty deceit, according to human tradition, according to the elemental spirits of the world, and not according to Christ" (Colossians 2:8). Because most of us have been indoctrinated into the scientific way of conceiving of reality, this presentation will likely seem downright weird and counterintuitive at first. However, what most scientists, philosophers, and indeed the majority of the world deem objective is in this view a subjective illusion. This book offers a clear accounting of a rigorous supernatural worldview.

I believe objective idealism is a rational way of thinking about the external world and how you perceive it, and it is supernatural. While it is impossible to know for sure, I truly believe this is much closer to the way Jesus saw the world. There are entire books written by philosophers that fail to really understand it. However, it is actually very simple to understand if you can let go of some of the alleged "common sense" notions that are, in truth, more common than sensible. In fact, anyone can understand this metaphysic and I think everyone *should*. If you truly believe in the God of the Bible, including the qualities of omnipotence, omnipresence, and omniscience, then you are 90 percent there. If you do not believe in God or perhaps do not understand what all of those "omnis" entail, then I hope to enlighten and persuade. The basic concept is very simple, but that doesn't mean it is easy. However, it is only difficult due to the baggage of philosophical naturalism that is misrepresented as common sense. Even if you ultimately reject this system of thought, it is well worth your time to consider. Patience and perseverance will be rewarded with wisdom. Please attempt to thoroughly understand what is presented before you dismiss it as fanciful.

I am suggesting the metaphysical stance called immaterialism or idealism. This metaphysic called *idealism* is often credited to Anglican Bishop George Berkeley for whom the famous University in California is named. Berkeley is best known for his controversial maxim *Esse est percipi*, "To be is to be perceived." He explained:

But, besides all that endless variety of ideas or objects of knowledge, there is likewise something which knows or perceives them, and exercises divers operations, as willing, imagining, remembering, about them. This perceiving, active being is what I call MIND, *spirit, soul,* or *myself.*

By which words I do not denote any one of my ideas, but
a thing entirely distinct from them, *wherein they exist*, or,
which is the same thing, whereby they are perceived—for
the existence of an idea consists in being perceived.[28]

In Berkeley's system, ideas are primary and matter is secondary.
This is where the famous question derives about a tree falling in the
woods: "If a tree falls in the forest and no one is there to hear it, does
it make a sound?" Most people, even trained philosophers, make the
mistake of assuming Berkeley was saying everything is subjective.
For example, they might argue, "George Berkeley would probably
say there was no tree at all." But they have missed Berkeley's point.
Berkeley would not only say the tree exists, but he would surely say
it made a sound. Why? Be because God was there to hear it. God is
the ultimate observer, and upon Him everything depends.

A modern idealist, Anglican theologian Keith Ward, explains:

An idealist, in the very widest sense, is a person who thinks
that mind or mind-likeness, something conscious and intelligent, perhaps capable of thought and feeling, is at the base
of reality and is the most real thing that there is. And matter
is somehow dependent on that or expresses that consciousness. Matter wouldn't exist without it.[29]

Follow the link in the endnote to hear Ward explain in more
detail. I first became fascinated with idealism when studying the history of ideas under theologian/philosopher R. C. Sproul. He explains:

Berkeley's theory is no simplistic retreat into subjectivism.
He denies, not that objective reality exists, but that objec-

tive reality can exist apart from its being perceived. He distinguishes between the activity of the mind *(percipere)* and the impression received by the mind *(percipi),* between the products of an active imagination, which are a matter of willful fabrication, and passively received sense impressions, which occur apart from one's volition.[30]

In philosophy, idealism is the group of philosophies that assert that reality, or reality as we can know it, is fundamentally mental, mentally constructed, or otherwise immaterial. Mind takes precedence over matter. In Berkeley's biblically consistent version, God as immaterial spirit not only preceded the material universe, He spoke it into being and so all matter is a product of His mind. This is an extremely rigorous form of twoism.

According to Berkeley, there are only two kinds of things: spirits and ideas. Spirits are simple, active beings that produce and perceive ideas; ideas are passive things that are produced and perceived.[31] Berkeley would tell the materialist that matter does not exist, he only perceives it in his mind—it is an idea. You do not see a tree out there—not really; the tree is an idea in your mind. This can get tricky, but technically Berkeley is correct. Think about it: There are many ways to fool our eyes. The tree could be a hologram or a model for a movie set. What you actually perceive is an idea constructed from the data gathered by vision. But sense perceptions can be fooled. In this way, your own thoughts are more certain than the external world.

For example, let's examine an apple. We look at the reddish, pleasant fruit carefully, but from a short distance there is nothing except the image of it, the feel of it, its taste and smell, and the noise it makes when we tap it or maybe even bite into it. There is no underlying apple "essence" or substrate that the sensory qualities inhabit. It is a group of sense experiences, perceptions that, when put together, tell us "apple." Therefore, the apple *is* the sensory experience of it. We have an *idea* of an apple and it exists in our mind (this implies metaphysical *idealism*). We cannot make sense of existence apart from our sensory experience of it. Hence, *esse est percipi,* or "to be, is to be perceived." Caution is in order because this is where mystics miss the boat and start to believe they create their own reality. Not so; in this version, reality is grounded in God. Berkeley was not advocating the subjectivism coming from the modern New Age quantum mystics. God wills and upholds reality and our human minds perceive ideas. Because Berkeley grounded ultimate reality in God, his idealism was entirely *objective.* Later philosophers lost sight of this and became lost in a morass of subjective idealism, and the idealist metaphysic was eventually crushed by reductive materialism.

Interestingly, many formerly materialist scientists now seem to agree with Berkeley based on the evidence from physics. Bruce Rosenblum and Fred Kuttner are professors of physics at UC Santa Cruz who wrote a recent book entitled *Quantum Enigma.* Although I would not call them idealists, the two university-trained physicists concede, "Today, quantum experiments deny a commonsense physical reality. It is no longer a logical option."[32] They explain in this way:

> Quantum theory tells that the observation of an object can instantaneously influence the behavior of another greatly distant object—even if no physical force connects the two. These are the influences Einstein rejected as "spooky actions," but they have now been demonstrated to exist. Quantum theory also tells us that an object can be in two places at the same time. Its existence at the particular place where

it happens to be found becomes an actuality only upon its observation. Quantum theory thus denies the existence of a physically real world independent of its observation.[33]

That sounds a lot like what Berkeley was saying! Atoms consist of electrons rotating around a nucleus made of protons and neutrons, which are composed of up and down quarks that are made of energy. *They have no size. All matter is actually made of energy that has congealed into particulate form.* In other words, that is what we are made of, energy. In addition, Sproul has pointed out a degree of absurdity in the scientific ontology for energy:

> We ask, "What is energy?" One may reply, "It is the ability to do work." But we push harder and say, "We are asking, not what energy can do, but what it is." One may then reply, "$E=MC^2$." But we become obstreperous and say, "We are asking not for energy's mathematical equivalent, but about its nature. What is the difference between energy and boojums? Between energy and animal spirits? Between energy and attraction?" We do not directly perceive energy, yet it is an unassailable doctrine of modern empirical science.[34]

If energy does not exist in an objective sense, then what about matter that is supposedly made of energy? Of course, it depends on whom you ask, but Max Planck, the German theoretical physicist who originated quantum theory and won the Nobel Prize in Physics in 1918, wrote this:

> There is no matter as such. All matter originates and exists only by virtue of a force which brings the particle of an atom

to vibration and holds this most minute solar system of the atom together. We must assume behind this force the existence of a conscious and intelligent mind. This mind is the matrix of all matter.[35]

I hope it is apparent that science is saying something very close to Bishop Berkeley. It works well with the apostle Paul as well: "And he is before all things, and in him all things hold together" (Colossians 1:17). Indeed, the transcendent mind of *Yahweh* prevails over matter. Everything exists only because His ultimate mind wills it. Apart from that vital mind of our Creator God, nothing exists. This is the depth of a Supernatural Worldview.

ity-

Notes

1. James Sire, "What Is a Worldview? "Christianity.com, http://www.christianity.com/christian-life/worldview/what-is-a-worldview-11627153.html?p=0. (accessed 05/23/13).
2. Mark I. Bubeck, *The Adversary: The Christian Versus Demon Activity* (Chicago: Moody, 1975) 47.
3. Ibid., 50.
4. Audio file: http://www.futurequake.com/Audio/FQShow142.mp3.
5. Peter Jones, *One or Two: Seeing a World of Difference* (Escondido, CA: Main Entry, 2010) Kindle edition, 1307–1308.
6. "Paganus," *An Elementary Latin Dictionary,* ed. Charlton T. Lewis (Medford, MA: American, 1890).
7. Jones, 151–157.
8. Ibid., 1210–1211.
9. See http://www.believersweb.org/view.cfm?ID=659 for an explanation of the scene in the made for TV film *Out on a Limb,* where MacLaine shouted "I am god, I am god," available on Youtube here: http://www.youtube.com/watch?v=ccb2GsnOoBM at the 3:25 time mark.
10. Jones, 151–157.
11. Ibid., 1213–1214.
12. Gary R., Habermas and Michael R. Licona, *The Case for the Resurrection of Jesus* (Grand Rapids, MI: Kregel, 2004) 50.
13. Ibid.,49.
14. Ibid., 61.
15. Ibid., 66.
16. Ibid., 69.
17. Ibid., 225.
18. Lee Strobel, *The Case For Christ* (Grand Rapids, MI: Zondervan, 1998) 201.

19. Habermas vs. Flew: http://www.youtube.com/
    watch?v=BVb3Xvny8-k.
20. Licona vs. Cavin: http://youtu.be/0rJqfsEN_Fo.
21. Craig vs. Spong: http://youtu.be/zsXzu4tcOTI.
22. Available here: http://www.lulu.com/us/en/shop/ray-boeche/
    journal-of-the-fortean-research-center-casebound/hardcover/
    product-20296798.html.
23. See Press Release here: http://www.google.com/url?sa=t&rct=j&q=
    &esrc=s&source=web&cd=1&ved=0CDsQFjAA&url=http%3A%
    2F%2Ffuturequake.com%2FPressReleases%2FPRESSRELEASE-
    RayBoecheInterview-FUTUREQUAKERADIOSHOW31MAY-
    4JUNE10.docx&ei=IRbrUqKFBcidyQHc-4GIAQ&usg=AFQjCN
    GV4zXp32CCa8XlQvnHXN1C99Exug&sig2=_wfX3l6N1GCAIo
    x_3ChDnA&bvm=bv.60444564,d.aWc.
24. See page 3 of this document: http://printfu.org/
    preview/?pdfurl=1qeXpurpn6Wih-SUpOGul6ynh7nEvLTCiLq2wY
    m4w7vHu6a4kbHYrpmfktiLqeegraGfjtfq2eSilJ_p4OWi2t3Sx9jQ2
    dDqydrc5pfR49Ok0tPP6NnR49jK1NvKndjV2OLS0d3q2KO1ur
    bBt52-1erf083b6ZSloZ2jobbP7cWmpp2fnebJ2oqg7Q.
25. http://www.huffingtonpost.com/2012/10/15/alien-believers-
    outnumber-god_n_1968259.html.
26. Remarks at the 2010 Last Days Conference in Nashville, Tennessee,
    verified in personal email.
27. Lesslie Newbigin, *Foolishness to the Greeks: The Gospel and Western
    Culture* (Grand Rapids, MI: Eerdmans, 1986) Kindle edition,
    801–803.
28. George Berkeley, *A Treatise Concerning the Principles of Human
    Knowledge*, (Project Gutenberg, http://www.gutenberg.org/catalog/
    world/readfile?pageno=13&fk_files=1983609) 13.
29. Transcribed from video Keith Ward, "Mind over Matter: The

Ultimate Nature of Reality," OPEN BIOLA, accessed January 20, 2013 http://open.biola.edu/resources/mind-over-matter-the-ultimate-nature-of-reality time mark 1:01–1:24.

30. R. C. Sproul, *The Consequences of Ideas: Understanding the Concepts that Shaped Our World* (Wheaton IL: Crossway, 2000), Kindle edition, 933–935.

31. T. M. Bettcher, *Berkeley: A Guide for the Perplexed* (London, New York: Continuum Publishing, 2008) 14.

32. Bruse Rosenblum and Fred Kuttner, *Quantum Enigma: Physics Encounters Consciousness* (USA: Oxford, 2006) 6.

33. Ibid., 7.

34. Sproul, 952–955.

35. Clifford Pickover, *Archimedes to Hawking: Laws of Science and the Great Minds Behind Them* (New York: Oxford, 2008) 417.

Appendix 1

DEMONOLOGY
by Alexander Campbell

FROM THE MILLENNIAL HARBINGER.
EXTRA
VOL. V.
BETHANY, VA., OCTOBER, 1841. NO. X.
DEMONOLOGY

AN ADDRESS delivered to the Popular Lecture Club,
Nashville, Tennessee,
March 10, 1841.

MR. PRESIDENT,
AN GENTLEMEN MEMBERS OF THE POPULAR LECTURE
CLUB,
WHILE the antiquary is gathering up the mouldering ruins of
ancient temples, palaces, and cities; or poring over the coins, med-
als, and statues of other ages, seeking to prove or to embellish some
theory of the olden times: while the astronomer is directing his largest
telescope to some remote ethereal field, far beyond the milky way, in
search of new nebulæ, unseen before, in hope to find the nucleus of
some incipient solar system: while the speculative geologist is delving
down to the foundations of the eternal mountains, in quest of new
evidences of his doctrine of successive and long protracted formations of the massy strata of Mother Earth, "rock-ribbed and ancient

as the Sun:" while the sceptic is exultingly scanning the metaphysical dreams of some imaginary system of Nature, or seeking in the desolations of the ancient Mythologies arguments against the mighty facts and overwhelming demonstrations of the Christian faith—may I be indulged, gentlemen, to invite you into the precincts of Demonology, and to accompany me in a brief excursion into the land of demons, whence, dark and mysterious though it be, we may, perhaps, guided by some friendly star, elicit some useful light on that grand and awful world of spirits, which, as we descend the hill of life, rises higher and higher in its demands upon our time and thoughts, as embracing the all-absorbing and transcendent interests of human kind.

Think not, however, that I intend to visit the fairy realms and enchanting scenes of wild romance; or that I wish to indulge in the fascinating fictions of poets, ancient or modern; think not that I am about to ascend with old Hesiod into his curious theogony of gods and demigods, or to descend with our late Sir Walter Scott to the phantasmatic realms of his Celtic and Scottish ghosts and demons. I aim at more substantial entertainment, at more sober and grave realities, than the splendid fancies of those gifted and fortunate votaries of popular applause, rather than of the approvals of the conscientious and sedate.

It is the subject of demons, as forming a portion of the real antiquities of the world—as connected with Pagan, Jewish, and Christian theology;—it is the subject of demons, sometimes called devils, not in their fictitious, but true character, that I propose to discuss: for even here there is the fact and the fable, the true and the false, the real and the imaginary, as in every thing else. The extravagant fancies of the poets, the ghosts and spectres of the dark ages, have spread their sable mantles upon this subject, and involved it all either in philosophical dubiety, or in a blind indiscriminate infidelity.

The inductive and Christian philosopher in this department, as in most others, finds both truth and fable blended in the same tradition; and, therefore, neither awed by authority, nor allured by the fascinations of novelty, he institutes an examination into the merits of a subject, which, if true, cannot but deeply interest the thoughtful; and which, if false, should be banished from the minds of all.

That a class of beings of some sort, designated *demons*, has been an element of the faith, an object of the dread and veneration of all ages and nations, as far back as all memory reaches, no one who believes in a spiritual system—no one who regards the volumes of divine inspiration, or who is only partially acquainted with Pagan and Jewish antiquity, can reasonably doubt. But concerning these demons, of what order of intelligences, of what character and destiny; of what powers intellectual and moral, or immoral, there has been much debate, and still there is need of farther and more satisfactory examination.

Before entering either philosophically or practically into this investigation, it is necessary that we define the true and proper meaning of the term *demon*. This word, it is said, is of Grecian origin and character—of which, however, we have not full assurance. In that language it is written and pronounced *daimoon;* and, according to some etymologists, is legitimately descended from a very ancient verb pronounced *daioo,* which means *to discriminate, to know. Daimoon,* or *demon,* therefore, simply indicates a person of intelligence—*a knowing one.* Thus before the age of philosophy, or the invention of the name, those were called demons, as a title of honor, who afterwards assumed the more modest title of philosophers. Aristotle, for his great learning was called *demon,* as was the celebrated Thucydides: hence among the Platonists it was for some time a title of honor. But this, it must be observed, was a special appropriation, like our use of the words *divine* and *reverend.* When we apply these titles to sinful men, who, because of their calling, ought to be not only intelligent, but of a divine and celestial temper and morality, we use them by a special indulgence from that sovereign pontiff with whom is the *jus et norma loquendi.*

 But as some of the Platonists elevated the spirits of departed heroes, public benefactors, and distinguished men, into a species of demigods or mediators between them and the Supreme Divinity, as some of our forefathers were accustomed to regard the souls of departed saints, this term began to be used in a more general sense. Among some philosophers it became the title of an object of worship; while, on the other hand, it degenerated into the genii of poetry and imagination.

 In tracing the popular transitions and transmigrations of words, permit me, gentlemen, to say that we are not to imagine that they very ceremoniously advance, as our naval and military officers, from one rank to another, by some systematic or conventional agreement, amongst the heads of the departments in the army of words and phalanxes of human speech. On the contrary, the transitions are exceedingly anomalous, and sometimes inverted. In this instance the term *demon,* from simply indicating *a knowing one,* became the title of a human spirit when divested of the appendages of its clay tenement, because of its supposed initiation into the secrets of another world. Thus a separated spirit became a genius, a demigod, a mediator, a divinity of the ancient superstition according to its acquirements in this state of probation.

 But we shall better understand the force and import of this mysterious word from its earliest acceptation among the elder Pagans, Jews, and Christians, than from the speculations of etymologists and lexicographers. Historical facts, then, and not etymological speculations, shall decide not only its meaning, but the character and rank of those beings on whom, by common consent, this significant title was conferred.

To whom, then, among Pagan writers shall we make our first appeal? Shall we not at once carry up the question to the most venerable Hesiod, the oldest of Grecian bards, whose antique style even antedates that of Homer himself almost one hundred years? Shall we not appeal to the genealogist of all the gods, the great theogonist of Grecian mythology? Who than he more likely to be acquainted with the ancient traditions of demons? And what is the sum of his testimony in the case? Hear him speak in the words of Plutarch:—"The spirits of mortals become demons when separated from their earthly bodies." The Grecian biographist not only quotes with approbation the views of Hesiod, but corroborates them with the result of his own researches, avowing his conviction that "the demons of the Greeks were the ghosts and genii of departed men; and that they go up and down the earth as observers, and even rewarders of men; and although not actors themselves, they encourage others to act in harmony with their views and characters." Zenocrates, too, as found in Aristotle, extends the term to the souls of men before death, and calls them demons while in the body. To the good demons and the spirits of deceased heroes they allotted the office of mediators between gods and men.[1] In this character Zoroaster, Thales, Pythagoras, Plato, Plutarch, Celsus, Apuleius, and many others contemplated the demons of their times.

Whoever, indeed, will be at pains to examine the Pagan mythologies, one and all, will discover that some doctrine of demons, as respects their nature, abodes, characters, or employments, is the ultimate foundation of the whole superstructure; and that the radical idea of all the dogmata of their priests, and the fancies and fables of

their poets, are found in that most ancient and veritable tradition—
that the spirits of men survive their fallen tabernacles, and live in a
disembodied state from death to the dissolution of material nature.
To these spirits in the character of genii, gods, or demigods, they
assigned the fates and fortunes of men and countries. With them a
hero on earth became a demon in hades; and a demigod, a numen,
a divinity in the skies. It is not without some reason that the witty
and ingenious Lucian makes his dialogist, in the orthodoxy of his
age, thus ask and answer the following questions:—*What is man? A
mortal god! And what is God? An immortal man.* In one sentence, all
Pagan antiquity affirms that from Titan and Saturn, the poetic progeny of Coelus and Terra, down to Esculapius, Proteus, and Minos,
all their divinities, were the ghosts of dead men, and were so regarded
by the most erudite of the Pagans themselves.

Think not, gentlemen, that because we summon the Pagan witnesses first, that we regard them either as the first in point of age or
character. Far from it. They were a pack of plagiarists, from Hesiod
to Lucian. The Greeks were the greatest literary thieves and robbers
that ever lived, and they had the most consummate art of concealing
the theft. From these Pagans, whether Greeks or Romans, we ascend
to the Jews and to the Patriarchs, whose annals transcend those of the
most ancient Pagans many centuries.

In the times of the Patriarchs, in the infancy of the Abrahamic
family, long before the time of their own Moses, we learn that in the
land of Canaan, almost coeval with the promise of it to Abraham,
demons were recognized and worshipped. The consultation of the
spirits of the dead, the art and mystery of necromancy, the species of
familiar spirits, and wizzards, are older than Moses, and spoken of
by him as matters of ancient faith and veneration. Statutes, indeed,
are ordained, and laws are promulged from Mount Sinai in Arabia,

from the voice of the Eternal King, against the worship of demons, the consultation of familiar spirits, the practice of necromancy, and all the arts of divination; of which we may speak more particularly in the sequel. Hence we affirm that the doctrine of a separate state—of disembodied ghosts, or demons—of necromancy and divination, is a thousand years older than Homer or Hesiod, than any Pagan historian, philosopher, or poet whatsoever. And so deeply rooted in the land of Canaan, so early and so long cherished and taught by the seven nations was this doctrine in all its branches, that, notwithstanding the severe statutes against it, traces of it are found among the Jews for almost a thousand years after Moses. Of the wicked Jeroboam it is said, "He ordained priests for the high places, and for the demons.["][2] Even David admits that his nation "learned the works of the heathen, served their idols, and sacrificed their sons and daughters to demons;" and he adds, "they ate the sacrifices of *the dead;*" a clear intimation that worshipping demons was worshipping the dead. Isaiah, too, lamenting their idolatry, asks the mortifying question, "Shall a people seek the living to the dead?"

But there is a peculiarity in the acceptation of this term among Jews and Pagans which demands special attention. Amongst them the term *demon* generally, if not universally, denoted an unclean, malign, or wicked spirit: whereas amongst the Pagans it as often represented a good as an evil spirit. Who has not heard of the good demon of Socrates, and of the evil genius of Brutus? While among Jews and Christians so commonly are found the *akatharta pneumata,* or the *ponera pneumata*—the unclean and malign spirits, that our translators have almost uniformly translated them *devils.*

In the Christian scriptures we meet the term *demon,* in one form or other, 75 times, and in such circumstances, as, with but one or two exceptions, constrain us to regard it as the representative of a wicked and unclean spirit. So general is this fact, that Beelzebub is dignified "*The Prince of the Demons*"—unfortunately rendered *devils*. This frequency of immoral and wicked associations with the word *daimoon* may have induced our translators to give us so many *devils* in their authorized version. But this misapprehension is now universally admitted and regretted: for while the Bible teaches many demons, it no where intimates a plurality of Devils or Satans. There is but one Devil or Satan in the universe, whose legions 'of angels and demons give him a sort of omnipresence, by acting out his will in all their intercourse with mortals. This evil spirit, whose official titles are the Serpent, the Devil, and Satan, is always found in the singular number in both the Hebrew and Greek scriptures; while *demon* is found in both numbers, indicating sometimes one, and sometimes a legion.

But that we may not be farther tedious in this dry work of definition, and that we may enter at once upon the subject with a zeal and spirit worthy of a topic which lays the axe at the root of the tree of modern Sadduceesism, Materialism, and Scepticism, we shall proceed at once to sum up the evidence in proof of the proposition which we shall state as the peculiar theme of this great literary adventure.—That proposition is—*The demons of Paganism, Judaism, and Christianity were the ghosts of dead men.*

But some of you may say, You have proposed to dismiss this work of definition too soon: for here is the horrible word *ghost!* Of what is that term the sign in your style? Well, we must explain ourselves.

Our Saxon forefathers, of whom we have no good reason to be ashamed, were wont to call the spirits of men, especially when separated from their bodies, *ghosts*. This, however, they did, not with the terrible associations which arise in our minds on every pronunciation of that startling term. *Guest* and *ghost*, with them, if not synonyms, were, at least, cousins-german. They regarded the body as the *house,* and therefore called the spirit the *guest;* for guest and ghost are two branches from the same root. William Tyndale, the martyr, of excellent memory, in his version of the New Testament, the prototype of that of king James, very judiciously makes the Holy Spirit of the Old Testament the Holy Ghost of the New; because, in his judgment, it was the promised guest of the Christian temple.

Still it is difficult, I own, to hear the word ghost, or demon, without the recollection of the nursery tales and fictions of our irrational systems of early education. We suffer little children to hear so much of

—"Apparitions tall and ghastly,
That take their stand o'er some new-opened grave,
And, strange to tell, evanish at the crowing of the cock,"

till they become not only in youth, but often in riper years, the prey and sport of idle fears and terrors "which scarce the firm philosopher can scorn." Not only the graveyard,

—"But the lonely tower
Is also shunn'd, whose mournful chronicles hold,
So night-struck fancy dreams, the yelling ghost!"

Imagination once startled,

"In grim array the nightly spectres rise!
Oft have we seen the school-boy, with satchel in his hand,
When passing by some haunted spot, at lonely ev'n,
Whistling aloud to bear his courage up. Suddenly he hears,

Or thinks he hears, the sound of something purring
  at his heels:
Full fast he flies, nor does tie took behind him,
Till out of breath he o'ertake his fellows,
Who gather round and wonder at the tale!"

Parents are greatly at fault for permitting such tales to disturb the fancies of their infant offspring. The love of the marvellous and of the supernatural is so deeply planted in human nature, that it needs but little cultivation to make it fruitful in all manner of fairy tales, of ghosts and spectres. But there is an opposite extreme—the denial of spirits, angels, demons, whether good or bad. Here, too, *media ibis tutissima*—the middle path the safer is. But to our proposition: We have, from a careful survey of the history of the term *demon,* concluded that *the demons of Paganism, Judaism, and Christianity were the ghosts of dead men.* But we build not only upon the definition of the term, nor on its philological history; but upon the following seven pillars:—1. All the Pagan authors of note, whose works have survived the wreck of ages, affirm the opinion that demons were the spirits or ghosts of dead men. From Hesiod down to the more polished Celsus, their historians, poets, and philosophers occasionally express this opinion. 2. The Jewish historians, Josephus and Philo, also avow this conviction. Josephus says, "Demons are the spirits of wicked men, who enter into living men and destroy them, unless they are so happy as to meet with speedy relief."[3] Philo says, "The souls of dead men are called demons." 3. The Christian Fathers, Justin Martyr, Ireneus, Origen, &c. depose to the same effect. Justin, when arguing for a future state, alleges, "Those who are seized and tormented by the souls of the dead, whom all call demons, and madmen."[4] Lardner, after examining with the most laborious care the works of these, and all the Fathers of the first two centuries, says, "The notion of demons, or the souls of dead men, having power over living men, was *universally* prevalent among the heathen of these times, and believed by many Christians."[5] 4. The Evangelists and Apostles of Jesus Christ so understood the matter. As this is a very important, and of itself a sufficient pillar on which to rest our edifice, we shall be at more pains to illustrate and enforce it. We shall first state the philological law or canon of criticism, on the generality and truth of which all our dictionaries, grammars, and translations are formed. *Every word not specially explained or defined in a particular sense, by any standard writer of any particular age and country, is to be taken and applied in the current or commonly received signification of that country and age in which the writer lived and wrote.* If this canon of translation and of criticism be denied, then we affirm there is no value in dictionaries, nor in the acquisition of ancient languages in which any book may be written; nor is there any confidence in any translation of any ancient work, sacred or profane: for they are all made upon the assumption of the truth of this law. We have then only to ask first for the current signification of this term *demon* in Judea at the Christian era; and, in the second place, Did the inspired writers ever give any special definition of it? We have already found an answer to the first in the Greeks and Jews of the apostolic age—also, in the preceding and subsequent age. We have heard Josephus, Philo, Lucian, Justin, and Lardner, from whose writings and affirmations we are expressly told what the universal acceptation of the term was in Judea and in those times; and in the second place, the Apostles and our Lord, as already said, use this word in various forms 75 times, and on no occasion give any hint of a special, private, or peculiar interpretation of it; which was not their method when they used a term either not generally understood, or understood in a special sense. Does any one ask the meaning of the word Messiah, prophet, priest, elder, deacon, presbytery, altar, sacrifice, sabbath, circumcision, &c. &c.? We refer him to the current signification of these words among the Jews and Greeks of that age. Why, then, should any one except the term *demon* from the universal law? Are we not, therefore, sustained by the highest and most authoritative decision of that literary tribunal by whose rules and decrees all works sacred and profane are translated from a dead to a living tongue? We are, then, fully authorized to say that the demons of the New Testament were the spirits of dead men. 5. But as a distinct evidence of the historic kind, and rather as confirmatory of our views than of the authority of the inspired authors, I adduce as a separate and independent witness a very explicit and decisive passage from the epistle to the Smyrneans, written by the celebrated Ignatius, the disciple of the Apostle John. He quotes the words of the Lord to Peter when Peter supposed he saw a spirit or a ghost. But he quotes him thus—"Handle me and see, for I am not a *daimoon asomaton*—a disembodied demon;"—a spirit without a body. This places the matter above all doubt that with them of that day a demon and a ghost were equivalent terms. 6. But we also deduce an argument from the word *angel.* This word is of Bible origin, and confined to those countries in which that volume is found. It is not found in all the Greek poets, orators, or historians, so far as known to me. Of that rank of beings to whom Jews and Christians have applied this official title, the Pagan nations seem never to have had the first conception. It is therefore certain that they could not use the term *demon* as a substitute interchangeable with the word *angel*—as indicative of an intermediate order of intelligent beings above men, and between them and the Divinity. They had neither the name nor the idea of an angel in their mythology. Philo the Jew has, indeed, said that amongst the Jews the word *demon* and the word *angel* were sometimes used interchangeably; and some have thence inferred lapsed angels were called demons. But this is not a logical inference: for the Jews called the winds, the pestilence, the lightnings of heaven, &c., *angels*, as indicative of their agency in accomplishing the will of God. In this sense, indeed, a demon might be officially called an angel. But in this sense demon is to angel as the species to the genus: we can call a demon an angel, but we cannot call an angel a demon—just as we can call every man an animal, but we cannot call every animal a man. Others, indeed, have just as fancifully imagined that the old *giants* and *heroes*, said to have been the fruit of the intermarriage of the sons of God with the daughters of men before the flood, were the demons of all the world—Pagans, Jews, and Christians. Their most plausible argument is, that the word *heroes* and the word *love* are the same; and that the *loves* of the angels for the daughters of men, was the reason that their gigantic offspring were called *heroes*. Whence the term was afterwards appropriated to persons of great courage as well as of great stature. This is sublimely ridiculous. But to return to the word *angel*. It is a Bible term, and not being found in all classic, in all mythologic antiquity, could not enter into the Pagan ideas of a demon. Now that it is not so used in the Christian scriptures is evident for the following reasons: 1st. Angels were never said to enter into any one. 2d. Angels have, no affection for bodies of any sort, either as habitations or vehicles of action. 3d. Angels have no predilection for tombs and monuments of the dead. In these three particulars angels and demons stand in full contrast, and are contradistinguished by essentially different characteristics: for—1st. Demons have entered into human bodies and into the bodies of inferior creatures.

2d. Demons evince a peculiar affection for human bodies, and seem to desire them both as vehicles of action and as places of habitation. 3d. Demons also evince a peculiar fondness for their old mortal tenements: hence we so often read of them carrying the possessed into the grave-yards, the tombs, and sepulchres, where, perchance, their old mortalities lay in ruins. From which facts we argue, as well as from the fact that the Pagans had neither Devil, nor angel nor Satan, in their heads before the Christian times, that when they, or the Christians, or the Jews spoke of *demons,* they could not mean any intermediate rank of spirits, other than the spirits of dead men. Hence in no instance in holy writ can we find *demon* and *angel* used as convertible terms. Is it not certain, then, that they are the ghosts of dead men?—But there yet remains another pillar. 7. Among the evidences of the papal defection intimated by Paul, he associates the *doctrine concerning demons* with celibacy and abstinence from certain meats, as chief among the signs of that fearful apostacy. He warrants the conclusion that the purgatorial prisons for ghosts and the ghostly mediators of departed saints, which, equally with commanding to abstain from lawful meats, and forbidding to marry, characterize the times of which he spoke, are attributes of the same system, and indicative of the fact that *demons* and *ghosts* are two names for the same beings. To this we add the testimony of James, who says *the demons believe and tremble* for their doom. Now all eminent critics concur that the spirits of wicked men are here intended; and need I add that oft-repeated affirmation of the demoniacs, "We know thee, Jesus of Nazareth; art thou come to torment us before the time?" Thus all the scriptural allusions to this subject authorize the conclusion that demons are ghosts, and especially wicked and unclean spirits of dead men. A single saying in the Apocalypse makes this most obvious. When Babylon is razed to its foundation it is said to be made the habitation of demons—of the ghosts of its sepulchred inhabitants. From these seven sources of evidence, viz.—the Pagan authors, the Jewish historians, the Christian fathers, the four Evangelists, the epistle of Ignatius, the acceptation of the term *angel* in its contrast with *demon*, and the internal evidences of the whole New Testament, we conclude that the demons of the New Testament were the ghosts of wicked men. May we not henceforth reason from this point with all assurance as a fixed and fundamental principle? It ought, however, to be candidly stated that there have been in latter times a few intellectual dyspeptics, on whose nervous system the idea of being really possessed by an evil spirit, produces a phrensied excitement. Terrified at the thought of an incarnate demon, they have resolutely undertaken to prove that every single demon named in holy writ is but a bold eastern metaphor, placing in high relief dumbness, deafness, madness, palsy, epilepsy, &c.; and hence demoniacs then and now are a class of unfortunates laboring under certain physical maladies called unclean spirits. *Credat Judæus Appella, non Ego.* On the principle that every demon is an eastern metaphor, how incomparably more eloquent than Demosthenes or Cicero, was he that had at one time a legion of eastern metaphors within him struggling for utterance! No wonder, then, that the swineherds of Gadara were overwhelmed by the moving eloquence of their herds as they rushed with such pathos into the deep waters of the dark Galilee! Great men are not always wise. The seer of Mesopotamia was not only admonished, but reformed by the eloquence of an ass; and I am sure that the Gadarene speculators were cured of their belief in eastern metaphors when they saw their hopes of gain forever buried in the lake of Gennesereth. It requires a degree of gravity bordering on the superlative, to speculate on an hypothesis so singularly fanciful and baseless as that which converts both reason and eloquence, deafness and dumbness, into one and the same metaphor. Without impairing in the least the strength of the arguments in favor of actual possession by the spirits of dead men, it may be conceded, that because of the similarity of some of the effects of demoniacal possession with those maladies of the paralytic and epileptic character, it may have happened on some occasions that persons simply afflicted with these diseases, because of the difficulties of always discriminating the remote causes of these maladies, were, by the common people, regarded as demoniacs, and so reported in the New Testament. Still the fact that the Great Teacher himself distinguishes between demons and all human maladies, in commanding the Apostles not only to "heal all manner of diseases—to cleanse the lepers, and raise the dead;" but also to "cast out demons;" and the fact still more palpable, that in number and power these demons are represented as transcending all physical maladies, precludes the possibility of contemplating them as corporeal diseases "When I read of the number of demons in particular persons," says a very distinguished Biblical critic, "and see their actions expressly distinguished from those of the man possessed; conversations held by the demons about their disposal after their expulsion; and accounts given how they were actually disposed of; when I find desires and passions ascribed peculiarly to them; and similitudes taken from their manners and customs, it is impossible for me to deny their existence, without admitting that the sacred historians were themselves deceived in regard to them, or intended to deceive their readers." Were it not in appearance like killing those that are dead, I should quote at length sundry passages which speak of "unclean spirits *crying with loud voices*" as they came out of many that were possessed, which represent unclean spirits falling down before Jesus, and crying, "Thou art the Son of God," and of Jesus "charging them not to make him known;" but I will only cite a single parable framed upon the case of a demoniac. It is reported by Matthew and Luke, and almost in the same words. "When the unclean spirit," says Jesus, "is gone out of a man, he walketh through dry places, seeking rest and finding none. Then he saith, I will return into my house from whence I came out; and when he is come he findeth it empty, swept, and garnished. Then he goeth and taketh with himself seven other spirits more wicked than himself, and they enter in and dwell there; and the last state of that man is worse than the first. Even so shall it be also to this wicked generation." On which observe, that "unclean spirits" is another name for demons—that is, a metaphor of a metaphor; for if demons are metaphors for diseases, the unclean spirits are metaphors of metaphors, or shadows of shades. Again, the Great Teacher is found not only for once departing from himself, but also from all human teachers of renown, in basing a parable upon a parable, or a shadow upon a shade, in drawing a similitude from a simile. His object was to illustrate the last state of the Jews. This he attempts by the adventures of a demon—first being dispossessed, finding no rest, and returning with others more wicked than himself to the man from whom he was driven. Now if this was all a figure to illustrate a figure, the Saviour has done that which he never before attempted, inasmuch as his parables are all founded not upon fictions, but upon facts—upon the actual manners and customs, the incidents and usages of society. That must be a desperate position to sustain which degrades the Saviour as a teacher below the rank of the most ordinary instructors of any age. The last state of the Jews compared to a metaphor!—compared to a nonentity!—compared to a fiction! This is even worse than representing a trope coming out of a man's mouth, "crying with a loud voice," "wandering through dry places"—unfigurative language, I presume—seeking a period, and finding a comma. At length, tired and fatigued, returning with seven fiercer metaphors more wickedly eloquent than himself, re-possessing the orator, and making him internally more eloquent than before. It will not help the matter to say that when a disease leaves a man it wanders through dry or wet places—through marshes and fens—through deserts and prairies—and finding no rest for its foot, takes with him seven other more violent diseases, and seeks for the unfortunate man from whom the Doctors expelled it; and, re-entering his improved constitution, makes that its eternal abode. In one sentence, then, we conclude that there is neither reason nor fact—there is no canon of criticism, no law of interpretation—there is nothing in human experience or observation—there is nothing in all antiquity, sacred or profane, that, in our judgment, weighs against the evidence already adduced in support of the position, that *the demons of Pagans, Jews, and Christians were the ghosts of dead men; and, as such, have taken possession of men's living bodies, and have moved, influenced, and impelled them to certain courses of action.* Permit me, gentlemen, to demonstrate that this is no abstract and idle speculation, by stating a few of the practical aspects and bearings of this doctrine of demonology: 1st. It relieves the Bible from the imputation of promulging laws against non-entities in all its legislation against necromancers, diviners, soothsayers, wizzards, fortune-tellers, &c. When Jehovah gave this law to Israel, he legislated not against mere pretences, saying, "You shall not permit to live among, you any one that useth divination, an enchanter, a witch, a consulter of familiar spirits, a wizzard, or a necromancer; for all that do these things are an abomination to the Lord: and because of these abominations the Lord thy God doth drive these nations out before thee." A divine law demanding capital punishment because of a mere pretence! The most incredible thing in the world! The existence of such a statute, as before intimated, implies not merely the antiquity of the fact of demoniacal influence, but supposes it so palpable that it could be proved by at least two witnesses, and so satisfactorily as to authorize the taking away of human life without the risk of shedding innocent blood. That there have been pretenders to such mysterious arts, impostors and hypocrites in necromancy, witchcraft, and divination, as well as in every thing else, I doubt not; but if the pretence to work a miracle, or to utter a prediction, be a proof that there were true miracles and true prophets, the pretence of necromancy, witchcraft, and divination, is also a proof that there were once true necromancers, wizzards, and diviners. The fame of the Egyptian Jannes and Jambres who withstood Moses in the presence of Pharaoh—the fame of the woman of Endor, who evoked Samuel, or some one that personated him—and of the Pythonic damsel that followed Paul and Barnabas, and who enriched her master by her divination, stand on the pages of eternal truth imperishable monuments not merely of the antiquity of the pretence, but of the reality of demoniacal power and possession. May I be permitted farther to observe on this mysterious subject, that necromancy was the principal parent of all the arts of divination ever practised in the world, and was directly and avowedly founded on the fact, not only of demoniacal influence, but that demons are the spirits of dead men, with whom living men could, and did form intimacies. This the very word *necromancy* intimates. The necromancer predicted the future by means of demoniacal inspiration. He was a prophet inspired by the dead. His art lay in making or finding a familiar spirit, in evoking a demon from whom he obtained superhuman knowledge. So the Greek term imports and all antiquity confirms. There are two subjects on which God is silent, and man most solicitous to know—the world of spirits, and his own future destiny. On these two subjects ghosts who have visited the unseen world, and whose horizon is so much enlarged, are supposed to be peculiarly intelligent, and on this account originally called *demons,* or *knowing ones.* But this knowledge being forbidden, kindly forbidden man, to seek it at all, and especially by unlawful means, has always been obnoxious to the anathema of Heaven. Hence the popularity of the profession of evoking familiar spirits, and hence also the indignation of Heaven against them who consulted them. Still we will be asked, Has any spirit of man, dead or alive, power to foresee and foretell the future? Does any one know the future but God? To which we cheerfully respond, The living and inspired prophets only knew a part of the future. God alone knows all the future. But angels or demons may know much more of it than man. How this may be analogy itself may suggest Suppose, for example, that one man possessed the discriminating powers of a Bacon, a Newton, or a Locke, only of a more capacious and retentive memory, had been coeval with Cain, Noah, or Abraham, and with a deathless vigor of constitution had lived with all the generations of men since their day till now, an inductive philosopher of course; what would be his comparative power of calculating chances and contingencies—the laws of cause and effect—and of thence anticipating the future? Still, compared with one who had passed that mysterious bourne of time, he would be but the infant of a day, knowing comparatively nothing of human destiny. But, indeed, the powers of knowing peculiar to disembodied spirits, are to us as inscrutable as the very elements of their spiritual forms and existence. But that they do know more of a spiritual system and more of human destiny than we, all antiquity sacred and profane fully reveals and confirms. 2. But a second practical aspect of this theory of demons demands our attention. *It is a palpable and irrefragable proof of a spiritual system.* The gross materialists of the French school, when Atheism triumphed over reason and faith, proclaimed from their own metropolis, and had it cut deep in marble too, that death was an eternal sleep of body, soul, and spirit, in one common unconsciousness of being. Since that time we have had the subject somewhat refined and sub-

limated into an intermediate sleep of only some six or seven thousand years, between our earthly exit and the resurrection morn.
These more speculative materialists convert demons into metaphors,
lapsed angels, or devils—into any thing rather than the living spirits
of dead men.

They see that our premises being admitted, there must be a
renunciation not only of the grosser, but of the more ethereal forms
of materialism of those who lull the spirit to repose in the same sep-
ulchre with its kindred mortality, in their opposition to the inhabita-
tion of the human body by any other spirit than its own. They make
but little argumentative gain who assume that demons are lapsed
angels rather than human ghosts: for who will not admit that it may
be more easy for a demon than an angel who has a spiritual body of
his own, to work by the machinery of a human body, and to excite
the human passions to any favorite course of action! Were not this
the fact, they must have tenanted the human house to little purpose,
if a perfect stranger to all its rooms and doors could, on its first introduction, move through them as readily as they

"If weak thy faith, why choose the harder side?"

To allegorize demoniacal influences, or to metamorphose them
into rhetorical imagery, is the shortest, though the most desperate
escape, from all spiritual embarrassment in the case. But the harder
you press the sceptical philosopher on the subject of his peculiar
idolatry, the more bold his denial of all spiritual influences, celestial or infernal; and the more violently he affirms that demoniacal
possessions were physical diseases; that necromancy, familiar spirits,
and divination, though older than Moses, and the seven nations of
Canaan, were but mere pretences; an imposition on the credulity

of man, as idle as the legends of Salem witchcraft, or the fairy tales of the mother-land of sprites and apparitions. But this, let me tell you, sceptical philosopher, relieves not the hard destiny of your case. Whether necromancy in all its forms was real or pretended, true or false, affects not the real merits of the question before us.

To me, in this branch of the argument, it is perfectly indifferent whether it was a pretence or a reality: for, mark it well, had there not been a senior and more venerated belief in the existence of a spiritual system—a general persuasion that the spirits of the dead lived in another world while their bodies lay in this, and that disembodied spirits were demons or knowing ones on those peculiar points so interesting and so unapproachable to man; who ever could have thought of consulting them, of evoking them by any art, or of pretending in the face of the world to any familiarity with them! I gain strength by the denial or by the admission of the thing, so long as its high antiquity must be conceded. I do indeed contend, and will contend, that a belief in demons, in a separate existence of the spirits of the dead, is more ancient than necromancy, and that it is a belief and a tradition older than the Pagan, the Jewish, or the Christian systems—older than Moses and his law—older than any earthly record whatever. Not a few of our modern sages ascribe to a Pagan origin that which antedates Paganism itself. They must have a Grecian, Roman, or Egyptian origin for ideas, usages, and institutions existent ages before the founders of these states or the inventors of their superstitions were born. No earthly record, the Bible alone excepted, reaches within hundreds of years of the origin of the idea of demons, necromancy, and of infernal as well as of supernal agency. Others there are who have more faith in what is modern than in what is ancient. They would rather believe their children than their fathers. The moderns, indeed, in most of the physical sciences, and in some of the physical arts, greatly excel the ancients. I say, in some of the useful and fine arts we may, perhaps, excel them as much as they excelled us in geometry, architecture, sculpture, painting, poetry, &c. &c. But though we excel them so much in many new discoveries and arts—in correct, traditionary, and spiritual knowledge they greatly excelled us; except always that portion of the moderns fully initiated into the mysteries of the Bible. Some seem to reason as if they thought that the farther from the fountain the waters are more pure—the longer the channel the freer from pollution. With me the reverse is the fact. Man was more intelligent at his creation and his fall in his own being and destiny than he has ever been since, except so far as he has been the subject of a new revelation. Would it not appear waste of time to attempt to prove that our national government is purer now than it was while its founders were all living amongst us? Equally prodigal of time the man who attempts to prove that the Patriarchal, Jewish and Christian institutions were purer five hundred or a thousand years after, than at, their commencement. With Tertullian I will say, that in faith, religion, and morality, whatever is most ancient is most true. Therefore the Patriarchs knew more of man living and dead, of the ancient order of things in nature, society, and art, than we their remote posterity. The age of philosophy was the era of hypotheses and doubts. Man never began to form hypothesis till he lost his way. Now having traced the belief in demons and necromancy beyond the age of conjecture and speculative reasoning, and located it amongst the oldest traditions in the world, we are compelled by the dicta of our own inductive and sounder philosophy to admit its claims to an experience, observation, and testimony properly authenticated and documented amongst the earliest fathers of mankind. One of the oracles of true science is, that *all, our ideas are the result of sensation and reflection, or of experience and observation;* that the archetypes of all our natural impressions and views are found in material nature; and therefore man could as easily create a world as a ghost, either by imagination, volition, or reason. Supernatural ideas must therefore have a supernatural origin. So speaks the Baconian system, and therefore its author believed in demons, spirits, and necromancy, as much as your humble servant, or any other living Baconian. When any man proves he can have faith without hearing and testimony—the idea of color without sight—or of hardness and softness, of heat and cold, without feeling, and understand all the properties of material nature, without any of his five senses, then, *but not till then,* he may explain how, without a supernatural influence of any sort, he may form either the idea or the name of a spirit, a ghost, or a demon—of a spiritual, invisible, and eternal system of intelligences of a supernatural mould and temper. He that can create out of himself the idea of an abstract spirit, or of a spiritual system of any sort, may create matter by volition, and a universe out of nothing. Dispose of the matter as she may, we affirm it as our conviction that Philosophy herself is compelled to admit the existence of demons, familiar spirits, and the arts of necromancy and divination, which all ancient literature and ancient tradition—all Patriarchal, Jewish, and Christian records assert. In this instance, as in many others, faith is easier than unbelief; and Reason voluntarily places herself by the side of Faith as her handmaid and coadjutor in sustaining a spiritual system, of which demons in their proper nature and character are an irrefragable proof.

3. A third practical tendency of this view of demoniacal influence is to exalt in our esteem the character of the Supreme Philanthropist.

We will be asked, Whence have all the demons fled? What region do they now inhabit! Have they not power to possess mankind as formerly? Is necromancy, divination, and witchcraft forever exiled from the abodes of men? Many such questions there may be propounded, which neither philosophy, nor experience, nor religion do infallibly determine. But we may say in general and in truthful terms, that the heralds of salvation, from the day of their first mission to the end of their evangelical labors, were casting out demons, restraining Satanic influence, and making inroads upon the power and empire of Beelzebub, the Prince of the Demons. The mighty chieftain of this holy war had a personal rencounter with the malignant chief of all unclean spirits, angelic and human, and so defeated his counsels and repelled his assaults as to divest him of much of his sway, as a presage and earnest of his ultimate triumph over all the powers of darkness. His success and that of his ambassadors on two occasions called from his lips two oracles of much consolation to all his friends; "I saw," said he, "Satan fall like lightning from heaven." This he spake when they told him, "The demons are subject to us through thy word." "Behold," he adds, "I give you power to tread on serpents and scorpions, and on all the power of the enemy, and nothing shall by any means hurt you." The partial dethronement of Satan, Prince of the Demons, is here fully indicated. The Roman orator uses this style when speaking of Pompey's overthrow. His words are, "He has fallen from the stars." And again, of the fall of the colleague of Antonius—"Thou hast pulled him down from heaven." So spake the Messiah: "I beheld Satan as lightning fall from heaven." His empire over men from that day began to fall. And on another occasion he says, "Now is the Prince of this world cast out." These, together with other similar indications, allow the conclusion that the power of demons is wholly destroyed as far as Christians are concerned; and if not wholly, greatly restrained in all lands where the gospel has found its way. With an old prophet or diviner who tried his hand against God's people once, we may say, "There is no

enchantment against Jacob—there is no divination against Israel."
Some arrogate to human science what has been the prerogative of
the gospel alone. They say the light of science has driven ghosts and
witches from the minds of men; whereas they ought to have said, the
gospel and power of its Author have driven demons out of the hearts,
and dispossessed them of their power over the bodies of men. The
error of these admirers of human science is not much different from
that of some European theologists concerning Mary Magdalene.
They suppose her to have been an infamous, rather than an unfortunate woman, out of whom were driven seven devils. They have dis-
graced her memory by erecting 'Magdalene Hospitals' for infamous,
rather than for unfortunate females; not knowing that it was the
misfortune, rather than the crime of Mary of Magdala, that seven
demons had been permitted to assault her person for the glory of the
Messiah and her own eternal fame. As to the abodes of the demons,
we are taught in the Bible what the most ancient dogmatists have
said concerning their residence in the air: I say we are taught that
they dwell *pro tempore* in the ethereal regions. Satan, their Prince, is
called "the Prince of the power of the air." The great Apostle to the
Gentiles taught them to wrestle against "wicked spirits that reside
in the air;" for, says he, "you fight not against flesh and blood, but
against principalities and powers, against the rulers of the darkness
of this world; against spiritual wickedness in high places"—properly
rendered, '*Against wicked spirits in the regions of the air.*' Paul's ship-
wreck at Malta by the Euroclydon, and Job's misfortunes by an Ara-
bian tempest, demonstrate the aerial power of this great antagonist
when permitted to exert it against those he envies and calumniates.

Evident it is, then, from such testimonies, facts, and allusions,
that the atmosphere, or rather the regions above it, the ethereal or
empyreal, and not heaven, nor earth, nor hell, is the proper residence

of the ghosts of wicked men. They have repeatedly declared their perfect punishment or torment as yet future, and after the coming of the Lord, when he shall send the Devil and his emissaries into an eternal fire. How often did they say to Jesus, "Art thou come to torment us *before the time?*" That they are miserable, wretchedly miserable, is inferrible from the abhorrence of the nudity and awful forebodings of their present position. They vehemently desire to be embodied again. They seek rest, but find none; and would rather possess any bodies, even the swine, than continue naked and dispossessed. Their prison is called by the Messiah, "outer darkness;" by Paul it is called *epourania, high places, aerial regions.* This is the, Hebrew-Greek name of that region where there is neither atmosphere nor light; for, strange though it may appear to uneducated minds, the limits of our atmosphere are the limits of all terrestrial light. These intervals between the atmospheres of the planets is what we would call *"outer darkness."* Could a person ascend only some fifty miles above this earth, he would find himself surrounded with everlasting night—no ray from sun, or moon, or stars could find him where there is no medium of reflection.

That they may still inspire oracles, as they were wont before the Christian era—(this, too, has been counterfeited)—and possess living men in heathen lands, or in places where Christianity has made little progress, is not altogether improbable. Of this, indeed, we have not satisfactory evidence, and therefore ought not to speak dogmatically. I know many affect to regard the whole matter as a piece of childish superstition, as did our two last great poets, Scott and Byron; who, nevertheless, like them, are under the influence of that same childish superstition. One thing is abundantly evident and satisfactory—that although the number of such spirits is vast and overwhelming, and although their hatred to the living is intense and enduring, the man of God, the true Christian, has a guardian angel, or a host of sentinels around him that never sleep; and, therefore, against him the fiery darts of Satan and the wiles of the roaring lion are employed in vain. For this we erect in our hearts a monument of thanks to Him who has been, and still is, the Supreme Philanthropist and Redeemer of our race. This view of demonology not only vindicates the law of Moses from the imputation of catering to the superstitious prejudices of mankind, by regarding as real the most idle fictions and pretences; and justifies Paul in placing witchcraft amongst the works of the flesh; it not only affords to weak and doubting minds new and striking evidences of a spiritual system; it not only develops our great indebtedness to the Author of the Christian faith in rescuing man from the tyranny of the arch apostate, the Prince of Demons; but it also inducts us into still more grand and sublime views of the magnitude, variety, and extent of the world of spirits—of our relations to them—and throws some light upon our present liabilities to impressions, suggestions, and influences from classes of agents wholly invisible and inappreciable by any of those senses which connect us with external and sensible existence. That we are susceptible of impressions and suggestions from invisible agents sometimes affecting our passions and actions, it were foolish and infidel to deny. How many thousands of well authenticated facts are found in the volumes of human experience of singular, anomalous, and inexplicable impulses and impressions wholly beyond all human associations of ideas, yet leading to actions evidently essential to the salvation of the subjects of them, or of others under their care, from imminent perils and disasters; to which, but for such kind offices, they must inevitably have fallen victims. And how many in the midst of a wicked and foolish career have, by some malign agency, been suddenly and unexpectedly led into the most fatal coincidences and suddenly precipitated to ruin, when such unprecedented exigencies are exceptions to all the known laws of cause and effect, and inexplicable to all their wonted courses of action! To assign to these any other than a spiritual cause, it seems to me, were to assign a *non causa pro causa;* for on no theory of mind or body can they be so satisfactorily explained, and so much in harmony with the Bible way of representing such incidents. Thus the angel of the Lord smote Herod that he died, and in various dreams admonished the faithful of the ways and means of escaping impending evils. Will it not be perceived and admitted that if evil demons can enter into men's bodies, and even take away reason, as well as excite to various preternatural actions, and if in legions they may crowd their influences upon one unhappy victim, spirits, either good or bad, may make milder and more delicate approaches to the fountains of human action, and stir men up to efforts and enterprizes for weal or woe, according to their respective characters and ruling passions. Certain it is that angels, beings, too, of a more embodied and less abstract existence, have not only demonstrated their ability to assume the human form, but to exert such influence upon the outward man as to prompt him to immediate action—as in the case of Peter, who was suddenly stricken on the side by the hand of an angel when fast asleep between a Roman guard, and roused to action. The gates and bars of the prison open at his approach and shut on his escape, touched by the same hand; and thus the Apostle is rescued from the malice of his foes. What an extended view of the intellectual and moral universe opens to our contemplation from this point! We see an outward, visible, and immense expanse every where, studded with constellations of suns and their attendant systems, circling in unmeasured orbits around one invisible and omnipotent centre that controls them all. Amazed and overwhelmed at these stupendous displays of creative power, wisdom, and goodness, in adoring ecstacy we inquire into the uses of these mighty orbs, which, in such untold millions, diversify and adorn those undefined fields of ethereal beauty that limit our ideas of an unbounded and inconceivable space. Reasoning from all our native analogies, and from the scattering rays of supernal light that have from suns unseen reached our world, we must infer that all these orbs are the mansions of social beings, of every conceivable variety of intelligence, capacity, and employment; and that in organized hierarchies, thrones, principalities, and lordships, they constitute each within itself an independent world; of which societies we are allowed to conclude that there are as many varieties of intellectual and moral organization and development as there are planets for their residence. In all these intellectual assemblages, spread over the area of universal being, there are but two distinct and essentially diverse confederations—one under the rightful sovereignty of Messiah the Lord of all, and the other under the usurped dominion of that antagonist spirit of insubordination and self-will which has spread over our planet all the anarchy and misrule, all the darkness and gloom, all the sorrow and death which have embittered life, and made countless millions groan in spirit and sigh for a discharge from a conflict between good and evil, pleasure and pain, so unequal and oppressive. This rebel angel, of such singular and mysterious character, is always found in the singular number—as *the Satan, the Devil,* and *the Apollyon* of our race. With him are confederate all disloyal spirits that have conspired against Heaven's own will in adoration of their own. In reference to this usurper and his angelic allies against the Lord's Anointed, we are obliged to consider those unhappy spirits, who, during their incarnation, took sides with him in his mad rebellion against the Eternal King. The number of angels that took part with him in his original conspiracy remains amongst the secrets of eternity, and is not to be divulged till the Devil and his angels, for whom Tophet was of old prepared, shall be separated from the social systems of the universe, and publicly sentenced to the bottomless gulph of irremediable ruin. The whole human race, at one time or other, have been involved in this war against Heaven. Many have, indeed, deserted the dark banners of Beelzebub, and have become sons of light. Hitherto, alas! the great majority have perished in the field of rebellion, and gone down to the pit with all their armor on. These spirits, shown to be the demons of all antiquity, sacred and profane, are now a component part of the empire of Satan, and as much under his control as the original conspirators that took part with him in his primeval defection and rebellion. How numerous they are, and how concentrated in their efforts, may be gleaned from sundry allusions in the inspired writings, especially from the melancholy history of the unfortunate Gadarene who dwelt among the tombs, tortured by a legion of them—not, perhaps, by six thousand demons in full tale, according to the full standard of a Roman legion; but by an indefinite and immense multitude. How innumerable, then, the agents demoniacal and angelic on Satan's side! What hosts of fallen men and fallen angels have conspired against the happiness of God's moral empire! No wonder that Satan is sometimes spoken of as omnipresent! If Napoleon in the day of his power, while in the palace of the Thuilleries, was said to be at work in Spain, in Portugal, in Belgium, and in France at the same time—with how much less of the figurative, and more of the literal, may Satan, whose agents are incomparably more multitudinous and diversified, as well as of vastly superior agility and power, be represented as wielding a sort of omnipresent power in all parts of our terraqueous habitation? And how malignant too!! The fabled Furies themselves were not more fierce than those unclean and mischievous spirits whose sweetest pleasure it was to torture with the most convulsive agonies those unhappy victims whom they chose to mark out for themselves. But here we must pause: and with this awful group of exasperated and malicious demons in our horizon, it is some relief to remember that there are many good spirits of our race, allied with ten thousand times ten thousand, and thousands of thousands of angels of light, all of whom are angels of mercy and sentinels of defence around the dwellings of the righteous, the true *elite* of our race. These we learn, from high authority, are ministering spirits waiting on the heirs of salvation. These attending spirits know our spiritual foes, and are able to cope with them: for when Satan and Michael fought for the body of Moses the fallen seraph was driven to the wall and lost the day. For how many services rendered, for how many deliverances from evil spirits and from physical disasters, we are indebted to the good and benevolent, though invisible agents around us, will never be known, and therefore never told on earth; but it may nevertheless be known and told hereafter.

And with what unspeakable pleasure may some happy being in this assembly yet sit down, side by side, with his own guardian spirit under the eternally verdant boughs of the life-restoring tree in the paradise of God, and listen to the ten thousand deliverances effected for him by the kind ministrations of that generous and beneficent minister of grace, that watched his path, numbered his steps, and encamped around his bed from the first to the last moment of his terrestrial day! With what grateful emotions will the ransomed spirit listen to the bold adventures and the triumphant rencounters with belligerent foes, of his kind and successful deliverer; and while, in the midst of such social raptures he throws his immortal arms around his kind benefactor, he lifts his bright and beaming eye of grateful piety to Him who gave him such a friend and deliverer in the time of peril and of need; and who, through such a scene of trials and of conflicts, brought him safely to the peaceful city of eternal rest!

NOTE.

The preceding essay bears the impress or an almost extempora-neous effusion on a subject requiring much and profound thought. The invitation to address THE POPULAR LECTURE CLUB of the city of Nashville, was received but a few evenings before its pronunciation. Meanwhile, having almost daily lectures on portions of the Christian system, I had leisure only to sketch, with much rapidity, at various intervals, the preceding remarks. True, indeed, the subject had been often on my mind, especially since the time of my writing a few essays on that sceptical and abstract something called *Materialism*. The facts and observations crowded together in this popular lecture are matters of grave and serious import, and not hasty or crude imag-inations, occurring at the impulse of the moment. True, indeed, I should rather have given them under more favorable circumstances, a more logical and philosophical form; but this is not the most popu-lar, nor, to the great mass, the most intelligible form. At the request of some who heard them, and of many who heard of them, I am induced to publish the identical draft which I read to the audience, with only a very few verbal alterations.

I think the subject of *demons* is one that fairly comes in the path of every student of the New Testament, and ought to be well understood; and as the reader will doubtless have observed, I regard it as constituting an irrefragable proof of a spiritual system, a full refutation of that phantasm called Materialism, to those who admit the authority of Jesus Christ and the twelve Apostles. To such it is more than a mere refutation of Materialism—it is a demonstration of a separate existence of the spirits of the dead—an unequivocal evidence of a spiritual system, and of a future state of rewards and punishments.

[*The Millennial Harbinger* (October 1841): 457–480.]

Notes
Appendix 1

(As appearing in original document)

1. Hence the saint worship and saint mediators of the dark ages, and of the less favored portions of our Anglo Saxon race.
2. Deuteronomy 18.10. Leviticus 17. 7, &c. 2 Chron. 11.15. Psalm 66.26–37.
3. De Bello Jud. cap. viii. 25; cap. vi. sect 3.
4. Jus. Apology, b. i. p. 65, par. 12, p. 54.
5. Vol. viii. P. 368.

Appendix 2

TOWARD A PHILOSOPHY OF FORTEAN RESEARCH
A CRITICAL EVALUATION OF RESEARCH
INTO UNEXPLAINED PHENOMENA

This paper was originally delivered as the keynote address at
Exploring Unexplained Phenomena III,
University of Nebraska Center for Continuing Education
May 17, 1991
© R. W. Boeche, 1991 All Rights Reserved

Preface

I believe it would be helpful to begin this paper with some brief explanatory remarks. Many of the concepts which will be discussed are complex and difficult to grasp. I do not apologize for this. I believe however, that being aware of this may help make it easier to follow the arguments which will be presented.

For those unfamiliar with the term Fortean, a brief explanation is in order. Charles Fort (1874–1932), was a journalist and short-story writer. A small inheritance allowed him to devote full time to research, particularly poring over scientific periodicals, and he spent nearly three decades collecting data which he referred to as "damned." These damned facts were eventually to be collected into four fascinating books: *The Book of the Damned* (1919), *New Lands* (1923), *LO!* (1931), and *Wild Talents* (1932).

These "damned" facts were those that were ignored, improperly explained, glossed over, or altered by the scientific community which sought to dismiss them—whether because they weren't easily assimilable into orthodox scientific models, or because they thought them to be tainted by some sort of pre scientific stigma.

Because my presentation will deal with the processes which underlie our interpretation of data, I will close this brief introduction to Fort with his own words.

"Here are the data. See for yourself. What does it matter what my notions may be? Here are the data."

I have, for the last three years (1988–1991) withdrawn from active investigative work in the field of Fortean research. This served a twofold purpose. First, it allowed me time to pursue graduate studies in philosophy and theology, and secondly, to create a coherent Christian foundation for research into the unexplained.

I do not dispute the existence of the UFO phenomena. People worldwide do observe bizarre unexplained flying objects in the sky and on the ground. I believe that the phenomenon commonly referred to as "alien abductions" are very real. I believe cryptozoology (the search for hidden or unknown animals) to be a valid area of scientific inquiry. Parapsychological events, animal mutilations, cases of spontaneous human combustion, and many other types of phenomena all deserve scholarly attention. The question is not, "Are these things happening?" but rather "What is the origin and cause of these events?"

Those areas of "Forteana" which provide us with tangible, physical evidence which may best be addressed by biologists, zoologists, pathologists, chemists, physicists, and practitioners of the other natural sciences are not my principle concern here.

I am interested in the interpretation and evaluation of data arising from human interaction with these strange events, as well as what may most accurately be termed "non-human entities." In a large number of these encounters, information is given to the percipient which has direct philosophical and spiritual implications. As a Christian, a minister of the Gospel, and a student of theology, it is incumbent upon me to assess and evaluate these encounters, the narratives arising from them, and their implications, in light of Holy Scripture—the final and ultimate authority of the Christian. This process and the foundational reasoning underlying it are my topic.

I have chosen *Toward a Philosophy of Fortean Research*, as my title, "toward" being the operative word. I do not consider this to be in any sense a complete philosophy to inform our research, but merely a starting point. Many comparisons have been drawn, and many examples taken from, the fields of philosophy and theology. Please don't be intimidated by these subjects. The classical disciplines have much to teach us about learning to interpret the world around us.

I ask only that in the spirit of true Fortean investigation, you keep your ears and minds open, and weigh carefully what is discussed in this presentation. Don't be too quick to jump to conclusions, or so anxious to agree or disagree with my position, that you fail to really hear what I am saying.

First Steps Toward a Philosophy

One of the greatest obstacles impeding not only those of us interested in these rather esoteric subjects, but our contemporary culture as a whole, is confusion. Confusion over how to think critically. Confusion over the consequences of philosophical positions. Even confusion over what explanation is, or is not, politically correct among one's peer group. The reality of the occurrence of various phenomena is not in dispute in this discussion. However, the interpretation and analysis of these events does need to be called into question.

In instances where physical traces can be observed, or samples and residues can be gathered and analyzed, the existence of tangible material simplifies, to some extent, the researcher's approach. In most situations, however, the student of the unexplained is dealing with an unrepeatable event, occurring in an uncontrolled environment, which leaves no physical evidence. How then, do we best deal with the information available in order to progress toward what I perceive to be our ultimate goal, the truth about the phenomena?

One phenomena very much in the news makes an excellent case in point—the so-called crop circles. Farmers, particularly in Great Britain, have been plagued by strange, symmetrical circles appearing in their fields for several years now. While some can be explained away as hoaxes, certain unique biological and physical anomalies in the affected plants and the soil in which they stand leave the origin of a great many of these perfect geometric formations shrouded in mystery.

So, if we find ourselves investigating crop circles, should we concentrate on attempting to prove a meteorological explanation, or perhaps a previously unknown magnetic vortex, or should we fall back on the old chestnut of trying to explain a mystery with a mystery, and blame it all on UFOs? And, regardless of which option we choose, or if we devise an entirely novel one of our own making, do we have a logical, definable, and defensible reason for preferring one over another?

In the area of UFO research, is it constructive to argue the question of whether aliens are A) sinister extraterrestrial over-lords who are seeking to destroy mankind from their underground bases in Nevada, or B) benevolent space brothers who are here to guide us into a fabulous Utopian paradise? Especially since at present we can in no way prove that UFOs are alien spacecraft, or that extraterrestrial life, let alone extraterrestrial civilization, even exists.

A recurring error in our thinking seems to be that of assumption. And, as I'm sure we all learned early on, when you assume, you make an 'ass of u and me.' I believe this charge of gross assumption can be laid at the feet of almost every area of Fortean research, and I believe it is a valid charge. There is a vast difference between what is apparently true, and what is actually true.

Because we, as researchers, should be attempting to discover the truth about the phenomena which so intrigue us, it follows that we should understand the nature and definition of truth itself. This is a subject about which volumes have been written. While an exhaustive study of truth is well beyond the scope of this paper, we can attempt to gain a basic understanding of truth this evening. I am going to focus on the concept of absolute, ultimate, foundational truth, but to get there, we need to establish a few definitions along the way.

Aristotle established a concept of truth which is eminently logical, and which helps to frame what I mean when I speak of truth. This concept is known as the Law of Non-contradiction. The Law of Non-contradiction states that the same attribute cannot attach and not attach to the same thing, in the same respect, at the same time. In other words, something cannot be and not be, simultaneously.

The ontological form of this concept (ontology relating to the state of being) is basic. How much more elementary can you get than the concept that something cannot be and not be at the same time? The purely logical form is, then, derivative. This concept becomes a law of logic, because it is first a law of being.

With the Law of Non-contradiction (which makes the existence of absolute truth indisputable) planted firmly in our minds, we can now turn to a closer examination of truth itself. Our next task is to determine whether a truth is relative or absolute.

Relative truth might be understood in two ways. Either truth is relative to time and space (it was true then but not now), or it is relative to persons (true for me, but not true for you). On the other hand, absolute truth implies at least two things as well: 1) whatever is true at one time and in one place is true at all times and in all places, and 2) that whatever is true for one person is true for all persons.

Relative truth is perfectly appropriate in statements such as "I have a great head of hair." In my case, that was true 35 years ago, but, unfortunately, not today. Or the statement "He has more money than he knows what to do with" may be true for Bill Gates, and several folks here in this audience today, but certainly not for me. There are truths which may be relative.

We discover a host of problems, however, when the idea of relative truth is applied to questions of a foundational nature. We are surrounded on all sides today by ethicists, sociologists, philosophers, cultural commentators, and sadly, legions of academics and clerics, who subscribe only to a relativist view of the truth.

The relativist position says, in essence, that "All truth is a matter of perspective."

One particularly thorny problem immediately presents itself in this view. Either the claim that truth is relative is an absolute claim, which would falsify the relativist's position, or it is an assertion that can never be made, because every time you make it you have to add another "relatively." It is the beginning of an infinite regress that will never result in a real statement.

There are, however, benefits to relativism. It means that you can never be wrong. As long as it is right for me, I'm right even when I'm wrong! Isn't that convenient? The only drawback is that I could never learn anything either, because learning means moving from a false belief to a true one—that is, from an absolutely false belief to an absolutely true one. I believe that the relativist should take a close look at the implications of his position.

Two other opposing views of truth must also be considered. The first, known as the correspondent view of truth, says that truth is what corresponds to reality. The other, the coherent view, says that a truth is true if it coheres, or holds together as an internally consistent set of statements. The correspondent view is foundational, basing truth on that which corresponds to reality. The coherent view compares truth to a chain, with each link dependent upon the others to make it all hold together.

The principal objection to the coherentist claim is that it makes truth dependent on an infinite regress that will never arrive at any truth. If every claim of truth presupposes some other claim, and so on, infinitely, then we can never be sure we have arrived at real truth. If we were to find an explanation that needed no further explanation, then we will have arrived at a foundation, a self-evident truth or undeniable first principle, and discover that the coherence view was false to begin with.

Truth by its very nature (remember the Law of Non-contradiction?) must be based on a firm foundation of self-evident truths or first principles that correspond to reality. Philosophically, lying is impossible without a correspondence to reality. If, in the coherentist view, our words do not need to correspond to the facts, then they can never be factually incorrect. Without a correspondent view of reality, there can be no true or false. Correspondence to reality is a philosophical prerequisite for truth itself, and for truthful communication.

The only logical view is that truth is absolute, and it is correspondent to reality. I would ask each of you, as we continue our discussion, to consider whether, or to what degree, this view of truth informs your view of the world. If it does not play a significant part in your thinking, I would ask you to please consider whether you can logically justify your current views of truth.

Philosophical Distinctions Between East and West

The concept of truth is a fundamental idea, our perception of which will certainly determine our basic concepts about life, ideas, and the world around us. These basic ideas, the "mental spectacles" through which we perceive the world, are known as presuppositions.

Based then, on one's views of truth, everyone has accepted or constructed philosophical presuppositions which color their thinking. Clear, intelligent dialogue cannot take place until an understanding is reached concerning the presuppositional views of each participant in a dialogue.

For example, by training, I am a theologian, and consequently a student of philosophy. My methodology presupposes the truth of Christian theism. From my point of view, then, regardless of any claims of "neutrality of thought" on the part of a non-Christian thinker, every viewpoint—the allegedly neutral one no less than any other—must presuppose either the truth or falsity of Christian theism.

The issues between Christians and non-Christians on any given concept cannot be settled by a direct appeal to facts or laws whose nature and significance are already agreed upon by both parties. The question becomes rather, what is the final reference-point required to make the facts and laws intelligible. The question asks what the facts and laws really are. Are they what methodology A assumes them to be? Are they what methodology B assumes them to be? Everyone looks through the eyeglasses of bias and presupposition.

Charles Fort turned a very neat phrase to describe the search for truth, when he said,

"We shall pick up an existence by its frogs. Wise men have tried other ways. They have tried to understand our state of being, by grasping at its stars, or its arts, or its economics. But, if there is an underlying oneness of all things, it does not matter where we begin, whether with stars, or laws of supply and demand, or frogs, or Napoleon Bonaparte. One measures a circle, beginning anywhere."[1]

One may measure a circle beginning anywhere, but I would issue a caveat: unless one has an absolute standard for the scale, the measurements tell you nothing. The question then becomes, what is that absolute standard going to be?

I maintain that the absolute standard by which all things must be measured is Truth. Absolute, correspondent truth. I emphasize that the worldview I will describe has a basic objectivism. It sees truth as unitary. By this, I mean simply that reality, and its corresponding truth, is what it is, independent of anyone's perceiving, understanding, appreciating, or accepting it. The knower's reaction to truth is important, but the truth is not dependent upon that reaction.

To begin an argument from a non-absolutist, or a relativist position is ultimately an exercise in futility. The Christian worldview teaches a created, sustained, guided universe, ultimately ruled in all aspects by the hand of an infinite, omniscient, omnipotent, omnipresent, sovereign, immanent and transcendent God. To think otherwise poses some very sticky problems about the very nature of existence.

Christian philosopher Cornelius Van Till provided a great illustration of the relativist's problem.

"Suppose we imagine a man made of water in an infinitely extended and bottomless ocean of water. Wanting to get out of the water, he builds a ladder of water. He sets this ladder on the water, and leans it against the water, and then tries to climb out of the water. This is the same kind of hopeless and senseless picture which can be drawn of one whose methodology is based upon the assumption that either time or chance is ultimate. On this assumption, even his own rationality is a product of chance. On this assumption, even the laws of logic which he employs are products of chance. The rationality and purpose he is searching for are still bound to be products of chance."[2]

The idea of chance as the ultimate foundation forms the basis for what I believe to be the fatal flaws which have not only Fortean research, but much of contemporary thought. The popularity in the United States since the 1960's of the Eastern philosophical concept that there is no absolute reality, that all is illusion, that we create our own reality, is patently false. Building on that kind of worldview, nothing of significance would ever be discovered. Mankind's current level of technological achievement was not attained because the great minds believed that they created their own reality. It was not achieved through the belief that truth is relative, that what is true for you is fine, but I may not perceive it as true, so my opposing truth is also true.

The very idea of reality being subjective, of existing only through a "veil of perception" as David Hume stated, is based on philosophical confusion: the fact that we do not always see things as they are does not give us license to infer that all we ever see are subjective appearances. Wittgenstein argued, "How do I, the lone, isolated conscious subject, know that an external world exists?" This question is simply answered—the use of the very linguistic concepts necessary for raising such a question presupposes the existence of an objective world of rules, and terms, and the criteria for using those terms.

The foundation upon which modern knowledge rests, no matter how vehemently many wish to deny it, is the concept of an ordered, structured universe, which has at its base Absolute Truth. The very fact that we live in a world governed by physical laws which possess ultimate predictability is the engine that drove science to further our understanding of the cosmos.

One can measure nothing with an ever-changing scale.

Relativism's Logical Flaws Lead To False Philosophies

We, as researchers, and our society as a whole, are pervaded by uncritical thinking. If we are to make advances in this field of research, and gain credibility for our efforts, we must cast off the tacky, out-of-fashion, "New Age" suit which many seem to wear with such pride. We must demonstrate that we are capable of critical thought, realize that intellectual discrimination is not wrong, and subject our efforts to keen, piercing scrutiny.

Lack of intellectual rigor, an acceptance of pragmatic, rather than definitive answers, and that old enemy, assumption, have combined to create the intellectual fog in which we, as an entire society, wander. I submit to you that possibly the greatest intellectual error of our time is the belief that the ultimate virtue which humanity can express is tolerance of anything and everything. Radical individualism, which denies any source of truth outside of the individual is disastrous to the pursuit of knowledge, and to humanity itself.

If you are willing to believe uncritically, and accept that everyone's views are equally true simply because they choose to believe them, then it logically follows that you must reject all absolutes. No absolutes means that you have no basis for accurate judgment.

I want to take a few moments to explain how our attitudes, are influenced, and in many cases dictated, by contemporary social views. As I review several of the dominant philosophical positions, and their chief proponents, please consider how they have helped to shape your world view. Our prevailing attitudes, or Zeitgeist, are formed from a concoction of the following:

Nihilism—the child of Friedrich Nietzsche, is a philosophy which says that truth does not exist, and that there is nothing of value. However, if truth cannot exist, then nihilism cannot be true.

Skepticism—not to be confused with a healthy, inquiring attitude, this school of thought, whose origins lie in ancient Greece, says that true knowledge is impossible. But we must ask, if this is true, then how can we possibly know that true knowledge is impossible.

Existentialism—a school whose chief proponents have included Karl Jaspers, Martin Heidegger, Jean Paul Sartre. Holds that human life is not exhaustively describable, that each man creates his own destiny; each man has only himself as his sole reason for existence; he exists without reference to others.

Agnosticism—The darling of the Enlightenment and such luminaries as David Hume, Immanuel Kant, and T.H. Huxley, asserts that one cannot know absolute truth absolutely. Agnostics may act on faith, but feeling that even though they have chosen to trust in that faith, they are prepared to be disappointed. I would ask simply, why bother?

Utilitarianism—championed by Jeremy Bentham, John Mill, and John Dewey, originated with the ancient Epicureans and taught that the ultimate goal was to achieve the greatest happiness and the least pain for the greatest number of people. It has over time degenerated into the concept that the pursuit of individual pleasure and happiness should be the dynamic which drives all men's actions. This is the "if it feels good, do it" philosophy. The question is, how do we determine when my need for pleasure outweighs your right to a lack of pain?

Secularism—maintains that values, rules, laws, and norms are constantly changing. Morality cannot consist of norms, values, and laws dictated by religious faith, but must be worked out freely and chosen by people for themselves. This is an excellent example of the glaring logical flaw of a relativist position supported by a contradictory, absolutist statement.

Humanism—From the Humanist Manifesto of 1933: "Humanism is faith in the supreme value and self-perfectibility of the human personality." I can only reply that I need an alternative to reliance on my self-perfectibility, because I know myself too well.

Totemism—Based on the ancient shamanistic ideas of transferring blame and responsibility to an inanimate object. For example: "People don't kill, guns do." "People are good, drugs corrupt them." Society would ask us to believe that there are no perpetrators, only victims. No one wants to take personal responsibility for their actions.

All of these concepts can be placed under the umbrella of relativism. Philosophical relativism says that all knowledge, but particularly judgments in ethics, science, and religion are not absolute, but absolutely depend upon a given culture's varying social perspectives. Relativists have quite a paradox on their hands.

G. K. Chesterton once said,

"There are many angles at which you can fall, but only one at which you can stand straight."

Relativism with its inherent logical flaws has wrought havoc with our society. The moral and ethical confusion created by these views is a scathing indictment of the abandonment of absolutes.

Let's make a brief examination of relativism's impact on society, the confusion it has created, and consider, in light of these examples, the impact which relativism has had on our attempts to reach true conclusions about the various phenomena we study.

The theory of Darwinian evolution, coupled with a gross misapplication of Einstein's theory of relativity to areas other than pure physics, has bred a hybrid form of thought which, as King Solomon once said, "…is a way that seems right to a man, But its end is the way of death." The false idea of our coming into being, and continuing to exist through chance and randomness, has opened a floodgate of relativism.

In June of 1990, Arthur Schlesinger was speaking at the inauguration of a new president of Brown University. His entire address was a tirade against moral absolutes, and those who believe in them. His whole argument was a diatribe in favor of relativism. His presentation is fascinating to read. In arguing the whole time against absolutes, all the while doing it absolutely, he has created a masterpiece of self-contradiction.

One cannot argue against absolutes without positing an absolute at the same time!

As a society, we are perilously confused by relativism. We do not know who we are, because we don't know what we believe. In the simplest terms, we are willing to die for a higher standard of living, and to live from a purely functional point of view.

Examine the issues confronting society today, and you begin to see the results of this. In problems of human sexuality, we don't seem to know what the answers are any more. Regarding the question of human life, we don't know when life begins, or, for that matter, when it ends. Considering society's ethics and the laws that are being enacted, we do not seem to know what is right or wrong anymore.

We have come unhinged from our absolute definitions of who we are and why we are here, and given it to chance. And as the British poet Steve Turner has written,

> If chance be the Father of all flesh,
> disaster is his rainbow in the sky
> and when you hear
> State of Emergency!
> Sniper Kills Ten!
> Crowds go Looting!
> Bomb Blasts School!
> It is but the sound of man
> worshiping his maker.

True relativism means giving every person permission to define his terms on what he sees as normative. If a man is truly relativistic in his thinking, then he ought to tolerate the person who disagrees with his relativism. Relativism, by its very nature, should give you the privilege of believing whatever you want. Almost all relativists, however, are in effect saying, "I will allow you to believe in anything you want, so long as you agree with me. You cannot believe in excluding what I believe." In doing this, the relativist ends up positing an absolute, exclusivist doctrine himself.

Trying to defend relativism is like trying to defend the existence of a one-ended stick. Ultimately, it doesn't exist. An absolute is like the law of non-contradiction in logic. That law says that something cannot be and not be simultaneously. Anyone who argues against the law of non-contradiction ends up proving it. One who argues against the existence of an absolute proves it.

Buddhism is an excellent example of an attempt to disprove the law of non-contradiction. The Buddha says, "When the mouth opens, all are fools." The problem is, his mouth opened to tell us that. The eastern mystic says, "He who knows, does not speak; he who speaks does not know." Again, the problem is, he spoke to tell us that. The essence is that you cannot argue against an absolute without establishing one at the same time.

We must have an unchanging, preeminent foundation on which to base our decisions, and our conclusions.

Plato said that transcendent values are the only possible foundation of civilization.

Aristotle promoted his idea of the "good life" as a society where people lived for virtue, and stressed values beyond self to be lived for.

Toward A Philosophy of Fortean Research

Let's consider, for just a moment, the existence of neutrinos—members of the family of sub-atomic particles known as leptons, which are particles found in what scientists call "weak reactions." The weak reaction most familiar to the layman, is radioactivity. In the beta decay reaction, a neutron will yield a proton, plus an electron, plus a neutrino.

Neutrinos, as members of this class of super-sub-atomic particles, play a significant role in our current understanding of the mechanics of the universe. But the point to remember, however, is that no one has ever seen a neutrino. Their existence is posited by a certain mathematical logic, which relies on postulations and extrapolations from observable, visible phenomena. Neutrinos are invisible, yet their existence is pointed to by those things that are visible.

An example of this type of situation drawn from my own field of expertise, theology, arose during the advent of theo-thanatology, in the mid-1960's. Theo-thanatology, or more simply, the death-of-God movement, spawned some lively discussion among theologians and philosophers.

One widely quoted argument in this discussion was put forth by the British philosopher Antony Flew. Two explorers, making their way through an area of almost impenetrable jungle, suddenly came upon a clearing that contained a well-tended, perfectly ordered garden. The first explorer said, "This is fantastic! We must camp here, and see the gardener who tends this plot." The second explorer objected, explaining that it was somewhat curious, but they really needed to press on with their expedition. But he acquiesced, and so they waited two, then three, then four days, and no one appeared.

The second explorer, eager to press on, said, "Look, there is obviously no gardener, this is simply one of those odd, Fortean occurrences, let's pack up and get on about our business."

The first explorer, noting that the garden was still in immaculate condition, said, "No, I want to wait. I believe that we must be dealing with an invisible gardener. We'll string a series of trip wires with bells attached, and when the invisible gardener comes to tend his plot, the bells will ring, and we'll have incontrovertible proof of the existence of the gardener."

Four more days passed, and still no sign of the gardener. No alarm bells sounded, nothing was seen, but still the plot appeared to be tended. The second explorer, his patience exhausted, said, "That's it, we must move on. There is obviously no gardener to wait for."

The first explorer, seized with a sudden insight, said, "No, we have to stay. You see, our plans to discover the gardener have failed because the gardener is not only invisible, but he is also immaterial!"

At this, the second exclaimed, "Wait a minute. Every time I raise a serious objection to the existence of your mysterious gardener, you give me a new qualification of his being; he's invisible, he's immaterial…Let me ask you, what is the difference between an invisible, immaterial gardener, and no gardener at all?"

That is where Flew left the parable. The death-of-God theologians felt that this argument made the point so strongly, that any further comment or defense of this position was unnecessary. They felt that those poor simple-minded folks who believed in God, were chasing a ghost, chasing their own tails to establish a doctrine of God, who, when they had invented Him, would have suffered, as Flew said, "the death of a thousand qualifications." After all, for all practical purposes, what is the difference between this spiritualized, invisible, immaterial being, and no God at all?

The first thought to strike me when I came across Flew's argument was that surely, since serious scientific inquiry began, and philosophical research was being carried on, this has to be probably the first, and certainly only the second century, in all of human history, in which people would be satisfied to respond to that statement with silence.

What is the difference between an invisible, immaterial gardener and no gardener at all? It is ludicrous to pose a situation and just let it hang in the air as a rhetorical question whose answer is obvious, the answer—at least for Flew—being that there is no difference.

But it is almost unthinkable, considering the history of philosophy, that anyone would state a question of that nature in such a rhetorical fashion, before the 19th century.

Any serious thinker prior to the 19th century would have immediately responded, "Sir, the answer to your question is so elementary, any school child would know it. What is the difference between an invisible, immaterial gardener, and no gardener at all? The answer is…the garden."

It couldn't be more simple. Throughout the history of western civilization, in the deepest attempts of humans to understand themselves and their environment, the presence of that garden—the very physical reality which surrounds us every minute of our lives—drove the greatest minds to the necessary conclusion of the existence of the gardener.

The field of Fortean research shares a major problem with theology. When we enter the realm of theology, the biggest obstacle we have, in speaking meaningfully about God, is that this God about whom we speak is invisible. We cannot have any direct perception of Him with any of our senses. We cannot see Him, we cannot hear His voice, we cannot touch Him, and even when we speak of feeling the presence of God it is tacitly assumed that these expressions are indications of an inner emotive, or affective stirring, not something we are doing with our fingertips.

A lack of tangible evidence is also an ever-present problem in most areas of Fortean research. We cannot produce a UFO on command, to be measured and examined. We are unable to materialize a Bigfoot, or schedule a demonstration of psychokinesis. The anti-supernaturalists take this as affirmation of the non-existence of these phenomena.

To answer these skeptics, these noisy negativists, let me parallel the results of this anti-supernatural stance towards the unexplained, with a very similar and appropriate philosophical problem. In every generation, the invisibility of God has been a difficulty for those who would seek to know Him. We, however, have a particularly excruciating problem with that in our own day.

We have, in our age, experienced an eclipse of the supernatural, a denial of that which transcends nature, primarily by the scientific and intellectual community. The Jewish existential philosopher, Martin Buber, wrote a book entitled, *The Eclipse of God*. Buber outlined in his work, an historical analysis of how theoretical speculation has come to produce the crisis of thought in which we find ourselves in these waning years of the twentieth century. The title of this book evokes a powerful image…the eclipse of God.

As we all know, an eclipse occurs when that which once was clear and bright is obscured and hidden from us by a shadow that covers its face. We as scientifically astute culture, know that in the case of a solar eclipse, this shadow does not annihilate the sun. The sun does not pass out of existence. The sun does not die, but rather, our view of it is obscured by something that is veiling its brightness.

What Buber was saying, was that things have happened in the history of thought that have cast a shadow over the face of God. That does not mean that God is dead, that He is destroyed, or that He has become impotent. It simply means that modern man's crisis is, that in a very significant way, man himself has obscured the reality of God, by his own faulty, illogical thought.

These events in the history of thought that, as Buber said, have cast a shadow over the face of God, have cast a shadow over every aspect of the supernatural; that which is above nature, the physical realm. Just because we can't touch, or measure, or control that which is super-natural, that which is above nature, doesn't mean that it isn't there. Our inability to physically study many types of Fortean phenomena does not negate their existence, any more than the inability to tangibly study sub-atomic particles forbids their existence, or unbelief nullifies the existence of God.

Let's turn the clock back just a bit, to the very beginning of the academic world. The academic world as we know it, began appropriately, in the groves of Academia, a grove of olive trees, in a suburb of the city of Athens. In that grove of trees, an Olympic wrestler opened a school called "The Academy." This Olympian, whose nickname was "broad shoulders," or in the Greek, Plato, affixed these words above the entrance to his academy "Let none but geometers enter here."

Geometry is the study of different forms, and their mathematical quantifications. When we think of Plato, we think of him as a philosopher, not a mathematician. The reason Plato made the qualification for entrance to his school a mathematical one, was that Plato was convinced that mathematics in the abstract, the quantification of forms, gave man the deepest insight possible into ultimate reality.

The assumption of Plato the philosopher was the same assumption of Plato the scientist or mathematician. As a Greek, he assumed that, as modern physics has reiterated in the twentieth century, the world in which we live is not ultimately chaos, but cosmos: the Greek word for order. There is an order, a symmetry, a coherence to all of reality. So if there are such things as neutrinos bouncing all over the place, the ultimate bounce that they have is not one of chaos. Plato sought the physical and mathematical forms that would define that which we see with our eyes, and touch with our fingers, and hear with our ears.

Plato, in his quest for truth, developed a concept that is effecting our lives right now. He said that the task of the scientist was a redemptive task, almost a religious task. That task is to "save the phenomena."

When Plato said that it is the task of science to save the phenomena, what he meant was this: We live in a world where we have perceptions of things outside of ourselves. As I stand here, I look out and see what appears to me to be a group of human beings: old human beings, young human beings, pretty human beings, not so pretty human beings, etc., etc. I see all different shapes and sizes.

I understand that all I am experiencing right now is external to myself. I don't believe that I have a projector inside my mind that is creating this crowd of people I am seeing. I'm not just dreaming you. You people are really there. I am not you, and you are not me. But, the only way I can know anything about you is from appearances, unless you choose to give me information about yourself that I cannot learn from simple observation.

The word phenomena refers now, as it did to Plato, to the external perceivable world. The world as it appears to the naked eye. That world does not include neutrinos, it does not even include atoms. It doesn't include gravity, or photons, or electrons, or anything else which we cannot actually perceive, though we theorize they must exist.

To explain this, Plato also used the well-known story of the cave. He said the person who lets his investigation of knowledge rest at the level of how things appear, is a person who will never get beyond opinion to the realm of truth. He is like someone chained, facing the back wall of a cave, who can only perceive shadows dancing on the walls, which he mistakes for the reality outside. Plato saw the task of science and philosophy as that of cutting the chains, and helping us out of the cave, in order for us to get in touch with ultimate reality.

Plato, and Aristotle, as different as Aristotle was from Plato, certainly agreed on this: *What you see is not necessarily what you get.* What you see is only the tiniest possible fragment of reality. No one, according to both Plato and Aristotle, can make sense of what they perceive if their vision is restricted to the phenomena itself. If all we look at are the visible things, we will end in chaos. Though philosophers differed in details, that was overwhelmingly the majority report of intelligent, thinking people, until the end of the 18th, and beginning of the 19th century.

Let's look at an example of "saving the phenomena."

Ptolemy was an Egyptian astronomer about 150 ad, who formu-

lated a system of cycles, epicycles and eccentrics to explain the movements of the stars through the heavens; to "save the phenomena."
His ideas emerged, down through the years, as a complex series of
crystalline spheres, which were hung with stars, and turned around
the earth. To explain the seemingly erratic movement of the planets,
which didn't conform to the motion of the stars, still more crystalline spheres had to be added to the model. Eventually some fifty-
odd spheres were needed to account for the apparent motions of the
heavens. Ptolemy had saved the phenomena.

For most of recorded history, that was the scientifically accepted
cosmological theory—that the earth is the center of the solar system, and that all other heavenly bodies move around us on these
crystalline spheres. Even though a Greek astronomer named Aris-
tarchus had suggested a heliocentric model for the solar system 300
years before Ptolemy, it met with little acceptance. Ptolemy held the
prevailing view until Nicolaus Copernicus appeared about 1400
years later.

But here's an interesting philosophical footnote to this scientific
history lesson. Copernicus shocked the world with his concept of
heliocentricity—the theory that the sun is the center of the solar
system. He said that we didn't need all of those crystal spheres to
explain these motions. He said that all we need to understand is that
the sun is the center of the solar system, not the earth, and then the
equations begin to make sense.

In Copernicus' system, the idea that the earth is moving around
the sun is a much closer understanding, to the best of our knowledge,
of what we call reality. I don't know anyone who is trying to argue
that the earth is the center of the solar system, and that everything
revolves around us. There may be someone out there who believes it,
but I am unaware of it.

However, and this is a crucial point to grasp: from a pragmatic, mathematical perspective, from the perspective of trying to save the phenomena, and make sense of the external world, the Ptolemaic system was better than the system of Copernicus.

Copernicus had made a gigantic error. He assumed that the orbits of the planets were circular rather than elliptical, and it took almost one hundred years, and the efforts of Tyco Brahe and Johannes Kepler to straighten it out.

The point you must grasp, is that even though the Ptolemaic view was further from reality, from truth if you will, than the Copernican system, it did a better job of saving the phenomena. That is, its mathematical models did a better job of prediction than Copernicus' first go-round.

What you see is not necessarily what you get.

Conclusions

What is the significance of all this? We must understand that it's possible to construct a hypothetical view of reality that for all practical purposes works, but in fact, is not true. You can postulate a view of reality that saves the phenomena, that works, but has no correspondence to reality.

It is fascinating to think of what will happen with the Hubble telescope. If things work, we are going to get an avalanche of new information. And, if the future is anything like the past, new theories will come, old theories will go, some will be vindicated, some disproved.

It is interesting to observe the efforts of modern thinkers trying to explain the universe, life, and ultimate origins. Some of them are very forthright and will say, "Our task is to save the phenomena.

It doesn't matter if our models are true, all that matters is that our models work mathematically."

There are people who believe that there are real particles called neutrinos. There are other people who say, "I don't believe they are real, I just believe they are mathematically necessary." Still others say, "Who cares? It doesn't matter so long as we have made the system predictable, and we have saved the phenomena."

For Plato, Aristotle, and the classical thinkers, one thing was clear. They recognized that the phenomena could be saved through theories that were not correct, but they also understood that for there to be phenomena to save—for there to be anything at all to study—there must be a transcendent, ultimate, causal being behind it.

For Plato, for Aristotle, for Plotinus, for Augustine, for all of the philosophers virtually, until Kant, the presence of phenomena demanded the prior assertion of being, of God. Scientists such as Newton based their work on the concept that the more we learn about the phenomena, the more we learn about the reality behind the phenomena. So Johannes Kepler could say, with full conviction, that "The task of science is to think God's thoughts after Him." By examining and pushing our understanding of reality further and further and further, we are driven, always and ever, (to borrow Kant's terminology) by the phenomena (the objective world) to the *noumena* (the spiritual realities behind the objective world): that is, to God.

If, in researching the unexplained, we are serious about arriving at the truth behind the phenomena, we must rethink our position. We can experience success in our investigative efforts, only if we recognize that there is an ultimate, transcendent truth underlying everything. This truth, as Fort implied, underlies stars, and laws of supply and demand, and frogs, and the existence of Napoleon Bonaparte.

The created realm clearly manifests the Creator. The visible world bears unmistakable witness to the invisible God. The phenomena, far from eclipsing God, are in fact, a vehicle of His revelation. We live in an age that asserts again and again, that all there is, is the phenomena. There is nothing behind the phenomena; or if there is anything behind the phenomena, we can't possibly attain knowledge of it, so that what you see is all you get.

I believe that only a Christian worldview can accurately "save the phenomenon" as well as clearly identify the noumenon—Let me summarize my position with 10 self-evident propositions:

I. Self-evident propositions about logic
   A. Law of non-contradiction
      (A is not non-A: i.e., something cannot be and not be simultaneously)
   B. Law of identity
      A is A: i.e., a thing is what it is)
   C. Law of excluded middle
      (either A or non-A: i.e., something either is or is not)
   D. Law of valid inference (the connection by which the conclusion of an argument is said to follow from the premises)

II. Self-evident propositions about knowledge
   A. Something can be known
   B. Opposites cannot both be true
   C. Everything cannot be false

III. Self-evident propositions about existence
   A. Something exists (e.g., I do).

    B. Nothing cannot produce something.

    C. Everything that comes to be is caused.

These principles are the foundation of knowledge. Unless we, as an active, responsible research community, are willing to be intellectually scrupulous, critically judge our observations, our research, our experiences, and our conclusions against an absolute standard of truth, and finally come to realize that what we see is most definitely not all we get, our research efforts will at worst be superstitious ramblings, at best expositions of opinion, and always and forever an exercise in futility.

    This field of research, as well as our entire society is rife with superstition. Whether it's based on old wive's tales or the current fads in the natural sciences, too many vague half-truths, based on misunderstandings and misinterpretations of scientific and historical fact, colored by fuzzy, non-critical illogical, relativistic thinking are paraded about as proven conclusions. As researchers, as a part of modern society, we must recognize and acknowledge that there is a transcendent source of absolute truth upon which we can, and must, base our investigations.

    What is the relationship of the Fortean's search for truth, compared to that of the theologian's? It is ultimately one and the same truth that is being sought, albeit by different avenues.

    The Fortean (whether he is willing to acknowledge it or not), is concerned principally with the revelation which God has given of Himself through nature; through phenomena which we do not understand at present. The theologian is principally concerned with God's particular revelation of Himself in Scripture.

    Both avenues, when properly pursued, must of necessity arrive at the same destination, the Creator God. The particulars of what

God has revealed in each arena differs vastly, of course, but they are not contradictory. Logic dictates that truth is an absolute, and God, by the very definition of His being must be absolute truth, therefore any search for truth is an ally, not an antagonist, of theology.

René Descartes' quintessential philosophical statement was, *"Cogito ergo sum,"*—I think, therefore, I am.

My attitude toward Christianity can be expressed as *"Cogito ergo credo,"*—I think, therefore I believe.

The view which I posit is this—the ultimate source and expression of truth is Jesus Christ.

Not some New Age Christ, but the Christ of orthodox, historic Christianity. I believe in His virgin birth, the deity of Christ, His vicarious, atoning death on the cross, His bodily resurrection, His imminent return, and the inerrancy and authority of His infallible Word.

It is only in working from this foundational truth that we can begin to truly research and understand such varied Fortean events as UFOs, spontaneous human combustion, and all the rest. We must work from a basis of absolute, unchanging truth.

I have been actively involved in the field of Fortean research for almost 30 years. Those years have been a search for the truth behind these puzzling events, an attempt to "save the phenomena."

I know that there is a truth which underlies all existence. So, with the understanding of a sovereign Creator God controlling the universe, and, through His sustaining power, providing a common thread through His creation, one can, as Fort said, "…measure a circle beginning anywhere."

Only in Jesus Christ, fully God, and fully man, the *logos*, the embodiment of absolute truth, do we have the unchanging standard by which we can begin to measure that circle.

As the late Francis Schaeffer, one of the greatest minds of the twentieth century put it,

"There is only one reason to embrace Christianity—it is the truth."

And, ladies and gentlemen, isn't that what we are all seeking?

Notes
Appendix 2

(As appearing in original document)

1. 1 Fort, Charles *Lo!,* Claude H. Kendall, New York, 1931.
2. Van Til, Cornelius, *The Defense of the Faith,* Presbyterian & Reformed Publishing, Phillipsburg, New Jersey, 1955.

Appendix 3

PAUL'S THORN IN THE FLESH: NATURALISM OR SUPERNATURALISM

By Cris Putnam

So to keep me from becoming conceited because of the
surpassing greatness of the revelations, a thorn was given
me in the flesh, a messenger of Satan to harass me, to keep
me from becoming conceited.
—2 CORINTHIANS 12:7

The purpose of this essay is to examine Paul's thorn in the flesh In
light of a Bible-believing supernatural worldview. This presentation
will first examine the overall concept of a biblical worldview and
then the context of 2 Corinthians 12 and offer several key points
of analysis on the nature of the thorn itself. The first point of analysis will be the terminology Paul employs for "thorn in the flesh,"
which naturally leads to his association of it with it as a "messenger
of Satan." Naturalistic theories will be contrasted with supernatural
ones. Finally, it will be argued that a supernatural worldview strongly
suggests that a personal demonic entity is involved. While there are
many theories about Paul's thorn in the flesh, a supernatural worldview leads one to include a demonic contingency.

Worldview

The term "worldview" is actually derived from a German word, *Weltanschauung*, which means a "look onto the world." It is the comprehensive set of basic beliefs in which one views the world and interprets experiences.[1] In Colossians 2:8, the apostle Paul issued a warning, "See to it that no one takes you captive by philosophy and empty deceit, according to human tradition, according to the elemental spirits of the world, and not according to Christ." The significance of his admonition is readily seen in the marketplace of ideas where biblical faith is increasingly marginalized. Belief in the supernatural is routinely ridiculed and dismissed as superstition.

While there is enough nonsense to warrant vigilant discernment, a Christian cannot afford to adopt a naturalistic mindset. Unfortunately, naturalism has made significant inroads into biblical hermeneutics and exegesis.

Naturalism is the philosophical position which holds that nature is the ultimate reality. Naturalists are typically atheists who collaterally deny the existence angels and demons.[2] Also, they typically deny the existence of a soul or afterlife and necessarily contend that consciousness is a phenomenon of the brain. The remarkable progress of science based on methodological naturalism has undone a great deal of superstition about disease and has afforded great progress. For this reason, it is entirely understandable that modern people including Christians have a tendency to think in naturalistic ways. Yet, naturalism is unsatisfying because it cannot even begin to address the big questions, the sorts of questions a child might ask like, "like why am I here?" or a philosophical ultimate like "why is there something rather than nothing?" The Bible answers these with authority, but is also replete with demon possession, mystical experiences, and the resurrection of the dead. The skeptic will default to naturalism when interpreting these passages, but this is not a viable track for those who accept the inspiration and inerrancy of the Bible. One cannot be a Christian and a naturalist.

Christianity is not only a personal relationship with Jesus Christ, it is a worldview. It is the lens through which one interprets reality. Because God has revealed Himself verbally in the Bible, Christians have answers to the most fundamental and ultimate questions in life that evade secularism. Neil Andersen writes:

The Christian worldview perceives life through the grid of Scripture, not through culture or experience. And Scripture clearly teaches that supernatural, spiritual forces are at work in this world. For example, approximately one-fourth of all the healings recorded in the Gospel of Mark were actually deliverances.[3]

The dilemma facing the Christian believer is finding the appropriate level of skepticism when faced with supernatural claims. The culture is abounding with everything from ghosts to space aliens and all sorts of fantastic nonsense. The skeptic would classify the Bible in the same category yet we argue that the existence of counterfeit does not preclude the genuine article. The cornerstone of the Christian faith is the resurrection of Jesus Christ and the historical evidence supporting it is quite powerful. Additionally, the record of fulfilled Bible prophecy provides convincing evidence for the veracity of the Bible's supernatural claims. The experience of the Holy Spirit also provides each believer with individual assurance. As Christians interpreting the Bible, it is imperative to not be taken captive by the naturalism of the age. The Christian worldview is a supernatural one and this presentation will argue for a supernatural interpretation of Paul's thorn.

Context of 2 Corinthians 12

Paul's challenges with the Corinthian church have provided the milieu for some amazing revelations. The book of 2 Corinthians' overall context is Paul's response to a good report by Titus concerning their repentance in response to no longer extant "severe" letter which scolded them (2 Corinthians 7:4–16). Paul encourages them to restore a repentant brother that he had addressed in the first letter. He explains the New Covenant and how it is superior to the old one. He encourages them to prepare for his next visit by taking up a collection for the church at Jerusalem. The mood is positive and encouraging until the focus moves to his opponents.

In chapters 10–13, Paul's tone changes so markedly that many scholars argue it was a subsequent letter which was later appended.[4] In response to the accusations of the false teachers, Paul challenges the church to consider carefully his personal life and ministry. He argues that his ministry is above reproach and his message true. Paul's opponents, described sarcastically as "super apostles," are accused of preaching a different Gospel (2 Corinthians 11:4). As inferred from chapter 11, they boasted of an Israelite heritage, from their criticisms it seems they were likely Hellenistic Jews, which leads scholars to think they were from the Jerusalem church. They challenged Paul's apostolic status and authority, took credit for his efforts in planting the church and even accused him of being timid and unreliable. Paul rhetorically assumes the role of a fool and begins to match them boast for boast. He calls them "false apostles" who are "masquerading

as apostles of Christ" (2 Corinthians 11:12). He then draws a fascinating comparison that has implications to this thesis. He argues,
"And no wonder, for Satan himself masquerades as an angel of light.
It is not surprising, then, if his servants also masquerade as servants of
righteousness" (2 Corinthians 11:14–15a). Thus, the passage infers
that Satan appears as an angel and that Paul's opponents are Satan's
servants. In chapter 12, he begins to boast in visions and revelations
of the Lord.

It is in this section of his defense that Paul relates the account of
his mysterious journey to the third heaven. While he insists that it is
worthless to prove his authority, he seems to be making sport of his
adversaries. His opponents had likely appealed to their own visionary
experiences exalting themselves while insinuating that Paul was inferior. In fact, it appears that Paul had likely kept this to himself for fourteen years (2 Corinthians 12:2). The nature of his vision is esoteric and
falls into well-known category of intertestamental divine encounters
(1 Enoch 39:3–4; 2 Enoch 7:1; 8:1).[5] Like Enoch, Paul says he was
"caught up" using is the same Greek word, *harpazo*, as in Acts 8:39,
Revelation 12:5 and the famous rapture passage, 1 Thessalonians
4:17.[6] He says he went to the "third heaven" (v.2) and "paradise" (v.3)
seemingly equating the two. This is likely a Semitic synthetic parallelism where the second term, "paradise," gives a more precise definition
of "third heaven."[7] The word "paradise" is a Persian loan word for garden which is used in the LXX for the Garden of Eden which is referred
to as the "garden of God" in Ezekiel 28:13 and 31:8. In intertestamental literature, paradise referred to God's abode (1 Enoch 60:23; 61:12;
2 Baruch 4:6) and it appears two other times as such in the New Testament (Luke 23:43; Revelation 2:7).[8] Even more mystical is his pondering
as to whether it was "in the body or out of the body." The typical Jewish
tradition presumes being raptured in the body (2 Kings 2:11; Hebrews

11:5; 1 Enoch 14:8) but there is also precedent for outside the body (Revelation 4:2; 1 Enoch 71:1).[9] He also says he heard divine secrets that can never be told, things so great that mere knowledge of them put him in danger of becoming conceited. As a precautionary measure he was given "a thorn in the flesh, a messenger of Satan to harass him" (2 Corinthians 12:7). The "thorn in the flesh" is the culmination of his argument. Its purpose is to keep him humble. He boasts in his weakness.

What Is the Thorn?

In regard to the exact nature of the thorn there has been no shortage of scholarly speculation. Most interpreters default to some sort of bodily ailment because the phrase "in the flesh" seems to support it. Consequently, his mention of a physical condition which hindered his Galatian ministry is frequently offered as a corollary (Galatians 4:13–14).[10] Suggestions have included poor eyesight, a speech impediment, epilepsy, solar retinitis, and depression.[11] For example, Ramsay famously argued that Paul suffered from a form of recurring malarial fever:

> Such an attack is for the time absolutely incapacitating: the sufferer can only lie and feel himself a shaking and helpless weakling, when he ought to be at work. He feels a contempt and loathing for self, and believes that others feel equal contempt and loathing[12]

Indeed, Martin calls Ramsay's hypothesis one of the more attractive options albeit listing a plethora of dreadful alternatives[13] In view of that, some sort of illness or health issue seems to have the most support amongst scholars.

Another popular view is that Paul was referring to his adversaries. This view has much to commend it, especially in light of the overall contextual polemic against his opponents. The church Father John Chrysostom would have none of the corporeal theories, "There are some who have said that Paul is referring to a pain in the head caused by the devil, but God forbid! The body of Paul could never have been given over to the devil."[14] He argued further that Satan should be understood in its Hebraic sense as "adversary" and that Paul's human opponents were in view. Mullins presents a cogent modern case for personal agency rather than a physical debility. He argues that there is no other place where Paul uses the term *angelos* in any other way but for an individual. He writes, "The normal, expected use of ἄγγελος is with reference to a person (whether to an earthly person or to a heavenly person is beside the point)."[15] But in this presentation it is decidedly not beside the point. It is the view here that Paul has told us clearly and specifically exactly what his thorn is albeit most interpreters balk; Paul's thorn is a demon.

The view argued here is that Paul means his "thorn in the flesh" is literally "a messenger from Satan." "Messenger" is rendered from the same Greek word which is also rendered "angel." Satan's angels are demons by definition. Thus, a plain reading of the text implies demonic oppression. Larry Richards writes:

> It's clear in this passage that what Paul experienced as a physical disability was an evil: It harmed Paul and caused him pain, and it was caused by one of Satan's angels. The phrase "to buffet me" indicates the demon's intent. Satan's motive was to do Paul harm, and perhaps to make Paul physically

repulsive so as to alienate potential hearers of the gospel. So Paul makes a direct connection between Satan, his angel (demon), and evil—the same connection that is made when Satan is called "the evil one" (John 17:15; 1 John 5:18).[16]

This view has many advantages in that it can account for all of the above arguments. That it is personal entity is supported by Mullins' treatment and all of the physical manifestations can be granted viewed as demonic harassment. In spite of Chrysostom's objections, it has ample biblical support. For instance, in Job 2:5 Satan is allowed to inflict sickness. Even more, in Luke 13 Jesus heals a woman who was bent over and could not straighten herself for eighteen years. Jesus laid hands on her and pronounced her healed. She is described by Luke as "a woman who had a disabling spirit" (Luke 13:11) and by Jesus as, "a daughter of Abraham whom Satan bound for eighteen years," (Luke 13:16). What appears natural may have a supernatural origin.

The demonic interpretation accounts for other views as well. Medieval scholars read the Latin *stimulus carnis* for "thorn in the flesh" and inferred a sexual temptation. Similarly, Calvin and Luther favored a spiritual temptation.[17] Yet, we know that Satan and his demons are tempters by trade (Matthew 4:1; Mark 1:13; 1 Corinthians 7:5). Commenting on Paul's thorn, Tertullian wrote, "The right to tempt a man is granted to the devil…whether God or the devil initiates the plan or for the purpose of the judgment of a sinner, who is handed over to the devil as to an executioner."[18] Furthermore, the function of the thorn to keep Paul from pride is reminiscent of Jesus' telling Peter that Satan demanded to "sift him like wheat" (Luke 22:31). The superior explanatory scope and coherence with a supernatural worldview give the demonic interpretation much force. Even more, it is well supported by exegesis.

Metaphors

That Paul is speaking metaphorically when he refers to his "thorn in the flesh" is not disputed by anyone. Yet, a metaphor is always figurative for some sort of real concrete thing. Most modern exegetes see "thorn", as a metaphor qualified by "in the flesh" which stands in juxtaposition to a second metaphor, "a messenger of Satan."[19]But does this really make sense grammatically or logically? A metaphor usually describes a referent which is overtly stated by the writer or is implicitly known to the reader. However, in this case interpreters would have one accept that Paul uses two metaphors describing one another with no tangible referent. This seems unlikely. Abermathy argues convincingly that, " 'thorn in the flesh' was the metaphor, and the second phrase 'an angel of Satan' was the concrete referent, the reality being described metaphorically by the first."[20] This argument is well supported by biblical evidence.

The biblical text supports this interpretation for both phrases. First, "thorn in the flesh" is best viewed as a single metaphorical expression, rather than metaphorical "thorn" as qualified by "in the flesh." The LXX has nearly identical uses of this type of phrase which were likely familiar to Paul. Ezekiel 28:24 describes Israel's disagreeable neighbors as "a thorn of pain." Numbers 33:55 and Joshua 23:13 speak of the Canaanites as "thorns in your eyes." Second, examining the phrase "messenger (angel) of Satan" the opposite is true. There are no biblical uses of this as a metaphor. It normally describes a supernatural being. In fact, as mentioned above Satan is described as an "angel of light" by Paul in this same letter (2 Corinthians 11:14). There is simply no precedent for *angelos* being used for anything other than a personal being. Thus, it is better supported exegetically that the "thorn in the flesh" is in fact a personal being of demonic origin.

Satan and Demons

A supernatural view has superior scope where naturalistic theories are inadequate. While natural pestilential conjectures abound, one marvels at how Paul could possibly endure all the physical trials he lists if he was so pathetic (2 Corinthians 11:24–27). Martin comments, "One wonders if a person who was so often on the 'battlefield' could have been so physically weak and still have withstood the rigors of Paul's life....Paul is one who must be seen as in robust health and with a strong constitution."[21] Accordingly, it seems more correct to believe that the harassment, *kolaphizō,* literally "beat"[22] delivered by the angel of Satan came in the form of the aforementioned hardships and his humbling is a direct result of being laid open to them. In this line of thought, Abermathy concludes:

He is saying that God, through Satan, gave him a demonic adversary to fight him every step of the way, and because of the resulting weakness, insults, hardships, persecutions and difficulties, his fleshly inclination to be puffed up with pride was punctured by the metaphorical "thorn" and Paul was a humbled man.[23]

After all, Satan tempted and opposed Jesus in a personal way (Mark 1:12–13) and as mentioned before, Jesus told Peter Satan had demanded to "sift him like wheat" implying a trial (Luke 22:31). It seems that God allowed this for Paul's ultimate benefit. Richards came to similar conclusion, "God did not do the evil to Paul. He permitted Satan to do the evil—and then God transformed the harm Satan intended into good."[24] It also seems fitting to recall Paul's message to the Ephesians, where he states that our battle is not as earthbound as it appears rather it is, "against the spiritual forces of evil in the heavenly places" (Ephesians 6:12b). Ironically, it seems almost as if Satan is unwittingly doing God's bidding.

The usual dualistic way to think of Satan and his angels is by juxtaposing them as the forces of evil against God as the power of good. But this can be erroneous as it affords him more than his due. Satan and demons are created beings, created by Jesus Christ (Colossians 1:16). Whether they know it or not, God employs them for his purposes. In Job, the term Satan is used in a legal way as "adversary" for an officer on the divine council.[25] But he functions in a much wider role than prosecuting attorney. He torments Job but only with Yahweh's permission.[26] There is also biblical precedent for the Lord's providential use of lying spirits (1 Kings 22:19–23) and in the case of another Saul to whom the Lord sent an evil spirit (1 Kings 16:14). In regard to Paul's thorn, Page argues:

> Paul views his experience of the thorn through the lens of Job's experience. Both Satan and God were involved in his suffering, as in the suffering of Job, but their purposes were very different. Satan sought to harm Paul, but God used the experience to promote Paul's growth in humility and dependence upon him.[27]

While Satan wanted Job to curse God, he opposed Paul to hinder the spread of the gospel. It seems odd that this is part of God's plan but it fits into the overall tension of the "already but not yet" paradigm inherent in New Testament theology. While Satan is a defeated foe (Colossians 2:15), he is still "god of this world" until the *parousia* (2 Corinthians 4:4; 1 John 5:19).

The Lord's providential use of Satan and demons has practical implications for believers. While it may at first instill fear that God would allow such a thing, it should ultimately bestow a stalwart sense of security like that found in Paul. Recalling that for Paul "to die is gain" (Philippians 1:21), it follows that once a person no longer fears death; the fear from evil is largely dissolved. In a text on spiritual warfare, Mark Brubeck comments concerning Paul's thorn:

> This tremendous passage affords great comfort to anyone undergoing a severe time of battle with Satan. We must see that God has a sovereign purpose in a believer's life, even during Satan's intense battle. He is working out His will in our lives, even when on the surface it looks like Satan is winning.[28]

Brubeck also argues that committed believers seem to experience a greater level of conflict with Satan's forces. He argues that because of the natural tendency toward pride, it is a difficult task for the Lord to prepare us to be blessed by Him.[29]

The lesson from Paul is that adversity and trials produce stalwart character and humility. It is not limited to apostles. Hymenaeus and Alexander were "delivered over to Satan, so that they may be taught not to blaspheme" (1 Timothy 1:19–20). The Corinthian who committed incest was delivered "to Satan for the destruction of his flesh, so that his spirit may be saved in the day of the Lord" (1 Corinthians 5:5). Another lesson is that things are often not as what they seem on the surface. When one views the world through the lens of a supernatural worldview, mundane challenges take on a new level of importance. A mission's pastor once remarked, "If you have any doubts about the existence of Satan, why don't you try opposing him for a little while?" Anecdotal reports from the mission field do reflect a more overt sort of spiritual warfare. While world evangelism is still incomplete, the work of men like Paul continues. Accordingly, one would expect similar demonic activity serving God's purpose. Paul asked the Lord three times to remove his oppressor but the Lord replied, "My grace is sufficient for you, for my power is made perfect in weakness" (2 Corinthians 12:9a). God uses adversity and opposition to sanctify and motivate believers. Accordingly Paul's "messenger of Satan" served to keep him humble and reliant upon God. Paul himself said he was a more effective in weakness than he would have been in his own strength (1 Corinthians 12:10).

Conclusion

This presentation examined Paul's thorn through a biblical worldview within the context of 2 Corinthians 12 and Paul's vision. It seems that a biblical worldview, with its inherent embrace of the supernatural, suggests that one must be open to the idea that Paul's thorn was a personal demonic entity opposing him. The terminology was examined and it was revealed that there is ample biblical precedent that "thorn in the flesh" is used metaphorically but no evidence that "messenger of Satan" is meant figuratively. It was argued that metaphors usually refer to a concrete and known item and it is most unlikely that Paul strung two metaphors in a row with no referent. Naturalistic theories lack explanatory scope and were revealed to be inadequate. Many examples of God's providential use of Satan and demons were discussed. Analysis was offered and it was revealed to be consistent with God's overall purpose of character development. The role of supernatural forces and spiritual warfare merits further study. It seems that Satan and demons seek to cripple the church by division, stall the mission of evangelism, and persecute individuals. Yet in all of these malicious disruptions, God's grace and providential sovereignty overrides, employing them to sanctify the believer, defeat the wicked, and ultimately show His glory.

Notes
Appendix 3

(As appearing in original document)

1. C. Stephen Evans, *Pocket Dictionary of Apologetics & Philosophy of Religion* (Downers Grove, IL.: InterVarsity Press, 2002), 124.
2. Evans, *Pocket Dictionary of Apologetics,* 79.
3. Neil T. Anderson, *The Bondage Breaker,* (Eugene, OR: Harvest House Publishers, 2006), 33.
4. F. F. Bruce, *Paul: Apostle of the Heart Set Free* (Grand Rapids: Eerdmans Publishing Co., 1977), 278.
5. Victor Paul Furnish, *II Corinthians: Translated With Introduction, Notes, and Commentary,* (New Haven; London: Yale University Press, 2008), 524.
6. James Swanson, *Dictionary of Biblical Languages With Semantic Domains: Greek New Testament,* electronic ed. (Oak Harbor: Logos Research Systems, Inc., 1997), DBLG 773, #1.
7. David E. Garland, *2 Corinthians The New American Commentary vol. 29,* (Nashville: Broadman & Holman Publishers, 2001), 514.
8. Furnish, *II Corinthians,* 526.
9. Furnish, *II Corinthians,* 525.
10. Garland, *2 Corinthians,* 519.
11. Clinton E. Arnold, Zondervan Illustrated Bible Backgrounds Commentary Volume 3: Romans to Philemon. (Grand Rapids, MI: Zondervan, 2002), 254.
12. William Mitchell Ramsay, Sir, *St. Paul the Traveller and the Roman Citizen,* "The Morgan Lectures for 1894 in the Auburn Theological Seminary, and Mansfield College Lectures, 1895." (Public Domain), 96.

13. Ralph P. Martin, vol. 40, *Word Biblical Commentary : 2 Corinthians*, Word Biblical Commentary (Dallas: Word, Incorporated, 2002), 414.

14. John Chrysostom, *Homilies on the Epistles of Paul to the Corinthians* 26.2, as quoted in Gerald Lewis Bray, 1-2 Corinthians, Ancient Christian Commentary on Scripture NT 7. (Downers Grove, Ill.: InterVarsity Press, 1999), 305.

15. Terrence Mullins "Paul's Thorn in the Flesh." (*Journal of Biblical Literature* 76, 4, 1957), 301.

16. Larry Richards, *Every Angel in the Bible*, Includes Indexes., Everything in the Bible series (Nashville: T. Nelson, 1997), 123.

17. Martin, *Word Biblical*, 414.

18. Tertullian, Flight in Time of Persecution 2.7, as quoted in Bray, 1-2 Corinthians, 304.

19. D. Abermathy, "Paul's thorn in the flesh: A messenger of Satan." (*Neotestamentica* 35, 1-2, 2001), 71

20. Abermathy, "Paul's thorn," 71.

21. Martin, *Word Biblical*, 415.

22. Swanson, Dictionary of Biblical Languages, DBLG 3139, #1.

23. Abermathy, "Paul's thorn," 76.

24. Larry Richards, *Every Angel in the Bible*, Includes Indexes., Everything in the Bible series (Nashville: T. Nelson, 1997), 123.

25. Michael S. Heiser, "The Divine Council in Late Canonical and Non-Canonical Second Temple Jewish Literature," (Ph.D. diss., University of Wisconsin-Madison, 2004), 58.

26. S.H. Page, "Satan: God's Servant," (*Journal of the Evangelical Theological Society*, 50, 3, 2007), 452.

27. Page, "Satan," 464.

28. Mark I. Bubeck, *The Adversary: The Christian Versus Demon Activity* (Chicago, IL: Moody Press, 1975), 85.

29. Bubeck, *The Adversary*, 84.

Appendix 4

ARGUMENTS FOR THE EXISTENCE OF GOD

While a skeptic might dispute each individual argument on specific details, the combined force of all the arguments together makes a formidable case.

Kalam Cosmological Argument

The goal of this argument is to show that the universe had a beginning in the finite past. The argument battles against the existence of an infinite, temporal regress of past events, which implies a universe that has always existed. As argued in chapter 2, this argument implies the existence of a supernatural first cause.

The form of the argument is:

Whatever begins to exist has a cause.

The universe began to exist.

Therefore, the universe has a cause.

Teleological Argument

The teleological (Gr. *telos*, "end" or "purpose") argument is also known as the argument from design. This argument moves from complexity and design to a necessary cause for such complexity and design. The force of the argument is that universe has discernable design, order, and arrangement which cannot be sufficiently explained outside a supernatural worldview. It is based on: "For his invisible attributes, namely, his eternal power and divine nature, have been clearly perceived, ever since the creation of the world, in the things that have been made. So they are without excuse" (Romans 1:20).

William Paley presented the watchmaker analogy in his Natural Theology (1802):

> Suppose I found a watch upon the ground, and it should be inquired how the watch happened to be in that place, I should hardly think…that, for anything I knew, the watch might have always been there. Yet why should not this answer serve for the watch as well as for [a] stone [that happened to be lying on the ground]?… For this reason, and for no other; namely, that, if the different parts had been differently shaped from what they are, if a different size from what they are, or placed after any other manner, or in any order than that in which they are placed, either no motion at all would have been carried on in the machine, or none which would have answered the use that is now served by it.[1]

Moral Argument

This argument argues from the reality of moral laws to the existence of a necessary moral law giver. The idea here is that if there are moral laws (murder is wrong, selfishness is wrong, torturing innocent babies for fun is evil), then there must be a supernatural explanation to justify such transcendent laws. Otherwise, they are merely social conventions that are not morally binding on anyone. However, since moral laws exist then there must be a moral law giver who transcends mankind and creation. This moral law giver is God.

If objective moral laws exist then a transcendent moral law giver exists.

Objective moral laws do exist.

Therefore a transcendent moral law giver exists, God.

Ontological Argument

The ontological argument is probably the most obscure because it seeks to demonstrate that God exists on the basis of that concept alone. It was first formulated by Anselm of Canterbury (1033–1109), one of the great medieval philosopher-theologians, in his *Proslogium*, chapter 2. Anselm's ontological argument rests on the identification of God as "that than which no greater can be conceived." Once it is understood that God is that of which no greater can be conceived, Anselm suggests, it becomes evident that God must exist. René Descartes articulated in this way:

We have the idea of an infinitely perfect Being. Since we are finite, and everything around us is finite, the idea of an infinitely perfect Being could not have originated with us or with the nature around us. Therefore the idea of an infinitely perfect Being must have come from such a being—God.[2]

Notes
Appendix 4

1. William Paley, *Natural Theology* (New York: American Tract Society, 1818) 25. ttps://archive.org/stream/naturaltheology00pale#page/n24/mode/1up (accessed 2/11/14).

2. "Descartes' Ontological Argument," *Stanford Encyclopedia of Philosophy* http://plato.stanford.edu/entries/descartes-ontological/ (accessed 2/11/14) 11.